Deconstructing Developmental Psychology

What is childhood and why, and how, did psychology come to be the arbiter of 'correct' or 'normal' development? How do actual lived childhoods connect with theories about child development? In this completely revised and updated edition, *Deconstructing Developmental Psychology* interrogates the assumptions and practices surrounding the psychology of child development, providing a critical evaluation of the role and contribution of developmental psychology within social practice.

In the decade since the first edition was published, there have been many major changes. The role accorded to childcare experts and the power of the 'psy complex' have, if anything, intensified. This book addresses how shifts in advanced capitalism have produced new understandings of children, and a new (and more punitive) range of institutional responses to children. It engages with the paradoxes of childhood in an era when young adults are increasingly economically dependent on their families, and in a political context of heightened insecurity. The new edition includes an updated review of developments in psychological theory (in attachment, evolutionary psychology, theory of mind, cultural-historical approaches), as well as updating and reflecting upon the changed focus on fathers and fathering. It offers new perspectives on the connections between Piaget and Vygotsky and now connects much more closely with discussions from the sociology of childhood and critical educational research. Coverage has been expanded to include more material on child rights debates, and a new chapter addresses practice dilemmas around child protection, which engages even more with the 'raced' and gendered effects of current policies involving children.

This engaging and accessible text provides key resources to inform better professional practice in social work, education and health contexts. It offers critical insights into the politics and procedures that have shaped developmental psychological knowledge. It will be essential reading for anyone working with children, or concerned with policies around children and families. It will also be of interest to students at undergraduate and postgraduate levels across a range of professional and practitioner groups, as well as parents and policymakers.

Erica Burman is Professor of Psychology and Women's Studies at Manchester Metropolitan University. She is an internationally renowned researcher, teacher and activist, as well as a group analyst. Her work supports critical and reflexive professional practice with and for disadvantaged women and children.

Every aspiring scholar of childhood should be required to read this book.
Radhika Viruru, Texas A&M University

Engaging with Burman's detailed and compelling arguments should be mandatory for all students and researchers of children's lives. A book to provoke, debate and inspire other ways to know and be with children.
Professor Glenda MacNaughton, Director of the Centre for Equity and Innovation in Early Childhood, Faculty of Education at the University of Melbourne.

This book is a vital resource for all who are engaged in trying to deconstruct and border cross the hegemonic role of developmental psychology in the field of early childhood education and childhood studies.
Gunilla Dahlberg, Professor of Early Childhood Education, Stockholm Institute of Education, Stockholm, Sweden

This version is even better than the first, with new, contemporary, compelling examples of the social-political context of developmental psychology. Burman is critical yet positive, bold yet thoughtful, provocative yet balanced, and deconstructive yet constructive. After reading this book you'll never think about attachment, families, or language learning in the same way again.
Patricia H. Miller, Ph.D., Professor and Head, Department of Psychology, University of Georgia

The first edition of this book was cutting edge and visionary in its sustained, critical analysis. This new edition takes forward its innovatory focus by updating the concerns of the first edition and situating them in changes in the geopolitical and developmental psychology landscape over the last 15 years. The relevance and scope of its coverage and the clarity of its writing makes it invaluable and accessible to both academic audiences and interested laypeople.
Ann Phoenix, Professor of Social and Developmental Psychology, the Open University and Co-Director of the Thomas Coram Research Unit, Institute of Education, University of London

Deconstructing Developmental Psychology

Second Edition

Erica Burman

Routledge
Taylor & Francis Group

LONDON AND NEW YORK

First published 2008 by Routledge
27 Church Road, Hove, East Sussex BN3 2FA

Simultaneously published in the USA and Canada
by Routledge
270 Madison Avenue, New York, NY 10016

Reprinted 2010

*Routledge is an imprint of the Taylor & Francis Group, an Informa
business*

Copyright © 2008 Routledge

Typeset in Times by Garfield Morgan, Swansea, West Glamorgan
Printed and bound in Great Britain by TJ International Ltd, Padstow,
Cornwall
Cover design by Sandra Heath

This publication has been produced with paper manufactured to strict
environmental standards and with pulp derived from sustainable
forests.

British Library Cataloguing in Publication Data
A catalogue record for this book is available from the British Library

Library of Congress Cataloging in Publication Data
Burman, Erica.
   Deconstructing developmental psychology / Erica Burman. –
2nd ed.
      p. cm.
   Includes bibliographical references and indexes.
   ISBN 978-0-415-39561-8 (hardcover) – ISBN 978-0-415-39562-5
(pbk.) 1. Developmental psychology. I. Title.
   BF713.B87 2007
   155–dc22

                                                  2007010337

ISBN 978-0-415-39561-8 (hbk)
ISBN 978-0-415-39562-5 (pbk)

Contents

PART III
Developing communication   179

PART IV
Cognitive development: the making of rationality   239

Preface to second edition

Welcome to the extensively revised second edition of *Deconstructing Developmental Psychology*. Although the chapter structure remains largely the same, its text has changed quite substantially. Thirteen years or so on from the first edition, the world seems a rather different place. The geo-political situation has changed quite dramatically, with major wars being waged (against 'terrorism'), accompanied by the rise of new racisms and new fundamentalisms. Neoliberalism has further penetrated the gross and intimate aspects of our lives, and there is a generalisation of the 'feminised' conditions of poverty and insecure, low-paid and part-time conditions of work such that these are now shared by many men. These changed conditions have highlighted further the major divisions between the rich and poor of the planet, which have been reflected in shifts within models of childhood. Alongside the general deterioration in personal and global security there is an intensification of the portrayal of childhood as a site of vulnerability and protection, albeit ambivalently so.

All these political 'developments' (or perhaps regressions?) have demanded some updating and modification of the claims I made in the first edition of *Deconstructing Developmental Psychology*. One major issue is that the publication of the first edition largely pre-dated the rise and impact of the child rights and childhood studies movements, although those perspectives (such as James and Prout 1990) informed the first edition (and my book in turn came to inform subsequent versions, Jenks 1996, 2005; Woodhead 1999). This second edition now engages with and references these debates – as vital contributions to current discussion of children and childhoods. It also has the advantage of now being able to connect with a substantial critical educational literature that takes further some of the practical consequences of this deconstructionist approach for nurseries and in schools (e.g. Dahlberg *et al.* 1999; Hultkvist and Dahlberg 2001; Moss and Petrie 2002; Dahlberg and Moss 2005; MacNaughton 2005), as well as further analyses that connect economic and political models of development with psychological ones. Indeed the companion volume to this book, *Developments: Child, Image, Nation* (Burman, in press) takes further the resonances between representations of childhood and national development noted here, with a focus on cultural-political debates rather than only specifically addressing developmental psychology.

Not only is this second edition therefore extensively revised and updated, it also covers debates that have acquired significance in the interim – both within developmental psychology and within public and social policy debates about children and childhoods. Chapter 7, the longest by far in the first edition, is now longer still, indicating the proliferation of attachment theory across the lifespan as well as into neurology, as also a reflection of the 'biological turn' in psychiatry and culture which renews such orientations within developmental psychology. New additions include neo-Piagetian studies in the form of 'theory of mind' (in Chapter 3) and the greater attention accorded to Vygotskyan-inspired approaches (in Chapters 9, 12 and 13). Fathers, once a small and rather marginal topic in developmental psychology, now exercise considerable academic as well as policy attention, and so this is reflected by more extensive treatment within the book (Chapter 8). The past 15 years have seen the consolidation of debates around child rights, alongside an increasing policy focus on child protection, and so this is now reflected throughout the second edition, in the form of the introduction of a new chapter (Chapter 5), as well as substantive treatment of notions of 'giving voice' to children (in Chapter 6). As Fortress Europe has closed its doors and draconian immigration measures combine with escalating racisms (notwithstanding the significant internal divisions also within the European Union), I also highlight further the ways exclusionary concepts of citizenship and nationality work to exclude many children access from such rights. Hence questions of 'culture', colonial legacies and the explicit mobilisation of new concepts of active childhood within neoliberal economic policies now form explicit topics within this edition.

Indeed contemporary policy figures much more visibly in this text than it did in the first edition and, while it may be inevitable that some parochiality creeps into the analysis when taking specific examples from national-level policies (on preschool provision or parent support programmes, for example), I hope that this is balanced by the more explicit connections made between individual, national and international economic development policies. Indeed perhaps Britain is a significant arena from which to formulate the arguments of this book, given that in a recent UNICEF report it was rated the worst of all economically advantaged countries for children to live, claiming that children are unhappier and feel less loved than anywhere else in the 'developed' world (UNICEF 2007). Above all we see how, far from receding from view, the figure of the child and approaches to child development are even more in dispute. It seems that, far from resolving the social problems that it came into being to address, developmental psychology has proliferated to accommodate their expansion. As the 'psy complex' comes to exercise an even greater grip on our lives, we have an even greater need for critical resources to interrogate and resist its presumptions.

This second edition of *Deconstructing Developmental Psychology* strengthens its position as a vital resource for childhood and educational researchers to scrutinise the developmental claims they may be tempted either to invoke or to refuse. Whichever, I think the vicissitudes of the past 20 years of critical engagement have shown that the developmentalist paradigm cannot be wished away, and – notwithstanding current attention to children's agency and participation, with the rise of the model of the child as 'competent social actor' – cannot readily be dispensed with.

This second edition has benefited enormously from critical and appreciative responses from international friends and colleagues, who have so continuously affirmed the relevance of its arguments, even when (or precisely because?) its critique of dominant Anglo-US developmental psychology is formulated from that context, and in English. These international networks reassure me of the enthusiastic audience for the arguments put forward here, even when more local contexts (especially within Anglo-US psychology) has sometimes seemed less receptive. My thinking (as well as my spirits!) have been enormously enriched by these international collaborations across countries as diverse as Australia, Brazil, Canada, Chile, China, India, Japan, Mexico, New Zealand, Pakistan, Puerto Rico, South Africa, the United States and Venezuela, as well as my Finnish, German, Greek, Norwegian, Spanish and Swedish friends and colleagues. I have also found support and inspiration from interdisciplinary discussions spanning development studies, geography, politics and especially women's studies. This revised edition cannot reflect just how much my thinking has been enriched by such connections, but I hope it at least gives some indications of this.

In particular, I want to express my deep thanks to Pam Alldred, Tom Billington, Karen Ciclitira, Khatidja Chantler, Babak Fozooni, Angel Gordo López, Peter Moss, Ann Phoenix, Vasu Reddy, Matthew Waites and Suzanne Zeedyk for their comments, suggestions for revisions for this book and in some cases even supplying material. I also want to thank my 'South African reference group' – Jill Bradbury, Jane Callaghan, Jude Clark and Ingrid Palmary – whose astute comments and perspectives in our work together over the past few years have helped to alert me further to the Eurocentric terms of developmental psychology. And my thanks – as ever – go to Ian Parker for his attentive companionship and support.

I dedicated the first edition of *Deconstructing Developmental Psychology* to my nieces and nephews, in the hope that by the time they were old enough to read it its contents would no longer be relevant. Sadly, the demise of oppressive developmental psychology has not yet arrived. Meanwhile Hannah, Rachel, David and Jonathan have become young adults, having negotiated their ways through the childhoods we made for them, and they made for themselves. I dedicate this second edition to the memory of Ann Levett, dear friend and also developmental psychologist, wise woman, activist, teacher, researcher and therapist, who first introduced me to South

Africa in 1994 where the politics of psychology has been so clearly connected with wider political struggles.

Erica Burman
May 2007

Acknowledgements to first edition

In addition to all the people whose work has been so useful, and influential, for me, I want to thank:

Kath Holland, Ian Parker and Sharon Witton for comments on the manuscript; Julian Pine for supplying lots of papers;

Liz Bondi, Katrina Long, Ian Parker and Diane Samuels for their general support during the process of its preparation;

Heather Walton and Berenice Burman for proof reading;

Valerie Walkerdine for her enthusiastic response to my tentative proposal to write this;

David Ingleby for the faxes full of comments;

Elena Lieven, John Morss and Rex and Wendy Stainton Rogers who, in addition to their constructive commentaries on earlier drafts, have encouraged me to realise that there really is a network of critical developmental psychologists; Sue Jameson for all those articles;

the library staff at Elizabeth Gaskell, the Manchester Metropolitan University, for discharging lots of books that have been so entertaining and useful;

the psychology technicians for the computer first aid;

successive cohorts of students taking developmental psychology on the BSc Psychology at the Manchester Metropolitan University who have been subjected to various forms of the material outlined in this book over the past six years, including the feminist students who, year after year, confirmed that it was important and worthwhile;

and the women I work with on the MA in Women's Studies at the Manchester Metropolitan University who display a healthy suspicion of psychology.

Erica Burman

Introduction

God forbid that any book should be banned. The practice is as indefensible as infanticide.

(Dame Rebecca West 1928)

Sooner murder an infant in its cradle than nurse unacted desires.

(William Blake, *Proverbs of Hell*)

Deconstructing Developmental Psychology is a critical introduction to developmental psychology: critical in the sense that it comments upon rather than replaces mainstream accounts of developmental psychology; introductory in the sense that it aims to present in an accessible way a synthesis of various existing critiques and discussions that are often complex and seemingly very specific in their remit, but which have major and important consequences for the project of developmental psychology and for all those involved with practices around children and child development that it informs. This book focuses on the relation between academic research and social policies and practices, in particular to highlight and often question the desirability of the effects of developmental psychological research (and also the possibility of the division between theory and application).

As the title suggests, my aim is to deconstruct developmental psychology, that is to identify and evaluate the guiding themes or discourses that structure its current dominant forms. To identify suggests an active search for patterning, while evaluation implies a process of commentary. I use the term 'deconstruction' in the sense of laying bare, of bringing under scrutiny, the coherent moral-political themes that developmental psychology elaborates, and to look beyond current frameworks within which developmental psychological investigation has been formulated to take up the broader questions of where these themes fit into the social practices in which psychology functions. I am using deconstruction here not as a formal analytical framework but rather to indicate a process of critique. This arises from a critical movement within psychology (exemplified by Henriques *et al.* 1984; Parker and Shotter 1990; Parker *et al.* 1995; Burman 1998a; Parker

1999) which takes as its topic the structure of psychological practice. Similar developments have since taken place in education, as exemplified by Davies (1994), Dahlberg *et al.* (1999), Hultqvist and Dahlberg (2001), MacLure (2003), Canella and Viruru (2004), Dahlberg and Moss (2005) and MacNaughton (2005).

In this book I will be addressing the discourses that developmental psychology both constructs and informs, using the term 'discourse' to refer to socially organised frameworks of meaning that define categories and specify domains of what can be said and done. Whilst the 'discursive turn' has now been extensively discussed (see Parker 1992a; Burman and Parker 1993; Davies 1994; Burman *et al.* 1996; MacLure 2003), my focus here is on applying these ideas to offer alternative readings of dominant Euro-US, or more specifically Anglo-US, psychology. I will be analysing developmental psychological texts, treating these not as transparent reflections of (logical or empirical) 'truths' but as *accounts* whose specific form can be understood as having wider significance. My concern with developmental psychological accounts is not simply in terms of the language within which these are cast, although this is important; rather this book addresses how these accounts reflect and engage with the practices associated with them. In this sense the key task here is to explore how, why and in what ways sets of ideas in developmental psychology have functioned outside as well as within its relatively restricted domain.

Developmental psychology, more than any other variety of psychology, has a powerful impact on our everyday lives and ways of thinking about ourselves. Its effects are so great that they are often almost imperceptible, taken-for-granted features about our expectations of ourselves, others, parents, children and families. Due to the divide in the West between the public world of work and the private, domestic sphere inscribed by industrialisation, the home and our actions within it carry so much emotional investment that evaluation of relationships and behaviours conducted within it (as mothers, fathers, children) is deeply felt, and often feared. Part of the imperceptibility lies in the ways in which developmental psychology has structured the standards and even the forms of state intervention that accompany welfare policies of protection and care. Acknowledging these issues means going beyond the representation of developmental psychological research as scientific and benign in its effects to consider its wider institutional and personal origins, and impact.

Organisation

The structure of this book reflects the main topics and categorisations employed by many widely available developmental psychology texts. In following this structure I do not mean simply to reproduce those categorisations, but rather to facilitate the co-ordination of this account with the others. Hence the titles of chapters and headings aim to highlight the discursive construction of topic areas. In commenting on these, the book traces the accounts of development along the semi-biographical or chrono-logical path typically elaborated by such texts for the notional 'child'. In Chapter 1, I start by exploring the historical background to the contem-porary role that developmental psychology and developmental psycholo-gists have played. This sets the focus for the first major section of the book, Part I, 'Constructing the Subject', which is concerned with how develop-mental psychology arrived at and investigates its unit of development. Here, Chapter 2 addresses this in terms of infancy research, Chapter 3 through discussions about social development and Chapters 4 and 5 by analysing historical and cultural influences that inform our conceptions of childhood and the limits of these conceptions.

Part II, 'Social Development and the Structure of Caring', focuses on the role accorded to, and particular representations of, families and parents. Chapter 6 examines the ways in which families are discussed in develop-mental psychological accounts. Chapter 7 analyses the literature on the formation and importance of relationships, and Chapter 8 evaluates the preconditions and consequences of the shift in cultural and academic focus from mothers to fathers.

Part III, 'Developing Communication', is devoted to the research on how children learn to talk (Chapter 9), and how child language can best be promoted (Chapter 10). Chapter 11 draws on a rather different set of per-spectives to argue for the importance of analysing the power relations that structure adult–child interaction, including that of psychologist and child.

Part IV, 'Cognitive Development: The Making of Rationality', deals with the role accorded to Piagetian and Vygotskyan theory within developmental psychology. Chapter 12 explores historical and cultural factors relevant to interpreting Piaget's and Vygotsky's work, offering some challenges to received understandings of their claims as well as critically evaluating the impact of their work in terms of how these ideas have been incorporated within social practices. Chapter 13 develops this further in relation to the impact of Piaget's and Vygotsky's work in educational contexts. Chapter 14 addresses the application of developmental models in the arena of morality through the work of Kohlberg, as illustrative of some of the major diffi-culties that the cognitive developmental approach involves. This question also brings us back to the moral status of developmental psychology and its collusion in the organised amorality of contemporary life. Methodological and political issues posed by the arguments put forward in this book are considered, including further clarification of the scope and limits of its claims (which are also further addressed in Burman, in press a).

Key themes

A number of key issues have structured the forms and functions of developmental psychology. These stretch across the seemingly (within current formulations) disparate arenas of social, cognitive or language development. While treating each topic separately I have tried to indicate continuities, highlighting the specific forms that the recurring structural themes take within particular domains. The repetition of these issues is in itself evidence not only of their pervasiveness, but also of the greater unity of preoccupations that developmental psychology has informed and reflected, as a vital contributor to modern state practices.

Put briefly, these themes are as follows: first, that tools of measurement produce research objects and research subjects. Developmental psychology has been driven by the demand to produce technologies of measurement. These methodological parameters have reflected broader ideological assumptions in selecting and abstracting child and mother as its units of enquiry. (And it should be noted that while my account is cast primarily in terms of biological mothers and fathers, the same literature and debates apply just as – if not more, given professional models – to adoptive or foster parents; see also Cradock, 2007.)

Second, in many respects mothers (and sometimes fathers) have come to replace children as the primary focus for developmental psychological investigation, reflecting wider themes of regulation – in terms of (a) active intervention in (especially) women's lives; (b) indirect impact through women's subscription to developmental psychological accounts about how children develop and what is 'best' for them; (c) the broader impact of developmental psychology as it informs the cultural climate and structure of provision and services available for children (and working mothers). It is the adequacy of mothering that developmental psychology is called upon to regulate and legislate upon, and the continuity with which this issue crops up across the range of topics in developmental psychology is a manifestation of the widespread and routine subjection of women to the developmental psychological gaze. As we shall see, fathers do not escape this gaze but are subjected to it in rather different ways. It could perhaps be said that we have seen a displacement in developmental psychology from 'the child' to other (responsible) parties engaging with this child, with the moral burden of this responsibility increasingly placed on families, within liberal democracies as much as countries that have no welfare state apparatus.

The third recurring issue is that normative descriptions provided by developmental psychology slip into naturalised prescriptions. These are fuelled by the appeal to biology and evolution, which is called upon in areas as diverse as attachment theory, language development and education. Representations of children frequently function as a projective slate on to which fantasies of nature and its relation to society are inscribed. Developmental psychology makes claims to be scientific. Its use of evolutionary assumptions to link the social to the biological provides a key cultural arena in which evolutionary and biologising ideas are replayed and legitimised. Closely associated with its technologies and guiding preoccupations has been its use to classify and stratify individuals, groups and populations so as to maintain class, gender and racist oppression. This is a central theme of this book which involves connecting the psychological project of describing individual development, which is usually cast in terms of child development, with policies and practices in international economic development. Developmental psychology forms an explicit resource within international aid and development policy, of course in relation to ameliorating child poverty and abuse and promoting child rights, but also within prescriptions for national development policies. Here we see how concerns around children and childhoods have always been, and continue to be, instrumentalised in terms of the fashioning of future citizens – including the generation of appropriate workers and consumers as well as promoting democratic participation.

A fourth strand within this book concerns the relation between psychology and psychoanalysis. A psychoanalytic reading of developmental psychology offers glimpses into the repressed themes of fear that underlie the scientific demand for control and prediction. Psychoanalysis is increasingly being used as a resource to critique psychology (Walkerdine 1990; Frosh 1997; Parker 1997; Parker 2004), including developmental psychology (see e.g. Henriques *et al.* 1984; Bradley 1989; Morss 1996). This enables a questioning of what lies behind the privileging of objectivity and control over the ambiguity, flux and ambivalence of the issues raised by caring for children.

However, it is important to note that this is a particular reading of the relationship between psychoanalysis and psychology that addresses the particular context of Anglo-US psychology. In other times and places, Latin America and South Africa, for example, psychoanalysis has been allied with psychology, and even is a dominant form of psychology. Although I argue in this book that psychoanalysis is the repressed other of psychology, this statement refers to a particular history of their relations. Hence there is nothing essential about the status of psychoanalysis as a critique of psychology. In psychology's Anglo-US 'centres', too, this relationship is undergoing considerable reworking, particularly in relation to developments in neuroscience that (for some) usher in the vista of connecting psychodynamics with neurophysiology and so putting psychoanalysis on a more 'scientific' footing. The so-called 'memory wars' of the mid to late 1990s around false/recovered memories illustrated new emerging disciplinary alliances between psychoanalysis and psychology (Burman 1997a, 1998b; Haaken 1998). Later in this book I discuss the seeming revival of the alliance between psychoanalysis and psychology within current developments around 'attachment'. This has occurred alongside wider cultural-political shifts that have brought questions of emotional regulation and literacy into social policy in new ways.

The fifth, and final, theme concerns how the selection of children as objects of developmental psychological enquiry leads to a failure to theorise the psychological context they inhabit. This contributes to individualist interpretations of socially structured phenomena that can lapse into victim blaming, as where mothers or families are treated as responsible for the social ills of the world in which they are trying to rear their children. Where the focus moves beyond the individual to consider class and culture, these have frequently, explicitly or implicitly, been treated as responsible for failures of child development or education, while the motivations or resources drawn upon by those who make such evaluations all too often remain unexamined. This book attempts to open up these structural themes for scrutiny, together with their underlying assumptions and the practices to which they give rise.

How to read this book

Children and childhood are rhetorically invoked in multiple ways for sometimes (as in my introductory quotations) divergent or contradictory purposes. Similarly, there are various ways of approaching developmental psychology: from the point of view of the child, from that of parents and families, and from the position of professionals or agencies directly or indirectly involved with children, while written from the third. Accounts are usually cast in terms of the first approach, of what the child is, does and what it will do next. In this book, I adopt the second position and explore the consequences of this for our focus on the child. These consequences are pervasive both for adults who do (and do not) care for children and for professionals involved with services for children. In fact, I will be taking the child-centred focus of developmental psychology as itself a topic of enquiry and critique.

This book therefore concentrates less on 'facts' that developmental psychology has unearthed than on how particular topics arise as interesting areas of enquiry. The perspective I am adopting is to look at developmental psychological knowledge as constructed within social practices rather than as a distinct content area. This means that this book is not only concerned with what developmental psychology has 'found' and the claims that it makes, but also considers the significance of the types of research and research outcomes in three ways: the circumstances in which the research was carried out; the social and political influences that made the topic seem relevant; and the role and impact of that research. In other words, developmental psychology is treated as a topic of enquiry in its own right, with objects and subjects of study (children, families, mothers, teachers, social workers, child therapists, etc.) constructed in relation to it.

My aim in this book, then, is to pose questions about what is all too often assumed to be given or obvious. For example: why is developmental psychology always presumed to be about 'the child'? What are the consequences of this for the theory and practice of developmental psychology? How would this be different from discussing 'children' or 'contexts in which people grow and change'? This book challenges the common-sense view of developmental psychology, treating this view as itself a resource through which to explore developmental psychology's project and practice.

In accordance with this perspective, I frequently refer to 'the child', the 'individual' or the 'subject' of developmental psychology using the feminine pronoun 'she'. This practice departs from the conventions used in many psychology textbooks – or certainly the ones I read as a student where the child was referred to using at best the 'generic' masculine pronoun 'he'. (I have been pleased to note that this new practice has been adopted within the Spanish translation of the first edition of this book, Burman 1998c.) In more general terms, this should lead us to consider *whose* development we are talking about – that of an individual? An abstract 'knower'? Everyone's development? (Are there claims to universality here?) Does it reflect all cultures? Classes? Men's and women's experiences? What are the consequences for developmental psychology of its forgetting of gender as a structuring dimension of development, instead of talking generally about children? Indeed should we not be specifying *which* children we are making claims about? Even the seemingly innocuous 'arrow' of time can be critiqued for its cultural masculinity (in the form of asocial individualism).

> The arrow metaphor expresses three contemporary explanations of developmental change: (1) biology, which launches movements; (2) an ideal solution to a cognitive task, which serves as the target for development; (3) linearity, which ensures continuity of travel. Arrows describe linear thought and linear development in a universal child. Arrows are also, of course, typically associated with aggression, domination, imposition of a view and penetration of an influence. An arrow expresses development as a push towards change, not as a force that simultaneously transforms and is transformed.
>
> (Kofsky Scholnick 2000: 34)

Here I want to note that the structure of this book departs from that of other more conventional developmental psychology texts by not having a chapter on gender. In part this is because gender issues are addressed throughout the text, and indeed feminist perspectives have been a key inspirational source for its arguments. But there are two other important reasons. First, gender issues infuse discussions of developmental psychology and child development so thoroughly that they cannot be simply relegated to a specific chapter. Rather their complexity is generated by the gendered structuring not only of childhoods, but also of parenthood, grandparenthood and professional relations. On this last point, we too often forget that professional titles obscure how nurses, health visitors, teachers and social workers are primarily women – and indeed the gendered character of this relationship can enter in covert and negative ways as when professionals attempt to ward off gendered identification with a neglectful or abusive parent they are working with by being unduly punitive (Dutton Conn 1995; Featherstone 1997).

The second reason is more analytical, but also makes a critical intervention. The discipline of psychology was given timely rejuvenation by the rise of 'sex difference' research in the 1970s – relying on research practices that were both methodologically and politically suspect, and confined to understandings of sex/gender that presume what they claim to study (see Kitzinger 1994): i.e. treating gender as (in its 'finished' form) a stable, fixed, singular identity framed within dominant discourses of heteronormativity. Developmental approaches to gender development have functioned as a key route by which to legitimate such conceptions, reading on to the development of the child the normative story of the emergence of adult gendered and (hetero)sexed categories. Put this way, its function in closing down the emergence, and appreciation of the emergence, of new forms of sexed/gendered subjectivities becomes clear.

Moreover, we should ask why it is that gender should function as the key axis of difference, often figuring in texts as a separate chapter whereas, for example, notions of classed or racialised/ethnic positions do not. Without in any way minimising the current significance of gendered identities and positions in structuring how we feel and act, and feel able to act, as well as structural positions and possibilities, it is worth pausing to consider how the privileging of gender can work in paradoxical ways: as the prototypical axis of difference it comes both to represent other such differences (and so is in danger of assimilating 'race' or class issues to the parameters taken by gendered analysis – which may well be related owing to axes of power, but are not identical) but thereby is also in danger of occluding these differences (see Burman 2005a).

For these reasons, unlike other treatments, the approach taken here does not focus on identity (and in that sense, as discussed later in this chapter, is not 'child centred' – see also Burman 1998b, 1999) but rather interrogates the disciplinary imperatives to generate accounts of subjectivity in such terms. As a final consideration, we might question why we should focus on gender, rather than, say, 'race' or class. An endless vista of proliferating identities thus opens up, revealing yet again a key limitation of psychological models that treat individual experience as a possession or property rather than the outcome of structural positions and relationships. There are, however, now many fine texts discussing the development of gender and sexuality (Stainton Rogers and Stainton Rogers 1992; Greene 2003; Shefer *et al.* 2006).

Throughout the book, I will be drawing links between what may seem like rather conceptual debates within the discipline and their effects within the practices in which developmental psychology participates. Developmental psychological knowledge informs a number of professional practices involved with health, education and welfare that touch everybody's lives. It informs everyday popular understandings with, for example, notions of emotional intelligence increasingly circulating in self-help but also in professional and policy contexts. These rely on notions of child development, as well as claims about (more and less) desirable models of communication (Burman in press b).

In particular, developmental psychology forms part of the knowledge base within so-called developed societies for health visiting and social work, as well as education and law. For example, on what basis do law courts arrive at an understanding of what constitutes a child's 'best interest'? Or, when is a child deemed to have sufficient understanding to be legally responsible for their actions? What underlies an education welfare officer's opinion that a child's 'social and emotional needs' will be better catered for outside mainstream school? What criteria do adoption agencies use in evaluating whether or not adoption is likely to be successful? What intellectual resources and expertise do legal and welfare professionals turn to when they seek to determine children's competence to participate in decision making? These are some of the ways in which developmental psychology reverberates far beyond the theory or the experimental laboratory, as well as beyond the pages of child advice magazines and toyshops.

To facilitate the connection between the arguments elaborated within the book and the general implications for theory and practice that flow from them, each chapter has suggestions for further reading, and practical demonstrations or activities that exemplify its key points. These activities can be used to structure individual or group work. They are based on my experience of teaching students of psychology, nursing, healthcare and youth and community work, and involvement in training teachers and social workers. They are intended as a resource that can be adapted or extended to a variety of audiences and contexts.

Cultural constructions

As already mentioned, the approach here is not the 'child-centred' variety generally found. (Indeed this book interrogates what 'child centredness' is.) Rather, the starting point is that children and childhood are *constructed*; we therefore have to study not only 'the child' but also the context (that is, the interpersonal, cultural, historical and political situation) that produces her. This book focuses on families and cultural-political practices; on the ways in which parents, and in particular mothers, are positioned in relation to children; and the effects that cultural prescriptions for 'good mothering' as relayed through developmental psychology have for women. It might be a surprise to some readers that it was Piaget (1950) who said: 'Child psychology is a branch equally of sociology and psychology, since the social environment is an integral component of development.' More recently, Goodnow and Collins (1990: 10) comment: 'For us an exclusively child-centered focus is limited. Child development is not the whole of developmental psychology. Moreover parents are interesting in their own right.

Their experiences, satisfactions and development are topics to be explored without any necessity to justify the exploration on the grounds of effects on children.' The developmental psychology generally studied is usually conducted on, and written by researchers from, Western societies. Indeed it is typically Anglo-US, and the bulk of this work is North American – although it exerts its influence throughout the English-speaking world. Thus the West is not only a geographical region (with significant class and 'race' variations), but also a form of knowledge practice (Venn 2000).

This point prompts a word on terminology. In this book I shift between formulations that try (inadequately) to grapple with this problem of the globalisation of specific, culturally privileged understandings. Thus, while I sometimes write of the West (meaning Europe and the US), I also sometimes refer to North–South relations which highlights the geographical distribution – across hemispheres of the world – of wealth, poverty and privilege (yet there are many political and economic 'norths' and 'souths' within the regional and political North and South). At other points I use the stark but I think rather telling descriptor of 'richer versus poorer', and sometimes '(over)developed versus developing' – both sets of comparisons working to draw attention to their relational character (whereby the inferiorised or immature status of 'developing' countries arises from the historical and current power wielded by 'developed' or more accurately – in terms of wealth and overconsumption – 'overdeveloped' countries). While there are problems with all these formulations they do at least highlight a key set of issues that – contrary to the universalised claims of most developmental psychology – we cannot ignore. So although there are clearly problems of egocentrism in talking of 'Western' societies (which are, for example, east of the Americas, and north of Africa), I retain this usage as a reminder of the constitutive relationship between orientalism and occidentalism as, I hope, affording a direct connection between psychology and post-colonial theory (see also Burman 1997b; Hook *et al.* 2004).

In the main, then, in this book I will also be drawing on culturally dominant Anglo-US sources, not because I wish to subscribe to the same assumptions, but rather because we need to analyse the structure of the dominant approach in order better to comment on its implications, especially in terms of its impact in post-colonial countries whose psychological services (and perhaps psychologies) are moulded by that colonial legacy. However, there is a longstanding (but until recently relatively separate and philosophically different) Soviet tradition (Valsiner 1988), and of course a Western European one. Later in the book I comment on the selective importing of Piaget's and Vygotsky's work and their subsequent insertion into existing practices. This offers a prime example of the cultural and philosophical tensions between different strands of developmental psychology.

This book focuses primarily on infancy and early childhood. Traditionally, developmental psychology has not only concerned itself with plotting the growth of individuals, but has also compartmentalised the human lifespan so that 'development' is usually portrayed as confined to early life, and psychological change during and after adulthood is limited to intellectual decline. In this, developmental psychology follows, and perhaps even informs, the earlier focus of UNICEF and other international child aid organisations on the early years. This has since been revised, with child rights and UNICEF now addressing the position of older children and young people. Moreover, the category of childhood has also expanded – especially in richer (over)developed societies – for significant reasons that will be touched on later. Such views have recently been disputed, and 'development' has come to be seen as a 'lifespan' affair. However, this tends to magnify rather than resolve the problems of naturalising the lifespan in the name of extending the trajectory of developmental progress. Yet lifespan models – in emphasising the significance of cohort and generational effects – have been methodologically important in demonstrating the inevitable cultural-historical influences on individual development (Baltes *et al.* 1980; Sugarman 1990; Berk 2007) and are allied to radical critiques challenging the individualism of dominant psychology (associated with the dialectical psychology movement initiated by Klaus Riegel (1975, 1977, 1979)). In this book, I will be principally problematising developmental psychology's study of the child as an isolated individual, rather than solely criticising the focus on childhood as a life stage. Nevertheless, the arguments elaborated in relation to childhood throughout this book also apply to the assumptions guiding the models of adulthood and ageing. These wider applications have been addressed by Lichtman (1987). Hence it could be even argued that lifespan psychology has played a role in deconstructing developmental psychology (Fozooni, personal communication).

Finally, this book highlights the nature of the normative assumptions guiding developmental theory and research, and assesses the impact of these on our understanding of 'the child' or 'the parent–child relationship' in relation to both the professional and non-professional social practices that developmental psychology informs.

Claims and disclaimers

While it may be tempting to treat this book as just a commentary on, rather than a contribution to, developmental psychology, it should also be considered as part of developmental psychology. A deconstruction of developmental psychology is no less a part of developmental psychology for that. These ideas should not be marginalised as 'outside' the discipline, for this would perpetuate the image of developmental psychologists as unreflexive, anti-theoretical empiricists. This book has been written out of a long engagement with and deep commitment to the ethical, political, epistemological and methodological concerns that drive developmental psychology. I do not claim that we should dispense with development, nor surrender claims to development – on which many ethical demands for justice and self-determination rely. Rather we need to be vigilant about the range of intended and unintended effects mobilised by claims to development, to be mindful of whose development is being privileged and, correspondingly, whose is marginalised.

Commentaries on the practice of psychology have for too long been seen as the province of sociologists and historians. There is now increasing recognition that behind the mask of detached, disinterested objective research lie interpretative and subjective features that, as is the way of repressed material, exert their influences in forms of which we are not aware. Rather than condemning developmental psychology to serving and reproducing this unconscious agenda, we should be moving towards some awareness of the historical and current reasons for the particular ways developmental research has been structured. This should enable a more informed revaluation of the possibilities and problems of developmental research.

The resources I have drawn upon in writing this book have been feminist and poststructuralist ideas (and in particular the feminist reworkings of poststructuralist ideas). In both dimly perceived and consciously developed ways, the history of my own (multiple and contradictory) subject position-ings within developmental psychological discourses – as child, daughter, sister, aunt, child-free, childless, part-time step-parent, daughter of single parent, feminist, child-centred, woman-centred and so on – has been instru-mental in the elaboration of this account. I list these not, or not only, to engage in the confessional mode of expression conventionally adopted within an Introduction, but to emphasise that I, as author, am as subject to the power of the discourses which developmental psychology produces and reproduces as the putative children and families I discuss in this book. I, like everyone else, cannot stand, or rather speak, outside them. But I can try to describe and analyse their consequences, and maybe by such reflections and interventions we can create new ways of doing developmental psychology.

1 Origins

Many experimental psychologists continue to look upon the field of child psychology as a proper field of research for women and for men whose experimental masculinity is not of the maximum. This attitude of patronage is based almost entirely upon a blissful ignorance of what is going on in the tremendously virile field of child behavior.

(Murchison 1933: x)

Nowadays the status of developmental psychology is not çlear. Some say that it is a perspective or an approach to investigating general psychological problems, rather than a particular domain or subdiscipline. According to this view we can address all major areas of psychology, such as memory, cognition, etc., from this perspective. The unit of development under investigation is also variable. We could be concerned with the development of a process, or a mechanism, rather than an individual. This is in marked contrast with the popular representations of developmental psychology which equate it with the practicalities of child development or, more recently, human development (with the relatively recent recognition that development is a 'lifespan' affair, Baltes *et al.* 1980; Berk 2007).

These paradoxical, mixed conceptions of developmental psychology testify to different aspects of its history. This chapter will show how deeply the discipline of developmental psychology, and indeed psychology itself, has been structured by its history. For if we look at the origins of developmental psychology we begin to get a picture of (a) the social movements from which it arose; (b) the social movements in which it participated; (c) how these have set the terms of developmental enquiry that reverberate even now. This chapter takes seriously calls to generate a 'critical social history of developmental psychology' (e.g. Bronfenbrenner *et al.* 1986), to elaborate how modern developmental psychology arose in the late nineteenth century to answer particular questions related to evolutionary theory and anthropology as well as philosophy. In so doing, developmental psychology participated in social movements explicitly concerned with the comparison, regulation and control of groups and societies, and is closely identified with the development of tools of mental measurement, classi-fication of abilities and the establishment of norms. It is associated with the rise of capitalism and science, subscribing to a specific gendered, alienated and commodified model of scientific practice (Parker 2007). All of these features are reflected in the terms of developmental research, including the reproduction of the division between rationality and emotion.

Child study

Ideas about children's nature and characteristics of course long pre-date modern psychology, and these were consistently concerned with how best 'to ensure that the person immanent in the child will become a responsible cultural heir and fulfil the necessary destiny envisioned for him by the family and the society' (Borstelmann 1983: 35). The new psychology of the mid- to late nineteenth century placed itself within and between various disciplines: natural history, anthropology, physiology and medicine. Most accounts take Charles Darwin as the author of the first child study with his 'Biographical Sketch of an Infant', which, though published in 1877, was based on notes made in 1840 (Riley 1983; Rose 1985; Walkerdine and Lucey 1989). Not surprisingly, Darwin's interest was in the relative contri-bution of genetic endowment and environmental experience – identifying the characteristics that differentiate humans (and human children) from animals, placing great weight on human ingenuity and creativity, especially as exhibited in language. This was one among many early observational, diary studies of young children, although, as Bradley (1989) points out, there had been many conducted earlier, especially by women, but these have been eclipsed from the history of developmental psychology. In retrospect, both this study and the importance it has been accorded can be taken as prototypical of the form developmental enquiry was to take.

First, the infant is depicted as a biological organism abstracted from its familial and material environment. By virtue of being very young, and having had less opportunity to learn, the infant is seen as close to nature, devoid of the trappings of adult training and (Western) 'civilisation'. In contradictory ways, romantic and scientific models combine to locate within the child both *more* knowledge ('the child is father to the man') and (by virtue of the child's lesser and different understanding) the *route* to knowledge. In this, developmental psychology naturalises the romantic fiction of children as innocent bearers of wisdom by producing them as objects and subjects of study.

The perspective underlying this project partakes of the theory of 'cultural recapitulation', that is, that the individual in her or his lifetime reproduces the patterns and stages of development exhibited by the development of the species – 'ontogeny recapitulates phylogeny'. The study of infants in the mid-nineteenth century, along with that of 'primitives' and of natural his-tory, was motivated by the quest to discover the origins and specificities of mind, that is, the human adult mind. This enterprise was related to similar ventures in anthropology and animal observation that were closely allied with European (and particularly British) imperialism, maintaining the hierarchy of racial superiority that justified colonial rule. The child of that time was equated with the 'savage' or 'undeveloped'; since both were seen as intellectually immature, 'primitives' and children were studied to illuminate necessary stages for subsequent development. As James Sully wrote in his 1881 article 'Babies and Science':

> The modern psychologist, sharing in the spirit of positive science, feels that he must, being at the beginning, study mind in its simplest forms. . . . [H]e carries his eye far afield to the phenomena of savage life, with its simple ideas, crude sentiments and naive habits. Again he devotes special attention to the mental life of lower animals, seeking in its phenomena the dim foreshadowing of our own perceptions, emotions etc. Finally he directs his attention to the mental life of infancy, as fitted to throw most light on the later developments of the human mind.
>
> (Sully 1881, quoted in Riley 1983: 47)

In addition, the apparently bizarre beliefs and behaviours of both 'primitives' and children were seen as relevant to the understanding of neurotic and pathological behaviour. As well as recapitulationism, Lamarckism (the belief in the heritability of acquired characteristics) underlay the new developmental psychology. Here it was the experience, rather than innate predispositions, that was seen as reproduced in childhood and in dreams. A set of equivalences was elaborated whereby the conception of the child was related to the 'savage', who, in turn, was seen as akin to the neurotic. Comparison between child, prehistoric man [sic] and 'savage' presupposes a conception of development, of individual and of evolutionary progress, as unilinear, as directed steps up an ordered hierarchy. This confirmed the intellectual superiority of the Western male. In such ways the project of individual (child) development became tied to a wider model of social and economic development. This model in turn reinscribed the gendered and racialised privilege of the cultural masculinity of the West as the normalised model of the nation state. 'Progress' is a key term that ties individual, social and national development together, as post- and anti-developmental critics of international economic development have noted (Sachs 1992; Mehmet 1995; Rahnema with Bawtree 1997).

The specifically Darwinian notion of natural selection, however, emphasises variability rather than uniformity. While Darwin's subscription to recapitulationism and Lamarckism was equivocal and implicit (Morss 1990: 14–16), these were the features taken up to structure the emergent developmental psychology. It should be noted that these views were widely held and that, among others, both Freud and Piaget subscribed to them in their writings.

While Darwin's study can in many ways be taken as prototypical (in various senses) of several others conducted by researchers such as Taine, Preyer and G.S. Hall in the 1880s (Cairns 1983; Riley 1983), John Morss (1990) argues that the effect of Darwin's work within the emerging developmental psychology was, paradoxically, to reinforce *pre*-Darwinian versions of biology, focusing on heritability rather than variation. Child study 'societies' soon flourished across Europe and the USA, observing children, weighing and measuring them, documenting their interests, states, activities. This development reflected the increasing importance of science – and a particular model of science at that – not only as a set of procedures for conducting research, but as a set of practices associated with the modern secular state.

The gendered division of labour and the scientific gaze

The child study movement 'observed' children. Guidelines on how to go about this emphasised the importance of being objective. In doing this a split or opposition was created in the process of knowledge construction – a gendered division. This also reflected the inferior position accorded women within models of competence and maturity – as closer to children and 'primitives'. Fathers were seen as having the necessary detachment and rationality to engage in scientific endeavour and mothers as too sentimental to participate. In his article (which was partly satirical – both of the practice of studying babies and of the current interest it was inspiring), Sully (1881) comments on the new phenomenon of the 'psychological papa':

> Men who previously never thought of meddling with the affairs of the nursery have been impelled to make periodic visits thither in the hope of eliciting important psychological facts. . . . [T]he tiny occupant of the cradle has had to bear the piercing glance of the scientific eye. The psychological papa has acquired a new propriety right in his offspring; he has appropriated it as a biological specimen. This new zeal for scientific knowledge has taken possession of a number of my acquaintances.
>
> (Sully 1881, quoted in Riley 1983: 48–49)

Kessen (1979) notes how the emergence of child psychology coincided with industrialisation. This brought about the separation between home and work, in turn engendering domestic labour as 'women's work' in the process of also consolidating the separation of women's and men's roles. Hence in terms of the early child study movement, as a 'scientific' enterprise, women were excluded because they were declared constitutionally incapable of regarding their children with the requisite objectivity. The mother's approach to infants:

. . . unfits her from entering very cordially into the scientific vein. She rather dislikes their being made objects of cold intellectual scrutiny and unfeeling psychological analysis. . . . To suggest a series of experiments on the gustatory sensibility of a small creature aged from twelve to twenty four hours is likely to prove a shock, even to the more strong-minded of mothers.

(Sully 1881, quoted in Riley 1983: 48–49)

Even if she does want to participate, her efforts are to be treated as suspect and as more of a handicap than anything else:

If the mother gets herself in time infected with the scientific ardour of the father, she may prove rather more of an auxiliary than he desires. Her maternal instincts impel her to regard her particular child as phenomenal in an extra-scientific sense. She . . . is predisposed to ascribe to her child a preternatural degree of intelligence.

(Sully 1881, quoted in Riley 1983: 48–49)

The Murchison quotation at the beginning of this chapter indicates how little had changed 50 years later. The equation between science and masculinity was so strong, and research practice so 'virile', as to be able to counter the supposedly feminising tendencies that proximity to children produces.

There are five ways in which the child study movement of the late nineteenth century prefigured the terms of developmental enquiry. First, it set out to investigate the mind, conceived of as singular, separate but universal. Second, the mind was seen as instantiated within the study of the development of the minds of children. Third, it researched knowledge, viewed as a natural and biological capacity – that is, subscribing to an assumption that there is a normal core of development unfolding according to biological principles. Fourth, it participated in the practices of education, welfare and medicine. Fifth, it institutionalised the ancient split between emotion and rationality, played out in the gendered practice of scientific research.

However, while the early child studies clearly privileged biological and universal questions concerned with the development of species, race and mind, there was still room to look at children's emotional proclivities and personalities. But by the 1930s clear lines of demarcation were being drawn between the elaboration of developmental norms for diagnostic use (seen as the domain of general psychology and medicine) and psychoanalysis (seen as the arena of the particular personality traits and specific idiosyncratic processes). The contrary and complementary relation between psychology and psychoanalysis came to reflect the split between the rational, conscious, uniform, individual subject of psychology, and the emotional, unconscious, contradictory, fragmented mental states associated with psychoanalysis (Urwin 1986).

The rise of psychology to meet the demands of prevailing social anxieties

The late nineteenth century was a time of social upheaval and unrest all over the world, and with revolutions brewing across Europe and anti-colonial revolts throughout the world. In England, for example, increasing urbanisation brought about by rapid industrialisation produced the appalling conditions of the Victorian slums, while the poor health of army recruits for colonial wars made the physical state of the general population a matter of widespread concern. Here we see how the colonialist imaginary connecting children, women and 'primitives' meets the regulation of the working classes at 'home':

> Fears for the military prowess of the imperial army were exacerbated by the Anglo-Boer war, with the attendant discovery of the puny physiques, bad teeth and general ill-health of the working class recruits. Motherhood became rationalized by the weighing and measuring of babies, the regimentation of domestic schedules and the bureaucratic administration of domestic education. Special opprobrium fell on 'non-productive' women (prostitutes, unmarried mothers, spinsters) and on 'non-productive' men (gays, the unemployed, the impoverished). In the eyes of policymakers and administrators, the bounds of empire could be secured and upheld only by proper domestic discipline and decorum, sexual probity and moral sanitation.
>
> (McClintock 1995: 47)

Politicians and the emerging social scientists focused their attention on the 'quality' of the population, in particular on those sectors of society considered unstable and unruly. The concern with the quality of the 'stock' and with the moulding, and ameliorating, effects of environmental conditions was reflected in the 'nature–nurture' couplet which was invented by Francis Galton in 1875, and which has since become the widely adopted formulation through which to pose questions about the origins of knowledge and learning in psychology. This early focus on change is somewhat ironic when it is recalled that 'nature–nurture' originates as a way of describing the *immutability* of human behaviour.

It has been widely documented (Meyer 1983; Walkerdine 1984; Hendrick 1990; Rose 1990) that the establishment of compulsory elementary schooling in the 1880s in England (and around the same time in France) reflected popular anxieties about 'pauperism' (seen as a trait rather than a set of circumstances) and crime. Popular education was seen as rectifying these tendencies by inculcating good habits, or at least keeping potentially disorderly groups busy and under scrutiny. Reading of the Bible was considered especially important, as well as learning skills suited to one's gender and station in life (Hunt 1985).

It is important to note here that such conceptions were not uncontested, or rather the criminalisation of the practices of the poor itself speaks to a particular set of transformations in the creation of a waged labour economy. In his meticulous documentary analysis of the trials of the London poor, Linebaugh (2003) shows how from the eighteenth century onwards the customary practice of workers being allowed to take home waste materials (whether the 'chippings' from ship-making or the tobacco and sugar from the lucrative spoils of early colonialism) was gradually outlawed. By such means workers were forcibly deprived of considerable sources of extra 'in kind' resources, on which their economic status had depended. These matters became warrants for hangings, and later transportations to the 'new world', while the forced erosion of this custom of privilege and 'perquisite' was central to the creation of an urban 'working class' whose labour would create the industrial revolution.

The notion of 'degeneracy' that now attached to the further impoverished poor elided mental and moral qualities to the extent that the object of political anxiety and scientific intervention became the 'feebleminded', who came to signify physical, moral, mental and political disintegration. In terms of the increasing currency of social Darwinist ideas (applying notions of 'survival of the fittest' to human societies), the fact that poorer sections of the population were reproducing at a faster rate than the educated middle classes provoked fears of contamination and upheaval equivalent to those of colonial occupiers seeking to maintain their rule. A state-of-the-art *Handbook of Child Development* (Pintner 1933) still devoted a chapter to 'The Feebleminded Child' in which there is a discussion of relation between feeblemindedness and delinquency. It ends with the following:

> Since feeblemindedness is not a disease that we can hope to cure, what methods are to be adopted to lessen the enormous burden that feeblemindedness places on the community? The only procedures seem to be training, segregation and sterilization. Training all the feebleminded as much as possible to reduce their liability to the community. The segregation of as many of them as possible is wise in order to diminish the chances of feebleminded offspring. The segregation of feebleminded women of child-bearing age is particularly necessary. . . . Perhaps the percentage is increasing in view of the very noticeable modern trend among the more intelligent families to limit the number of offspring, with little corresponding limitation among the less intelligent families.
>
> (Pintner 1933: 837)

Controlling and regulating those social elements considered potentially unruly presupposed the means to monitor them. Nikolas Rose (1985) discusses how 'individual psychology' emerged to fulfil this role of classification and surveillance. The psychological individual was a highly specified and studied entity whose mental qualities and development were understood by virtue of comparison with the general population. So knowledge of the individual and the general went hand in hand: each required the other, and each was defined in terms of the other. The division of the mad from the sane, the criminal from the lawful and educable from the ineducable, shifted from moral-political criteria to the equally judgemental, but scientific, evaluation of mental testing.

Catching them young: mental testing and the production of the normal child

The psychology of the individual, then, was the forerunner of the arenas now known as personality and developmental psychology, and depended heavily on testing for both its knowledge base and functioning – though psychology did not achieve its monopoly on testing without a struggle (Rose 1985). Individual psychology in late nineteenth- and early twentieth-century Western Europe reflected and translated the social preoccupations with population quality and mental abilities into policy recommendations, prescriptions on infant and child management, and education. As Donna Haraway (1989: 236–237) notes: 'Comparative psychologists have been extraordinarily creative in devising testing situations and technology: the testing industry is central to the production of social order in liberal societies, where the prescriptions of scientific management must be reconciled with ideologies of democracy.' But the technology of testing both requires and relies on the very institutions that permit its administration. Hence 'individual psychology' became central to the existence of the mental hospital, the prison, the school and the child guidance clinic. The emergence of both the individual and the child as objects of social and scientific gaze was therefore simultaneous.

> Developmental psychology was made possible by the clinic and the nursery school. Such institutions had a vital role, for they enabled the observation of numbers of children of the same age, and of children of a number of different ages, by skilled psychological experts under controlled experimental, almost laboratory, conditions. They thus simultaneously allowed for standardisation and normalisation – the collection of comparable information on a large number of subjects and its analysis in such a way as to construct norms. A developmental norm was a standard based upon the average abilities or performances of children of a certain age in a particular task or a specified activity. It thus not only presented a picture of what was *normal* for children of such an age, but also enabled the normality of any child to be assessed by comparison with this norm.
>
> (Rose 1990: 142)

By virtue of producing the unit of enquiry, the standardisation process set up a reciprocal dependence between the normal and abnormal: it is the normalisation of development that makes abnormality possible; and vice versa – in the sense that the special education system has always deeply structured, rather than merely supplemented, the mainstream schooling system (Ford 1982). So, despite the current image of 'special' schools as some extra or distant facility drawn upon in exceptional circumstances, they are what make mainstream schools 'mainstream': that is, the latter function as 'normal' schools precisely because they are bounded by institutions for those designated as 'abnormal'. In 1956 a book appeared by an erstwhile President of the British Psychological Society, C.W. Valentine, entitled *The Normal Child and Some of his Abnormalities*, which went through 11 reprints up to 1974. As the editorial foreword by Professor C.A. Mace puts it, the book sets out to answer a question of great concern to parents and teachers today: *Is this child 'normal' or shall I take him to the clinic?* (Mace, in Valentine 1956: 9). Hence 'the clinic' becomes the arbiter of 'normal' development through its position as the domain of its converse, 'the abnormal'.

Moreover, this process of normalisation prompted a naturalisation of development, overdetermined by two related factors. The new psychology's claims to be a science of the mental sought to emulate medicine's status as a science of the body. This emulation was expressed within the confounding of the notions of medical with mental through the hybrid notion of mental hygiene. This endowed a scientific legitimation upon practices of social regulation, social division and (supposed) reform.

Kindergarten cops: the naturalisation and regulation of development

There were two key ways in which development was naturalised: the creation of the notion of 'mental life', and the medicalisation of mental life, via the subsuming of the mental to the physical. First, the notion of mental age underlying IQ tests, considered as analogous to chronological age, assumed that ability could be distributed (at quantifiable and equal intervals) on a quasi-physical scale. The work of North American psychologist Arnold Gesell was highly influential in drawing up the norms and 'milestones' that underlie developmental health checks, and in promoting a maturational view of development as a process of natural unfolding whereby development is equated with growth. The blurb to the fourth (1971) edition of *The First Five Years of Life* (Gesell 1950) claims that it contributes 'more than any other book to the foundations of systematic developmental psychology'. While (in contrast to more behaviourally oriented positivist researchers) he favoured 'naturalistic', clinical interviews over psychometric tests, Gesell presented descriptions (or what he called 'characterisations') of development as absolutely age graded. Years and months dictated capacities and achievements. The following example, while meant to ring a lighter note, highlights more general themes. The abstraction of developmental time is associated with that of exchange, such that developmental maturation is linked to the return on a financial investment. Child development parallels capitalism: 'Three is a delightful age. Infancy superannuates at Two and gives way to a higher estate' (Gesell 1950: 40).

Second, the production of the individual mirrors the incorporation of the mental within the medical: the natural has to be closely scrutinised to prevent it lapsing into the pathological. The presumed equivalences between mental and physical development systematise the scrutiny of children, extending beyond the measurement of apparent to hypothetical qualities, and beyond the child to the family in ways that are now central to welfare policies. Note how the emphasis on care subsumes the mental within the physical and reinforces the role of the expert as empowered to make family interventions in this extract from the aptly titled *The Handbook of Child Surveillance*:

> Child health surveillance is a programme of care initiated and provided by professionals, with the aim of preventing illness and promoting good health and development. . . . [A]lthough we have described some of the methods of early detection in detail, we have also stressed the import-ance of primary prevention and of working with parents as the most effective means of helping children.
>
> (Hall *et al.* 1990: x)

The normal child, the ideal type, distilled from the comparative scores of age-graded populations, is therefore a fiction or myth. No individual or real child lies at its basis. It is an abstraction, a fantasy, a fiction, a production of the testing apparatus that incorporates, that constructs the child, by virtue of its gaze. This production, rather than description, of the child arose from the technologies of photography by which hundreds of children doing the same tasks could be juxtaposed, compared and synthesised into a single scale of measurement, from one-way mirrors through which children could be observed, and of psychometric tests. The production and regula-tion of children extended beyond testing environments to the settings by which children were cared for and instructed. Gesell (1950) provides plans of the prototypical nursery school, the complex design of which is struc-tured around a hidden child observation room. All child behaviour is available to be documented, becomes normalised into child development, and child development comes to inform the mundane minutiae of childcare.

Not all children were the objects of such fascination though. Early photographic records of colonial travellers in Africa are virtually devoid of children (contrasting with the contemporary saturation of images of African children within Western media). Indeed Beinart (1992: 225) notes that 'many Europeans regarded children as a less interesting species of local fauna . . . photographs of pets and dead "game" greatly outnumber those of children'. This was perhaps indicative of the general infantilisation of Africans within the colonial imagination (as 'less developed' than Westerners), as indicated also by the demeaning address to African men as 'boys'. Beinart's study of nineteenth and early twentieth century photographs of mothers and children taken by European colonialists to Africa documents equivalent regimes to 'improve' and regulate through maternal education and, especially, intervention:

> The notion of saving the sick African child through health interventions appears as an extension of educational programmes of transformation. Acceptance of Western medicine for the child, according to this reading of the images, places on the child's kin an obligation to acknowledge the dominance of Western scientific thought.
>
> (Beinart 1992: 237)

While Beinart reminds us that such photographic records reflect colonialist desires (rather than actual effects), nevertheless they do illustrate the increasingly political role according to children as '"go-betweens", whose image grew in importance in the colonial lens as the need to establish a dialogue increased in the face of the growing movement for self-determination in the colonies' (Beinart 1992: 237). As Urwin and Sharland (1992) argue from their analysis of the British child guidance movement in the inter-war years, the organisation and arrangement of the body was taken as the route to the regulation of the mind.

Jagged edge? Conflicts and continuities

In drawing out these connections, no causal determination can be attributed to the psychological study of children, but rather this is simultaneously both a reflection of the wider preoccupations and an instance of strategies developed to further them. As Valerie Walkerdine puts it, political motivations cannot be said to have:

> caused in any simple sense certain developments in the science of the individual. Rather each should be taken as mutually implicated, making and remaking the other possible, intertwining to produce a discursive and political nexus. The rational, the savage, the animal, the human, the degenerate, the normal, all become features of the modern scientific normalization and regulation of children.
>
> (Walkerdine 1984: 173)

Moreover, highlighting the continuities between past and present forms of developmental psychology should not lead us to underestimate shifts and conflicts between them. The child study movement, based on the accumulated observations of individual children and inspired by evolutionary ideas, focused initially on questions of heredity. But soon afterwards its attention was devoted to the role of education in alleviating or compensating for the deficiencies of heredity (Riley 1983). Cyril Burt is now infamous for the falsification of his twin studies (Hearnshaw 1980; Rose *et al.* 1984), but was responsible in large part for creating the profession of psychology in Britain. (Later, the British Psychological Society, which condemned Burt, was under pressure, against the background of a revival of streaming and testing in British schools, to rehabilitate him.) While adhering to a notion of a fixed, quantifiable and heritable cognitive capacity, he also subscribed to a staunch environmentalism by which hereditary dispositions could be mitigated. Philanthropic and innatist perspectives can coincide with as well as contradict each other.

With the impact of behaviourist ideas from the 1910s onwards, environmental – meaning school as well as family – influences became the main focus of developmental psychological accounts. Child training accompanied improvements in sanitation and social reform. Education (of the child and the parents) gradually superseded segregation as a strategy of demographic management – though, as the above examples indicate, it was nonetheless regulatory. If anything, a strategy of education rather than segregation required a commitment to greater intervention and control. It should nevertheless be recalled that many of the founding fathers of statistics, and of individual psychology, such as Galton and Pearson, were in the forefront of the eugenic movement in Britain. Rose (1985) discusses in detail why and how the more 'enlightened' ideas of the reformers prevailed over those of the eugenicists even before those ideas were further discredited by their application in Nazi Germany, and Ulfried Grutier (1987) documents the flourishing of psychology in Nazi Germany. The point is that modern psychology came of age with the political utility of mental testing. As Lewis Terman, himself responsible for the development and popularisation of one of the foremost standardised tests, asserted in 1920:

> It is the method of tests that has brought psychology down from the clouds . . . that has transformed the 'science of trivialities' into the science of human engineering. The psychologist in the pre-test era was, to the average layman, just a harmless crank, but now that psychology has tested and classified nearly two million soldiers, has been appealed to in the grading of nearly two million children, is used everywhere in our institutions for the feebleminded, delinquent, criminal and insane, has become the beacon light of the eugenics movement, is appealed to by congressmen in the shaping of national policy on immigration . . . no psychologist of today can complain that his science is not taken seriously enough.
>
> (Terman, quoted in Olsson 1991: 191)

While hailed by some as the forum in which to resolve age-old philosophical questions about what knowledge is innate and what acquired, the emergence of modern developmental psychology was also prompted by other more pragmatic concerns to classify, measure and regulate, in particular, those populations deemed a social threat to the prevailing order. Hence the division between theory and its application becomes unimportant, since the social need for the technology and data provided by individual psychology constituted the condition and rationale for its existence (Ingleby 1985). This continues with the drive towards increasingly biological explanations for societal problems, as indicated by Shonkoff and Phillips (2000) in the child development text entitled *From Neurons to Neighborhoods*. This infusion of scientific enterprise with social-political agendas is not, of course, specific to psychology nor to the development of testing. Richards (1997) concludes from his detailed assessment of psychology's relationship with scientific racism as follows:

> Psychology may be better seen reflexively as an arena in which the cultural 'racial' preoccupations of Europe and North America have been articulated and played out. There are many such arenas, from the street to the theatre, the school to the concentration camp. What is different about Psychology is that it has, until very recently, seen itself as the site where such issues can be submitted to truly scientific, objective, scrutiny and research. The articulation and playing out of cultural concerns in Psychology thus acquired a rather refined character precisely because it was supposed to be something else – dispassionate objective science. Ironically this rendered the underlying anatomy of the issues peculiarly visible.
>
> (Richards 1997: 309)

Science, as the tool of reason and progress fostered and harnessed by the modern state, put into practice enlightenment philosophies of protection and care of citizens, the realisation of which presupposed greater monitoring and control. Even the authors of the early child studies were quick to move from observation to advice, from empirical 'fact' to social application. As Kessen (1979), in his now classic article 'The American Child and other Cultural Inventions', pointed out:

> Tolstoy said that there is no proletarian literature; there has been no proletarian child psychology either, and the ethically imperative forms of child psychology, our messages to practice, have ranged from pleas for the equitable treatment of all children to recipes for forced assimilation to the expected forms of child behavior. Once a descriptive norm has been established, it is an antique cultural principle to urge adherence to it.
>
> (Kessen 1979: 818)

What is perhaps different about standardised testing is that the moral evaluation which underlies the description is rendered invisible and incontrovertible through the apparent impartiality of statistical norms. Their administration, through the power of the institutions, enforces statistical description as moral-political *pre*scription. There is a central ambivalence here about the relation between the natural and the nurtured that mirrors the tension between scientific objectivity and social application structuring psychological research: it seems that the natural course of development has to be carefully monitored, supported and even corrected in order to emerge appropriately. That which is designated as natural or spontaneously arising is in fact constructed or even forced.

As Adrienne Harris (1987) suggests, the drive towards rationality in models of development may be a reflection of the rationalisation of the capitalism taking place at the level of individual psychic, rather than industrial, processes. The norms and milestones that structure developmental psychology present a picture of orderly, progressive graduation through stages to ever greater competence and maturity. We can see here the modelling of an ideal-typical citizen-subject who is knowable, known, docile and productive.

Moreover, in addition to being the modern economic strategy for efficient production, rationalisation is also, in psychoanalytic terms, a psychic *defence* against anxiety, that is 'the process by which a course of action is given *ex post facto* reasons which not only justify it, but also conceal its true motivations' (Rycroft 1974: 136). In psychoanalysis we can infer from defences the structure of what it is that is repressed. What is wilfully left out or repressed from developmental psychology is the chaos and complexity (including the emotional chaos) of the research and developmental process. The investment in portraying development as progress works to deny our histories of the personal costs in 'growing up'. More than this, turning the complex disorder of individual development into orderly steps to maturity reflects explicit social interests in maintaining social control within and between social groups and nations. The technologies of description, comparison and measurement of children that underlie the descriptive knowledge base of developmental psychology have their roots in demographic control, comparative anthropology and animal observation that set 'man' over animals, European man over non-European, man over woman, as well as politician over pauper. So the history of developmental psychology offers glimpses of its structural and structuring influence in its coming of age as the authoriser and arbiter of child, family and professional relations within the capitalist and now neoliberal state apparatus. The next step is to look more closely at how these origins are sustained or transcended in contemporary developmental psychology.

Further reading

On the preoccupations that prompted and maintained the emergence of developmental and individual psychology, the most accessible and relevant resources remain:

Cooter, R. (ed.) (1992) *In the Name of the Child: Health and Welfare 1880–1940*, London: Routledge (a useful collection addressing historical and cultural perspectives).

Rose, N. (1985) *The Psychological Complex: Psychology, Politics and Society 1869–1939*, London: Routledge & Kegan Paul.

—— (1990) *Governing the Soul: The Shaping of the Private Self*, London: Routledge (see especially Chapter 11).

On the selective interpretation of Darwinian biology and its implications for developmental psychology, see:

Morss, J. (1990) *The Biologising of Childhood*, Hillsdale, NJ: Lawrence Erlbaum Associates, Inc. (especially Chapters 2 and 11).

On the relations between representations of femininity, childhood and the colonial project, see:

McClintock, A. (1995) *Imperial Leather: Race, Gender and Sexuality in the Colonial Contest*, New York and London: Routledge.

On the child study movement, see:

Cairns, R. (1983) 'The emergence of developmental psychology', pp. 40–101 in W. Kessen (ed.) *Handbook of Child Psychology, Vol. 1: History, Theory and Method*, New York: Wiley.

Riley, D. (1983) *War in the Nursery: Theories of Child and Mother*, London: Virago (especially Chapter 3).

Urwin, C. (1986) 'Developmental psychology and psychoanalysis: splitting the difference', in M. Richards and P. Light (eds) *Children of Social Worlds*, Oxford: Polity.

On opportunities generated by a critical, reflexive practice for intervention in educational and child psychology assessment and practice, see:

Billington, T. (2000) *Separating, Losing and Excluding Children*, London: Falmer Press.

—— (2006) *Working With Children: Assessment, Selection and Representation*, London: Sage.

Billington, T. and Pomerantz, M. (eds) (2003) *Children at the Margins: Supporting Children, Supporting Schools*, Stoke-on-Trent: Trentham Books.

Suggested activities

1 Drawing on Rose (1985), Rose (1990) and Cooter (1992), comment on extracts illustrating psychology's preoccupation with population regulation and control. Contrast with current articles (e.g. Slaughter-Defoe *et al.* 2002) which connect arguments for girls' schooling with fertility rates and national development.

2   Drawing on extracts from Van der Eyken's (1973) *Education, the Child and Society: A Documentary History 1900–1973*, such as Cyril Burt on 'mental deficients', or another such documentary resource, comment on the underlying assumptions and discourses that structure these accounts. Drawing on Newnes and Radcliffe (2005), contrast these with current explanations for attention deficit hyperactivity disorder (ADHD).

3   Discuss the changing lexicon of 'special education', highlighting the relations between terminology and social practices (e.g. 'imbecile', 'feebleminded', 'degenerate', 'mentally retarded', etc., to the more recent formulations of 'children/people with learning disabilities or specific learning difficulties'). Note that this does not involve claims that the language is being used somehow to refer to what is essentially 'the same' entity – this would run counter to the ideas elaborated in this chapter about the constitutive effects of psychological discourses. The issue is not to trace continuities or homologies, but to explore the positions set out within the different practices. Indeed, the current proliferation of diagnostic labels – from 'educational and behavioural difficulties' to specific learning difficulties – including autism, dyslexia, Asperger's, dyspraxia and the like testify to a more fragmented, 'specialised' and hard-wired set of classifications.

4   Contrasting the accounts of Billington (1996) and Timimi (2002), evaluate the possibilities and limits of using standardised tests to ward off, as well as identify, particular classifications of childhood abilities and behaviour.

Part I

Constructing the subject

This part addresses the theoretical and practical consequences of developmental psychology's identification of the individual child as its unit of study, exploring the implications of this in relation to the study of infancy (Chapter 2) and of social development (Chapter 3). Chapters 4 and 5 highlight how developmental psychology both draws on and feeds into dominant images of childhood.

2 Researching infancy

But trailing clouds of glory do we come
From God, who is our home:
Heaven lies about us in our infancy!
(Wordsworth, *Ode, Intimations of Immortality*, 1807)

I was born yesterday but . . . Babies know a lot more, a lot younger than we used to think.
(*Independent on Sunday*, 10 March 1991)

The baby has become the guardian of stability in an uncertain life.
(Kessen 1993: 425)

Most contemporary accounts of infancy start with the derivation of the Latin word 'infans' meaning literally 'without speech', the period which used to be taken to refer approximately to the first 18 months of life. But since developmental psychology is discovering so much about babies' abilities, the age at which particular achievements occur is ever earlier, so that there is a continual danger that infancy research will collapse back into neonatal (first two weeks) examination, and even earlier. I will be suggesting that this dynamic follows from the earlier practices and assumptions I identified in Chapter 1. This chapter draws on that historical framework to trace briefly the phases and fashions of infancy research. After this broad survey, classic research studies are discussed, as paradigmatically illustrating more general features of infancy work. Continuities are identified in the topics the research addresses, which in turn raise further questions about the significance of its sustained preoccupations and its absences.

Trends in infancy research: absolute beginners?

Psychology, and in particular developmental psychology, is heir to a long-standing set of philosophical, epistemological questions about the nature and growth of knowledge, and indeed was hailed from the start as the forum in which to test out competing theories (much as computer modelling is claimed to do now). By this account, biology and epistemology meet in the study of developmental psychology. Taking a broad look at twentieth-century Anglo-US and European psychology, general social preoccupations and moral orientations are reproduced within the history of infancy research. The child study movement of the late nineteenth century and early twentieth century was motivated by questions drawn from evolutionary theory, that is, comparing animals and humans, and different groups of humans, to evaluate the role of heredity. But, from the 1920s until approximately the 1960s, behaviourist ideas shifted attention away from genetic endowment to environmental history, with a corresponding preoccupation with child training. The model of the child was as a passive recipient of experience, with emphasis placed on quality of environment such that parents were seen as responsible for moulding and producing an appropriate moral character. The philosophical framework for this model of the child was empiricism, where the mind is conceived of as a blank slate (Locke) or, in pragmatic varieties, as 'blooming, buzzing confusion' (James). Since the behaviourists were reluctant to attribute any internal structure or organisation to the 'organism' – consistent with their denial of unobservable mental activity or events (which was in part their 'response' to introspectionist approaches) – the acquisition of knowledge was held to occur through conditioning, that is, through selective reinforcement based on environmental contingencies or learning from experience.

While it would be simplistic to treat these as sequential shifts, broadly speaking the 1970s saw a change of model from an incompetent infant assumed to know nothing, to a competent infant depicted as arriving already equipped with, or at least predisposed to acquire, sophisticated skills. This change arises in part from technological developments which could attest to the complex capacities of even newborns, but it also reflects the eclipse of behaviourism and the rise of cognitive psychology. The reversal of perspective (from blank slate to preprogrammed) is evident in the moral tone of righteous indignation with which books like Stone *et al.*'s (1973) *The Competent Infant* are presented. The very term 'competent' is used 'to stress that, from his [sic] earliest days, every infant is an active, perceiving, learning and information-organising individual' (Stone *et al.* 1973: 4). Accounts of this period celebrate the achievements of modern science as miraculously transforming the understanding of infant development: 'all at once it seemed possible to obtain empirical answers where previously there had been largely theoretical speculation and inference . . . in what had previously seemed to be chaotic variability of response and responsiveness took on new meaning and order' (Stone *et al.* 1973: 6). Science promises order in measuring the individual via infant research, and the metaphor of comprehension becomes almost literally a process of grasping the mystery of infancy by means of new techniques. Technology is accorded a key role in revising the image of the newborn:

Still another handle was fashioned by the electronic transformation of autonomic (particularly cardiac) measures and instrumentation . . . . aided by measures of brain electrophysiology it became possible to determine what infants, even neonates, could see or hear, or otherwise take in . . . . new approaches and methodologies in learning have transformed our understanding of the young infant's capabilities.

(Stone *et al.* 1973: 6)

While new technologies undoubtedly played an important role in generating new research, the driving force behind the 'discovery' of neonatal qualities was not only to do with the accumulation of more facts from the accelerating pace of infancy studies but was also due to the replacement of behaviourism by biologism and cognitivism.

The rhetoric of wonder and (self-)congratulation of the 1970s technical reports has been continuously replayed in subsequent popular accounts: 'Born brilliant. It's amazing what your newborn can do' reads the November 1989 cover of *Practical Parenting*, with the inside story starting: 'Just arrived – isn't he clever! A newborn baby is much more interesting than anyone could imagine. . . . Take time to study your baby, get to know him and discover the many different ways that make him unique'. Another account reads: 'Baby brilliance – the secrets revealed. Exciting new research suggests that babies know more and learn much faster than we think?' (*Under Five*, November/December 1990). Further technological developments such as ultrasound have rendered the embryo not only visible but also amenable to investigation (Franklin 1997; Hepper 2005). The modern commitment to science as progress, with developmental psychology accumulating facts on the way to complete knowledge, is thus reinscribed within the process of documenting the individual infant's increasing maturity.

From the 1970s, as a corollary of the representation of the ever-more-able child, a new research ethos emphasised how the infant takes an active role in moulding the environment in which she participates. The 'child effects' work (Bell and Harper 1977) investigated what the child elicits from her caregivers, rather than solely her adaptation to them, and began to piece together a picture of reciprocal learning histories of both caregivers and their charges: how each responded to and learned from the responses of the others. Subsequently, infancy research from the mid-1970s onwards became the forum to test out and develop Piagetian theory, since the sensorimotor period was seen as the arena where Piagetian claims are at their most specific (e.g. Butterworth 1980).

The late 1970s to 1980s saw a diversification of research. One strand continued with an unabated cognitivism, combining the test and application of Piagetian theory with cognitive science (Leiser and Gilliéron 1990). A second strand, influenced by hermeneutics (e.g. Newson and Shotter 1974), tried to achieve a reprieve-by-synthesis of (cognitive) innativism and (behaviourist) environmentalism, that is, to move beyond the positions which either denied any structure in the child's head (behaviourism) or put it all in her head (1960s–1970s cognitivism). After all, if the attributes and capacities are already there, what is it that could be said to *develop?* The reaction to behaviourism thereby threatened to fall back into innatism, and most developmental psychologists wanted to avoid this.

So notwithstanding the contested claims arising from neurophysiological research and evolutionary psychology (see later), most current developmental psychological claims about infant capacities waver somewhere in the space between child and environment, which is also the space between child and adult caregiver. The fact that this is represented as a *space*, and that child and adult are treated as prior categories, is itself part of the problem because these categories reproduce the divisions they strive to repair. As we will see in subsequent chapters, the current emphasis following from this is on communication, and on the processes by which infant behaviour is interpreted. This has given rise to a focus on adult expectations, attributions and framing of child activity which are taken up in Chapter 3, although this has witnessed a neo-cognitive return to innatist explanations. But before we look at this, we need to explore how infancy research continues to reproduce the theoretical frameworks that initially gave rise to it.

Hangovers: continuity of questions addressed by infancy research

Throughout the study of infancy, research has been organised around a recurring set of preoccupations which include: first, depicting infancy as the evolutionary baseline; second, treating infancy as providing insight into adult development; and thereby, third, demonstrating the association between research and its application.

Infancy as evolutionary baseline

The study of infancy was explicitly undertaken to illuminate the old philosophical debates about the nature and development of knowledge: What is innate? What is acquired? What is the role of experience in the construction of knowledge? These were transformed into specific questions, such as the extent of early plasticity of the nervous system, and age limits on learning capacities. Developmental psychology positioned itself as the testing ground for these age-old epistemological preoccupations, and in so doing it took on board the nineteenth-century framework of comparative psychology, comparing rates of development or states of knowledge between different (age and cultural) groups and species. Different approaches have emerged to investigate these questions. Some researchers engaged in the experimental study of sensory deprivation in animals, from which it was claimed relevant extrapolations could be made. Examples of this work include Colin Blakemore's report that cats raised in visual environments consisting only of vertical and horizontal stripes behave as though they are blind to diagonals

(Blakemore and Cooper 1970) or Harry Harlow's (1959) maternal deprivation studies with rhesus monkeys (discussed in Chapter 7).

A second, supposedly less interventionist, approach was the ethological study of animals (Blurton Jones 1972), especially those designated as the primate evolutionary ancestors to humans. This comparative framework can also extend (by a worrying set of associations) to the study of human societies still living in the 'ecological niche' within which Homo sapiens *is* said to have evolved, that is, hunter-gatherer societies. Note the implied relation suggested between these two groups – with resonances of the nineteenth-century hierarchisation of societies (Gould 1984). Ethological work has also been applied to the analysis of infant and child behaviour as a set of observational techniques that claim to provide neutral descriptions of clusters of actions, rather than preconceived interpretative categories (Hinde 1983).

Later neonatal research claimed to move away from evolutionary explanations in accounting for early infant behaviours such as the neonatal stepping and rooting responses previously designated as 'reflexive' (Bremner 1988). Instead these became interpreted as having specific individual functions, so that, for example, the stepping is said to help the foetus turn in the intrauterine environment, which, it is hypothesised, may, in the early stages of prenatal development, prevent adhesion to the wall of the womb and later facilitate engagement of the head in the cervix in preparation for labour. The tone of this interpretation is that we have outpaced evolution in ontogenetic development, that spontaneous foetal activity arises as adaptation to the womb and that there are continuities between prenatal and neonatal behaviour. However, despite the explicit distancing from evolutionary accounts and their assumptions, including the appeals to the 'primitive', the emphasis on the *function* of behaviour in specific contexts still harks back to evolutionist assumptions about adaptation and survival value which structure the agenda of infancy research in particular directions. Overall, the commitment to an evolutionary framework prioritises 'the biological' and accounts for the heavy emphasis on physical, and especially perceptual, abilities in the early infancy literature. This also assumes that perception is more 'basic', and therefore simpler to investigate. This trend was maintained within the arena of artificial intelligence – although here the emphasis on vision and sensory research was also related to other, military, interests (Bowers 1990).

Although evolutionary psychology flourished in the 1990s, this too lays claim to more complex forms of interactionism rather than genetic or biological determination (Buss and Reeve 2003). Yet popular sociobiological accounts of mate preference, gendered predispositions to monogamy and polygamy and the like have certainly championed genetic over environmental explanations. It is relevant to observe two key cautionary notes put forward by prominent researchers in the field. In a review of progress and claims made for developmental research, Michael Rutter (2002) criticises the recent 'evangelism' over claims of early experience determining brain development, including how this tends to overlook how we continue to learn throughout our lives, commenting: 'Knowing that a trait is genetically-influenced, however, is of zero use on its own in understanding causal mechanisms. The same, of course applies to parallel claims with respect to environmental influences' (Rutter 2002: 4). He specifically counters some of the claims made for having discovered brain mechanisms determining specific forms of behavior, noting: 'It should be added that although it is obvious that the workings of the mind must be based on the functioning of the brain, remarkably little is known about structure–function links' (Rutter 2002: 13). In relation to the benefits brought by technological innovations such as magnetic resonance imaging (MRI) he adds:

> The technique is often 'sold' as a means of actually the brain in action, but this is not quite so. What MRI does show are changes in blood flow and oxygen take-up, which reflect metabolic activity, but produce only a very indirect means of investigating brain physiology and neuro-chemistry. It is important, also, to appreciate that just because changes in brain function can be seen does not necessarily mean that the biology of the brain has caused whatever changes in psychological functioning are being investigated.
>
> (Rutter 2002: 14)

This implies that the measures used are not as direct or unmediated as they are claimed to be, since brain biochemistry may reflect, rather than cause, environmental changes.

Equivalent criticisms emerge from that bastion of sociobiology, comparative anthropology. Sarah Blaffer Hrdy (2003) has taken issue with Pinker's (1997) claims about the genetic determination of mate selection by showing how female animals' mating preferences are dependent on the gendered character of social structure. Thus claims for the supposed evolutionary preference for 'wealthy' providers may more likely be explained as opportunistic adjustment to 'patriarchal social structures (meaning patrilocality, patrilineal inheritance and institutions and belief systems biased in favor of male reproductive interests and control of resources' (Hrdy 2003: 128). She concludes that even evolutionists have to take history – including the historically structured ways in which unequal access to resources enters into contemporary gendered relationships – into account.

Blooming babies and adult aids

The contemporary version of the nineteenth-century notion that 'the child is father to the man' takes the form that babies can tell us how we come to know what we know, how they are more receptive to learning and how we might learn from them for (their and our) later remediation. Claims are made for the study of infancy as providing insight into the development and functioning of adult capacities which may be so skilled as to be automatic. To take some widely cited classical examples, Tom Bower's studies with infants just a few weeks, sometimes days, old led him to suggest that they use almost the same repertoire of visual cues as adults do to interpret depth (though not to the same extent), in the form of interpreting virtual images of cubes of varying sizes and distances away, and show the same susceptibility to visual illusions. The measure used as the index of this knowledge was (operantly) learnt by association with a friendly (female) experimenter playing 'peekaboo' (Bower 1966: 40).

Moreover, close study of infants has been used to challenge some of the dominant assumptions of psychological models. For example, it was assumed that sensory knowledge (touching, seeing, hearing, etc.) is acquired in separate modalities which are only later combined (matching what you hear with what a particular object looks like; knowing how to make your facial expression correspond to that of your conversational partner). Research in the 1980s, by contrast, suggested that the starting point was one of an initial intersensory co-ordination which only subsequently separated into specific modalities. Meltzoff (1981), working on cross-modal matching, controversially claimed that infants less than one month old could imitate the facial gesture of an adult on their own face, which of course they could not see. Since they cannot see their own faces, this early imitation would therefore involve the infant possessing an abstract representation of something she has not seen. But, theoretically important though these issues may be, they are nevertheless cast within an evolutionary perspective by which the study of infancy is seen as the route to understand the adult course of development.

In addition, work on how infants conceptualise and discriminate 'the world' has been directed towards the early identification of delay and handicap, the development of remedial devices and therapeutic interventions. A celebrated example of the practical application, as well as test, of intersensory co-ordination reported by Bower (1977) involved babies being fitted with devices emitting ultrasonic waves which bounced off objects and were reflected back to the wearer's head. The device then picked up the waves and translated them into sounds which conveyed auditory information about the layout of the environment. Bower (1977) used the device with blind babies and young children of ages varying from a few months to a few years old and reported that all those fitted could translate this auditory information back into information about the visual world, sometimes within minutes of being fitted. The applications for children who have visual impairments are manifest (though, after the equipment's promise had been demonstrated, its expense meant that the applications for a long time remained potential rather than actual). But, at the level of theory, Bower claimed that infants a few months old can respond to abstract properties of sounds and translate them into visual information, reporting that adults fitted with the device took weeks of training before they could accomplish this, and thus arguing for the greater sensory plasticity of infants. The theoretical implications of this were taken to present a direct challenge to the dominant model of the construction of knowledge and perception, although, after the initial enthusiasm, it seems that both theoretical claims and results may have been overstated (see Bremner 1988: 92–99). Infancy research has since continued to document increasingly nuanced permutations of infant/maternal activity, and pushed back the chronological boundaries of investigation to now claim to analyse foetal psychology (Hepper 2005).

The relevance of this work for our purposes here lies as illustrative of the ways different questions – some theoretical about the course of development and others 'applied' for remediation purposes – are fused together. As the research literature suggests, it is important to see that what is at stake in interpreting an infant gesture (as, for example, defensive or indicative of awareness of an impending collision) are key theoretical issues about the origins and nature of knowledge. But, and this is a big but, perhaps this is not the only way to ask these questions. These are not the only ways to interpret the infant's actions.

Cliffhangers: fear of falling?

At this point I want to develop the argument by looking in some detail at an early classic infancy experiment, Gibson and Walk's visual cliff (1960) which set out to address the question of how we see in three dimensions, that is, how we perceive depth. This experiment is classical in the sense that it continues to be described in current developmental psychology textbooks (e.g. Siegler *et al.* 2006: 191–192; Bee and Boyd 2007: 133–134; Berk 2007: 142) complete with diagrams and details of the apparatus. It therefore takes on a pedagogic role as a memorable experiment combining those vital ingredients for success in infancy research: ingenuity and technology. Its underlying assumptions are correspondingly maintained and reproduced within successive cohorts of students who read and learn about it.

Gibson and Walk couched their question, which they trace back to the Greek philosophers, as a nature–nurture issue: Is the ability to process and interpret visual cues about depth innate or learned? It was also posed as a comparative question within an evolutionary context: What is the species variation in this ability, and how is this related to differences in species habits and habitats? They developed an apparatus to investigate this: a simulated 'visual cliff' which permitted control of optical auditory and tactile stimuli, while also protecting experimental subjects from harm (by suspending the checked board indicating depth on the underside of a heavy glass sheet). Later versions permitted adjustment of the depth so that this too could become an experimental variable. The researchers observed the behaviour of infants on this visual cliff, placing each child on the centre of the board (a 'safe' area), asking the baby's mother to call the child to her, first from the 'cliff' side and then from the 'shallow' side of the board. Out of the 36 infants tested, the authors reported that all of the 27 who moved off the board crawled out on the shallow side at least once; only three crept over the cliff side; many crawled away from their mother when she called from the cliff side; others cried because they couldn't come to her without crossing an apparent chasm (Gibson and Walk 1973: 19).

The researchers claimed this demonstrates that most infants can discriminate depth by the time they can crawl. This, in turn, indicates dependence on vision for depth discrimination: although the infants could touch a solid surface, they refused to cross because of the visual depth cues. They also argued that awareness of depth precedes the locomotor abilities to act on that knowledge, in that many of the infants might have had a nasty accident while they were deciding which way to go had it not been for the protection of the glass. They did not, however, claim to have proven that depth discrimination and cliff avoidance is innate, since they acknowledged that by the time infants can crawl they will have had a substantial visual and locomotor experience.

Gibson and Walk continued with many permutations on the same theme, investigating the role of specific pattern cues, the effect on animals reared in the dark (so depriving them of visual experience on which to apply any visually based predispositions) and so on. But it is worth reflecting for a moment to see what this work indicates about the styles and preoccupations of infancy research.

Evolutionary or communicative test?

First, there is clearly an explicit continuity of interest in comparative work and evolutionary considerations. The entire study was cast within the framework of nature and nurture, of relating response to species and species lifestyle. Age of onset was related to that of autonomous locomotion, interpreting reactions in terms of the necessity to each species tested. Kittens, chicks, turtles, rats and goats were all compared to see the extent to which onset of responsivity varied. For example, Gibson and Walk suggested that night foragers, like rats, might rely primarily on tactile information from their whiskers, while predators like cats which depend on vision may be more susceptible to the illusion. Apparently, turtles were unperturbed by the 'cliff', which the authors interpreted as arising either from the fact that they had no need to fear a fall or because the glass reflections gave the impression of water.

Second, there are problems with casting this investigation as a global nature–nurture question. Identifying the different prerequisite abilities presumed for the target behaviour (in this case discriminating between 'shallow' and 'deep' sides of the cliff) raises difficulties of what in experimental terms would be interpreted as either spurious or artefactual indicators of 'knowledge' (false positives) or failure to respond appropriately for reasons other than the variable under manipulation (false negatives). Gibson and Walk investigated infants who could already crawl and therefore cannot be said to have addressed whether appreciation of depth is innate (nor did they claim to have done so). Turning to animals to investigate neonatal responses leaves them open to the criticism of making unwarranted extrapolations from animals to humans. They relied on a fear response, but it is possible that infants could register and even use the depth information and that they merely might not yet have learned to associate this information with danger. A subsequent study, using younger infants who were placed on different sides of the visual cliff, reported a change in heart rate according to the side on which they were placed. However, the direction of the heart rate change – deceleration – is conventionally interpreted as an interest rather than a fear response (Wolman 1982).

Criticisms so far have been of the classical scientific variety. But as important for present purposes is a third problem, that this framework suppresses the analysis of the task as a social situation. The emphasis on the problem of perceptual discrimination leads to a failure to consider the construction of the laboratory test as a social situation. A subsequent study applying some of the research on face recognition to the 'visual cliff' experiment suggested that the infants' reaction (whether or not they are willing to cross the deep side of the cliff) depended on the (standardised) facial expression the mother (and it was only done with mothers!) had been trained to assume (Sorce *et al.* 1985). When the infants' mothers assumed an expression considered to indicate fear, none of the infants crossed the cliff, whereas nearly all of them (14 out of the 19 in that condition) crossed when she smiled; most of them crossed when she looked interested, but rarely when she looked angry (understandably since anger might serve as a restraint, prohibiting approach towards the mother); where the mother looked sad six of the 18 infants in this condition crossed towards her, but they looked at their mothers more frequently than any other group, suggesting that they were puzzled or uncertain. Whatever the limits of such facial recognition tasks, what this study intimates is that presenting the task as an epistemological enquiry ignores motivating factors, and reduces what is clearly a complex communicative encounter, dependent on particular aspects of a relationship, to a question about individual perceptual competence.

It is most revealing that research should first have concentrated on the issue of babies' depth discrimination and only much later begun to appreciate the children's sophisticated abilities to interpret their mothers' facial expression – which seems at least as impressive. Moreover, this experiment illustrates how misleading it is to regard the infant alone as the appropriate unit of analysis. Rather we must look at the whole material and communicative system within which the infant acts. We will return to the 'maternal-referencing' paradigm in Chapters 3 and 7, to consider its applications within attachment research where – as we shall see – simply acknowledging the interactive elaboration of infant capacities may not be enough to ward off innatist explanations. But for now let us reflect on the relations between what, and how, we know about babies.

Problems of infancy: technical or conceptual?

Developmental research, with infancy as its prototype, can be seen as a paradigm example of both experimental ingenuity and ambiguity. In this sense it occupies a key place in demonstrating the credibility and renewal of experimental psychology. Indeed a typical account of infancy research starts at precisely this point in the narrative, discussing the difficulties of researching a subject population where there is a very limited behavioural repertoire to use as measures (hence earlier underestimations of infant abilities) of what infants 'know'. Much literature deals with the problem of interpreting infant behaviour, highlighting also the complex relationship between different response measures, a relationship which is confounded both by differences in relative maturation of response systems and because the same reaction can have different meanings at different ages. Heart-rate change is taken as indicating that the infant has registered a difference, but the basis on which she has discriminated a difference may be less easy to determine. Overall, debates in the literature have been preoccupied with the problem of determining between competing interpretations for the same experimental result: whether, for example, a reaction of head retraction is defensive, indicating awareness of impending collision with a virtual object moving towards them (also eye widening, hands in front of face) in Bower *et al.*'s (1970) looming object procedure, or simply arises from infants' visual preference for the edges of objects, so that they draw their heads back to watch the edges recede as the object moves away. By one account the response indicates 'fear' and by the other the 'same' response indicates 'interest' (the latter arising from features irrelevant to the investigation of infants' depth-perceiving abilities).

But, more than anything else, what these debates illustrate is the preoccupation of the infancy literature with methodological issues, with major sections of research reports devoted to descriptions of apparatus and techniques. While this is undoubtedly important, the focus on method and technology distracts attention from reflection on the rationale for the experimental question – which is largely taken to be self-evident. Either it is assumed that the earlier a behaviour can be documented the closer it is to being innate, or research on infancy is presumed to have implications for later intervention, with early detection contributing to later remediation, irrespective of whether it is clear that the behaviour under investigation is necessarily and solely indicated as the antecedent of the later difficulty.

While there is no doubt that infancy is a challenging and difficult area of human development to investigate, it could be argued that it simply represents in a particularly graphic form what are general problems for psychological investigation. Problems cited include those of variable and conflicting results, whereby slight differences in a baby's age, state of arousal, birth factors, posture, stimulus materials, techniques and so on all produce ambiguous and conflicting measures. But rather than being seen as technical difficulties to be overcome, what these difficulties demonstrate is that we cannot make a clear distinction between what a baby somehow 'knows' and how that knowledge is obscured by so-called 'performance variables', since the two are much more deeply interrelated than the split between these two terms would suggest.

If we take as a further illustration of this DiPietro *et al.*'s (1987) study of behavioural and heart-rate differences between breastfed and bottle-fed infants, we see the relationship between environmental issues of method of feeding and seemingly internal issues such as temperament as inextricably involved. In this study the authors reported that birth factors, such as the type of delivery or the drugs taken by the mother during or after childbirth, were reflected in the state of the breastfed baby. Method of feeding was related to how fussy, active or placid a baby rated. Hence, factors associated with the circumstances of the birth become interpreted as a property of the child in the classification of neonatal temperament. Generalising this further, it seems that casting discussions in terms of traits and behaviour, inside and outside, and even organism and environment sets up oppositions which treat as separate those entities that may be far less clearly differentiated.

Discussions about the indeterminacy of early responses, then, highlight that there is no such thing as 'raw potential': the behaviour we see exhibited by an infant can occur only within a social situation that, first, elicits it and, second, interprets it, thereby constructing it. It is now well established that environmental events can modify infant behaviour from the earliest moments of life – seen in the DiPietro *et al.* (1987) bottle-feeding versus breastfeeding study and also, for example, in the Sandler *et al.* (1970) study where newborns were found to exhibit different rates of crying in relation to different caregivers, or where change of maternal diet over the birth period is related to difficulties in establishing breastfeeding (Hepper 2005). One theoretical consequence of this is that there is no easy separation between internal and external, and that the exhibition of infant – and even foetal – behaviour must be regarded as both reactive and interactive.

New visions of infancy?

Attending to Ben Bradley's (1989) claim of the irreducibly rhetorical character of models of infancy, we should pause to reflect both on what the emerging representation of infancy achieves and the implications this has for the knowledge claims concerning the rest of 'development'.

Adrienne Harris (1987) has argued that the dominant conception of infancy portrays it as the atomistic acquisition of skills, built up in steps that link to later, more complex skills. She suggests that the research preoccupation with tracing skilled performance mirrors the societal value placed on productive aspects of labour, while the negative, maladaptive features of infant action are screened out of the picture (see also Bradley 1991). The cognitive model of the infant as problem solver mirrors that of the assembly worker, with research privileging those activities and products which will enhance performance. The result is that the indeterminate, ambiguous and non-instrumental features of infant behaviours are suppressed. The effect of this, Harris suggests, is that it encourages parents to see the technological capacities of their offspring at ever earlier ages, contributing to the compression of developmental time in the rush to competence and 'mastery' (with its masculine connotations).

Even when apparently describing infant activity, then, our interpretive framework is structured around features of the adult whom the baby will become, rather than what the baby is or does now. This is what James and Prout (1990) have criticised as a failure to engage with children of the present and currently lived childhoods. Inscribed within models of the infant, then, are a cluster of problems. The dynamic of changing models is towards a reflection of rational, industrial capitalism, with, as we shall see in Chapter 3, the psychological subject portrayed as separate and endowed with a rational and adaptive agency. Perhaps even more significantly, as demonstrated in the interpretation of the Gibson and Walk study, it has rendered the context in which the infant acts invisible, thereby both nullifying and naturalising the work of early 'parenting' – which is, within prevailing social arrangements, (still) usually mothering. Instrumental agendas, it seems, inform our visions of infancy. But the societal focus on progress remains constant. As Vandenberg (1993) notes:

> The 'child as developing organism' situates the psychological study of children within a biological (progressive) evolutionary framework, and therefore affords a measure of security for inferences about the ethical nature of human life, These issues, however, are no longer an explicit aspect of developmental theory. But while they are less visible, they are no less powerful. The shape of contemporary developmental theory has been profoundly influenced by historiography, theology and the idea of progress.
>
> (p. 199)

So (albeit implicitly) biologically framed, this apparently universal and culture-free account of infancy in fact bears the hallmark of the rise of the American dream. Its sustained theme of technology as saviour in the search for the truth reflects a particular progressivist narrative of science as the tool of the emancipation of humankind, as Kessen noted in this now classic paper (which formed the inspiration for Kessel and Siegel's 1983 landmark collection):

> The United States developed, and *developed* is the word of choice, from an isolated agricultural dependency to an aggressive and powerful state. Technology and science joined the industrial entrepreneurs to persuade the new Americans, from abroad and from the farm, that poverty was an escapable condition if one worked hard enough and was aggressively independent.
>
> (Kessen 1979: 816)

Situating the themes of infancy research within a broader political context offers new vantage points to understand what is at stake within prevailing conceptions of infancy and childhood. In a later paper, Kessen (1993) argues that locating previously undiscovered skills and qualities within the child serves an additional function of warding off contemporary anxiety about the adequacy of conditions and care in which we are rearing children. This is expedient in a context where the modernist narrative of scientific and technological improvement is now in trouble, both within the discipline of psychology (where the role of interpretation is increasingly acknowledged) but particularly in a political context of increasing volatility and unpredictability that makes the parental task of preparing a new generation for the life ahead particularly fraught:

> The assignment of cognitive capabilities to the new infant frees the baby of dependence on environmental – specifically cultural and parental – influences; his intellectual growth is safe regardless of variations in his surrounding context. Whether or not western culture is the epitome of historical evolution, whether or not American child-rearing patterns are optimal, the child contains shielded knowledge that will exist independently of his nation or handling . . . Nor does the assignment of cognitive richness to the infant escape political implications; the new baby of current research is conservative, protected from the vagaries of an unpredictable environment, holding the truths steady in the winds of cultural change.
>
> (Kessen 1993: 424–425)

More recently, developments in neuropsychology and scanning have documented even more neonatal capacities and achievements. According to Kessen, the 'competent infant' of the 1970s has expanded to become a 'full infant', invoked to cover the gaps in developmental theory and method, as much as the shaky confidence in the benevolence of our times. A model of the infant as fully equipped, he argues, 'may even have been constructed to save us from the disorder of no longer having shared conceptual models, or even assured research procedures' (1993: 415). We need this 'smart' child to compensate for the deficits of our social conditions and empirical shortfalls, but as we shall see this model of the independent, active child has other consequences too. Harris's (1987) association between the conceptual models of infancy and the factory assembly worker turns out to have resonances with more contemporary re-structuring of work and welfare.

Further reading

On the rhetorical and ideological status of babies, see:

Bradley, B. (1989) *Visions of Infancy*, Oxford: Polity Press.
Burman, E. (1999) 'The child and the cyborg: metaphors of abjection and subjection', in A. Gordo López and I. Parker (eds) *Cyberpsychology*, London: Macmillan (see also Burman 1998b).
Harris, A. (1987) 'The rationalisation of infancy', in J. Broughton (ed.) *Critical Theories of Psychological Development*, New York: Plenum.
Morss, J. (1990) *The Biologising of Childhood*, Hillsdale, NJ: Lawrence Erlbaum Associates, Inc. (especially Chapter 6),

On qualitative approaches to developmental psychology, see:

Burman, E. (in press b) 'Developmental psychology', in W. Stainton Rogers and C. Willig (eds) *Handbook of Qualitative Psychology*, London and Thousand Oaks: Sage.

Suggested activities

1 Taking classic accounts such as those reproduced in T. Greenough (ed.) (1973) *The Nature and Nurture of Behavior: Developmental Psychobiology* (San Francisco: Freeman), or L. Stone, H. Smith and L. Murphy (eds) (1973) *The Competent Infant* (New York: Basic Books) or other more current texts, explore the relevance of the arguments outlined in this chapter in relation to the following questions:

- What claims is infancy research used to warrant?
- What models of the relation between infant and adult capacities are being invoked?
- What other interpretations can be put forward for the phenomena described (with particular reference to features of the experimenter/caregiver/child relation)?
- What issues and features are absent within (a) the topics of and (b) the relationships set up within infancy research?

2 On wider social themes mobilised by models of the infant, child and society, contrast:

Kessel, F. and Siegel, A. (eds) (1983) *The Child and Other Cultural Inventions*, New York: Praegar.

with

Hultqvist, K. and Dahlberg, G. (eds) (2001) *Governing the Child in the New Millenium*, New York and London: RoutledgeFalmer.

3 Attributing sociality

So runs my dream: but what am I?
An infant crying in the night
An infant crying for the light:
And with no language but a cry.
                    (Alfred, Lord Tennyson 1860)

A baby's smile is a language everyone understands.
                    (Salada teabag tag 1991)

Two main aspects of the legacy of nineteenth-century developmental psychological research form the focus for this chapter. One is the division between social and 'non-social'. The second is the priority accorded to biology in accounts of infant and early child development. I will explore the forms these take through discussion of classical (iconic and widely cited) studies, to consider how these link with recent themes of developmental psychological research, finishing by evaluating some efforts made to escape the terms in which these questions were posed.

The developmental psychology of the early 1970s assumed the human infant started as a biological organism which had to be incorporated into an already existing social system. Drawing on work on attachment theory that harks back to evolutionary and animal work, researchers in this paradigm emphasised how the human infant is born equipped with a reflexive repertoire of behaviours that function to elicit care, nurturance and attention. This is interpreted in an evolutionary framework as being of 'survival value' to the species as well as to the individual (since the child is portrayed as the species' future). For example, there is research which documents distinctively different crying patterns exhibited by neonates that adult caregivers rapidly learn to differentiate and so attend more effectively to the infant's needs (Wolff 1969). By this kind of account, then, there is an attempt to overcome the split between the biological and the social by referring to the adaptedness of the neonate for human social interaction, with this seen as functioning as a social signal to caregivers. The infant is viewed as making a gradual transition from a biological to a social being. The efforts that researchers made to overcome this divide between the biological and the social are reflected in the titles of books of this period. To take as indices the titles of two well-known and influential works of this period, Rudolph Schaffer's (1971) *The Growth of Sociability* suggests a development from lesser to greater involvement with and awareness of the social world, while Martin Richards' (1974) edited collection *The Integration of the Child into a Social World* conjures up the image of a transition from isolation into sociality, with the epithet 'social' qualifying 'world' functioning retrospectively to designate the world the child had previously inhabited as pre- or non-social.

The problem with this genre of research is that it was surprisingly unspecific in its analysis of what it was that made the social world social or what demarcated it from any other variety of world. The 'social' here staggers under a heavy theoretical load, coming to mean communication, enculturation, participation and (bearing in mind the political preoccupations discussed earlier in this book) adaptation. In Chapter 1, I discussed how, with the advent of cognitivism, 1970s developmental psychology superseded earlier behaviourist accounts of infancy, claiming that they provided an impoverished picture of children's abilities. This trend was also reflected in the investigation of children's social development as much as in the attention to the diversities of that social world. I will outline some of this work now to illustrate its variety and the corresponding fluctuations of the image of the child on offer.

Innate predisposition to being social: born to party?

Corresponding with the 'discovery' of infants' competencies, a narrative of neonatal and infant development emerged which traced the adaptedness of the young child for social interaction, an adaptedness that in some sense was regarded as genetically 'prewired', but that formed the basis for involvement and then interaction with others. Infants were shown to distinguish between and orient towards human voices. The key studies – which continue to be cited as classic work even today – made claims about infants selectively attending to faces (Fantz 1961), and exhibiting different patterns of behaviour towards 'social' and 'non-social' objects, where these terms mapped on to animate (persons) versus inanimate (things) (Brazelton *et al.* 1974). A rather different line of work, but one that also sprang from the technological revolution of infancy research brought about by film and video, was the 'micro-analysis' of infant–adult behaviour. Continuing Gesell's paradigm of photographic records, this was based on close scrutiny of film played at slow speeds (or even frame by frame). Researchers made startling claims about regularities they could pick out in mother–infant interaction.

Two key strands of micro-analytic work were elaborated. Condon and Sander (e.g. Condon 1977) applied the work on interactional synchrony of body movements with talk to the caregiver–infant context. Social psychological research had already suggested that as adults we move our bodies in subtle but characteristic ways when we are speaking, and listeners move in similar ways as if in sympathy with the speaker (that is, in relation to changes of tone, etc.). Condon and Sander claimed to be able to see similar patterns at work in the movements of infants whose mothers were talking to them (see Condon 1977). They argued that this synchronous matching of movement with speech constitutes a basic form of social response which is fully functional at birth. Within these claims, then, what is social is accorded so pre-existent a role that it is threatening to lapse back into biology.

In a similar vein, and equally widely cited, Colwyn Trevarthen's work (e.g. 1977) argued for the existence of an innate predisposition for co-operative turn-taking exchanges, which were regarded as paving the way for linguistic dialogue. This was interpreted in terms of the development of mutual intentionality, that is the sharing of mental states and purposes, whereby (consistent with the 'child as agent and contributor to her own development' reaction to behaviourism) the infant is depicted as interpreting the actions of the caregiver as well as vice versa. The emphasis in Trevarthen's analysis was on the active involvement of the infant in communicative interaction – with partners negotiating together to achieve 'joint action', that of constructing and elaborating joint purposes.

Ben Bradley (1989) provides a more extensive review and commentary on the presuppositions and adequacy of this work. For present purposes a few points should suffice. First, unlike Condon and Sander, Trevarthen described several different stages in the development and achievement of intersubjectivity (sharing of mental states) rather than postulating that all was present and ready from birth. They were of course formulating their claims in the context of the new cognitivist focus in psychology. However, in different ways these accounts present an impoverished and insufficiently analysed understanding of what it means to be social and, in their efforts to connect early infant reaction patterns to later interaction, they fail to specify what it is (if anything) that by their account distinguishes sociality from biology. Perhaps another way of reading this is as an illustration of some of the difficulties with maintaining the opposition between a social and a biological realm. Dissolving one into the other, as these accounts threaten to do, will not solve the problem once it has been cast in this frame – although for these researchers, who were working at the advent of cognitivism – a lapse 'back' into biological explanations of sociality was perhaps preferable to eliminating any such explanation. As we shall see in later chapters, while the more recent focus on communicative development may seem to depart from the biological and evolutionary concerns of the early work, it nevertheless retains some of the same starting assumptions, albeit now cast in more neutral terms.

Problems: qualifications and modifications

The claims of infant predisposition to sociality have been subject to a number of other criticisms. First, there has been a failure to replicate some of the key studies which inform the theoretical account. So, there are disputes about the specificity of response to animate and inanimate objects (Sylvester Bradley 1985), and about the interpretation of infant movements from the micro-analytic studies. Bradley (1989) argues that the process of selection of material for analysis both reflects and contributes to a sanitised and romanticised representation of infant lives (and of the lives of those who look after them).

Related to this, a second point is that determining what an infant response 'means' is not a 'biological given' or inevitability, so it is not sufficient to invoke some kind of innate pre-adaptedness. For example, the meaning of a particular action may be culture bound and state dependent. Classic cross-cultural studies highlighted how in many cultures babies are in constant physical contact with their mothers who carry or strap them on their bodies (Konner 1977; Whiten and Milner 1986). Despite the 'culture-free' and universalist terms of the developmental formulations, then, crying need not necessarily serve as a signal to bring the parent to the baby, as the evolutionary theorists suggest, nor to signal hunger. What crying means will be defined by the particular circumstances of its exhibition and cannot be entirely pre-ordained by some genetic programme. This has implications for how we research and interpret parental behaviour, in particular for more recent discussions of 'maternal sensitivity', a 'quality' that, it is claimed, can be tested and measured and related to child social awareness (Yarrow *et al.* 1975; Light 1979). If we take the notion of the social construction of meaning seriously, a mother who does not immediately respond to her child is not necessarily 'pathological' or 'insensitive', since signalling systems are a matter of cultural definition and individual elaboration by mother and child. This perspective on the research on 'sensitivity' is a theme we shall be returning to in subsequent chapters.

All this highlights the difficulty of identifying a specifically *social* response. Fantz's pioneering work on the visual preferences of infants for face-like patterns was soon revised on the grounds that it seemed that the crucial factor was the complexity of the experimental stimuli rather than a specific response to face-shaped configurations (Cohen *et al.* 1979). Perhaps the clearest illustration of this comes from the literature on smiles.

Smiling, the development of smiles and their interpretation have occupied many pages of social developmental psychological texts from the 1970s onwards. Thus a key 1970s study noted that mothers' voices were the most effective at eliciting smiles from infants of five weeks old (Sroufe and Waters 1976). Smiling in infants has been seen as an index of recognition which has been used as an illustrative measure of infant capacity to discriminate specific individuals (Lamb 1988). While smiling is a very rewarding response for caregivers, since we interpret it as communicative, it is not only communicative. It may not even *be* communicative. Infants have been observed to smile in so-called 'non-social' contexts at the point at which they seem to have solved a problem or (in behavioural language) detected a contingency relation. These so-called 'smiles of successful cognition' are reported as exhibited in circumstances where infants learnt that they could control the sound or movement of a mobile above them by operating a micro-switch at the turn of their heads (Hunt and Uzgiris 1964). The crucial factor in eliciting the smile seemed to be control, and in other studies of developmentally delayed or visually impaired babies, their first smiles were elicited in those contexts of discovery in which an action on their part produced a particular (and presumably pleasurable) result (Watson 1973). Now, rather than engaging in the elusive quest for the quintessentially social smile, the variety of contexts in which this index of sociality is exhibited must lead to a questioning of the viability of the social versus non-social distinction, or at the very least a closer inspection of the criteria by which such demarcations are made.

Some of this theoretical work has been carried out in debates as to the status of ascriptions of intentionality to infants. When can an infant be said to be purposive or intentional in its behaviour? There is a danger of going overboard in reacting to the outside-in approaches of the behaviourists in returning to an already constituted, socially mature model of the child. This would simply be a backdoor way of returning to the biological determinism of an inside-out approach, since all the qualities defined as constituting sociality are portrayed as already built-in (as in the Condon and Sander study). By depicting the child as already social, the category social is being collapsed back into the biological and thus rendered meaningless. At an intuitive level, there is a clear difference between interpreting the howls of a three-week-old baby as meaning 'I want to be fed', and interpreting an eight-month-old baby's actions as intentional when she crawls to the door, looks back at you, looks at the door again and starts to cry. In the second case we would perhaps feel much more confident about attributing purposes, goals and communicative intent. But we must be clear that *we* are doing the attributing and have our own investments in reading actions in this way.

Research in the 1980s recognised and tried to address these problems by emphasising the as-if quality of early parent–child interaction: how we treat infants as if they were fully initiated social partners, as if they were able to participate in a social system. This work claimed that it is by treating the infant as socially competent that she becomes so.

Fruitful illusions: adult attributions and self-fulfilling prophecies

I am going to take Kenneth Kaye's (1982) book *The Mental and Social Life of Babies* as indicative of a genre of research which emphasises how infant behaviour is framed within a context of adult attribution and interpretation. This is a good example of a constructionist approach which I analyse here to identify residual tensions and challenges for this project. By this account, initially the caregiver does all or most of the interactive work in maintaining the communication or activity, but gradually the infant assumes more responsibility for this. Such ideas are now widespread in developmental psychology, as extensions of Jerome Bruner's notion of 'scaffolding' in the precursors to language development (see Chapters 9 and 10 for more detail), and Kaye presents an influential account which attempts to elaborate precursors within prelinguistic activity for the emergence of communication (including language) and sense of self. Kaye sets out to elaborate what he calls a 'holism without romanticism', to provide an account of how infants are initiated and come to participate within the social world. He attempts to do this without either postulating the infant as a pre-given separate (asocial) unit or resorting to the claim that the newborn baby arrives equipped with all human social characteristics and skills. In other words, he explicitly rejects some of the earlier (what he calls 'romantic') claims of primary intersubjectivity and interactional synchrony. The account blends evolutionary concerns about species adaptation with information-processing models to present a 'holistic' approach whereby the primary unit is the social system rather than individual interactants, out of which the 'personhood' of the infant gradually emerges. Hence, by treating the baby as social it becomes so:

> The human infant is born social in the sense that his [sic] development will depend from the beginning upon patterns of interaction with elders . . . . interaction does begin at birth but . . . infants only become individual partners gradually, as a direct result of those interactions.
>
> (Kaye 1982: 29)

This seems a promising start, particularly because Kaye presents a clear analysis of what he considers a social system is, and elaborates criteria for different levels of participation within it. For Kaye, the two key features of properly social systems are sharing a history and common ends. He discusses examples which fall within each section of a four-by-four matrix of separate/shared purposes versus shared/independent development. Since his examples are worthy of some scrutiny, I summarise them as follows: Enemy armies share a history in the sense of participating in the same battle, with rather different goals but with their fates intertwined; a wolf and caribou (a variety of Alaskan deer) share neither the same history nor the same goals, even if they share the same habitat – the wolf that preys on the lame and straggling deer relies on an understanding based on species knowledge rather than a specific relationship with each deer; strangers in an elevator share a goal in the sense of wanting to go to the fifth floor, but the history of that journey is (usually) independent in the sense of not requiring the other for it to take place. Bees are excluded from being social on the grounds that their mutual functioning and adaptation arises from the evolution of roles (drone and worker) within the species rather than from relationships between individual members. In summary, members of the system are portrayed as requiring some knowledge of it and their place in it before it is truly social – hence the gradual emergence of the mother–infant interaction as a social system:

> Members of a system know when other members are or are not performing their roles. And it is not enough for only one member to be responsible for that awareness: A mother and infant do not begin to be a social system until the infant, too, has expectations of how the mother will behave. These must be expectations based on experience together, not genetically programmed information like the expectations spiders have about the behaviour of flies.
>
> (Kaye 1982: 35)

(The example of a social system that receives the most elaboration in this account is about softball. It is fortunate that Kaye's discussion is concerned with accounting for the emergence of culturally specific knowledge as well as developmental regularities that are continuously produced and repro-duced across cultures!) We will return to these examples later, after we have considered his model in more detail.

Kaye applies this perspective to an arena for which claims of the earliest pre-adaptation between adult and child have been made – namely breast-feeding. He claims that the infant's pattern of sucking in bursts and pauses, combined with the mother's tendency to jiggle the nipple of her breast (or the teat of the bottle) during the pauses, constitutes the earliest form of mutual adaptation and turn taking. Apparently all mothers tend to jiggle and all babies tend to pause after jiggles, but within the first few weeks of their infant's life mothers learn to adapt their jiggles to maintain feeding because pauses after jiggles tend to precipitate a resumption of feeding. Hence the infant reinforces the cessation of the jiggle. Kaye goes on to claim that this pattern has evolved specifically to set up feeding as a primitive turn-taking interaction, since there seems to be no physiological reason for the burst–pause alternation (babies breathe while they suck). Rather, the pauses function to 'prompt mothers to fit into infants' patterns' (Kaye 1982: 40), that is, 'to bring the mother into the feeding as an active taker of turns with the baby' (p. 89). The mother *adjusts* her jiggles to contingencies she learns about the infant's sucking patterns, and hence comes to *share and organise* the infant's world by structuring and partici-pating in the feeding rhythm. What was initially a neurologically organised patterning provides, by virtue of the mother's anticipation and engagement (that is, the adaptation of the rhythms of her jiggles), the rudiments of a socially structured patterning. By treating her infant as a turn taker, the narrative goes, she starts to give the infant turns to take, setting up patterns so that eventually, in terms of other behaviours, the infant will start to take her own turn and assume her place in the social world.

The account goes on to highlight how adults supply, frame and place stimulation to entice infants into social participation as a self-fulfilling prophecy, extending in the rest of the book from the establishment of the earliest feeding patterns to face-to-face interaction, game playing, language development and even the development of 'selfhood' and clinical implications. Here we will leave it to take stock for a minute.

Pausing to jiggle and think

While Kaye's account offers considerable improvement over earlier ones in terms of clarity both of definition of sociality and of the evolution–learning relation, it is still caught within the framework of the very biological-social opposition it tries to transcend. First, the preoccupation with biological and evolutionary issues remains with the concern to sort out how neurological responses by babies come to function as social, through mothers' adaptation of their 'instinctive' action (jiggling) to the infants' reactions (sucking and pausing).

Second, although developmental psychology is hailed as providing the way out of the teleology of philosophy (by attending to the how rather than the why of development), the focus is still on the route by which the finished adult mind emerges – which still preserves a privileged status for the 'finished product' in guiding the investigation. Moreover, there is a lapse back into biologism since the existence of the current final product is held to arise from its adaptive value for our evolutionary ancestors, presumably because it must have been adaptive to have endured (Kaye 1982: 15). Despite Kaye's efforts to avoid this, then, there is a short step from what is to what has been, and therefore from what is to what is best. A thoroughly normative account of development is thereby produced. Ultimately, the goal seems to be about demarcating humans from other kinds of animals and confirming the specialness of 'man' which is seen to reside in 'his' adaptability, particularly in relation to communicative and symbolic capacities.

Further, the conception of evolution here has extended from the 'baggage' a child brings with her on her developmental journey to construct the environment in which she travels and arrives. Kaye discusses this in terms of intrinsic and extrinsic functions which he claims are not the same as nature versus nurture. The reason for this, as it turns out, is that *both* are regarded as innate. Paradoxically, in formulating what initially looks like a thoroughly social approach to development it collapses back into being even more biologically determined. The explanation for the fit between parent and infant is one of mutual evolution; the mother's reaction (jiggling) to the neurological response by the baby (sucking) is also 'instinctive':

Certain social mechanisms – interaction mechanisms for feeding, play and instruction – are the products of evolution every bit as much as those features we think of as innate to the individual organism. In fact it can be argued that such jointly evolved social mechanisms are likely to be more stable, once evolved, than particular traits intrinsic to either infant or the adult alone.

(Kaye 1982: 24)

While Kaye is careful to disclaim the developmental fallacy that earlier behaviours must be causally related to subsequent developmental achievements, nevertheless this research falls into the classical model of identifying the earliest exhibition of a basic unit of interaction (turn taking) which becomes the building block for everything else. In the very analysis of what makes the system social, we return to the project of partialling out the biological and the social. While in this account, unlike many previous ones, the individual is seen as produced by rather than pre-existing the social, nevertheless the biological and evolutionary perspective reduces culture to biology. Although 'the human infant is born social in the sense that his [sic] development will depend from the beginning on patterns of interaction' from which 'infants only become individual partners gradually as a direct result of those interactions' (Kaye 1982: 29), the impetus towards sociality is analysed only in evolutionary terms (instead of in terms of the social demands of, and for, interaction from others – as addressed later in this book in the chapters on language development.

The tensions and contradictions within this otherwise very interesting account point to a more general trend towards biological reductionism. The problems elaborated above indicate the conceptual and theoretical difficulties that lie within efforts to connect the biological and the social, and it is ironic that Kaye frames his project of 'holism without romanticism' as one of rescuing empirical scientists (who treat the child as an isolated unit) from the romantic (read unscientific) humanists. In terms of connections with broader themes taken up throughout this book, this evolutionary perspective should also be noted as both fragmenting cultural variation into individual differences and moving the focus of the analysis once again away from difference in favour of cultural universals. These are seen to owe their status not to their cultural reproduction, but to a biological ordination: 'the universal aspects of infants' culturally transmitted nurturing environments turn out to be also a matter of nature' (Kaye 1982: 29).

Beyond good intentions: the return of the native

This covert return to biology and the flattening out of cultural variations inform subsequent developments in this area. These have taken two forms. A first key strand of current research has largely assumed intentionality on the part of the infant, with debate focusing on definitional differences and their consequences. Indeed as Zeedyk (1996) has noted, the fact that there is less dispute over the developmental sequences observed than their interpretation reveals how what is at stake is the meaning researchers make of this (rather than what the infant or (m)other means!). Among new contenders in the intentionality debates are ecological approaches which frame intentionality in terms of behaviour-in-context, rather than mental states, and so emphasise bodily activity (e.g. Vedeler 1991). Also, dynamic systems approaches analyse how change and development of specific components of activity interact to produce greater competence – as in specific development of bone and muscle co-ordination needed to become more adept at reaching and grasping, for example. Such approaches largely draw on Vygotskyan perspectives emphasising the material, interactional context of the production of such individual accomplishments (see Chapters 12 and 13) rather than the mental equipment of infant and (m)other. While the structuring of research around specific prototypical tasks shifts the domain of explanation from a stage model to one of skills development (component skills to adequate demonstrate intentionality), neither approach can explain *why* certain behaviours develop. So we see developmental models – notwithstanding the claimed focus on change – slipping in practice from a preoccupation with 'why', to the more descriptive 'when' and 'how' questions.

Notwithstanding these, innate intersubjectivity models (claims of innate predispositions to sociality) largely continue to hold sway, attracting particular attention within the psychotherapeutic world. In particular the work of Daniel Stern (1985) – as both developmental psychologist and psychoanalyst – has been very influential. It has afforded a key crossing point between the two disciplines, and the lure of empirical grounding for psychoanalytic phenomena (in terms of documenting affect attunement – or divergence) has produced claims of seeing maternal–infant intersubjectivity at work that aim to close the gap between behavioural genetics, developmental psychology and developmental psychopathology (e.g. Stern *et al.* 1998).

However, what is not always clear is that a psychotherapeutic understanding of intersubjectivity (e.g. Stolorow *et al.* 1994) is not always the same as a psychological one. The former focuses on relationship, whereas the latter has tended to be more concerned with the infant's capacities to form and conduct relationships. Thus key analytic distinctions are in danger of being overlooked in the rush towards attaining scientific legitimacy for elusive interpersonal, psychoanalytic phenomena (see also Cushman 1991; Burman 1998a). But when empirical developmental psychology is invoked to identify developmental disorder, as in Stern *et al.*'s (1998) and Fonagy and Target's (2004) accounts, the two models are in danger of becoming fused (especially within current all-encompassing discussions of 'mentalisation'). We will see later on (especially Chapter 7) how this closer scrutiny of adult–child interaction has not always brought positive effects, especially for mothers. But if innate intersubjectivity theories affirm the social as biological, they also abstract the cultural specificity of their own values and contexts to (so to speak) render that nativism 'native', and so – in their presumption of its generality and normality – they privilege Western culture in their portrayal of early childcare and relationships (see also Chapter 14).

Theory-theory: mind-reading or malignant mirroring?

An alternative approach, which treats the social as cognitive, has flourished over the past decade or so. This work explores children's 'theory of mind' (ToM), or how they represent others' mental states. As well as sometimes being known as 'theory-theory', it now extends into work addressing 'mentalisation' (Fonagy and Target 2004.). Reddy and Morris (2004) note that a staggering 1 per cent of all psychological research referring to infants or children published in 2003–4 also referred to 'theory of mind'. Leudar *et al.* (2004) note the speed with which this line of work appears to have acquired the status of orthodoxy, attracting almost no critical evaluation. In accounting for the rise and popularity of this research paradigm, Costall and Leudar (2004) highlight how it rejuvenated an experimental developmental psychology that was running dry on Piagetian permutations. A relevant point is that it combines developmental psychological concerns with those of developmental psychopathology (always a winner!) and has been especially important within models of autism (e.g. Baron-Cohen *et al.* 1985; Baron-Cohen 1995). Indeed Costall *et al.* (2006) comment on the unintentional irony of theory of mind advocates, for in claiming to investigate how infants come to apprehend the mental states of others through the motif of 'mind-reading' the conundrum they find themselves in is the *reductio ad absurdum* of cognitivism (p. 166).

There are indeed several key logical problems with this work. First, it presumes what it sets out to investigate. That is, the problem they try to account for is how infants can infer the mental states of others. Not only does this rely upon a kind of circular reasoning, but it also maintains a dualist separation between minds and bodies, that then becomes part of what has to be bridged:

> The experiments do not just test the theory, but themselves reproduce the unnoticed assumptions of the theory. The ToM approach and false belief tasks both intellectualize intentionality and put abstract solipsistic reasoning about solipsistic mental states on the centre stage.
>
> (Leudar *et al.* 2004: 574)

The narrative of ToM is that the problem posed for the child is the same one as that faced by the (cognitively inclined) psychological scientist: how to go beyond the interpretation of observable behaviour to infer hidden mental events. In this sense, as Costall and Leudar (2004) point out: 'Thus Theory of Mind seems so refreshingly democratic. Rather than trying to find a place for people within science, it apparently founds a scientific practice upon human nature' (p. 635). The problem is that the experimental paradigm already so frames the representation of human nature that it assimilates the latter into it:

> Once Theory of Mind was adopted by experimental developmental psychologists, this assumption became attached to and partly transformed, the psychological experiment itself. In turn the psychological experiment has provided a 'paradigm for the researchers, not just in the sense of a procedure for testing knowledge of other minds, but as a tacit model of what making sense of other people must entail.
>
> (Leudar *et al.* 2004: 632)

Here we see a methodological framework governing the theory of the social that can emerge. Moreover, the assumptions structured into the model are not value neutral:

> Both the idea that understanding requires a theory and the idea that the theory is about other minds reflect the Cartesian assumption of one individual mind looking out at external reality to represent it as truthfully as possible. Knowledge of other minds is from this perspective highlight problematic. This representation of the problem incorporates the strong northern value of *individualism* as well as of *disembodied minds*, or, in psychological terminology, of cognitive autonomy and primacy of the individual over the interpersonal.
>
> (Nelson *et al.* 2000: 67)

It is unfortunate that experimental psychologists are particularly bad at viewing their experiments as social events, including involving interaction and relationships with participants:

> We note a curious inversion: psychologists' accounts of mundane communication are modelled on practices of experimental psychological investigations rather than experiments analysed dialogically. Yet studies of the dialogical engagements of experimenter and participants would inevitably throw many of these experiments in doubt, as incoherent and as investigating possibilities that the experiments themselves presuppose.
>
> (Leudar *et al.* 2004: 615)

A key feature of this paradigm, noted also by Zeedyk (1996), is that it has its own brand or experimental device which forms the focus of studies: the false belief task. This acquired the force not merely of research procedure but as a *criterion* of understanding other minds (Leudar *et al.* 2004: 63). What this fetish of experimental science achieves is the masking of the subjectivities informing the experiment, and the maintenance of the illusion of neutral, objective science.

Further, Reddy and Morris (2004) argue that the focus on theory leads to an ignoring of the child's actual behaviour and the interactional engagement that elicits it and makes it intelligible. This, they suggest, would be better explained by analysing interactional engagement. Reddy (2007) further challenges the dualism inherent within the ToM framework and suggests a second person, i.e. interactional, alternative. She focuses on the logical incoherence and cultural presumptions structured within the model, instead positing an approach which rejects the dualist 'gap' between mind and body, rejects the assumption of singularity of other minds (as 'the' other) structured within developmental models, and treats the process of emotional engagement as constitutive of, rather than supplementary to, developing minds. Both Reddy and other critics indicate some serious ethical-theoretical concerns prompted by the model of social disengagement effectively put forward by psychologists and its possible self-fulfilling effects. For if a child is related to as though its internal states are not connected to those around her, she may be less likely to be actively engaged in interaction and this may offer reduced opportunities to learn how to do so.

Bradley's (1991) earlier but prescient critical account airs similar concerns, but in rather different terms. He portrays the theory of mind research as an expression of experimental psychology's narcissism, magnanimously offering to extend its own theory of mind to others:

> What sets the agenda for the idea that children have 'theories of mind' is experimental psychologists' own preferred image of themselves. 'Theory of Mind' is a portrait of the child which serves as an Imaginary object to bolster the image of the scientists in an illusory and idealized self-identity as – like anyone else who is 'normal' – naturally immune from fantasy and unproblematically able to deduce the mental state of others.
>
> (p. 507)

Moreover, he points out how this works not only to deny the influence of the researcher's own subjectivity within the design and conduct of the research but also to suppress the other's difference. The other can only become known as a reflection of the self. In a self-confirming move, the theory of mind confirms the mind of the psychological researcher's theories of others' mental states, foreclosing the possibility of encountering or actually finding out anything about those others.

Nelson *et al.* (2000: 78) conclude in terms remarkably prescient of Canella and Viruru's (2004) post-colonial analysis of childhood:

> In this sense the child is the Other in developmental research in a way analogous to the subjects of anthropological research into other

cultures. In one sense, we know the child intimately, both because we have all been children at one time (thus dominated by adults) and because many of us have children of our own or have close child relatives, and have faced the challenge of communicating with and interpreting those Others regarding everyday practical concerns. But the demands of scientific developmental research require that we make the child Strange.

Notwithstanding these problems, the theory of mind framework is acquiring increasing credibility through the resource to neurological claims, linked particularly to the 1995 discovery of 'mirror neurons' – cells which 'seem to directly reflect acts performed by another in the observer's brain' (Rizzolatti *et al.* 2006: 50), which, it is claimed encode templates for specific actions that underlie recognition of intentionality. Indeed, as Ramachandran and Oberman (2006) point out, ToM accounts of autism go little beyond merely redescribing its symptoms, while claiming that they have identified the brain mechanisms matching the functions disrupted in autism. These accounts make the ToM framework seem more robust than they are. We need to keep in mind the significant conceptual problems underlying ToM, especially as this has major consequences not only for ordinarily developing children, but also for those carrying the label of autism (and related disorders). ToM work has also been influential within recent developments of attachment theory, as discussed in Chapter 7.

Love island? The social as interpersonal

Overall, the confusion between the social and cultural (with its attendant corresponding homogenisation of difference) arises from the impoverished representation of the social on offer. In the first place, the social is reduced to, or seen as quintessentially represented by, the dyadic. Further, the social is equated with communication, which is seen only as the 'interpersonal'. The dyad of 'social' developmental research is almost always the mother–infant. This suppression of other relationships that surround and involve infants and young children is an overwhelming illustration of the permeation into research of particular ideological assumptions about the structure of families, about which relationship is the most important for a child and how the social world is categorised into the domestic and the public (see Chapter 6).

Despite the proclamations of wonder and congratulation at maternal skills and responsivity (a double-edged commendation – for woe betide you if you lack them), mothers are continually depicted in the literature as almost appendages, pieces of furniture constituting children's environments. For example, in the Sorce *et al.* (1985) variation on the visual cliff experiment discussed in Chapter 2, the narrative slips in its reference, moving from designating the infants as the 'subjects' to designating the mothers, who thus become research subjects (and so objects) of the experiment – as if the mothers had no existence independent from the babies:

> Subjects were middle class volunteers . . . whose infants were normal at birth. In response to postcard inquiries, they had expressed an interest in participating in studies of normal psychological development. Subjects coming to our laboratory were included if (a) they did not become too distressed at any time prior to noticing the drop-off, (b) they spontaneously referenced the mother's face after observing the drop-off.
>
> (Sorce *et al.* 1985: 196)

Moreover, the knowledge produced by developmental psychological accounts itself contributes to the ways a mother complements and completes her infant's actions, since she is exhorted to orient her child rearing around it:

> Since it is usually the child's mother who is his [sic] guide during the early years, it becomes extremely important for her to have a knowledge of the general route along which he is travelling . . . . If she has in mind a preview of the genetic sequence through which a behavior is likely to develop, she is in a position to foresee and interpret the developing behavior in all its variations.
>
> (Gesell 1950: 240)

In addition, accounts analyse dyadic relationships as if they take place in a social vacuum, ignoring how they are structured by culture. Here, returning to Kaye's (1982) matrix, we might note that in his system the examples of a social system he provided are all of the dyadic variety. Taking his specific examples we might ask: Are we dealing with one social system or many? In what senses do husbands and wives necessarily share the same goals or the same history? Do pupils and teachers always mesh together so congruently? In the effort to account for a shared social reality, developmental psychological accounts occlude variability of perspective and position. The conception of the social as the extrapolation of the (already sanitised) interpersonal promotes an over-harmonious view of relationships – eliminating all traces of conflict and disharmony in psychology's representation of relationships (a point taken up in Parts II and III). The focus on the interpersonal dyad leaves out of the picture the wider social structural relations, relations of power (in Kaye's examples gender, age and professional relations), and thus correspondingly works to obscure the ways in which those wider structural relations enter into and are (re)produced within micro-social relations. Lacking that broader perspective, interpersonal relations and interactions become rendered simply as the exchanges of separate equals. A very *particular* social system (the biological mother in the home) is thereby depicted here as *generic* (as if no other caregiving systems are possible). A liberal model of society as consisting of separate, autonomous agents engaged in joint activities for mutual benefit is reproduced within a developmental model seeking to describe processes of engagement and enculturation. There is a failure to treat the representation of this 'social system' as itself historically and culturally constructed. This omission, combined with the social role model that underlies both this analysis of social systems and its liberal model of social exchange, works to naturalise patriarchy and capitalism, and to flatten out social relations within it as equal and harmonious.

Even in Kaye's model, which in many respects presents a much more sophisticated and elaborate constructionist account than previously of the creation and emergence of the autonomous child, the project still boils down to apportioning responsibility to the partners in the interaction. Like other developmental models it tends towards being drawn back into the framework of preconstituted individual agents, rather than focusing on what it is that is achieved. In some respects, this impetus towards individualisation and atomism is itself a product of the social role theory that underlies Kaye's model in his exemplary social system. The mechanism for learning is socialisation, and the norms for behavioural performance are roles (albeit now reconceptualised as a mutual process). Since the account cannot provide a socially structured explanation of the emergence of the roles (owing to the absence of a wider conception of the social), to postulate that the capacity of the system functions as if the infant were playing the role, as well as flowing from the infant's own readiness, does nothing to help ward off the divisions and dualisms of individual and society, and of biology and society. It is this failure to treat the typical categories of psychological research – of parenthood, personhood, gender, class, etc. – as discourses that are reflected in, and in part produced by, developmental psychological practices that facilitates the incorporation of this constructionist model into the dominant atomistic and individualist approach.

It is now beginning to be recognised that people other than 'the mother' interact with and provide the environment for an infant. When the category of the social is extended beyond the dyadic to consider the relationships between father and children and between siblings, we begin to see how highly selective and impoverished are the topics that have been the preoccupations of developmental psychology. In particular, we see the consequences of the emphasis on the physical, its separation from the emotional and the suppression of the emotional in developmental psychological investigation. Judy Dunn and Carol Kendrick's (1982) and Dunn et al.'s (1991) pioneering analyses of sibling relationships, for example, provide a picture of children's social awareness, capacity to interpret another's emotional state and to empathise with one another at ages when such skills of understanding of 'social cognition' had previously been considered impossible. While still harking back to an evolutionary framework, their work also strongly suggests that we need to restore the study of emotions to the developmental agenda, and to reconsider our conceptualisation of the emotion–cognition relation. They highlight how traumatic events such as the birth of a sibling can herald rapid developmental advances rather than the regressions that are typically expected or noted. Yet as was argued in Chapters 1 and 2, the question of what is considered 'progress' or 'regress', and why, restates rather than resolves problems about the construction and categorisation of development.

Baby bio? The general and the particular in developmental psychology

The tension between the biological and the social is inscribed within psychology in general, and in developmental psychology in particular. This tension is reflected in the general psychological project to explain both the general and the particular in the human condition. Psychology has tended to deal with this tension by suppressing the particular, i.e. the cultural, historical and the emotional. Despite its name, the 'psychology of individual differences' (of which developmental psychology is a key component) addresses similarity rather than differences, with difference explored only in relation to technologies of scores on attitude tests, personality tests or ability scales. Emotions become stable, generalisable variables conceived of as analogues to relatively fixed cognitive processes. In this chapter I have discussed how this contributes to a psychology which has abstracted its unit of analysis such that its notions of 'interaction' and 'the social' are highly impoverished. So far in this book I have tried to point out how these considerations have been both reflected in the historical origins of developmental psychology and reproduced within its recent history. We can see the culmination of this failure to theorise the social, and the abstraction of the 'individual' as the unit of analysis, in the way computer programs are regarded as being capable of modelling thought processes. Written into the history of artificial intelligence is a dramatic illustration of psychology's models of the individual and all that this fails to address: the computer metaphor provides a representation of the human mind as individual, rational, isolated and disembodied – modern Western subjectivity writ large. Moreover, as will be discussed in more detail in Chapter 4, the individualist assumptions that permeate developmental psychology both feed into and are reflected by the rhetoric of child rights. Judith Ennew and Brian Milne (1989: 48) provide a dramatic illustration of the direct consequences of these theoretical issues. They claim that the 'individualism' of the international human rights policies on children facilitates the abstraction and dislocation of children from their nationality or culture, which have made practices of transracial and/or transnational adoption a matter of only recent debate.

Any adequate developmental psychology has to address the question of the relationship between the biological and the social, but the failure of so much developmental psychological research so far lies in how it has regarded these as polarised factors of development that somehow combine in an additive way. Without a more through-going conceptual revision, even so-called 'bio-psycho-social' models that claim to integrate rather than separate these domains turn out to so privilege the 'bio' as to really be 'bio-bio-bio' models (Read 2005). In this chapter we have seen how impoverished developmental models are when they attempt to graft the biological on to the social – the language of 'socialisation' falls into this, with the social portrayed as a layer around, or coating over, the biological (rather like a choc-ice). What we have to get away from is a conception of biology as somehow prior to or underlying the psychology, to rather, as Denise Riley (1983) argues, how it is lived out in particular times, places and conditions.

The seemingly abstract concerns of developmental psychological research have their reflections in the wider cultural arena. In terms of more popular representations, the social world of children, especially infants, is almost always one where 'parent' signifies mother, and where mother and child are used to convey meanings of purity and naturalness. Developmental psychology both partakes of and informs cultural representations of the origins and nature of social organisation that are recycled within models of social development. But just as it is by no means clear that we can determine if a baby's cry or smile has meaning, and, even if it has, that this is not fixed or shared except by historical and cultural convention, so significations of children, including what childhood is and what meaning this holds, are by no means as stable and homogeneous as has been assumed – as we will see in Chapters 4 and 5.

Further reading

Bradley, B. (1989) *Visions of Infancy*, Oxford: Polity Press.

Kaye, K. (1982) *The Mental and Social Life of Babies*, London: Methuen.

Morss, J. (1990) *The Biologising of Childhood*, Hillsdale, NJ: Lawrence Erlbaum Associates, Inc. (see Chapters 6 and 9).

Nelson, K., Henseler, S. and Plesa, D. (2000) 'Entering a community of minds: theory of mind from a feminist standpoint', pp. 61–84 in P. Miller and E. Kofsky Scholnick (eds) *Towards a Feminist Developmental Psychology*, New York and London: Routledge.

Reddy, V. (2007) *Feeling Other Minds: How Babies Understand People*, Cambridge, MA: Harvard University Press.

Riley, D. (1983) *War in the Nursery: Theories of Child and Mother*, London: Virago (see especially Chapter 2).

Suggested activities

Examine a range of developmental psychological textbooks, both current and from the 1960s onwards, exploring definitions of what it means to 'become social' and the positions set out for the 'socialising agent'. What conception of society is on offer? Contrast this with the kind of account provided within a Vygotskyan-informed perspective (see, e.g. R. Harré (1986) 'Steps towards social construction', in M. Richards and P. Light (eds) *Children of Social Worlds*, Oxford: Polity Press; and F. Newman and L. Holzman (1993) *Lev Vygotsky: Revolutionary Scientist*, London and New York: Routledge).

4   Discourses of the child

Once upon a time we all lived in the land of childhood.
(*Adolescence*, Channel 4, 26 April 1992)

Childhood is the kingdom where nobody dies
Nobody that matters, that is.

(Edna St Vincent Millay 1892–1950)

The child shall have a better time than his parents; he shall not be subject to
the necessities which they have recognized as paramount in life. Illness,
death, renunciation of enjoyment, restrictions on his own will, shall not
touch him; the laws of nature and of society shall be abrogated in his favour;
he shall once more really be the centre and core of creation – 'His Majesty
the Baby,' as we once fancied ourselves.
(Sigmund Freud 1914/1957, 'On Narcissism: An Introduction', p. 91)

Discourses of childhood are central to the ways we structure our own and
others' sense of place and position. They are part of the cultural narratives
that define who we are, why we are the way we are and where we are going.
This chapter addresses the range of ways childhood is depicted, the extent
to which developmental psychological accounts reflect these representations, and the consequences of this for the adequacy of current forms and
functions of developmental psychology, and the social policy and professional practices it informs.

   The definition and demarcation of childhood are replete with social and
political meanings. Whether cast in terms of nostalgia or repugnance, the
category of childhood is a repository of social representations that functions
only by virtue of the relationship with other age and status categories: the
child exists in relation to the category 'adult'. While most developmental
accounts treat movement within, and transition beyond, childhood as
largely maturationally determined (as reflected in the chronological organisation of textbooks), a moment's reflection reveals that the membership
prerequisites and privileges associated with the entry to adulthood are only

tenuously linked with some criterial common point. As Jo Boyden and Andy Hudson note:

> The distinction between children and adults is given as a basis on the one hand for granting additional rights (for instance, the first to receive relief in times of distress), and on the other, for restricting both the enjoyment of certain rights and the exercise of certain obligations.
>
> (Boyden and Hudson 1985: 4)

To take just a few contemporary and immediate examples, in Britain today there are a number of competing definitions of adult maturity simultaneously applied to different spheres of activity which vary in the age of maturity employed: political majority, legal responsibility and sex. In the last case it should be noted that different criteria for maturity have typically been employed depending on whether your sexual partner is of the same or opposite sex (see Waites 2005). The entry limits on these three arenas of adult activity vary within Western Europe as well as across wider cultural spheres. There is variation within systems as well, with different criteria employed on the basis of gender. In Judaism, for example, boys are considered adult in terms of obligations for religious observance at age 13 while girls attain this status at 12. At a more general level, to take perhaps the most telling example, in many countries, the UK included, young men of 16 are treated as too young to vote or marry without permission, but old enough to kill or be killed for their country. So even before we look to 'other' cultures or to history, a diversity of definitions of maturity is apparent. To what extent is this diversity reflected in developmental psychological accounts? The question of whether 'we all lived in the land of childhood' (as the documentary claimed) turns out to be indissociable from that of who 'we' are, and which land it is.

Developmental psychology and the cultural categorisation of the lifespan

Do children grow or are they made? This variant of the nature–nurture question is what structures both the popular and the academic imagery of child development. The cover of one textbook (Dworetzky 1990) shows a budding flower emerging from the soil beneath the beneficent glow of a sun (with bud and sun of the same colour) – all this in a naive childlike style. Another (Kaplan 1991), entitled *A Child's Odyssey*, conveys a picture of development as a journey, beset with difficulties and dangers, which are, moreover, negotiated sequentially and separately. Reproductions of Impressionist rural and garden scenes are interspersed throughout this text. Such themes are maintained by Siegler *et al.* (2006) depicting children playing on a beach in a blurry naive-style oil painting, and Bee and Boyd's (2007) cover photo of a multiracial group of children tumbling together in the pose of a frolicking scrum. The cover of Berk's (2007) text on lifespan developmental psychology sports that quintessential motif of the naturalisation of the lifecourse, a tree (reminiscent of the same kind of oak tree that was adopted as the symbol of the British Conservative party in 2007) – its single image divided into four quadrants reflecting change throughout the four seasons.

The nuances of nostalgic romanticism and naturalisation mobilised by these images underscore how as readers we learn about developmental psychology through the lens of our own recollected childhood, as retrospectively reconstituted within dominant models of the child. Small wonder perhaps at the alternation between a rhetoric of mystery or wonder and businesslike calculation of how much further there is yet to go.

The important point here is that both varieties of account portray development as natural and inevitable. The trajectory of development is seen as basically uniform, with 'cross-cultural perspectives' appearing as optional extras within 'applications' sections, in which it is largely child-rearing and educational strategies or differences in moral codes that are presented for consideration. That is, cultural issues are treated as informing the 'content' of development rather than entering into its structure in any more fundamental way. Further, the distinctions most textbooks make between the main account and 'applications' or 'issues' maintains an implicit assumption that developmental psychological knowledge is not otherwise informed by 'applied' interests or values – an assumption that was put into question in Chapter 1.

One reason why culture can be portrayed as a kind of optional or exchangeable extra in this way lies in the structure of the texts. First, most textbooks follow a chronological format from birth (or even conception) to adolescence or, with the recognition that development is 'lifespan', to death. Some accounts even specify age limits on the periods they distinguish, as in Dworetzky and Davis (1989) who distinguish 'Beginnings: 0–1 years; Early Childhood: 1–6 years; Middle Childhood: 6–12 years; Adolescence: 12–18 years; Early Adulthood: 18 years; Middle Adulthood: 40–65 years; Late Adulthood: 65+ years of age' (pp. vii–x). It is impossible to read this without noting at the very least the remarkable lack of sensitivity to cultural and class variation in life expectancy. Most accounts distinguish between early and middle childhood, with 'toddlerhood' emerging as a new category between infancy and early childhood (e.g. Kaplan 1991). At a more detailed level, Fogel's (1991: ix–xiv) account of infancy breaks this period down into seven sections, each of which is accorded not only age limits but also a specific subjective orientation (in some instances even assuming the 'voice' of the infant), with 'The psychology of the newborn (the first two months)'; 'Attention and anticipation (two to five months)'; 'The origins of initiative (six to nine months)'; 'Becoming a cause and becoming vulnerable (ten to twelve months)'; 'Expression, exploration and experimentation (twelve to eighteen months)'; 'Conflict, doubt and power (eighteen to twenty four months)' and 'I'm not a baby anymore (twenty four to thirty six months)'.

In one sense this kind of 'developmental tasks' approach simply represents the application within an age category of what is frequently portrayed as the preoccupations that separate and govern age categories. But how much do these actually have to do with chronological age? Dworetzky and Davis (1989) treat 'Loving and working' as the subtitle for 'Early adulthood' (p. xx) with the 'Applications' section devoted to 'Finding your one and only'. In 'Late adulthood' (subtitled 'Relationships and retirement'), the 'Applications' is about 'Stopping elder abuse'. Are these inevitable, or even prevalent, features of the human lifespan? Surely 'elder abuse' can occur only in societies where older people are demeaned and treated as dispensable, rather than integrated and revered, and where human nature is measured in terms of economic productivity. Important questions arise from these reflections. What we have here are features of white middle-class US society mapped on to models of development which are then treated as universal. What are the effects of condensing the intervals between stages from multiples of years to mere months, as in the infancy example? The earlier in the lifespan, the more crucial it seems the developmental achievements must be within an ever-contracting period of time. Are these achievements as culture free as they are represented? What kinds of injunctions do they make to parents?

Second, the categorisation into age-graded intervals brings with it a further segmentation of developmental description. Many of these comprehensive texts subdivide each period into 'physical, 'cognitive' and 'psychosocial' (or 'social and personality'), in some cases with a chapter on each (e.g. Seifert and Hoffnung 1987; Bee and Boyd 2007), but more often combining the treatment of 'physical and cognitive development' and 'social and personality development' or 'emotional and social development' (e.g. Dworetzky and Davis 1989; Santrock 1989; Dworetzky 1990; Kaplan 1991; Berk 2007)). There are two features to note here: first, the connection between the cognitive and the physical works to privilege the realm of the cognitive as the primary arena for psychological development (and incorporates the physical within this), and places it in linear succession to the emphasis on biology in development; second, it reinstates the now familiar division between the rational and the irrational, that is, the cognitive and the emotional (see Chapter 2), with the first seen as essential and the second as contingent, as indicated, for example, within accounts of notions of emotional intelligence (Goleman 1996; Matthews *et al.* 2002), seen as a variant of cognitive processing (Burman in press b).

Bringing up baby: variability in childcare advice

A rather different picture emerges from the history and sociology of childhood. Here, debates focus on the extent and variability of conceptions of childhood, conceived of as a modern Western notion (Ariès 1962). While it is not possible to make a simple translation from representations (whether pictorial or literary) of children to child-rearing practices, or from news-paper accounts to what parents actually did to and felt for their children (Pollack 1983), nevertheless childcare advice does constitute an important resource from which to speculate about the cultural content of, and importance accorded to, childhood and parenting practices. Indeed Elias' (2000) account of the development of 'civility' and social etiquette contains much analysis of advice on child-rearing practices. He embeds this within a fine-grained comparative review of the different historical forms these have taken according to the different political structures within Europe, develop-ing his theory of the societal management of aggression after feudalism through increasingly elaborate codes of conduct. Moreover, his analysis attends to the particular forms these codes have taken in specific national contexts, as well as reflecting and contributing to class and gender strati-fications. Hence childcare advice can therefore provide an alternative vantage point from which to look at contemporary developmental psycho-logical accounts.

Various models have been put forward to categorise historical fluctu-ations in childcare advice discernible even within England and the USA. Newson and Newson (1974) and Hardyment (1983) write in terms of prevailing moralities which have governed approaches to childcare. From the mid-eighteenth century to mid-nineteenth century they identify a 'religious' morality, with a focus on preparing children for death since, with the high infant mortality rates of the time, a parent's duties were seen as best fulfilled in striving to ensure their child's life in the hereafter. With the prospect of little time to prove a child's goodness in life, a battle ensued to save the child's soul. For some this means there was little scope for indulgent, permissive parenting. As Susanna Wesley wrote to her son John (founder of the Methodist movement) 'Break his will now and his soul will live' (in Newson and Newson 1974: 56). Child activists Ennew and Milne relate the powerlessness of children to their status as legal minors in every society, pointing out that in eighteenth-century Europe:

> Child theft was not theft unless the child was wearing clothes. Other-wise child theft was like the theft of a corpse. The body was not inhabited by a legal person in either case.
>
> (Ennew and Milne 1989: 12)

After World War I medicine succeeded religion as the dominant moral authority governing childcare. This is sometimes attributed to a decline in infant and child mortality rates due to sanitation reforms in the mid- to late nineteenth century (combined with a general crisis of faith from the war), but it should be recalled that the highest recorded infant mortality rates in Britain were reported in the first part of the twentieth century (Rose

1985). The narrative of modern scientific and technological progress that sometimes informs these accounts of childcare advice must therefore be problematised.

With the shift from medical to mental hygiene, the emerging psychology partook of medicine's authority to promise earthly survival in return for adherence to 'scientific mothercraft'. The earlier preoccupation with hereditary inclinations and predispositions was superseded by the application of behaviourist principles to childcare. The work of Watson and the New Zealand stockbreeder Truby King, who applied principles he developed rearing cattle to the upbringing of children, advocated 'regularity of habits' and gave rise to what Daniel Beekman (1979) has called the 'mechanical' child:

> The establishment of perfect regularity of habits, initiated by feeding and cleaning by the clock is the ultimate foundation of all round obedience. Granted good organic foundations, truth and honour can be built into the edifice as it grows.
>
> (Truby King 1937, cited in Newson and Newson 1974: 61)

The authoritarian religious expert on child development was succeeded by the equally authoritarian medical expert. But the 1930s to the 1950s saw the rise of a different moral orientation towards children, emphasising children's 'needs' and 'natural development'. This was the period when psychoanalytic ideas were beginning to make their impact in early child education and with this came the importance accorded to play, to emotional as well as physical needs, and to continuity of care (Urwin and Sharland 1992). As Newson and Newson put it: 'At last the dirty, happy, noisy child could be accepted as a good child' (1974: 63). A less punitive approach was advised in dealings with children, particularly in relation to those enduring preoccupations of childcare advice: toilet training, thumb sucking and masturbation. But this was uttered in no less coercive pronouncements to parents.

The final period Newson and Newson (1974) distinguish is what they call 'Individualism and the fun morality' which they identify with the period after World War II. In part they attribute this change to the inward turn towards personal, domestic matters as an escape from recalling the atrocities of Hiroshima and Nazi death camps, and otherwise as part of a new confidence and assertiveness that marked this more affluent (for some) period. These developments (in 'choice' and consumption) were reflected in the childcare advice: first, in the less authoritarian tone of address and, second, by an emphasis on flexibility rather than prescription. While Alldred (1996) has identified resources that mothers draw upon to resist childcare advice, the problem here is that enjoying parenting has become mandatory. In terms of the contemporary situation, the current vogue for *Supernanny* shows indicates rumblings of a backlash to permissive parenting in favour of more punitive parent-centred approaches, with the spectre of out-of-control children linked with moral panics about childhood crime and failure at school. Significantly these debates arise alongside the increasing diagnosis of childhood conduct disorders such as ADHD (Timimi 2005), while the reality television parentcraft shows reiterate the familiar theme of locating the problem within the parent–child relationship, rather than exploring any interaction with school or societally based issues (such as bullying or racism). Contrariwise, in publicity about child abuse, moralities of 'natural needs and development' are still very much in evidence (Kitzinger 1990; Stainton Rogers and Stainton Rogers 1992).

Reflecting on this brief review, it seems that – even within a relatively homogeneous cultural group – different historical periods have represented the process of rearing children very differently. While only one of these periods employs an explicit rhetoric of needs, it is important to recognise that all types of advice laid claim to the moral authority to define the requirements not only for good parenting, but also for what made an appropriate child, albeit often concerned with what the children would become rather than how they fared at the time. In this sense, the rhetoric of children's needs, while attractive, has been invoked over the years in quite diverse and often conflicting terms. There is a corresponding danger that children's 'needs' become some kind of inviolable category that is treated as self-evident rather than as informed by and reflecting the socio-political preoccupations of particular cultures and times (Woodhead 1990). Its seeming incontrovertibility masks other, more appreciative, models of childhood in circulation even within Europe – of enrichment rather than deficit (Moss *et al.* 2000). Indeed the discourse of 'needs' reflects a model of children and childhood as passive, to be serviced, protected and provided for, rather than to be engaged with as active participants (Moss and Petrie 2002).

Childhood as dependency

Changing images of the child can be related to broader social tensions within emerging modern industrialising states. There are three points to note here. First, the contrasting models frequently coexist and compete, rather than succeed each other in a harmonious fashion. Second, and following from this, there are continuities between images at different times – many conceptions reverberate on in powerful ways today. Third, debates about the nature of the child have been central to the ways the state has interacted with, and regulated, its citizens. The eighteenth-century French philosopher Rousseau is credited with inventing the modern notion of childhood as a distinct period of human life with particular needs for stimulation and education. In contrast to evangelical doctrines of 'original sin', this model upheld the innocence of the child, the proximity of children to nature and their freedom from contamination with the ugly lessons of civilisation. But this was not all it achieved, for Rousseau's ideas (which were still religious but installed a vision of original innocence instead of sin) also had implications for the position of women as mothers:

> The new child was a figure of the 'Cult of Sensibility' associated with Rousseau. . . . At the basic level, therefore, this construction related to the contest for a particular kind of society – for a particular kind of beliefs – which was to stand between eighteenth century rationalism and nineteenth century industrialisation.
>
> (Hendrick 1990: 38–39)

Industrialisation in the late eighteenth century ushered in the formalisation of child labour in factories. Outrage over the conditions of child labourers had less to do with exploitation than with fears of unruly and potentially undesirable activities made possible by an independent income. Indeed when children were no longer needed in the factories there developed a fear of – especially – young men roaming the streets. This was alongside the ways in which women's and children's waged labour participation was seen as competing with men's and so not only limiting the availability of work but also depressing wages. Martin Hoyles (1989) relates the invention of childhood innocence to the cult of the 'infant Jesus' which worked to eclipse children's active political resistance. Harry Hendrick (1990) argues that a debased version of the eighteenth-century philosophy of child nature was invoked to justify making children dependent through schooling, imposing a middle-class ideal of childhood as a period of helplessness. This was then treated as a cultural universal to block the reproduction of working-class resistance through controlling the activities of young people:

> They [eighteenth-century notions of child nature] were thoughtful expressions of a developing social and political philosophy (extending well beyond a concern with children) which was finding an audience among a class anxious about what it deemed to be the rebellious and aggressive attitudes and behaviours of young people (and of their parents). Thus juvenile lawlessness was seen as one of the heralds of political insurrection.
>
> (Hendrick 1990: 44–45)

This was achieved through the introduction of compulsory mass schooling, linked to a theory of child nature which presented the initial state of the child as ignorant (thereby disenfranchising their community and 'street' knowledge) and positioning the working-class child as in need of education and socialisation. A standard curriculum produced a segregated and surveyed population with an emphasis on Bible study, along with gender-appropriate training suited to working-class boys' and girls' allotted station in life (Hunt 1985). A national childhood was constructed through schooling, which, although it was officially classless, rendered the child (and therefore the family) always available for reformation of their working-class morals. The process of schooling demanded a state of ignorance in return for advancement of opportunities for a limited few. In terms of the impact on children at the time, Hendrick (1990) suggests that the main effect of the introduction of compulsory schooling was to diminish children's sense of their own value and take them out of the sphere of 'socially significant activity':

> [T]here was nothing coincidental in mid-century penologists and social investigators seeking to return children to their 'true position' (to their nature), as it also involved making them more amenable to the class-room. . . . The reconstruction of the factory child through the prism of dependency and ignorance was a necessary precursor of mass education in that it helped prepare public opinion for shifts in the child's identity (from wage-labourer to school pupil), for a reduction in income of working class families (as a result of the loss of children's earnings), and for the introduction of the state into childrearing practices.
>
> (Hendrick 1990: 46)

Zelizer's (1985) influential analysis of the rise of the notion of the 'price-less child' explicitly ties the rise of child abuse to the decrease in children's economic value within the labour market. Indeed Qvortup (2000) addresses the contemporary reversal of the school–work relationship for children by controversially proposing that, since children's work is now schoolwork (often in the early years through the medium of 'play' – see Chapter 13), children should be paid to go to school. (This could be linked to other discussions of monetarising contexts of education and care, as in the discussion of 'wages for housework' in Chapter 6.)

So we can see that current anxieties with children's antisocial activities are nothing new, but rather the latest challenge to the recent hegemonic view of childhood innocence. For example, a similar erasure of young people's active political contribution to social transformation is happening now in South Africa, where the eclipse of youth mobilisation and action in the anti-apartheid struggle is now giving rise to a criminalisation of young people's activities (Marks 2001). In the UK, the anxiety generated in 2005/6 by the wearing of a 'hoodie' (hooded top) has marked the shift in perception from child as victim of violence to child as perpetrator (although that child might now be called a 'youth' or a 'yob'). A raft of legislation aimed at controlling young people's activities has been introduced. There is a new British system of applying anti-social behaviour orders (popularly known as ASBOs), designed to monitor and survey behaviour by imposing limits on what can be done, and where. Nearly half of these ASBOs have been issued to children (Lister 2006), while significantly curfews and parenting orders make the children's parents responsible for ensuring compliance. Their ambiguities have been highlighted (if also probably overstated) by reports that the ASBOs are seen as a 'badge of honour' rather than shame by young people themselves (Barkham 2006a). But beyond this the familiar theme of adult identification with, and so covert toleration or even incitement of, young people's exuberance or rebellion is indicated by the availability of greetings cards for purchase that are cast in the format of an ASBO – with the precise details of the misdemeanour to be completed by the sender.

Childhood as universal

The specific historical picture of childhood based in mid-nineteenth century Europe therefore saw a move away from a diversity of class and cultural conceptualisations of childhood to the imposition of a standardised model that drew together a set of concerns with child education, management and control as well as philanthropy. This standard childhood, as administered in part through schooling, achieved uniformity and coherence among urban and rural populations. It reflected the Victorian domestic ideal of the family – based on order, respect and love – with corresponding organisation around age and gender asymmetries; and it made possible the twentieth-century construction of the compulsory relation between family, state and public welfare characteristic of Western liberal democracies. Childhood, conceived of as a period of dependency, meant that education and socialisation were required to lead and train the child in the 'appropriate' direction. Hence representations of childhood were central to social policies.

It is worth reflecting on the links between notions of childhood, schooling and child labour when considering contemporary debates on the welfare of children in Third World countries. The mass media encourage us to think about 'all our children' (the BBC leaflet to the series of this name was subtitled 'A guide for those who care'), and charitable aid to Third World countries is focused on the welfare of children (as in sponsoring a child: 'Experience the joy of sponsorship says Michael Aspel', advertisement in the *Guardian*, 13 February 1992). We are exhorted by Plan International UK to 'change the world . . . one child at a time', to consider ourselves 'A World Family'. Cosy and caring as this 'world family' sounds, it ignores cultural and economic differences and the complexity and inequality of power relations structured within this new diaspora space (Brah 1996). For example, consider how the 2005 Live 8 benefit concerts – organised to precede the G8 Conference and Summit held in Scotland to 'make poverty history' – portrayed 'Africa' as if it were one country, rather than a continent. Such popular approaches treat economic inequalities outside the history of colonialism and imperialism which produced the impoverishment of the Third World in the first place. They risk positioning those countries as responsible for their own 'underdevelopment' instead of recognising the vested interests that maintain Third World countries as dependent markets and sources of cheap labour – primarily that of women and children, but with the rise of the practice of 'outsourcing' business to sites of low-cost labour this is now extending to men. In evaluating the significance of the suppression of the impact of imperialism within these texts, we should recall that children are directly involved in the sex tourism industry which was made possible by imperialist (often specifically US) wars in South East Asia (Boyden and Hudson 1985), as was international trafficking in children (Ramirez 1992). Moreover, additional consequences follow from this focus on the child. Social change is rendered gradual, discretionary and individual through working at the level of 'one child at a time'.

Indeed within economic dependency models, the Third World is itself infantilised by its position as recipient of aid (Reeves and Hammond 1998). This interpretation is not only bolstered by the ways in which images of Third World children are used as signifiers of need in fund-raising campaigns (Burman 1994a, 1994b, 1994c), but also because – in part due to low life expectancy as well as high birth rates – poor countries of the world have massively younger populations. Reciprocally, anti-colonial (e.g. Fanon 1952) and post-colonial analyses of orientalism (Said 1979) and subalternity (Spivak 1993) can be applied to the analysis of children's positions. Childhood has emerged as a domain to be colonised and 'civilised', its mysterious and alien features rendered legible and docile, its 'voice' only able to be spoken within adult-defined and regulated discourses (Canella and Viruru 2004).

In these ways the child *as child* functions as an index, a signifier of 'civilisation' and modernity, while the child remains the key arena in which to instill such civilisation (Elias 2000). Yet as exemplified by the current rush for US celebrities (such as Madonna) to adopt African children, the 'right' to childhood is adopted as a transcultural universal that links First and Third Worlds in a relationship of patronage and cultural imperialism. The adoption of this notion (which is structured in the 1959 UN Declaration of the Rights of the Child and the 1989 Convention on the Rights of the Child) bears witness to interests which, while seeking to enable and protect children, are also in danger of rendering them passive, dependent and malleable (Freeman 2000). Indeed while currently championing the convention and its implementation and monitoring, it is interesting to note that UNICEF was initially very opposed to it on the grounds that the convention might distract from its work on child survival. Until recently the focus of UNICEF's work was on early childhood. This has now changed, and with the attention to older children (with the category of child defined as under 18 years old) and youth (extending to late 20s) has brought in a new focus on participation.

Significance of advice literature

What bearing do these historical and cultural analyses have on our understanding of the changing, and proliferating, advice given to parents?

First, there is the significance of its presence (and volume). Newson and Newson (1974) comment on how little there was of this literature prior to the mid-twentieth century. They provide a useful reminder that the preconditions for a psychology of child development, with its concerns about psychological adjustment and abilities, are a low rate of infant mortality and an adequate standard of living. Consider then what they term the 'cult of child psychology', the explosion of popular as well as academic literature that assaults us in supermarket queues and newsagents, and finds its way among the recipes and quizzes in general newspapers as well as in those magazines specifically directed to women. Developmental psychology participates within the everyday popular understanding of parental roles, family relations and indeed personal identities of mothers, fathers, children and all who are involved in teaching or caring for them in contemporary Western culture. In 1990s Britain, the Royal College of General Practitioners approved a publication, *Emma's Diary* (Lifecycle Marketing 1991), available free in doctors' surgeries and clinics. This contains adverts not specifically associated with childcare as well as a week-by-week description of the progress of pregnancy and childcare. The demand for information about childcare and development was presented in newspaper coverage as aiming 'to satisfy pregnant women's craving for facts about parenthood', with pregnant women described as 'information guzzling' (*Independent on Sunday*, 16 February 1992: 24). The popular notion of pregnancy as producing compulsive appetites is here extended to include women's desires to know. So essential is the role currently accorded to knowledge about child development that it can even be represented as part of a pregnant woman's bodily needs. Nested within these ideas is a form of biological reductionism which collapses the biological fact of pregnancy into a period of receptivity to information about children (shades here of Winnicott's 'primary maternal preoccupation', and of the attachment and 'bonding' research discussed in Chapter 7). Following from the biologistic analogy, the notion of critical periods, or deadlines by which this knowledge must be demonstrated, is maintained. These trends were also noted by Marshall and Woollett (2000) in their review of pregnancy texts.

But, second, what functions does this advice play? Do we find it helpful, reassuring? How can we understand the development of this eager market? It has been suggested that one reason why mothers (and fathers) turn to books arises from the erosion of extended family ties within which cultural understandings of child rearing would otherwise be communicated. Indeed, distinct class differences have been noted between those mothers who rely on their mothers' advice and those who seek out professional sources of information (Vukelich and Kumar 1985; Jones 1987). Again this is a useful prompt to recall the (classed, gendered and racialised) social divisions that make spurious simple descriptions of 'society' as homogeneous even within one geographical area. While the readership of the early child manuals was primarily middle class, one clear reason for the increasing dependence on professional advice lies in the ways this explicitly devalues oral sources as uninformed and old-fashioned, cautioning women not to rely on their mothers' or older women's advice. In this sense the advice literature is self-maintaining.

It is clearly difficult to assess the impact or 'effects' of this literature. Marshall's (1991) analysis of the content of some influential British sources highlights their dominant themes. Motherhood is presented as a woman's 'ultimate fulfilment', with mother love as 'natural' (and, correspondingly, failure to love as requiring psychiatric treatment). There is an emphasis on 'modern' motherhood, with a dependence on professional experts for advice, and the desirable forum for the bringing up of a child is defined as a happy, heterosexual, nuclear family. This is presented as both inevitable and enduringly stable, wherein the expressed commitment to flexibility and 'sharing the caring' in the accounts gives way to positioning the mother as primarily and ultimately responsible for the 'normal development' of her child through actively stimulating, as well as caring for, her child. Rather as indicated by the slip in the Sorce *et al.* (1985) study discussed in Chapter 3, her identity as a woman is absorbed into that of mother: she is treated as responsible for her child's subsequent deeds and misdeeds through the emphasis on the importance of early experience. She is drawn into the discourse of developmental psychology through this positioning, as both originator and monitor of her child's development.

Marshall speculates whether, given this load, it is possible for a woman to feel confident that she is fulfilling her maternal duty. While the women in Cathy Urwin's (1985a) study report consulting manuals for reassurance, these are also the source of considerable anxiety. Developmental milestones structure mothers' observations of their offspring, such that they worry about the rate of progress, and induce competition between parents by inviting comparisons between children, reflecting the structuring of 'normal development' as measurable through the ranking of individuals. Development thus becomes an obstacle race, a set of hoops to jump through, with cultural kudos accorded to the most advanced, and the real or imagined penalties of professional intervention or stigmatisation if progress is delayed. Small wonder, then, at the marginalised position of 'learning disabled' children and their families. As well as the tendency to load responsibility for the next generation's moral performance on women, and to locate social problems within 'faulty mothering', this account also fails to accord any role to societal and structural influences.

The cultural organisation of development

The popular and 'academic' literature on how children develop reflects dominant cultural assumptions about children's natures and treatment. It also informs these to the extent that they become the resource for the circulation of everyday understandings about what children (and through them mothers, fathers and others) around them are like. The variability of advice gives rise to variability of practice. Newson and Newson (1974) take as their example the case of breastfeeding, which has been subject to fluctuation according to class and generation. While in the 1920s and 1930s bottle-feeding was a means for the British middle classes to display their status as able to afford the technology to feed and manage babies, by the 1980s breastfeeding had come to be associated with a middle-class commitment to the notion that 'breast is best' (Stanway and Stanway 1983). This conveyed a principled desire to give your baby the best start to life, backed up by studies correlating breastfeeding with subsequent cognitive performance. The point here is not to advocate one form of feeding over another, but to indicate how the fluctuating demands on women made by medicine and psychology neglect the social factors that constrain women's choices, and thus often function simply to stigmatise further those who fail to measure up to this moral imperative.

A major consequence of this variability is that women are segmented and separated from each other's experiences and solidarity, both by generation and by class. First, women who adhered to the expert advice of their day, by, for example, staying home with their child rather than engaging in paid work, are now portrayed as overinvolved and clinging while, before them, their mothers who had not indulged their children and had fed them by the clock had gone on only to be later positioned as cruel and heartless – as testified by the agonised accounts of mothers quoted by Newson and Newson (1974). Meanwhile, within the current rhetoric of 'flexibility', women are presented with the 'choice' about feeding method (Alldred 1996; Marshall and Woollett 2000). But the decks are heavily loaded in favour of breastfeeding: what mother can resist the injunction to foster the development of her child or, worse, impede it by failing to provide 'baby's birthright'? What of the mothers who do not have 'the choice' not to work, or who cannot for other reasons breastfeed their babies? This is not to condone the cynical peddling of baby milk substitutes to poor women in the Third World. Rather, in both contexts, the rhetoric of freedom of choice functions as a more subtle form of oppression by failing to recognise the inequality of access to the conditions it presupposes.

Gill Craig's (2004, 2005) research with families with children who have severe disabilities is instructive in this regard. She worked with families where the child's disabilities (usually cerebral palsy) were so great that they experienced dysphagia (i.e. problems with swallowing and eating). Feeding these children orally was not only excessively time consuming (some mothers spent between five and seven hours a day doing this), but also involved discomfort and coercion. Clearly the use of force would appear to conflict with child-centred discourses of nurturing and even child rights. Given other possibilities – such as nasogastric tubes (where a tube is inserted through the nose and passed into the stomach) and ultimately gastrostomy (where a feeding tube is surgically inserted into the child's stomach), it would be expected that families would take advantage of other modes of enabling their children to be fed. Yet although some were happy to accept this, other mothers in Craig's study resisted such feeding technologies, to the mystification of the medical personnel.

From analysis of detailed longitudinal interviews conducted with these women it emerged that their commitment to the onerous and sometimes dangerous practice of oral feeding (since the child could choke, and often would not get sufficient nutrition) arose from the meanings they accorded feeding as a time when they could feel that their child was normal, and where they could engage in the kind of normal mothering practices that would enable them to feel good, proper mothers, with a child who was accessing at least one of the experiences (i.e. eating) shared by ordinarily developing children. So it emerged that the paradoxes of coercion in the name of care, and resistance to an apparent health-promoting intervention (although it should also be noted that gastrostomy operations are not without risks, so that the mothers were facing a very difficult decision), could only be understood in terms of how their sense of stigmatisation for having a disabled child was in some senses briefly alleviated by being able to feed the child 'normally'. The introduction of this technology ruptured this sense of normality and rendered their child as somehow less childlike and even less human, and confirmed their own pathologisation as failing mothers. On the other hand the technology also facilitated the possibility that the child would look more 'normal' (by appearing less thin and malnourished). So rather than being the lifesaving measure it was often portrayed to be, it is clear that the mothers faced a number of complex dilemmas. What this study documents, then, is how powerfully images of what 'proper children' are like inevitably enter into parental self-understandings, and how the sense of evaluation by others works to regulate them.

Consequences

This chapter has focused on the forms and variations of discourses of childhood, and the significance of these variations. Three main issues emerge. First, definitions of childhood are relational, they exist in relation to definitions of adults, of mothers and fathers, of families, of the state. These relational terms of child, adult and the state have come to function in mutually dependent, mutually constitutive ways. While this may be an easy point to accept at an intellectual level, its ramifications are far-reaching. Discussions of children's natures necessarily reflect, and invoke, models of political organisation. Just as the needy, dependent child requires the attentive, indulging mother, so the child on whom environment inscribes its learning schedules requires the regulating, training mother. As Niestroj (1994) highlights: 'the making of the European mind and the *discourse* of the mother–child relationship are profoundly related . . . '*Maternal love' is not modern . . . but the belief in its influence on the developing mind is'* (pp. 294–295).

Second, as feminists have recognised (Thorne 1987), changes in gender relations bring about changes in our conceptualisation of children. Developmental psychology's commitment to a view of children and child development as fixed, unilinear and timeless is not only ethnocentric and culture-blind in its unwitting reflection of parochial preoccupations and consequent devaluation of differing patternings, but is also in danger of failing to recognise changes in the organisation of childhood subjectivity and agency. Ann Solberg (1990) documents the increased power gained by the greater participation in household labour of Norwegian children of dual-earner parents, as indicated both by their own and their family's perceptions. This study involves analysis of the subjective meanings invested (by children as well as adults) in being older or younger, or more or less big or grown up. It is indicative of a specifically Northern European tradition of developmental psychological investigation that documents and analyses the daily routines of children's lives in order to understand better how childhood is lived and experienced. Not surprisingly, a more competent model of childhood emerges from these studies (see also Kjorholt 2005; Andenaeas in press), for the participation of women in paid work outside the home in the socialist democracies of Northern Europe, in a context of national planning for childcare provision, has created the conditions for new forms and variations of childhood to emerge. If childhood is seen as static, universal and timeless then this can only be viewed as an aberration to be deplored. But to do this would be to proscribe any change from existing social arrangements and to refuse to recognise opportunities for the development of new subjectivities. Further, the fact that Solberg's study appeared so novel in testifying to a relation between children's productive labour and enhanced social position itself speaks volumes about the ignorance or repression of the fact that most of the world's children work. That is, we fail to recognise the cultural specificity of our developmental models, which are not only partial and unaware of this, but also function oppressively, in prescribing what are Western norms for Third World countries (see Chapter 5 for more on child labour).

Third, and finally, there is the question of the positioning of children and knowledge. Children are defined as lacking knowledge, hence requiring protection and education. To challenge this conception may seem to render children responsible for the difficulties that befall them, as is evident in discussions of child abuse (Kitzinger 1990). In their textbook, Seifert and Hoffnung (1987), alongside a section on 'The concept of childhood in history', present an account of the modern construction and institutionalisation of children as benign, noting that:

> In the twentieth century, society became increasingly concerned about protecting children from the harsh world outside the family. Children

were thought to need the special protection of parents and institutions dedicated to serving children, such as schools.

(Seifert and Hoffnung 1987: 12–13)

Attribution of knowledge to children is bound up with images of the child and what we imagine them and ourselves to be. Discourses of childhood function as regulatory both overtly and internally. They produce a sense of adulthood and childhood not only for us but also for children. Accounts such as that quoted above fail to distinguish between a variety of social relations, both within and between cultures, that constitute a 'society'. They portray as unproblematic both the position of the family as a haven in a heartless world, and the state as involved in protecting and educating children. These are the issues to which we turn next.

Further reading

Elias, N. (2000) *The Civilising Process*, Oxford: Blackwell.

Hendrick, H. (2003) *Child Welfare: Historical Dimensions, Contemporary Debate*, Bristol: The Policy Press (reviews of changing models of childhood and the conditions that gave rise to them from the 1880s to the twenty-first century).

James, A. and Prout, A. (eds) (1997) *Constructing and Reconstructing Childhood*, 2nd edn, Basingstoke: Falmer Press (a fascinating and wide-ranging collection, all of which is useful in the elaboration of issues raised in this and other chapters in this part).

For accounts that specifically address childcare advice, see:

Alldred, P. (1996) 'Whose expertise? Conceptualising resistance to advice about child-rearing', pp. 133–151 in E. Burman, G. Aitken, P. Alldred, R. Allwood, B. Billington, T. Billington, A. Gordo-Lopez, C. Heenan, D. Marks and S. Warner (eds) *Psychology, Discourse Practice: From Regulation to Resistance*, London: Taylor & Francis.

Marshall, H. and Woollett, A. (2000) 'Fit to reproduce? The regulatory role of pregnancy texts', *Feminism and Psychology*, 10, 3: 351–366.

Thom, D. (1992) 'Wishes, anxieties, play and gestures: child guidance in inter-war England', in R. Cooter (ed.) *In the Name of the Child*, London: Routledge.

Urwin, C. and Sharland, E. (1992) 'From bodies to minds in childcare literature: advice to parents in inter-war Britain', in R. Cooter (ed.) *In the Name of the Child*, London: Routledge.

Suggested activities

Gather together a selection of childcare advice literature from the key books – ranging from current (such as those by Gina Ford and Jo Frost), to those of the 1980s (such as Hugh Jolly and Penelope Leach), to the 'experts' of the 1950s and 1960s such as Benjamin Spock and earlier. Many public and college libraries have endless amounts of such material, while websites are also devoted to such issues. Students may also have access to such materials as well. It is also useful to include literature that is provided free of charge at health centres, doctors' surgeries or family planning clinics, or distributed by health visitors, and to analyse material in childcare magazines, of which there are currently many. Having allocated this material to individuals or pairs, address the following questions:

- What is the gender of the child depicted (and how do you know)?
- What is the gender of the primary caregiver?
- What is the gender of professionals (if they are depicted)?
- What is the tone of the advice offered?
- What models of family relations are represented?
- How culturally specified is the form of childhood depicted?
- Which kinds of childhood would be privileged, and which marginalised, in each account?

Simple questions such as these can generate interesting commentary and debate, particularly if the material under scrutiny spans a significant period of time, or is clearly addressed to different audiences (as in those who buy versus those who are statutory recipients of services). Tensions or contradictions can also be fruitful, as in variation between articles and advertising copy within a single text such as a magazine, or between narrative and image. An exercise like this can bring to life questions about variety and variability of childcare literature over time and within and between cultures that make the discursive construction of childhood and the correlative positions elaborated for mothers, fathers and others very concrete. As examples of such work, see:

Dolev, R. and Zeedyk, M.S. (2006) 'How to be a good parent in bad times: constructing parenting advice about terrorism', *Child Care, Health and Development, 32, 4*: 467–476.
Skeggs, B. and Wood, H. (2004) 'Notes on ethical scenarios of self on British reality TV', *Feminist Media Studies, 4, 1*: 201–208.

5 Models and muddles
Dilemmas of childhood

Innocent child – Children must be cared for. THAT'S IT

The text above features as the sign of a building round the corner from my workplace. It gives voice to the widespread view that children demand unconditional support. The fact that this slogan has a subtitle, 'international humanitarian relief', announces this as the office of an aid organisation, but it also speaks to the role of the appeal to the child as the quintessential deserving human subject, with the modal verb 'must' combining with 'THAT'S IT' to convey this as an absolute, incontrovertible imperative. So powerful is this that the motif of the child is sometimes mobilised in favour of aid for deserving parties generally. But are all children 'innocent'? And what happens to the injunction to 'care' if they are not? (Does it then become discretionary or dispensable, and what exactly constitutes 'care'?) And who is it who 'must' do the caring?

This chapter builds on the discourses of childhood discussed in Chapter 4 to address some of the conundra set up by the dominant model of the happy, playing and developing child. The chapter first considers the emergence of the inner child and its implied 'others', and then addresses its relationships with non-normative childhoods framed by discourses of abuse and exploitation. A key feature of this analysis is the exploration of how the focus on the child and family works to eclipse wider social explanations and social processes (including varieties of state exclusionary practices), and serves a particular role within contemporary social policy.

The inner child

Terry Gilliam's (2005) film *Tideland* follows the activities and subjectivity of a little girl fending her own way in rural America when her parents die of drug overdoses. As its director, he opens the film with the comment that, at the age of 64, he has discovered his inner child. Indeed (with interesting cross-gender inflections 'allowable' to maverick celebrities – though that also confirms the association between femininity and childhood) this inner child is a little girl.

The inner child connects ideas about the childhood we (adults) had, or rather that we wished we might have had, with ideas of the true self – the ideal version of ourselves that perhaps remains secret or carefully protected, that lies within us as something special or potential. Significantly, then, this separates notions of children and childhood from real children's lives.

Obvious and self-evident as this notion of the child as exemplar of the true self may seem, in fact it has very particular (cultural and historical) origins. It is tied up with the development of a sense of interiority, of feelings stored and sustained 'inside' (within the head or body), ideas which originated within the development of the precursors to science and psycho-analysis in eighteenth-century Europe. This notion of interiority connects contemporary therapeutic and popular self-help concerns with arriving at a narrative of one's own history that is self-affirming. Steedman (1995) has traced the emergence of this notion through the analysis of literary, technical and popular European texts. She argues:

> The child was the figure that provided the largest number of people living in the recent past of Western societies with the means for thinking about and creating a self: something grasped and understood: a shape, moving in the body. . . something *inside*, an interiority.
>
> (Steedman 1995: 20)

Thus actual personal and social history, and actuality (one's 'real', historically lived childhood), is subordinated to some fantasy child. Steedman proposes that children – especially little girls – signify not only the inner, fragile self, but also have come to express longing and loss within the modern Western imaginary:

> The child within was always both immanent – ready to be drawn on in various ways – and, at the same time, always representative of a lost realm, lost in the individual past, and in the past of the culture. . . The idea of the child was used both to recall and to express the past that each individual life contained: what was turned inside in the course of individual development was that which was also latent: the child *was* the story waiting to be told.
>
> (Steedman 1995: 10–11)

Here developmental psychology meets psychotherapy, as fantasy and history converge. The gendered character of this personification of the fragile self is of course deeply significant. Moreover, notions of the inner child form a key segue between popular self-help and professional psycho-therapeutic discourses. While the credibility of psychotherapeutic practices underwent a battering under the barrage of scrutiny and criticism generated by the disputes over false/recovered memories (with the memories of women claiming to have recovered memories of abuse at issue), the motif of the child as personification of the true self appears to have remained unscathed, as – significantly – has the reputation of developmental psychology – positioned as the arbiter of knowledge about children's and adults' memorial capacities (Burman 1997a).

Given the disjunction between this notion and the real lives children lead, one can only speculate about what is at stake in the adult investment in this notion. But the celebration of those qualities now associated (within the Western imagination) with childhood – of play, indulgence, consumption and irresponsibility – has acquired a wide cultural circulation (think of the youth culture subversion of the young children's television series *Teletubbies* in the late 1990s, for example, or the fashion for young people going clubbing to wear dummies; see also Burman 1992b; Gordo Lopez and Burman 2004). Such ideas have flourished alongside, or perhaps precisely because of, an alternative representation of the self as fragile and wounded, in need of particular nurturance and care (Furedi 2004). In a sense this notion of the inner child offers a diagnosis of the dissatisfactions and thwarted longings of adult lives under advanced capitalism, rather than any depiction of children. To this extent, then, it serves as a key warning of the need to distinguish between fantasy notions of children and childhoods and the actual lived experiences of real children.

The child has been recruited into a culturally sanctioned form of secular spirituality in an increasingly individualised world, so that self-help books, such as the one below, exhort us to nurture our inner child, and sing songs to it:

> *The Song of the Child* is, then, an attempt to speak for the child, but in a way in which the child could not – yet – describe herself. It is '*the invisible*' that is – and which is trying to become – living within the child which seeks to find expression in *The Song of the Child*. There is no little risk, of course, in claiming to have the very *soul* of the child speak to us adults in a mediated way. Indeed, the only way of so doing must necessarily lie crucially *beyond the intellect*, beyond analytical consciousness, and, instead, must needs embrace a kind of empathically intuitive *Verstehen* through which the child is enabled to speak *through* the adult in a relatively unmediated way, unhindered by adult-centric consciousness . . . championing *the sanctity, mystery and wonder* of childhood in the face of modernity's multiple challenges.
>
> (Hétu 2004, www.urpublications.com, accessed 23 August 2006)

Moreover, as we have seen, this inner child is gendered. In a neat twist which reads fully formed adult gendered identities back on to depictions of early childhood, and so renders them essential and natural, men and women are invited to rediscover a (usually) gender-appropriate (but usually pre-sexual) inner child. Such claims are not only explicit in their gendered allocation, but also in the kind of qualities so associated. Marketing strategies now address the boy the man was, or would have wanted to be, in (the self-ironised) depiction of cars or new technological gadgets as 'boy's toys' (which does not of course preclude them finding different ways of addressing women). Here it is the rebellious, non-conformist, fearless and spontaneous 'boy' qualities that are invoked, claiming a childhood omni-potence that, by definition, has disappeared (as in the Peugeot advert slogan 'Remember that feeling of total control?'; Burman 1995a). By contrast, the feminised inner child signifies an emotional and physical vul-nerability that fits well with a wider cultural model of subjectivity empha-sising victim status: the adult as the victim of the vicissitudes of a cruel and uncertain world. In this sense, it fits well with the 'full child' of contem-porary developmental psychology discussed in Chapter 3, even if – or precisely because – this prior fully formedness is invoked to compensate for current insufficiencies. Some varieties of feminist therapy advocate attending to one's inner needy little girl (Orbach and Eichenbaum 1982). This little girl may be angry and assertive as well as 'needy', and her 'needs' may precisely be to express this, but it is significant that it is because this lays claim to the status of 'need' that it demands redress. And as we have seen, this discourse of needs has acquired culturally incontrovertible status.

These essentialist engenderings, far from being incompatible with post-modern renderings of flexible gendered subjectivities, coexist comfortably with them. The adventurous, fearless inner boy may be as much a precious and secret inner vulnerability as it is a culturally celebrated genre. It complements current social policy concerns in many Western societies on the self-destructive health and mental health vulnerabilities of young men.

Endangered/dangerous children?

As I write this, a new debate about the status of childhood is happening in Britain. A lead 'Letter to the Editor', signed by 110 'experts' published on 12 September 2006 in the *Daily Telegraph*, complained of the erosion of child-hood and promotion of mental health problems in children due to a 'lack of understanding, on the part of both the politicians and the public, of the realities and subtleties of child development'. The letter called for a public debate on 'child-rearing in the 21st century' to generate ways of improving children's well-being, thus moving swiftly from a critique of contemporary social life to imposing greater responsibilities on parents. A feature article claimed 'Junk culture "is poisoning our children"' (Fenton 2006), while the editorial column that day led with the title 'Lost childhoods', taking up such diverse themes as junk food, the displacement of recreational play by computer games and television, consumer overindulgence 'to such an extent that those same minds are stunted, and the opportunity to enjoy the simply, outdoor life of play that was once a child's perceived birthright is lost'. A flurry of letters appeared across the British press proclaiming and disputing children's natures, parental involvement and state responsibilities. Calls for a national inquiry into children and childhood emerged from across the political spectrum, with even the Archbishop of Canterbury participating in the media discussion. A daily radio series discussed the controversies over what childhood is, has been and what is at stake in such concerns. British journalist Anne Karpf comments on the debate, highlighting that the lost childhood at issue appears to derive from the childhoods of the authors of the initial letter, and points out 'Why pick on kids when you could say the same about all of us?':

> There's a real danger that, in these admittedly troubled times, we resort to an idealised, nostalgic view of childhood – one which, if it existed at all, did so only for a relatively short period of time and only in certain parts of the world . . . It hasn't always been the 1950s.
>
> (Karpf 2006: 12)

Whatever the truths and merits of attending to the increased educational pressures upon and mental and physical vulnerabilities of children, there is discernible slippage in the portrayal of this 'toxic childhood' (cf. Palmary 2006), from the child as *subject to* social problems to the child *as* a social problem. Indeed at exactly this time, new educational reforms were announced that abolished continuous assessment by coursework in national school assessments, but the rationale here was – significantly – less to do with the continuous pressure that children are subjected to by such measures than the problems with detecting the (allegedly) increased rates of plagiarism made possible by home-based work in the age of the internet. Thus what seems clear from all this is that childhoods are not only unstable, but their instability within the national and international imaginary generates considerable anxiety.

A historical perspective on legal and social policy indicates that ambivalence about the state's role in relation to children is nothing new. While the model of the vulnerable, ignorant child positioned them as requiring protection, children were also portrayed as a source of disruption requiring control and discipline. In their analysis of policy and welfare practices relating to children that have given rise to legislation in Britain, Dingwall *et al.* (1984) argue that childhood has generally been treated as a 'social problem' whereby the dominant focus of social policy and practice has been on the perceived capacities of young people to threaten public order. Children's problems of abuse and neglect have tended to be collapsed together with the treatment of the child *as* a problem, as reflected even now within the types of care and provision available. Indeed, Franklin (2002a) has noted a shift over the past 15 years in the UK away from the cultural demand for indulgence towards children and towards an increasingly punitive stance. We can see such elisions happening on official notices in institutions which warn parents that the premises are not adapted for children (Burman and MacLure 2005). In these examples, measures taken apparently to protect children actually exclude them from accessing facilities (and often exclude their parents too, if they cannot bring their children with them).

Equally problematic are those cases where children appear to be actively transforming their status as 'sufferers'. The story 'Child charity warns of "Ritalin for CDs" trade' (*Guardian*, 27 July 2003) blames drug dealers, rather than children, for this trade – since the ADHD treatment drug Ritalin is an amphetamine. Yet from the reports it also seems likely that children themselves are dealing the drug at school, so turning the stigmatised status of having a diagnosed behavioural difficulty into a financial asset. Significantly, the report also noted that girls are using it as a 'diet pill' because of its appetite-reducing effects. This example also shows that – contrary to the prevailing assumption that involvement in education and labour are mutually exclusive – schooling is not necessarily incompatible with income generation, nor that the escalating rates of medication of children (Black 2003) guarantee docility. In terms of gendered motifs, girls are positioned as the unfortunate dupes of the dealers and of the fashion industry (i.e. as 'victims'), while boys and men are implicitly positioned as the reprehensible dealers.

This connects with the wider cultural theme of girls as victims noted above. This happens most explicitly in discussions of abuse, particularly sexual abuse. Clearly the escalating rates of sexual abuse demand urgent attention and intervention. But the fact that little boys and girls are presumed innocent and without sexual urges is not always helpful. For as the judge's comment 'She's no angel' referring to a pre-teen girl raped by her babysitter indicated, any evidence of awareness prejudices claims to victim status: knowledge is, apparently, incompatible with exploitation. Such dichotomies are of course not only false but give rise to a double bind: for failure to 'know' can put children in more danger.

Policies around child protection have struggled with these socio-cultural paradoxes. In particular anxieties around children's suggestibility coexist with extensive legal requirements for professionals to report any suspicions of abuse. These competing demands create difficulties for them to know how to relate to children. There is an understandable desire not to have to invoke the intrusive, protracted and expensive apparatus of child protection procedures, alongside a fear of being prosecuted for failing to do so. This gives rise to a kind of defensive practice that privileges bureaucracy over relationships and prevents, rather than promotes, engagement. As a specific instance of the ways in which the discourse of 'risk' has come to be embodied and attached to individuals (rather than societal conditions, see later), the 'child-at-risk' has become a 'risky child'. This is a particularly pernicious reversal that also covertly works to penalise children as victims, and threatens to treat them as unworthy victims at that.

Thus the current focus on child protection (and its struggle with more libertarian approaches) poses a key question: is protectionism winning over participation in an era of defensive practice and 'risk'? As Munro (2004) and Rustin (2004) note, bureaucratic proposals for better interprofessional relationships and tracking of families cannot address the problem: for the real issue is that at a personal, psychological level (because it is unbearable) and an institutional level (it is too expensive), we often do not really want to know what is happening to children. Thus 'protecting' children can function as a way of pre-empting answers/silencing children, so closing down rather than opening up arenas for discussion with children since parents/guardians are required to be present (see also Stainton Rogers and Stainton Rogers 1992; Warner 2000). As Munro (2004) comments:

> The public have unrealistic expectations about protecting children. Abusive parents work hard to deceive and, however expert the professionals, some abusers will escape detection. Public intolerance of failure leads to defensive practice. Fear of missing a case of serious abuse makes professionals adopt a low threshold for triggering a full investigation. Consequently many families are subjected to a painful intrusive inspection and, in the majority of cases, either no abuse or low level abuse is found and no further help is offered. Investigations absorb so many resources that few services are available for families with lower level worries.
>
> (Munro 2004: 183)

Increasing regulation of both families and social work interventions will not necessarily improve matters, for under market economy conditions British social workers have to comply with specified limits on the time they are allowed to devote to any single case. The emphasis on 'throughput' and the promotion of autonomy reflects the prevailing neoliberal model of the subject, with its emphasis on self-sufficiency. But as the dominant cultural context for the delivery of social work interventions – alongside unmanageable workloads and lack of supervision – this does not facilitate the development of good quality relationships and service partnerships upon which social work assessment and service provision inevitably rely.

Both institutionally and personally, then, what is being avoided here is the inevitable ambiguity and emotionality of work with children. Fear and pain are inevitably generated by child protection work, but this work cannot adequately be done without human engagement, as Cooper (2005) emphasises:

> I do not believe it is possible to do effective child protection work, or supervise and manage it, unless there is a capacity to experience and engage with intense emotional pain, anger, disbelief, the desire to

punish and retaliate, and the balancing impulse for compassion . . . this means the capacity to both endure intensity of emotional and intellectual pain and turmoil, and exercise measured thought, analysis and judgement. The answer lies not in one or the other, but in both.

(Cooper 2005: 5)

The longstanding awareness of child abuse throughout history perhaps also challenges professional and popular sensibilities of the enlightened superiority of modern Western societies (Calder 2005). Given the understandable desire to avoid such engagements and demanding judgements, it is often easier to fail to recognise a child's distress:

The question which must be borne in mind when we remove our attention from the suffering of the child is do we do this in the service of helping the child or in the service of protecting ourselves from our own suffering? Good child protection work is always poised somewhere on this difficult boundary.

(Cooper 2005: 6)

Moreover, child protection is not always a uniformly applied right. The case of Victoria Climbié, an 8-year-old child who died in London in 2000 as the result of injuries inflicted by her great-aunt and the latter's partner when living in their custody, indicates how some children are considered more valuable or in need of protection than others. Within current British social policy agendas that position many migrants as having 'no recourse to public funds', children whose claims to citizenship or residency are questionable may not be deemed deserving. That Victoria Climbié and her guardian were African (from the Ivory Coast) rendered their entitlement somehow in question, despite the fact that (through colonial legacies) they had EU visitor status. As Rustin (2004) notes:

Although public responsibility for the well-being of a child was accepted, at least to a degree, it seems possible that some of the stigma and hostility being more broadly attached to refugees at this time was a factor in the misrecognition of and official indifference to the situation of this family . . . The Inquiry Report does not explore the possibility that animosity towards refugees in this period may have been a contributing factor to the neglect of Victoria's needs, or indeed that other children who are in this situation might now for the same reasons be at risk.

(p. 11)

Chapter 6 takes up the question of whether 'every child matters', by offering further perspectives on this and other child protection issues.

Working children: working to live, working to play and learning to earn

All this is useful in evaluating current discussions of child labour in Third World countries, which Boyden with Holden (1991) claimed involves around 150 million children, but is probably now significantly more. Moreover, prevailing ideas of 'work' equate this with paid work, so making invisible the domestic labour of especially girls and women. Indeed the labour of women and children is better seen as the last resource left to poor families the world over (Nieuwenhuys 2000). The issue here is to proscribe exploitative and dangerous work practices rather than pathologise Third World cultures and families for failing to uphold modern Western notions of childhood as a period of dependency, play and irresponsibility. We might recall how the abolition of child labour was central to industrial reform in nineteenth-century Europe (Steedman 1983, 1995). Indeed current debates surrounding young carers of disabled or chronically ill parents/siblings echo the arguments put forward a century ago (Olsen 2000).

Moreover, in a transnational context, the scandalisation that surrounds discussions of child labour all too often works to protect national market monopolies, where, for example, calls to boycott products from a country in which children work function to exclude that country from trade (O'Neil 2004). The real challenge is to change the exploitation of the poor rather than proscribe child labour (which is impossible anyway). Hence this is more a matter of transforming geopolitical relations of inequality than only child victimisation. What Boyden (1990) has called the 'globalization of childhood' functions as a medium for perpetuating ethnocentric and racist assumptions and prevents us from attending to the specific conditions and meanings of children's participation within local economies, without which little real aid and action is possible (see Park 2006 and Chapter 14 for more on these issues).

Hence the current position taken by many on child labour is that total abolition is neither possible nor desirable. Indeed – in the right circumstances – work may be an arena for learning a range of valuable social and technical skills, and gaining social status. Nevertheless within the popular imagination it is assumed that only poor children, and especially children from so-called Third World countries, work. And it is also assumed that engaging in work is incompatible with schooling. As we have seen, schooling has come to be seen as central to the promotion of child development and child rights – although the poor quality of many schools must surely make this presumption questionable.

Rather than contributing to stealing children's childhoods – as the dominant discourse would have it (which only serves to stigmatise working children as somehow not quite proper children), these activities can offer useful experiences and opportunities. However, this rationale has also been put forward to warrant the (financial and other kinds of) exploitation and appropriation of children's labour in the form of expecting them to do low-paid, piecemeal and often unpleasant or dangerous tasks. Indeed Morice (2000) argues that this is even invoked as a patriarchal right:

> Let us not forget that childhood is a temporary condition, not a social class. Like their mothers, they have no 'natural' place in the labour market; so one is 'doing them a favour' by granting them access to it, and that favour is already something of a payment.
>
> (Morice 2000: 198)

That this work is shared by other marginalised and disenfranchised groups reveals how this is a matter of social status, and that blanket abolition will merely make such exploitation worse:

> The young children breaking rocks in Asia today have taken over from the Cayenne convicts; the only difference being that they are cynically refused the worker status that is supposed to be protecting them from exploitation. Finally, from the point of view of labour law, they and illegal immigrants share the plight of being non-persons.
>
> (Morice 2000: 198)

Far from being an exception, then, child labour can be seen as a structural feature of capitalist societies.

While it is clear that gender and class issues structure the child labour debate (Elson 1992; Lavalette 2000), we will see later (in Chapter 13) how play and work are less opposed than they immediately appear. Further, despite this association of child labour with the poor countries of the world, probably all children work everywhere – although we may not always see this as work (including housework, childcare, running errands, 'helping' in the family shop, as well as paper-rounds, etc.). There is a clear differentiation, though, in the function of the work that children undertake across the world: while children in poor countries work to live, in the sense of sustaining their own and their families' survival, children in (over)-developed countries work to play, in the sense that their paid labour is typically undertaken to fund leisure activities and supplement 'pocket money' (Mizen *et al.* 1999). Indeed children and young people are increasingly targeted as independent possessors of finance in marketing, alongside their role as 'pester power' in affecting their parents' consumer choices.

Current moves in social policy across liberal-left governments of the world aim to tie welfare entitlements increasingly to labour market participation. A model of citizenship rights based on individual income generation is increasingly emphasised. This gives rise to further pressure to be economically active as the measure of social participation (Cradock 2006). My local adult education college currently carries the slogan 'Learn2Earn' (www.mancat.org). The 'smart child' of the twenty-first century does not simply go to school to learn, she learns in order to earn. Debates about child labour not only offer key diagnostic resources about legitimate and illegitimate childhoods that are theoretically and methodologically important for developmental psychology (Burman 2006), they also graphically illustrate how childhood is gendered, with girls' and boys' working lives differentially structured and acknowledged. Moreover, by virtue of the relational, mutually constitutive character of the constructed categories of child and adult, we can also see what is at stake in the role of work in adult lives. If the discussion on child labour presumes that work is the prototypical activity of adults, not only can we question this as an exclusion of children from what is a socially relevant and valued activity, but – as policy debates on 'work–life' balance (to which psychology is a key contributor) indicate – we can also ask why we should frame our adult subjectivities in these terms. In a transnational political climate where welfare entitlement is increasingly predicated on individual economic productivity, do we really want to offer further legitimation to a model of life as living to work? (cf. Lafargue 1883).

Childsize: shrinking the social

There are further ways that contemporary political conditions have come to limit the conceptions of the social that enter into the ways we think about children. Let us consider three examples: firearm deaths, bullying and child poverty.

In March 2006 a 66-year-old Cincinnati man shot dead Larry Mugrage, a 15-year-old boy who had walked across his lawn on his way home. Clearly this senseless act could not have happened without the ready availability and culturally sanctioned use of firearms. In the USA more than 40 per cent of adults own a gun. It is claimed that a child is killed by a gun every three hours, with nearly 1000 children under 19 shot dead every year, another 800 using guns to commit suicide and a further 160 dying in firearm accidents (Borger 2006). Moreover, when in August 2006 plans were announced in Dallas, the most dangerous US city (with murders running at four times the national average), to ban replica guns there was an outcry claiming loss of innocence for childhood games of cowboys and Indians and even that this was a 'criminalisation of nostalgia' (Luscombe 2006). Surely there is something a little peculiar about attempting to redress massive crime and violence by legislating against children's toys. As the International Action Network on Small Arms (IANSA, www.iansa.org, accessed 9 September 2006, which organises youth-led groups to mobilise against the production, circulation and use of firearms) makes clear, individual explanations and interventions are insufficient to address this large-scale problem, and young people should be engaged with rather than legislated against.

To take the second example, there has been a massive increase in discussion of bullying. Indeed bullying seems to have become the route by which societal violence can be talked about, with the paradigm institutional context of the school now generalised from children to adults, to include work-based bullying. It seems significant that this development has happened at the same time that discussions of racist and sexual harassment in British schools seemed to become more problematic. Social-structural issues such as racism, sexism or heterosexism are stripped of their political framework and rendered only personal within the discourse of bullying (McLaughlin 2006).

Finally, in late 2003 the British children's charity Barnardos launched a campaign on child poverty ('No silver spoon'). Yet this was banned on the grounds of being too offensive (Carvel 2003). The image of a baby with a cockroach in its mouth was apparently deemed more shocking than general popular culture condoning the eroticisation of little girls, and the equation of youth with beauty and so sexual attractiveness. The idealised conception of children and childhoods disallows association with poverty and deprivation. This is despite the fact that across richer and poorer countries more children are living in poverty than ever before (Penn 2005).

Overall, we seem to be more comfortable thinking of abuse as individual or familial than as systemic or structural. Moreover, Calder (2005) suggests that there is also a disjunction between popular and professional perception. Professionals seem particularly subject to their own paradigms of disbelief:

> We have never had any trouble in believing in the existence of abuse in institutions for children when it comes to literature. It occurs, of course, in such acknowledged classics as *Oliver Twist* or *Jane Eyre*, but when we read of an orphanage in children's literature it is almost invariably a place of horror – a place to run away from. Not only do we have no difficulty in entertaining the idea of institutional abuse, we positively expect it. The rather alarming conclusion here seems to be that professionals find it harder to accept the reality of professional abuse than the rest of us. It may be that we should look to the exalted educational and social status of the professional as a partial explanation of this, and that their lack of contact with the general public on equal terms makes it hard to tap into the knowledge of abuse that has always existed in wider societies.
>
> (Calder 2005: 119–120)

Defending against the 'risky' child

More generally, the focus of discussions of abuse privileges the familial over the social such that the general risks and dangers posed to children from environmental degradation, wars and political instability tend to be downplayed, except in contexts of international child concern, and even then only at opportune times. Indeed societal anxieties about personal, environmental and national safety are projected on to children, and abstracted from their social and political conditions through their association with children (Burman 1994a, 1994c). As argued above, children come to be the source of professional anxieties, which can get in the way of providing for them. As already mentioned, Munro (2004) is critical of proposals for professional tracking of children's welfare, on the grounds that this is founded on the unrealistic assumption that serious abuse is always preventable (thus giving rise to defensive practice) and such 'tracking' also disempowers parents by surveilling them. The implication that parents are to blame for most of a child's difficulties also ignores or minimises other social-structural forms of abuse (for which the state is clearly much more responsible). She argues that the focus on identifying abusive parents is disproportionate, and minimises other forms of societal abuse and degradation affecting children's welfare:

> We need to remember that serious parental abuse is only one cause of children's problems. Some are harmed by lower level forms of abuse, some as a consequence of parental problems such as poverty or chronic illness, but many are harmed by factors outside the family – crime, racism, poor schools. The Green Paper ['Every Child Matters'] muddles together the problem of identifying dangerous parents with the problem of identifying children showing low level concerns. It consequently gives the impression that parents are to blame for most of a child's difficulties. This is then used to justify the need to distrust parents and establish a national system for professional tracking of children's welfare.
>
> (Munro 2004: 183)

It has been suggested that the undermining of parental authority reflected in current child rights legislation arises from a model of society that is disillusioned and disempowered, that is thereby positioned as in need of support from professional experts (Pupavac 1998, 2002b). Indeed it is unsurprising that parents seek advice about how to bring up children given how two centuries of developmental psychology have told them they do not know how to do it. In a context where the global 'war against terror' comes to be reflected in the insecurity of personal and familial relations, this may herald a return to a new, but less confident, individualism that is all the more intent on regulating children, and – through (or 'for the sake of') the children – their families. Yet this focus on families also ignores the situation of children who have lost, or been separated from, their families – as in children whose parents have died of AIDs-related illnesses, and unaccompanied child asylum seekers (see later). As Moss and Petrie (2002) point out, such wider crises appear to enter into our models of services such that – especially in the UK – we have come to think of services *for* children, with children positioned as passive consumers in need of being contained and protected, instead of creating spaces for children to explore and interact with each other and with others. This greater segregation, protectionism and surveillance of children may also play a part in the documented increase in diagnoses of childhood conduct disorders such as attention deficit hyperactivity disorder (Timimi 2005). The need for docile, manageable children in the classroom, especially in a context of increased class sizes, arises alongside increasingly circumscribed places for children to be active. Here too we see the links with the current health policy concerns with childhood obesity: in conforming to their prescribed role, the passive, docile child has become a couch potato.

So, returning to the developmental psychology textbooks, a similar elision is distinguishable. Dworetzky and Davis (1989) move from discussing children's needs in early life to taking as their 'Application' for their 'Adolescent Social and Personality Development' chapter the question of 'Preventing teenage pregnancy'. British government policy on sex education in schools takes the form of interventions to prevent teenage pregnancy in a context where – notwithstanding the massive negative publicity around this topic – actual rates of teenage pregnancy have halved over the last 30 years (David *et al.* n.d.; Stronach *et al.* 2007). It is worth pointing out here that the majority of the world's children are born to women under the age of 20 (Phoenix 1991), and that this is the time considered by most cultures as appropriate for childbearing. So whose development is being depicted here? 'Sexual precocity' is, however, a threat to the dominant, sanctified, passive model of childhood. More recent arrivals within US child development texts are coverage of 'teenage suicide' (Seifert and Hoffnung 1987; Dworetzky 1990) and 'childhood obesity' (Kaplan 1991), both of which are considered escalating problems in the West (but while most of the world is starving and struggling to survive). In Bukatko and Daehler (1992) the chapter on 'Social Cognition' treats this as equivalent to 'self-regulation'. Issues of social inequalities, disaffection and unemployment are alluded to in the last of the new (to the second edition) sections on 'The Child and the Year 2000' in Kaplan (1991). These, however, are presented as choices or almost life careers for young people, with the headings 'The non-college bound student'; 'Gender and achievement; minorities in high school; dropping out of school'; and 'Delinquency'. The focus on individual development leads to an acknowledgement of structural disadvantage only insofar as it is treated as a property of the individual; yet another reminder of the problems with opting for a model of change (as Plan International puts it) 'one child at a time'.

Developmentality: how babies make pensions

We have seen in this chapter how the proliferation of models of childhood has given rise to complex professional and cultural dilemmas. A recurring theme has concerned gendered conceptions of childhood and how they figure within discussions of child abuse and child exploitation (particularly in relation to work), while the appearance and disappearance of social structures and relationships has been in focus. We have troubled dominant narratives of children at risk and risky children, showing the connections between these. One key question remains concerning the status of the 'girlchild'. For while the little girl may have figured as the personification of the inner child of the industrialising West, girl children occupy an anomalous role within international development policy – as both in need of particular kinds of support and intervention, and as subject to particular kinds of intervention – as potential mothers. In this sense 'the girlchild' is not quite a child, as indicated also by her linguistically 'marked' status (since we rarely see attention to 'the boychild'). Indeed 'she' is often addressed within aid and development policy in terms of her future motherhood status rather than her current situation (or else provision in relation to the latter is warranted in terms of the former). What is missing from this, as with the other topics addressed in this chapter, is how children's developmental entitlements are predicated on and instrumentalised by models of national development (see Burman 1995a, 1995b, 1995c, in press a).

If developmental psychology's earlier formulations fitted well with conceptions of the liberal subject of bourgeois capitalism, more contemporary conceptions can be said to coincide with neoliberalism. National policies around childcare and education not only privilege nursery provision to increase women's labour participation, but also configure the child as an active and autonomous agent and point of 'social investment', whose life-long welfare support will be generated from future economic activity rather than from any entitlement from the state (Jenson and Saint Martin 2002; Lister 2006). Hence at the 'Progressive Governance Summit' of eight key liberal-left world leaders held in London in 2003, the then trade secretary Patricia Hewitt invoked the idea of early brain development affecting future cognitive performance as part of the rationale for childcare provision:

> Arguing the case for better pre-school support, she said almost half the brain's power is developed by the age of six, yet from birth nearly 20% of children in Britain and the US are en route to disaster . . . Referring to the ageing population and falling fertility, Ms Hewitt argued that better pre-school provision also provided the solution to the growing pension problem. "The problem starts with helping with babies, so making it possible for women to reconcile work and family."
>
> (*Guardian*, 14 July 2003)

The ideal-typical neoliberal subject, like the liberal one, is autonomous but she is also flexible and emotionally literate. Currently, girls now appear to be outstripping boys in high school achievement, although this effect is largely mitigated when balanced for class and 'race' (Epstein 1998; Lucey 2001). Similarly, the gendering of the normative developing subject seems to have undergone a recent shift from being culturally (and classed) masculine to feminine (Burman 2005a). This model of the subject is clearly more suited to deal with the insecure, typically low-waged and part-time conditions of labour, long associated with women and children's work and now extending to men's. Lifelong learning may be extending the developmental trajectory in ways that prolong previous understandings of development beyond adolescence, but it also implies a sense of immaturity and incompletion, or in Fendler's (2001) terms 'developmentality', that involves the injunction to continuously work on oneself.

This chapter has reviewed tensions and contradictions within current models of childhood, attending to how these set up both different positions for children and different relationships towards children who do not 'fit', or deviate from, these models. Particular attention was paid to the contrast between idealised childhoods mobilised within notions of 'the inner child' and the escalating discourses of 'risk' and danger that surround actual children. In particular, the positions of working children and an example of the management of a case of child abuse were discussed. Overall, what emerges is that the idealised childhood of innocence is itself not so innocent, in the sense that it carries major consequences for the evaluation of children's lives who fail to 'fit' this. Childhood as a state is not only endangered, but children themselves can acquire the pathologised status of 'risk'. This is all the more paradoxical in the current political context where neoliberal state policies increasingly aim to mould 'active' and flexible children for the creation of autonomous and economically self-sufficient citizens.

Further reading

Burman, E. (in press a) *Developments: Child, Image, Nation*, London: Routledge.

Burman, E. and MacLure, M. (2005) 'Deconstruction as a method of research: stories from the field', in B. Somekh and C. Lewin (eds) *Research Methods in the Social Sciences*, London and Thousand Oaks: Sage.

Canella, G. and Viruru, R. (2004) *Childhood and Postcolonization*, New York and London: RoutledgeFalmer.

Penn, H. (2005) *Unequal Childhoods: Children's Lives in Poor Countries*, London: RoutledgeFalmer.

Reavey, P. and Warner, S. (eds) (2003) *New Feminist Stories of Child Sexual Abuse*, London: Sage.

Schlemmer, B. (ed.) (2000) *The Exploited Child*, London: Zed Books.

Suggested activities

There are many possible activities that can highlight the contests and multiple agendas fulfilled by interventions around children and families. These could include the following:

- Assembling a range of standard developmental psychology and child development textbooks and analysing the images on their covers. Questions here might include: What models of childhood are set in circulation? Which are privileged and which are marginalised?
- Analysing an episode of a television series such as *Supernanny, Wife Swap* or *Fat Families* to explore the ways in which families are positioned as in need of professional help, with particular attention to class, gender and cultural issues.
- Taking a policy or official document on child custody, or proposals for the curriculum on sex educations in schools, and analysing the assumptions structured around gender and sexuality involved.
- Analysing different versions of the same fairy story, attending to their differently nuanced representations of childhood.
- If working in a group, discussing the range of histories and definitions of work you have all experienced, attending particularly to those features that may not originally be thought of as 'work'.
- Analysing a media campaign involving the representation of children, childhood or in some other way relevant to children (i.e. children may not be actually visible, which may be even more interesting).

Part II

Social development and the structure of caring

Along with 'the child', developmental psychology constitutes homes and families as its object of enquiry. This part correspondingly explores the impact of developmental psychological research on families in Chapter 6, highlighting in Chapter 7 what this has meant in terms of its conceptions of mothers and mother–child relations and, in Chapter 8, of its depiction of the role of fathers. Particular connections are made with issues of policy and practice.

6 Familiar assumptions

> Parents . . . remain the most cost-effective social service for children's well-being.
>
> (Whitfield 1980: 108)

Representations of children function in relation to representations of those who look after and live with them. Indeed, a family is often defined in terms of caregiving roles for dependent children, to the extent that couples living together without children are rarely classed as a 'family' (Van Every 1992). We saw in Part I how the individual-centred focus of developmental psychology sets up an opposition between 'child' and 'environment' such that the separation between 'child' and 'context' seems taken as pre-given. This 'context' has come in for much scrutiny and evaluation, not least in terms of its purported child-rearing qualities. While the 'environment' for children's development has often been treated as synonymous with the mother (e.g. Yarrow *et al.* 1975), the family as the context for child rearing is central to social policy and welfare provision and is also the site for heated debate about social relations and social change. The significance of these national and international social policy debates – in particular at the level of specific national policies – and the ways they enter into developmental research is the topic of this chapter. State and family interact in complex ways.

The state of the family

While the Right claims a special allegiance to it, social commentators of all political persuasions see the family as the basic unit of social life, and political parties compete to be the party of 'the family' (Egerton 1991). Yet discourses of 'the family' function in contradictory ways, positioning it sometimes as a refuge from the stresses and strains of the outside world, and sometimes as a threat to its orderly functioning. Alongside its associations with security, commitment and romantic love in which the home is depicted as a conflict-free haven, there are continuous anxieties about the 'break-up' of the family through rising divorce rates and rising numbers of young, 'teenage' mothers. Domestic violence and claims of child abuse are increasingly being taken seriously as widespread phenomena. Before entering the debate about whether families are really disintegrating, we need to consider the extent to which families have changed and are variable.

Discussions about families often treat the family as a universal, common and unchanging structure without reference to cultural or historical specificity. Yet patterns of mortality and fertility dramatically affect the composition of families. In the 'developing' world today (as in the northern hemisphere in pre-industrial days) where infant and child mortality rates are high, parents are more likely to have more children in the hope that some will survive. Indeed anthropologist Nancy Scheper-Hughes (1989a: 10) has suggested that a high birth rate may well be a *response* to a high death rate. So we see how the South is accorded disproportionate blame for the dwindling of the world's natural resources because of its rising population, despite the fact that the North consumes massively more resources per capita.

Changes in life expectancy alter the age and composition of families. While the key demographic issue currently preoccupying the rich, industrialised countries of the northern hemisphere is an ageing population, with people living longer, its preoccupation with the impoverished South is with reducing the birth rate. As Diana Gittins (1985) points out, 'till death do us part' has a different meaning in modern technological societies where, with increased life expectancy, a marriage can last 60 or 70 years. It is in this context that moral panics about divorce rates and 'broken' homes need to be evaluated.

Economic factors enter into the structure and composition of families. Historical accounts of the family generally point to the role of industrialisation not only in bringing about the transition from village to urban life for most people, but also as creating the division between the 'public' sphere of work and the 'private' realm of home – coinciding with the greater separation of and segregation between women's and men's labour. It is instructive to see how shifts of urbanisation and family forms documented in the South existed in pre-industrial Europe. Productive activity was carried out in or near the home, and all family members worked, although tasks varied according to age and skill (Gittins 1985). Families were often distributed by sending children into service (for girls) or apprenticeship (for boys), and might be extended by the inclusion of servants who were treated as part of the household (but not necessarily equally). Hence household size would vary according to the number of dependants and servants it could support. Variation in land ownership and inheritance patterns affected who was able to marry and when. For example, women have only relatively recently been able to own and inherit property in their own right (from 1870 in England), and a woman with no dowry might have been unable to marry. Marriage has therefore played an important role for women as a source of material security, and as almost their sole route for social mobility. (This is the point that Hrdy 2003 uses to ward off evolutionary psychology claims of female 'innate' preferences for wealthy male mates, discussed in Chapter 2.) The different histories and political role of both aristocracy and bourgeoisie in Britain and France owe much to variation in inheritance laws (with land passing to eldest sons in Britain and divided equally between all sons in France, for example). Elias' (2000) detailed study of the development of etiquette or 'civilised' codes of conduct from medieval to modern times specifically highlights how different configurations of nature, culture and 'civilisation' emerged in Britain, France and Germany as a result of their differing property and power relations between monarchs and aristocracy, as well as structured through different forms of colonialism. Finally, it must be remembered that a large proportion of the population (up to 20 per cent) remained single in pre-industrial Europe: celibacy (irrespective of how celibate people actually were) was seen as a chosen and valued way of life, often but not always linked to religious devotion.

While, contrary to some contemporary commentators, it is unlikely that there was ever an idyllic 'golden age' of happy and supportive extended families (Abbott 1989) as some critics of modern life suggest, it is clear that families have taken and do take on different forms according to culture and historical period. Moreover, attending to this history indicates that the nuclear family, composed of man and woman plus children, with the man as breadwinner working outside the home and the woman responsible for housework and childcare, is itself a family form which came to prominence in Europe in the late nineteenth century. It is not possible to make absolute distinctions between varieties of family forms at different historical periods, since these forms are both more continuous and less uniform over time (according to economic factors among others) than has usually been assumed. Nevertheless, there is no doubt that the nuclear family emerged as the privileged form. Gittins (1985) notes that, while the industrial revolution was spurred on by the low waged labour of women and children, the call for a 'family wage' was a central demand of the developing trade union movement. Echoing the middle-class norm of women and children as dependants of their husband/father, this demand called for men to be treated as primary wage-earners. Since most families could not afford to live on one income alone, an ideal of family life was being promoted that few could attain. In addition to naturalising women's roles as mothers and homemakers, the model of the nuclear family therefore reinforces the low-waged status of women workers. It should also be noted that the so-called 'third industrial revolution' of the computer age relies on the low-paid labour of southern hemisphere women and children (Mitter 1988).

The devaluation of childcare and housework as women's work has prompted much debate, including among feminists. It has given rise to demands that women should be paid 'wages for housework', for example, as a way of recognising the financial value of women's reproductive labour, and compensating women for their loss of earnings. This proposal for the commodification of the work of 'love' has generated much controversy among feminists, with some criticising this as supporting the further penetration of capitalist commodity relations into the domain of intimate human relationships and others. But, even apart from this, it is still unclear how the work of cleaning and childcare can be transformed to acquire equal status. As Riley (1987) graphically comments:

> The very term 'childcare' has a dispiriting and dutiful heaviness hanging over it which resists attempts to give it glamour or militance alike. It is as short on colour and incisiveness as the business of negotiating the wet kerb with the pushchair; and it has some of the awful blandness of the 'caring' voiced in the language of psychologized social work, and increasingly, by anyone else wanting to lay claim to possessing a professional humanity. 'Childcare' has the ring of something closed-off, finished, which some people – mostly mothers – know all too much about, and from which other people shy prudently away.
>
> (Riley 1987: 181)

This 'dutiful heaviness' is not mitigated by the increasing emphasis on getting women (back) into paid work outside the home, tied in the UK, as liberal social democracies worldwide, to a neoliberal economic policy of welfare entitlements linked to individual earnings. It is echoed by what Moss and Petrie (2002: 78) call the 'joylessness of children's services', linked to managerialism and instrumentality:

> Joy, spontaneity, complexity, desires, richness, wonder, curiosity, care, vibrant, play, fulfilling, thinking for yourself, love, hospitality, welcome, alterity, emotion, ethics, relationships, responsibility – these are part of a different vocabulary which speaks about a different idea of public provision for children, one which addresses questions about the good life, including a good childhood, and starts with ethics and politics.
>
> (p. 79)

Moreover, despite current so-called 'family-friendly' policies promoting flexible working and leave, research published by the UK Institute of Fiscal Studies in January 2006 confirms that not only does having a baby bring a break from income generation but also that it is associated with long-term lower pay and career prospects (Barkham 2006b). Notwithstanding the political pressures on women to 'return to work' outside the home, then, it is not always economically viable for many mothers to pay for childcare – since this often costs more than they themselves could earn.

Familiar assumptions

Perhaps the most pervasive assumption about families is that they are necessary. The idea that we could not do without such important and worthwhile social institutions is based primarily on the mere fact of the continuing existence of families, although, as we have seen, they are not fixed in structure and composition. 'Functionalist' approaches to the family within sociology (such as those of Parsons and Murdock) assume that the family is a universal and basic social unit as the site for co-operation and exchange of resources and services. The allocation of resources is taken to include money, food, skills and space, while services range from the division of labour between production and reproduction (i.e. childcare, household labour versus paid work) to sexual relations. These assumptions clearly legitimise the maintenance of traditional gender and age roles. They present a sanitised image of the home as a conflict-free arena, thus ignoring power relations between family members, and presume that all members share the same interests (Brannen and Wilson 1987).

Yet the very assumption of co-residence as a criterion for constituting a family both includes those who would not consider themselves a family (such as prisoners) and excludes those who would (where one parent works away from home, or a child attends a residential school). It also ignores the complexity of children being between households in the context of joint custody agreements following divorce (see e.g. Smart 2004). Indeed the assumption of co-residence is now undergoing revision in a context of massive labour migration, giving rise to cross-national families, with mothers as well as fathers absent for long periods of time. As Hochschild's (2000) and Morokvasic's (2004) studies highlight, wealth structures access to socially valued models of the family with an available mother. It is a sharp irony that many women migrate to work as nannies and au pairs to enable middle-class women in richer countries to work outside the home. This 'global care chain' thus maintains the feminisation of childcare precisely as it recapitulates the power relations between First and Third World. Moreover, while such analyses were focused around childcare they extend also to other feminised and so low-paid caring work such as nursing (Yeates 2004).

Further, the emphasis in functionalist accounts on the family as a site of 'co-operation' ignores other sources of co-operation and support and suggests that it functions autonomously, thus failing to recognise both the interrelationships between families and state incentives which bolster and maintain this particular form of social organisation. For example, notwithstanding the recent introduction of civil partnerships in the UK, as in other countries, it is still the case that marriage status is important to pension arrangements.

The model of the nuclear family, consisting of heterosexual couples with their genetic, 'naturally' conceived children, with the man bringing home the wage and the woman keeping the home, is increasingly recognised to be a fiction. By the 1990s over a third of children in Britain were born to single mothers, over a third of marriages ended in divorce (more in the USA) and 70 per cent of women were economically active, part time or full time (Equal

Opportunities Commission 1991). Also as Robert Dingwall (1989) has pointed out, over a quarter of a million children in Britain live in residential institutions (especially if we include young people in boarding schools). Yet the nuclear family continues to lie at the centre of social policy in terms of defining relationships and responsibilities (with women rendered economically dependent on men, and men emotionally and physically serviced by women), and children treated as the property of their parents.

The power of this model of the family makes itself felt more on those who fail to conform to it than those who do (Van Every 1992). Clause 28 of the British Local Government Act of 1987 defined lesbian and gay relationships as 'pretended families' and until 2000 lesbians and gay men were precluded from fostering or adopting children, although the fact that – at the time of writing this – Catholic adoption agencies in the UK are attempting to claim exemption from placing children with gay and lesbian couples on religious grounds shows that this debate is far from over. The furore over 'virgin births' which hit the British press in March 1991 (with periodic revivals since) highlighted widespread outcry at the possibility of women having babies without sexual contact with a man, while justification for donor insemination (DI) and calls for infertility treatments to be selectively available to women in heterosexual relationships have been made on the grounds that such a relationship will satisfy the child's 'need' for a father. Indeed recent legislative changes that now require sperm donors to be identifiable highlights how a discourse of children's rights to 'identity' fuses biology with psychology in ways that – among other consequences – may discourage donation.

The definition of a normal mother as married and in her mid-twenties positions young mothers, most of whom are single, as 'social problems', particularly in terms of being presumed to be likely to be inadequate parents and dependent on state benefits. While both of these assumptions are questionable (Phoenix 1991), single mothers are thereby either rendered invisible within normative definitions of mothering or recognised only in order to be treated as deviant – thus appearing in policy and research literature in terms of a dynamic of 'normalised absence/pathologised presence' (Phoenix 1987).

Familial organisation is of course culturally as well as historically variable, as are age of marriage, structure of living arrangements, styles of management of behaviour and definitions of family responsibilities. This is clearly relevant to policies and practices around childcare and families within contemporary 'multicultural' societies. It is dangerously simplistic to generalise within and between cultural groups, especially since migration changes the availability of extended family networks and physical organisation of characteristic childcare and rearing practices (Platt 2005). Nevertheless it should be noted that women-headed households are a predominant family form for many people of African-Caribbean descent, and this renders black women subject to further stigmatisation and pathologisation within contemporary familial ideology (Phoenix 1987; Burns 2000).

Lutrell's (2003) ethnographic study of a US school programme for pregnant teenagers in Piedmont, North Carolina, highlights the burden of stigmatised representations that these (mainly black) young women daily negotiate – both literally (in terms of the school desks that do not fit) and interpersonally. She graphically shows the impact this can have in suppressing their creativity and corresponding educational possibilities.

In contrast, research into children's own ideas about families indicates that children are aware of normative definitions of families, but that their definitions reflect their own experiences. For example, O'Brien and Alldred (1991) report that children's drawings of their families were not always confined simply to the people they lived with, and that in group discussion they employed variable definitions at different times and expressed awareness about the complexity and diversity of family relationships.

Developmental psychological research and the family

There is now some acknowledgement within developmental psychology that families are both changing demographically and constitute differing environments for the different individuals within them that also vary over time (Daniels and Plomin 1985; Cohen 1987). Despite this, until recently most developmental psychological research conformed to dominant familial assumptions of the nuclear family containing a male breadwinner and female childcarer. This connects with dominant definitions of femininity which characterise motherhood as women's ultimate fulfilment, a characterisation to which all women, mothers or not, are subjected (Phoenix *et al.* 1991). It also gave rise to suspicion as to whether gay male or lesbian couples could be adequate parents. Indeed it has taken considerable amounts of research to prove this otherwise (Tasker and Golombok 1997; Golombok 2000; Tasker 2004), with textbook accounts of this work emphasising that children brought up in gay and lesbian households are no less likely to be heterosexual (e.g. Bee and Boyd 2007: 383). However, as Anderssen (2001) and Anderssen *et al.* (2002) have pointed out, this frames the representation of lesbian and gay parents from a heterosexist-centred perspective (and also, on the way, essentialises sexual identities).

Practical as well as ideological motivations inform the mother-focused orientation of most research. Until recently (and probably still primarily), it has been mothers rather than fathers who have tended to be at home during the working day, and who therefore have made the most convenient research 'subjects' for developmental psychologists, while limiting the study to mother and child is held to reduce the complexity of data collection and analysis (White and Woollett 1992). As Penny Munn (1991) points out, the overwhelming emphasis of developmental psychological research on the early years of child rearing produces an impoverished conception of the family unit as 'mother and child', ignoring the fact that most women have more than one child, and that therefore the familial context in which most children develop – even within exclusive childcare by mothers – is far from dyadic (see Chapters 9 and 10 for a discussion of the consequences of this on child language research). A consequence of the 'normalised absence/ pathologised presence' of black, single, lesbian and working-class mothers within developmental psychological research is a homogenisation as well as normalisation of accounts of mothering and children's development:

> We have less information about normal interaction patterns in unconventional families and problems in normal families, so we do not have a good basis for assessing the relative advantages and disadvantages of different family forms.
>
> (White and Woollett 1992: 11)

The terminology used within developmental psychology texts reflects dominant familiar assumptions, with 'normal' family meaning 'nuclear' family, and variations correspondingly defined in relation to that noun. An 'intact' family is a nuclear family, which can be 'broken', 'reconstituted' or 'extended' (see e.g. White and Woollett 1992). 'Non-traditional' families, even when they are studied (e.g. Lamb 1982), until recently rarely 'varied' beyond cohabiting couples, and lesbian and gay parents are only now making an appearance in current developmental psychological texts (gaining a brief mention under 'other types of family structures' in Bee and Boyd 2007: 383; as a section entitled 'Gay and Lesbian Parents' in Berk 2007: 488; and on 'Lesbian and Gay Parents' in Siegler *et al.* 2006). Women have been so absorbed into definitions of mothering that research investigating their specific identities *as women* who are mothers is important, rather than homogenising all mothers as the same (e.g. Phoenix *et al.* 1991). However, acknowledgement of the recent 'expansion' of women's economic and political roles can turn into a position which treats attention to the conflicting interests of family members, particularly of women and children, as unhelpful (Dornbush and Strober 1988). The changing conceptions of the relation between the interests of women and children have been taken up by Singer (1992) who traces their historical construction and by Burman (2007d) in relation to children's rights.

Familialism and imperialism

Setting up the division between public and private serves many functions. While the relationship between these is complex historically, ideologies of femininity and family have long been seen as central to doctrines of racial supremacy. As noted also in Chapter 1, the overwhelmingly white imagery of the cultural icon of mother and child functions as the conjoined index of both 'nature' and 'civilisation'. These twin (and contradictory) notions tie patriarchal ideologies of femininity and family to the specifically racialised configurations set up by colonialism.

McClintock (1995) discusses how the nineteenth-century trope of the family worked in two key ways: first, to sanction social hierarchy via invoking an 'organic unity of interests' (p. 45). Thus nationalist and imperialist claims of the 'natural' character of women's subordination to men, and children's to adults, worked to legitimise exclusion and hierarchy outside the family. Second, once inequalities within familial relations were configured as natural, this allowed for historical change and power inequalities to be portrayed as inevitable, rather than as constructed, and amenable to challenge and transformation:

> Projecting the family image onto national and imperial progress enabled what was often murderously violent change to be legitimized as the progressive unfolding of natural decree. Imperial intervention could thus be configured as a linear, nonrevolutionary progression that naturally contained hierarchy within unity: paternal fathers ruling benignly over immature children.
>
> (McClintock 1995: 45)

Thus the naturalisation of inequalities *within* the family, alongside its rendering of this as timeless, offered a key 'alibi of nature' (p. 45) that was not only central to state imperialism, but also to the rationality of its claims:

> After the 1850s, the image of the natural, patriarchal family, in alliance with pseudoscientific social Darwinism, came to constitute the organizing trope for marshalling a bewildering array of cultures into a single, global, narrative ordered and managed by Europeans. In the process, the idea of divine nature was superseded by the idea of imperial nature, guaranteeing henceforth that the 'universal' quintessence of Enlightenment individualism belongs only to propertied men of European descent.
>
> (McClintock 1995: 45)

Hence not only did being white become identified as the norm, but the white couple of mother and child came to signify vulnerability and the need for protection from unnamed dangers outside. Vron Ware's (1992) analysis of varieties of British and US femininities within the context of eighteenth- and nineteenth-century imperialism demonstrates the central role this iconography played within the terrorism of colonial rule, so that the subjugation of black people (as, for example, through the threat or actuality of lynching) was defended on the grounds of claiming to protect white women:

> One of the recurring themes in the history of colonial repression is the way in which the real or imagined violence towards white women became a symbol of the most dangerous form of insubordination. In

any colony, the degree to which white women were protected from fear of sexual assault was a good indication of the level of security felt by the colonial authorities . . . Protecting the virtue of white women was the pretext for instituting draconian measures against indigenous populations in several parts of the Empire. . . . White women provided a symbol of the most valuable property known to white man and it was to be protected from the ever-encroaching and disrespectful black man at all costs.

(Ware 1992: 38)

Recently we have seen how imperialist agendas selectively and opportunistically mobilise calls to action in the name of emancipating women as the rationale for the invasion of Afghanistan in 2001, whilst doing little to combat the impact on them of the re-Talibanisation process in 2006.

The family and the state

Hence the definition and boundaries of families connect with wider institutions and practices. While the general shift to the Right in Britain is not yet sufficiently organised, successful or monolithic to constitute (as in the USA) a 'moral majority' (Durham 1991), policy and legislative changes already reflect ideological assumptions about appropriate and desirable citizens – that have been extended, rather than dismantled, under New Labour (Franklin 2000). The nuclear family reflects heterosexist and ethnocentric assumptions. The recent effort in Britain to chase up fathers who default on maintenance payments for children whom they are no longer jointly parenting, while presented as a measure to support mothers, has forced some women into unwanted negotiations with their ex-partners, and children to see abusive fathers (Aitkenhead 2006). Notwithstanding state support for children's centres and the 'rolling out' of early intervention programmes such as Sure Start (Lloyd *et al.* 2003), this is clearly driven by an agenda to move financial responsibility for provision from the state to individuals (see also Chapter 8).

More recently, increasing attention to children's rights has generated policies such as 'Every Child Matters' (in the UK) and 'No Child Left Behind' (in the US). Yet families are still positioned as the primary site for the socialisation of children to such an extent that there are recurrent calls for parents to be legally responsible for children's bad behaviour, as in the recently introduced 'parenting orders' which compel parents to attend parent programmes if their child has offended. Indeed since over three-quarters of those attending such programmes are mothers, it has been suggested that they should more properly be called 'mothering orders' (Lister 2006). Moreover, in a climate of increasing privatisation and reduction of welfare services and benefits, the rhetoric of family support clearly works to exonerate the state from its responsibilities (Lister 2005; Parton

2005). While kinship has functioned and continues to function as the basis on which to organise financial and caring support, this is by no means automatic or unchanging (Finch 1989). Not only do recent welfare policies position women as responsible for childcare (Moss 1990), but it has become increasingly clear that 'care in the community' for people who are physically and mentally disabled rests on unpaid care by women (Finch and Groves 1983; Dalley 1988) and sometimes also children (Olsen 2000).

While the sanctity and privacy of the family is contrasted with the public arena (to the extent that wife battering is frequently condoned and rape in marriage has only recently become illegal in Britain), those who infract the dominant norms of child rearing and parenting are subject to intervention by a variety of professional and welfare agencies. State provision of childcare is primarily directed at those families deemed to have 'special needs'. These women are correspondingly accorded less 'privacy' than those who can afford nannies or au pairs:

> So while provision of council day nurseries seems benevolent, and is indeed essential to some women who live in poverty, they also allow easy surveillance of the children being placed in them. . . . What is being suggested is that the privatization of 'the family' together with social constructions of 'good parents' which omit many mothers, particularly those who are black, working class and single, makes some mothers liable to state intervention based on their structural position rather than because they are inadequate.
>
> (Phoenix and Woollett 1991: 20)

If structural disadvantage is in danger of being rendered a personal deficit, then migrant and minoritised (i.e. cultural minorities of non-dominant) families may be especially reluctant to access or be recruited into services. It is ironic that in Northern contexts cultural minorities are typically blamed for being particularly oppressive to women and children when social policy and political theory the world over, with developmental psychology providing a key rationale, has treated the mother as responsible for cultural as well as biological reproduction (Yuval-Davis 1997). As McClintock's (1995) analysis illuminates, the hidden (because naturalised) player in this is the imperial state, and its legacies remain in the discourses of national identity that inform national social policy on the family worldwide.

Thus since families, and within existing childcare arrangements particularly mothers, are seen as reproducers of culture (Yuval-Davis and Anthias 1989), professionals have long regarded educating parents as preventive social work. Bowlby was active in developing the profession of social work for this purpose (see Chapter 7). As the extract at the beginning of this chapter indicates, 'Education for Parenthood' programmes aim to create responsible and autonomous families, in which developmental psychology (in the form of knowledge about child development and maturation), along with nutrition, domestic technology, economics and health care, is seen as a vital resource to foster appropriate moral reasoning within the child.

The boundary between public and private perhaps becomes most controversial in cases of (suspected) child abuse. Handelman's (1989) key analysis of the management of a case of suspected child abuse highlights how 'caring' professions such as child protection workers, health visitors or social workers are embedded within a bureaucracy of 'helping' services that are structured around the bipolar dimensions of punishment and rehabilitation. The tension between care and coercion is epitomised by the use of the term 'co-operation' as a description of the recipient of the service's response to the intervention. This can mean either partnership or submission to authority under threat of losing the child. The fact that these two rather different reactions are treated as equivalent highlights the elision between punishment and support within the services. Handelman traces how the bureaucratic procedures for the management of a 'case' and the corresponding structures of professional accountability can construct, rather than prevent and aid, the situation (in this case of child neglect) they are designed to ameliorate. Her analysis is based on the example of a mother whose resistance to professional involvement is pathologised to such an extent that she is eventually compulsorily admitted to a mental hospital. The structures for prevention of child neglect and maternal deprivation had created the very phenomena they supposedly set out to prevent.

The UK national response to the UN Convention on the Rights of the Child was the England and Wales Children Act 1989. This was introduced within a market-oriented context, extending economic relations of exchange to social theory, to try to balance up 'rights' of parents with those of children. Despite the overt separation between economic and social spheres (with the market regulating the public sphere and the family the social), commentators suggest the Act has worked to bolster the authority of the state in the name of protecting individual rights and liberties (Parton 1991). Here the regulation of families becomes particularly overt within policies which have abandoned thoroughgoing policies of childcare provision to focus simply on child protection:

> The more voluntaristic indirect and universal childcare services have been remodelled and refashioned to meet the needs of the child protection system which emphasises much more of the targeting of provisions and concentrates on the direct observation and regulation of behaviour. Nowhere is this more evident than in the replacement of day nurseries with family centres.
>
> (Parton 1991: 207)

Since then, in the UK we have seen this policy dynamic extended with Sure Start schemes and mandatory parentcraft classes for caregivers designated inadequate. Sure Start is the flagship New Labour scheme aimed at children under four years, and families in disadvantaged areas. Central to the boundary between family privacy and state intervention is conformity to normative definitions of acceptable family organisation and relations which, although regulated by social workers, draw upon developmental psychology as an academic resource which then gets recycled into common-sense norms about what proper parenting and families are like:

> What the recent very public debates about sexual abuse and parental rights have provided is not simply a vehicle for constructing and re-thinking the nature of child protection practices and social work, but the form and nature of the family itself. If governing the family is to be successful, it means that most of us must know what good childcare and good parenthood is and what constitutes normal family rela-tionships without ever having contact with a social worker.
>
> (Parton 1991: 214)

It seems we have now become self-governing families but, as a particular example of how the (repudiation and identification of the) 'abnormal' produces the 'normal', child abuse now structures models of the family. Indeed Featherstone (2006) summarises widespread concern over how contemporary social policy seems to operate with a split model of the family which on the one hand portrays families (and families with fathers) as the best place to bring up children, and on the other is reluctant to connect this with escalating rates of domestic violence and its increasingly acknowledged effects on children (Mullender 2004).

Rights and wrongs: does practice make perfect?

Developmental psychology therefore both contributes to and reflects dominant assumptions and debates about families, both in structuring research agendas and in informing practice. As already noted in Chapter 3, discourses of 'rights' and 'liberties', reflecting the worldwide move towards so-called 'free' market economies, figure prominently in the political arena, in which the struggle to determine children's rights constitutes a key area for the definition and legislation of familial ideology. While the normative role of developmental psychology in this is usually tacit, it becomes much more explicit where it informs legal discussions about children's rights, needs and 'best interests'. Parents and children may not share the profes-sionals' view of the nature of the problem. In the early days the influence of individual psychology and family therapy in social work training could 'lead to a social worker being preoccupied with relationships and family malfunctioning, whilst in stark contrast the preoccupation of many of their clients is lack of money and balancing of budgets' (Fletcher 1982: 2).

Nowadays, budgets are also likely to figure just as much within social work agendas. While early 'extreme' discussions of children's rights assumed the form of children potentially being able to divorce their parents, the more common applications have, for example, been in terms of consultation with children over consent to medical procedures. Here children have demonstrated capacity for understanding and decision making far beyond that accorded by developmental psychologists (Alderson 2002). Similar claims inform other practices of professional engagement with children and young people in arriving at arrangements that concern them (e.g. in the youth justice and care systems).

Historically within the British legal system (as many others), children, like women, were seen as the legal property of men, except where the child was conceived outside marriage, when the father could disavow responsibility (Lowe 1982; Freeman 1989). The move towards according children rights, as in the British Children Act 1989, redefines parents as having *responsibilities* towards children, which they forfeit in circumstances where they fail to meet their parental duties. On the other hand, children are positioned as having responsibilities such that when family or, still more significantly, foster care arrangements fail, they have little recourse to state support (Cradock 2007). Further, Parton (1991) argues that in practice the responsibilities accorded to parents towards children are undermined by a consumer model of partnership borrowed from discussions of parental involvement in services for disabled children. The result is that the rights of parents are privileged over those of children, as has been confirmed by recent research with children investigating their experiences of joint custody arrangements (Smart 2004). Further, the shift towards defining child abuse as a socio-legal rather than a socio-medical issue extends the power of the 'psychological complex' (Rose 1985), in which, as we have seen, developmental psychology is a vital ingredient. This is because, paradoxically, in spite of the widespread criticism heaped upon social workers, they now play an even greater legal role in determining state intervention within families through the importance accorded to 'social assessments' which report on children's and families' welfare and development.

Indeed, as Pupavac (1998) points out, it is significant that children's civil rights are based on their presumed *in*capacity rather than attributing children with rights to self-determination. This in effect produces a greater paternalism towards children. Moreover, an adversarial position is assumed between parents and child, amenable to mediation by the state, rather than protection from state intervention. Pupavac points to how the rise of the discourse of children's rights is linked to a context of welfare reforms which have actually worsened child poverty and therefore increase children's dependency on their families. She points to the paradoxical state injunction around increasing rates of participation in higher education:

> Implicitly and in practice, eighteen to twenty five year olds are becoming more dependent on their parents, although there is no explicit legal obligation to do so after eighteen; for example, university grants are

means-tested on the basis of parental education. The expansion of higher education and the erosion of university grants in the last decade have meant that there has been a dramatic rise in the numbers of young people dependent on their parents.

(Pupavac 1998: 10)

Objective and indisputably right as affirming 'children's rights' sounds, then, the call contains an irreducibly moral-political component which can be enlisted into different agendas. This is illustrated by the varying definitions of parental and child rights within criteria used for awarding the custody of children. Contrary to received wisdom, it is only comparatively recently that women have tended to get custody of their children. Within English law until the mid-nineteenth century the family was considered the father's 'empire', and fathers' legal rights over children and women were upheld irrespective of child welfare considerations. The Infant Custody Act 1839 first allowed courts to award custody of children under seven to women, but this was subject to the proviso that they had not committed adultery. Legislation in 1886 permitted courts to award custody of all children under 21 to their mothers. As Nigel Lowe (1982) has pointed out, while this legislation extended the courts' powers to grant custody orders in favour of mothers, this was only at the courts' discretion and did not amount to any affirmation of mothers' custodial rights. In fact the equalisation of parental rights was achieved within English law only in 1973. Rather it has been the emergence of the 'child welfare principle' formulated in the 1925 Guardianship of Infants Act that has changed women's custodial positions (see Freeman 2002).

In their analysis of key cases in English courts from the mid-nineteenth to the mid-twentieth century, Dingwall and Eekelaar (1986) document how normative and contradictory assumptions about what constitutes a proper family have entered into custody settlements. Consequently, varying definitions of children's best interests have been deployed, with factors such as financial provision (usually advantaging men) or living in a nuclear family (where the father has remained) prevailing over continuity of relationship and the child's 'need' for her biological mother. Women's success in custody disputes over the last 40 years derives from 'the primary caretaker' rule, by which the child is awarded to the parent who has played the major role in day-to-day care, which within current arrangements is usually the mother (Smart 1989). While some fathers' rights groups are arguing that this constitutes discrimination against men, Holtrust *et al.* (1989), Graycar (1989) and Boyd (1989) all argue that so-called egalitarian moves towards joint custody arrangements prevalent in Europe, Canada, North America, Australia and now emerging in Britain (Lyon 1989) advantage men (who had previously lost out according to the 'primary caretaker' rule) and increase the likelihood of the harassment of women and manipulation of children. Maureen O'Hara (1991) takes this further to argue that the rhetoric of children's rights can work as a cover to assert the power and control of men, and renders even more vulnerable the custodial rights of lesbian mothers.

The problems with determining children's 'best interests' become most evident where the children, for reasons of age or disability, are unable to make their own opinions clear. One strategy put forward for dealing with this has been to appoint child advocates. However, as Martha Fineman (1989) argued from the North American experience, what this does is to create a further layer of professionals through which ideas about children and families are mediated. For what resources can a 'child advocate' draw upon except those already popularised by the childcare and welfare 'experts', then recycled as the child's putative wishes? While it may have the potential to do other things, child advocacy therefore threatens simply to strengthen the legitimacy of, and to naturalise, psychology in social policy.

The discourse of rights presumes that individual interests can be treated as isolated and separable from others. This is a particularly difficult model to maintain when dealing with children, whose material and psychological existence is constituted through relating to others (Roche 1989). We have seen how developmental psychology tends to reproduce this model by researching the child as separate and abstracted from social relations. This has key implications for the production as well as the topic of psychological research. Abramovitch *et al.* (1991) report that children who consent to participate in developmental psychological studies rarely understand the consequences of this and do not feel they have a genuine choice, especially if their parents or teachers have agreed. Waving the banner of freedoms, rights and choices simply cannot remove the issue of power relations between the parties whose rights (actually or potentially) conflict.

Giving children 'voice'

Much current work claims to consult with and enable child self-representation, often using the rhetoric of giving 'voice' to children (Cullingford 1991). Attractive though this sounds, it can mask rather than dismantle prevailing power relationships that structure adult–child relationships. We need to ask: Whose voice is privileged in such accounts? The researcher, or the researched? For such work still cannot escape the work of interpretation. Instead of remaining complicit with how unequal power relations outside the research relationship structure access to representational arenas, this kind of research attempts to use the power of legitimation that research is accorded to re-present the accounts of, and so advocate for, children as a relatively marginalised and disempowered group. But conceptually and methodologically there are some risks in this.

Feminist research in particular has exposed the paternalism that can underlie the drive to conduct emancipatory research whereby the very desire to 'give voice' to the disempowered paradoxically reiterates those power relations, through the presumption of the power to bestow them (Bhavnani 1990). Thus the claim to conduct egalitarian research threatens to disguise the power relations always set up (though not in unidirectional ways) by research (Ribbens 1989; Wilkinson and Kitzinger 1996).

Moreover, as well as potentially confirming the power of the advocate or professional, notions of 'voice' are in danger of underestimating the role of others in producing it. Thus – contrary to some romanticised or essentialised claims – the child's 'voice' is neither authentic nor anterior to sociocultural conditions and relations (Canella and Viruru 2004; Alldred and Burman 2005; Clark *et al.* 2005). For example, in her study investigating children's accounts of being excluded from school, Marks (1996) was surprised to find that, instead of generating accounts of defiance or indignation, many of the young people's (mainly boys') accounts apparently concurred with their detractors as to the reasons and justification for their exclusion. How was she to make sense of this?

Rather than invoking claims about the young people's beliefs or self-images, she attempted to analyse further the broader cultural contexts mobilised within the interviewing situation. From this, it became clear that it is far from unusual for those subject to a regulatory practice to position themselves accordingly. This 'confession' is surely the expected framework within which the participants had likely rehearsed, and perhaps had to rehearse, their account of what had happened. As much as giving 'voice', through her research she was *producing* a subject; a subject constituted in forms of talk as institutional practice. Alldred and Gillies (2002) develop this argument further to highlight the fundamental ambiguity of consent and compliance within educational research practice (see also David *et al.* 2001; Alldred and Gillies 2002). Further, such strategies can be consciously deployed by children, as was highlighted by Silverman *et al.*'s (1998) conversational analysis of children's silence in parent–teacher consultations about them. In such contexts, rather than signifying incompetence, silence can work to successfully resist enlistment into a moral discourse which children want to avoid (see also Chapter 12). While such incitement to speech may be a familiar parental and pedagogical strategy, from a child rights perspective we should note how 'giving voice' may function to disempower, rather than empower.

The social and the cultural

It is vital that we address the dominance and power accorded the nuclear family, and their wider reverberations. Occluded from this model of care-giving are cultural and historical practices of collective or distributed childrearing – including the 'othermothering' performed by fathers, grand-mothers, aunts and other (usually but not only kin related) women in black and working-class communities the world over (cf. Hill Collins 1990: Chapter 6). Just how such arrangements enter into the psychic structuring of affectivity and relationships has scarcely figured on the developmental research agenda, owing to its Western, middle-class and heternormative frame. Yet such contexts offer profound opportunities to highlight specificities and limits of prevailing developmental (and psychoanalytic) conceptualisations (Kurtz 1992). Moreover, such examples not only highlight questions of culture, but also import a dynamic, relational and sometimes conflictual model of the social, involving migration, adversity, poverty and racism, as highlighted by Watt's (2002) study of three generations of Jamaican heritage women in Manchester (UK) (see also Reyolds 2005). As we have already seen, the assumption that childcare and child rearing involves intergenerational relations on which the weight of enculturation (or socialisation) depends is belied by the fact that in many parts of the world, through maternal employment, migration or death, children head households and care for each other.

That such contexts do not figure in developmental psychology texts only underscores the idealised and abstracted model of the social they presume, and reproduce. A significant example of this can be seen in the amendment made to Bronfenbrenner's (1979) influential 'ecological intervention' model as presented within (and to inform) aid and development models. A key amendment made to his diagram of concentric circles of state, community and family surrounding the basic unit of (m)other and child – the macrosystem, exosystem, mesosystem and microsystem respectively – renders the 'inner circle' (the microsystem) as comprising the child alone (Burman 1996b). While this may be because many standard introductory texts also amend it in these ways (as in Siegler *et al.* 2006: 359), this rather significant conceptual change not only returns the model to the isolated, abstracted individualism it set out to avoid, but its misinterpretation implicitly does the work of globalising through their insertion within international development policy of the very norms that Bronfenbrenner was criticising.

Once culture is excluded from investigation, it returns only in pathologised forms. So the Inquiry investigating the death of 8-year-old Victoria Climbié (Laming 2003), which was discussed earlier in Chapter 5, noted that cultural explanations were put forward to justify why social workers had not intervened earlier: 'The social worker dismissed nurses' concerns about Victoria's subservient behaviour when her great-aunt visited her in hospital on the grounds that it was typical of her African culture to show respect for elders' (Munro 2004: 181).

'Culture' thus acquires the status of a mitigating variable, according to which standards of child rearing could be moderated, rather than being seen as a relational, contestable set of practices (Burman 2005b). Obviously a child rights model would absolutely refuse this approach, and moreover there can indeed be problems of cultural imperialism in the identification and approaches to intervention in cases of child abuse (Levett 2003). But these problems can take a subtle and quite perverse form. In the case of Victoria Climbié the minoritised and marginalised status of this child and her caregivers (as Africans in the UK) appeared to function as a warrant for welfare professionals to avoid stepping in. Indeed such concerns with cultural sensitivity appear to have worked to prevent co-ordination across professional groups too:

> It [The Inquiry] refers for example to the difficulties of joint working between social services and police brought about by ethnic dimensions – for example, the reported suspicion by social workers of police insensitivities and prejudices towards black people, and some consequent police reluctance to work with social services staff.
>
> (Rustin 2004: 10)

Clearly it is important for welfare agencies to be aware of the ways that black and minority ethnic families and communities have been disproportionately scrutinised and pathologised, most particularly in relation to child care and custody issues. Indeed, as Powell (2003: 137) notes, rather than (minority) cultural practices, it may be that dominant cultural norms around children (which by virtue of their dominant status remain unacknowledged and so uncontested) were more relevant: 'While acknowledging the fact that Victoria was black, the most important cultural factor in her case may have been the Western culture and belief that children should be seen and not heard.' In this tragic example, however, claims around the desire to 'respect culture', alongside a covert consensus that a refugee child of questionable residential status was not important or did not qualify for societal responsibility, functioned to prevent or exclude intervention.

In this sense the Climbié case is indicative of the broader function of the discourse of culture (seen as attaching to a cultural minority) in four ways. First, that minority ethnic cultures, traditions and often also religion are elided together, so that white professionals become wary of criticising familial practices for fear of being (accused of being) racist. Second, as long as dominant cultural norms surrounding children and childcare remain unacknowledged, 'culture' remains figured only as pathological, abusive or inferior. Third, rather than being seen as an individual, tragic example of familial and state neglect and abuse (that no 'culture' or tradition would sanction), such moves to treat it as 'cultural' contribute to the pathologisation of a wider community that in turn helps to silence disclosure of abuse for fear of further fuelling racism (Burman *et al.* 2004). Fourth, we see how the discourse of culture has become attached to that of the minority group, such that the cultural norms of organisational systems and bureaucracies become invisible as assumed, and so naturalised, professional models of practice. Moreover, such norms rely upon models of service provision that are increasingly predicated on a model of national citizenship such that the current discourse of 'social inclusion' in fact works in exclusionary ways. In the UK young asylum seekers are now being held in detention centres (www.noplaceforachild.org), and recent legislation allows children of asylum seekers to be taken into care as a strategy to pressurise their families to agree to be repatriated to their country of origin. At the time of writing this in August 2006, it was announced that unaccompanied refugee minors to Britain may now be deported back to their country of origin, returning them to the very circumstances that generated their transnational cycle of exploitation, with children trafficked from Vietnam to the UK being the first such candidates. Indeed in the case of unaccompanied young people there is a key tension between their status as children vis-à-vis their status under immigration law. In the UK, immigration status takes priority as the government reserves the right to exclude asylum-seeking children from entitlements claimed under the UN Convention on the Rights of the Child (Jones 1998; Martin 1998). This, as Chantler (personal communication) points out, is a very practical example of when a 'child' is not a child.

Cultural differences?

The above example graphically shows how political considerations structure who is allowed the status of childhood. These also enter into the assessment of a young person's age, for the purpose of determining eligibility to services. (Below the age of 18 social services have responsibility to provide care, while if assessed as over 18 years unaccompanied children can be detained in centres with adults and are disallowed social service provision.) UK social workers are currently required to conduct age assessments where requested by the Home Office or other government agencies. There are no statutory guidelines on which these should be based. Here not only are 'cultural differences' very much at issue but developmental psychological expertise is also acquiring privileged status, in part because medical staff have made it clear that there is no 'medical' test that can reliably determine age. Immigration officials tend to base their 'age assessments' on appearance alone plus documents (such as passports and birth certificates). Social workers are expected to conduct 'Merton compliance assessments' (named after a legal case in 2003 – B, R (on the application of) v London Borough of Merton) which means that age assessments should also take a social history of the young person, including family history, educational background, activities the young person has undertaken shortly before arriving in the UK and behaviour. Clearly normative judgments inform understandings of what is age-appropriate experience.

Singer (1993) discusses the difficulties that developmental psychologists have had in addressing social and cultural differences in child-rearing norms. She sees this as linked to the ways claims to expertise universalise what are in fact particular cultural norms. A key way of addressing this has been via cross-cultural psychology. The paradigm of cross-cultural psychology has a long history (almost as long as modern colonisation). As Hogan and Sussman, reviewing its origins, note:

At its most basic level, cross-cultural research had its inception when one group, with certain folkways and language, began to observe another group, with somewhat different characteristics. When the observations became part of a record, usually with a view to promoting the superiority of one of the groups, the history of cross-cultural psychology began.

(Hogan and Sussman 2001: 16)

However, these authors do not quite admit how this was the dynamic structuring Western contact with Africa and Asia. In terms of the assessment and evaluation of parenting, Singer (1993) notes:

Most psychologists do not accept that children from poor families need different (psychological) abilities to survive than middle-class children. They do not see that other values apply in worlds where there is no certainty of the basic requirements of life, such as a doctor in times of illness, sufficient food or adequate housing, If psychologists are to intervene effectively, these values would have to be recognized in their programmes. They would have to distance themselves from their claim of being more expert than parents, and to acknowledge that their theories can yield no neutral advice. But this is rare.

(Singer 1993: 436)

However, there are now efforts to research cultural practices around child rearing without simply presuming Western practice as the standard from which to evaluate other cultures. Drawing on anthropological contributions – and turning the tables from prescribing to, to learning from, parents – a recent research trend positions parents as worthy informants of their own theories of development. As mediators and moulders of development, parental accounts indicate socio-cultural norms and standards. For example, Keller's (2003) study documents how parental evaluations of caregiving practices are structured by distinct cultural norms related to particular economic and cultural conditions. She videotaped mother–child interaction in a rural traditional subsistence-based community and an urban (post)industrial context. Since these two groups were considered to have different socialisation goals, so they espoused correspondingly different notions of competence. Framed as an investigation of parents' own cultural assumptions (or ethno-theories), she presented to groups of seven to ten women extracts of the videos showing typical interactional situations with three-month-old babies from each cultural environment, inviting comments from each woman on 'what they had seen (what they find good or bad, or whatever comes to their mind)' (p. 293). Not surprisingly, the mothers from each cultural group could offer clear analysis and justification for the practices from their 'own' group. More interesting was their emphatically negative view of the other group. While this approach runs the risk of homogenising each community and over-polarising possible cultural differences (through selection of two opposing cultural practices, rather than researching across contrasts of class and region intraculturally – see Neff 2003; Gjerde 2004), it at least shows how the evaluation of child-rearing practices can be situated within locally defined norms.

Family resemblances?

In this chapter we have seen how developmental psychology has enlarged its focus of enquiry from the abstracted child to the 'context' only to halt at his or her immediate social surroundings of family, rather than examining the social-historical influences that construct the family unit. This has led to a failure to see the variety of forms of family organisation as connected with cultural and economic issues. In turn this leads to an idealised model of the family which perpetuates age and gender asymmetrical relations, ignores conflicts and stigmatises and pathologises those who fail to conform to this model.

We have already considered a number of key examples that highlight the real effects of the arbitrary and discretionary character of the systems of evaluation and intervention around children and families that developmental psychology informs. A final illustration comes from the provision of educational psychological services dealing with children identified as 'having problems'. These either treat the child with *problems* as *being* the problem or else position the child's family as responsible for creating the problems (Marks 1993a, 1993b; Billington 2000). Yet it is now increasingly recognised that the identification of children's needs is a matter of resources rather than flowing from anything intrinsic to the child or family, so that professional assessments are constrained by the knowledge of the limited forms of provision available (Wolfe 1981). A consequence, then, of developmental psychology's inability to theorise the relation between the individual child and the wider social and political context is an academic and welfare discipline that blames difficulties on either child or family, or both, and fails to implicate the wider social forces which construct and maintain the child's relations within his or her family. The rhetorical use of the term 'family' functions to tie individuals together into small units, to deny their relation with broader social action and reaction and to act as a buffer zone to mask wider social responsibility. Hence 'community care' means care by families (that is, usually women). So by this account we do not need social services (except where families are not doing their job properly) and we do not need social change.

Clearly the ties that hold women, men and children together are not only self-imposed. Mothers and fathers are glued to the family through discourses of family structure, and within that structure the child is glued in particular to the mother through discourses of attachment. This is addressed in the next chapter.

Further reading

Dahlberg, G. and Moss, P. (2005) *Ethics and Politics in Early Childhood Education*, London and New York: RoutledgeFalmer (contains many practical examples, as well as accessible accounts of theories about why and how we should engage in participatory work with children).

Franklin, B. (ed.) (2002) *The New Handbook of Children's Rights*, Oxford: Routledge (offers a timely commentary on the progress of child rights across a range of legal, cultural, health and welfare sectors – primarily but not exclusively from a UK context).

Hendrick, H. (ed.) (2005) *Child Welfare and Social Policy: An Essential Reader*, Bristol: The Policy Press (a big compilation of key texts on social policy, children's rights and political analysis – as its title suggests).

Phoenix, A., Woollett, A. and Lloyd, E. (eds) (1991) *Motherhood: Meanings, Practices and Iideologies*, London: Sage (remains a very useful and diverse collection).

On unaccompanied minors and age assessments see: http://www.childrens legalcentre/com and also: http//:www.asylumsupport.info/specialfeatures/children/htm

Suggested activities

1   Using the cases of the kind discussed by Dingwall and Eekelaar (1986) or Aitkenhead (2006) (including more recent cases initiated by children themselves under new legislation), construct vignettes and ask individuals or small groups to consider what factors they would consider relevant to the decision making, and, if possible, what decision they would favour. If, as is likely, they feel they need more information on which to base their decision, then ask them to specify what further information they require and how it would inform their judgement – which becomes an extra resource for discussion later. Then discuss the actual outcomes, and the factors that were considered relevant at the time. This exercise draws attention to the variation in cultural-political preoccupations over time which throws into question often unanalysed assumptions about mothers' or fathers' rights, and economic over affectional considerations (and the role played by developmental psychology within this; see Chapter 7).

2   Drawing on Lutrell's (2003) account of the experience of schoolgirl pregnancy, design an educational programme for young mothers, also addressing the methodological and ethical issues posed by and for the researchers.

7   Bonds of love – dilemmas of attachment

> It has been the fate of mothers throughout history to appear in strange and distorted forms. They may appear as larger than life or as invisible; as all-powerful and destructive; or as helpless and angelic. Myths of the maternal instinct compete, historically, with myths of a universal infanticidal impulse. Some of these contradictions and psychological projections can be found in the scholarly literature as well.
>
> (Scheper-Hughes 1989a: 3)

> Harlow's imaginative research on the attachment behavior of infant monkeys brought the emotional and social development of the infant out of the field of clinical inference and speculation and made love an acceptable variable in the experimental laboratory.
>
> (Stone *et al.* 1973: 6)

> Misogyny is deeply implicated in the dream structure of the laboratory.
>
> (Haraway 1989: 238)

Within the tripartite structure of 'physical, 'cognitive' and 'emotional' development set up by developmental psychological accounts, relationships between parents and children necessarily figure strongly in descriptions of children's social selectivity and responsivity. Mothers, positioned as the objects and sources of children's affections, feature in terms of their success or failure in promoting the child's development. While the claim that children need warm, continuous and stable relationships seems indisputable, the precise arrangements that fulfil these conditions continue to be a matter of fierce dispute, and many children grow up without them. The debates around childcare constitute a key arena for the interplay between developmental psychological research, social movements and social policy, with controversy focusing on how competing interpretations carry dramatically different implications for women's employment. But, central as this issue is, it is also a symptom of a more general and familiar agenda.

   This chapter largely follows the chronology of the historical emergence of key themes and debates on attachment, from the formulation and reception of the theory in the mid-twentieth century to its shifting, but especially vibrant, forms in the early twenty-first century. The story of attachment theory is perhaps a case example of the relationship between theory and policy, and of sensitivity to crossdisciplinary developments. This chronological narrative traces the development of an increasingly important area of psychological (and psychoanalytic) theory that has found particular resonance within policy and service provision so that, where relevant, particular points of connection with later developments will be highlighted. This is important because attachment can be seen (in Butler's 1997 sense) as the trope, lynchpin or turning point around which not only are mothers, in particular, evaluated and regulated, but – through recent extensions of attachment theory to the retrospective analysis of adult attachment histories (through, for example, the adult attachment interview) – also the means by which relationships surrounding children come to be figured as individual, and even neurophysiological, properties. As we will see, such moves take a measure of an emotion or relationship very far from its psychoanalytic origins. Hence the first part of this chapter reviews the themes characterising the research on attachment, while the second evaluates the assumptions guiding the research and the procedures which generate it.

Jobs for the boys?

Free and available childcare has long been a demand of the feminist movement as a necessary prerequisite for women's liberation. At the same time, feminists have challenged the assumption that women are responsible for childcare (New and David 1985). It is therefore not surprising that psychological theories which appear to confirm women's place in the home, which claim children suffer if they are not in the full-time care of their mothers and which suggest children who have personal or behavioural problems in their later lives have been inadequately mothered have attracted particular criticism. The popularity of John Bowlby's theory of maternal deprivation in the 1950s, at a time when men were returning from fighting in World War II, appeared to provide justification for excluding women from the (often heavy industrial) jobs they had taken over 'for the war effort'. While there is no doubt that most nurseries set up during the war to enable women to work were closed shortly afterwards, and that the 1950s was a period which glorified motherhood (as both the bearing of and caring for babies), to regard developmental psychology as responsible for this would be to overstate its influence and to underestimate other important influences, such as the institutionalisation of psychoanalytically informed 'family fables' (Rose 1985). Narratives of love going wrong employed by such services as child guidance clinics (Thom 1992; Urwin and Sharland 1992) all acted to perpetuate the assumption that women's futures lay in motherhood. Nevertheless, psychology played its part in the post-war celebration of home and hearth which defined and regulated women's fitness as mothers.

Clearly, as Denise Riley (1983) argues, the process by which a set of ideas gets inscribed within policy is not a simple translation process, nor can it be reduced to the efforts or the creativity of a single author. Rather what has to be addressed is the question of what social-historical conditions made possible the emergence and reception of those ideas (Urwin 1985b). What this perspective means is that we cannot postulate an absolute separation between theory and its application. In this case, the primary theorists of attachment and maternal deprivation, John Bowlby and Donald Winnicott, were very active in the promotion and popularisation of their ideas, writing newspaper columns and doing radio broadcasts. They were aware of the implications of their pronouncements for women's economic and social roles. But there is also a more complicated story of the interlinking of individual ideas, theoretical frameworks and social policy arrangements that needs to be told.

Home alone

Bowlby's work on the effects of maternal separation was a major influence in reforming residential and hospital practices for the care of children. His conclusions in his 1951 *Maternal Care and Mental Health* report commissioned by the World Health Organization were based on studies of children evacuated from the cities away from their parents, demonstrating yet again psychologists and psychoanalysts benefiting from war as providing 'natural experiments' (Wexler 1983) and an investigation into the backgrounds of children who had histories of stealing and involvement in petty crime. From these, he argued that separation from mothers was an inherently traumatic experience for children, that children who failed to establish a firm attachment by the age of three would be unable to do so subsequently and would suffer severe psychological problems (in his terms would become 'affectionless psychopaths'), and he urged early treatment and prevention programmes on the basis of early identification (he claimed by age three). He reflected current norms about family organisation, arguing that a bad home was better than a good institution (the wisdom of which has increasingly been challenged). In some circumstances, however, blood ties were not enough. In accordance with dominant moral codes, he urged that unmarried mothers should submit children for adoption in the interests of securing a stable family life for their child. In this sense, Bowlby followed and confirmed developmental theory in assuming the presence of mothers at home, an assumption that was addressed or problematised only when a woman's full-time availability or devotion to motherhood was put in question.

While formulated to draw attention to the plight of children in residential care, Bowlby's ideas about care imposed impossible demands on the conscientious mother. With a familiar elision of mental and physical development, maternal care was likened to vitamins for the healthy growth of the young child, and the criteria for continuity of care were vague. Brief, regular and absolute separation were all lumped together so that day care, brief separation and death or divorce were treated as having equivalent effect and significance. As a result, any absence, brief or prolonged, was invested with the possibility of producing far-reaching effects and was inadvisable. The good mother must therefore be always available and always attentive. This rendering of the cosy world of innocent and dependent childhood both reproduces and produces the division between public and private realms. Women were portrayed as devoted to, attending to and attuning to their children; they bask in her presence while she orients to their unspoken needs:

> She is his whole world, and the little excursions he makes beyond her are rooted in confidence that she is nearby to give him full protection. He has been weaned from the breast, but is still unwearied from complete dependence on the protection and love of this one person. . . . He is not far from her skirts all day, and in this close relationship she acts intuitively to meet his physical and emotional needs.
>
> (Robertson 1958: 4)

For Gesell, the intermeshing of minds and reading of needs takes on an almost physical quality: 'It is almost as if the child's nervous system were completed by his mother, her part being that she must think ahead for the child' (Gesell 1950: 240).

  Significantly, it is knowledge of child development that is held to provide the resource for mothers to know what lies ahead. The dutiful, attentive mother provides a secure environment in which the child learns the control and regulation of emotions. But separation, lack of bonding or emotional disturbance on the part of the mother would give rise to criminality and pathology. It followed that the roles of devoted mother and working woman were divergent and incompatible. The upshot of such a model was that any later moral or psychological aberrations exhibited by the child were attributable to the mother. This positions women as responsible for the ills of a world their maternal duties proscribed them from participating in: 'Through the child, the mother was made responsible for violence and social chaos in the world outside the family, a world from which she was more or less excluded' (Singer 1992: 99).

  As indicated in Chapter 3, the reduction of the social to the interpersonal, with the partner of the child in his [sic] environment defined as the mother (or else the environment is assumed to comprise the mother), adds up to a seemingly coherent theoretical whole, with the well-being of society identified with women at home (Walkerdine and Lucey 1989). As we shall see, notwithstanding shifts in prescriptions about women and work, the definition and regulation of what constitutes good, sensitive mothering structured, and continues to structure, both discourses of child development and, through these, discourses of childcare provision and femininity. Maternal presence therefore functions as the essential feature in the maintenance of the social-political order. Mothers were, and still are, positioned as the relay point in the production of 'democratic citizens', that is, adults who will accept the social-political order by imagining that their concurrence is through independent choice rather than coercion. Once again, we see how definitions of child and mother on offer within developmental psychology work to maintain existing social relations and forms of organisation.

Watch with mother

Subsequent studies modified the original gloomy picture, arguing that Bowlby's work should be regarded as an indictment of institutional rather than maternal deprivation (Clarke and Clarke 1976), that separation need not be damaging (Rutter 1982) and that secure relationships can be formed in later childhood (Tizard 1991). Nevertheless, contemporary research on childcare continues to be dominated by a restricted range of questions that betrays a theoretical legacy which positions women as responsible not only for the care of their children, but also for their current and future development. Day care has been researched within a paradigm presuming damage limitation, portraying it as a risk factor (Belsky and Rovine 1988), or else day care was investigated in terms of the way it affects children's attachment to their mothers, rather than exploring the more useful questions concerning what different organisations of attachment relationships and caring contexts offer (Hennessy *et al.* 1992; Singer 1993).

Despite women's increasing participation in paid work outside the home, until recently there has been little corresponding development of preschool childcare provision. While there are significant variations in policy and provision across Europe and increasing national government pressures for 'family-friendly' policies (of flexible working to allow for childcare commitments) as part of national policies to increase women's labour participation, it is important to note that the trend in childcare provision is increasingly to configure this as an employer, rather than state, responsibility. The policy move is to constitute childcare as a work-related provision, as a key expression of a neoliberal model that ties service provision to economic productivity.

As Chapter 6 indicated, the introduction of schemes such as Head Start (in the US) and Sure Start (in the UK) target and so – at least potentially – differentially regulate and stigmatise disadvantaged families. A commitment to preschool education has given rise to the proliferation of playgroups and children's centres, but these only function for limited hours. Provision has been structured around the assumption that children are primarily to be cared for by their mothers, with care outside the family provided as an extra resource for children's development, not for mothers' convenience (Singer 1992). Not only are mothers disenfranchised from participating in the productive sphere of paid work by employers' expectations of their engagement in full-time childcare, but those who do work have been correspondingly positioned as morally *reprehensible*. Even where these assumptions are starting to be eroded, with childcare provision so minimal, or else – if privately purchased – exorbitant, those for whom it is provided are thereby designated as inadequate. How much more pathological a mother must be if she needs to be taught what is supposed to 'come naturally'!

As Barbara Tizard (1991) notes, the attribution of the origin of adult problems to inadequate mothering in early life works to 'champion children at the expense of imposing guilt on mothers' (p. 183). It also treats social problems as originating in the individual. There is every indication that 'mother blaming' remains a pervasive and enduring explanandum in a wide range of clinical literature (Caplan 1985). More recently, with the research trend towards communicative development, and the tendency to collapse development into ever earlier stages, the domain of early care is increasingly taken to include education, such that nursery and preschool provision are now regarded as indistinguishable (Hennessy *et al.* 1992; Dahlberg *et al.* 1999). Research sets out to link early childcare with later social and cognitive development, enlarging the arena for which mothers can be held responsible. Jerome Bruner, known for his commitment to environmental 'compensation', illustrates how the onus for species-appropriate development lies in the mother's hands: 'the child's transition from his primate background into the use of the powerful cultural tool of language depends upon the development, indeed, the exploitation of the mother–infant bond' (Bruner 1978: 63).

She's gotta have it

The current policy emphasis promoting women's economic productivity in the public sphere precisely underscores the power of earlier gendered models of childcare. Mothers have been portrayed as so central to, and absorbed within, their children's development that any assertion of power or independence on their part appears to be at the expense of damaging children. Mothers' needs must be assimilated to those of their children for them to avoid censure as 'bad mothers':

> In this way a mother's own will, her (career) wishes, activities and thoughts, are cast in a negative light, as characteristics of a nonsensitive mother – they should be hidden. Conceptualized in this way, self-confidence is something for which the child has no model in the mother. In fact it is based on an illusion. The mother must act as though she has no power. If her power becomes visible it is thought to be 'unnatural' and dangerous for the child's self-confidence.
>
> (Singer 1993: 434)

As many critics point out, children separated from their mothers in residential care are also separated from their fathers and other friendship and family ties (e.g. Tizard 1991). However, the focus on the uniqueness and exclusivity of the mother–child relationship has excluded men from having a role in childcare and child rearing, while also sealing the separation between the worlds of work and home and the division of roles between breadwinner and childcarer. Until recently, the beneficent gaze of the mother (aided and regulated by professional experts) relegated fathers' contributions to childcare to financial provision and emotional support to mothers (though see Chapter 8 for further developments). On a number of counts then, the term 'maternal deprivation' is something of a misnomer. Under current arrangements surrounding the status and support for children and childcare, mothers (and fathers) could be said to be more deprived by their caregiving role than depriving. Yet, as we have seen from contemporary social policy, women continue to be regarded as responsible for both children's upbringing and childcare provision. Despite the crucial role accorded to childcare in social policy, and its supposedly fulfilling qualities, its lack of value is reflected in the low pay of professional childcare workers (usually also women).

Even when, late in his life, he was challenged to address methodological and political criticisms of his work, Bowlby remained unrepentant about his claims of the irreconcilability of combining motherhood with career. From this it is clear that he regarded women who draw upon other sources of childcare as not only surrendering their proper childcare responsibilities but as also demonstrating their lack of care and commitment to their children's development. Any woman who asserts her right to have an existence independent from her child is dismissed as abandoning her, with a clear dichotomy set up between women who put childcare first and those who will not, as 'extreme feminists who take the line "I can have children, I needn't look after them, I'm going to go ahead with my career and I'm damned if I'm going to be handicapped by looking after them"' (Bowlby *et al.* 1986: 51). It is worth contrasting this point of view with that put forward by Riley (1987):

> Why has it been such an enduring charge, that feminism has nothing to say to or about women with children? An impression of child-dumping was conveyed, for some, by one of the original four demands of the women's liberation movement: that for 'twenty four hour nurseries'. This was, I think, conceived in the wish for some unchallengeable flexibility for mothers . . . Against that, though, can be set the far greater evidence of extensive feminist work, not only against the myth of 'maternal deprivation' and the rosiness of domestic life, but, for instance, for child benefit to go on being paid to mothers, for better conditions for unsupported mothers.
>
> (Riley 1987: 177)

Weird science

According to the theory, the securely attached child is endowed with the confidence to be able to leave mother and explore his or her surroundings, whereas the insecurely attached child is 'clingy'. While babies and young children usually protest at being separated from familiar caregivers, from around two and a half years old children are expected to be able to adapt to the absence of their mothers. The paradigm by which attachment is investigated was developed by Ainsworth as a test of Bowlby's theory (e.g. Ainsworth *et al.* 1974). Typically, the reactions of children are observed, first, when they are brought into an unfamiliar setting with their mothers, second, when a strange adult enters the room and, third, when the mother leaves the child alone with the adult. If the child will not settle to play at some distance from her mother while she is there, the attachment is considered insecure. Conversely, this conclusion is also drawn if the child fails to protest at his or her mother's departure. It is important to note (for our subsequent critical evaluation) that the key observation on which the classification of attachment is based is the reunion with the mother; and from this the classification of ambivalent or avoidant attachment (for example) is determined. Moreover, although the original attachment sequence was designed around 12 month olds, it is now used longitudinally alongside other methods for investigating the attachments of older children (including interviewing caregivers). Such methodological shifts, from observations to analysis of interviews, also shape the direction of attachment theory towards (as we will see) increasingly cognitive forms.

Clearly the ethics of treating children's distress as the variable under both investigation and manipulation should be questioned. Moreover, using this procedure to compare the strength of attachment relationships between children of employed and non-employed mothers is also methodologically suspect. Children of employed mothers may not experience separation as stressful since it is a regular part of their daily life. It seems paradoxical that children's success at adapting and gaining greater independence from their mothers should then be treated as a measure of disturbance. Furthermore, not only does the 'strange situation' test not take account of individual separation histories, it also fails to reflect real-life caregiving contexts when children are generally left with caregivers with whom they have some familiarity and in contexts to which they have become accustomed. As Alison Clarke-Stewart (1988) has argued, this throws some doubt on studies claiming that children of employed mothers are less securely attached to their mothers.

Cultural connections

Ainsworth's (1967) studies in Uganda are often heralded as one of the early examples of cross-cultural psychological research. Of late, attachment theory has been resurrected from the margins of psychoanalysis and psychology (and ethology) into a burgeoning field that also claims connections with neurology and evolutionary theory. Here claims are being made: from stability of patternings (albeit with variations) across species, to across cultures, and now over time. These dramatic claims generate speculations considered to be of predictive and forensic importance (see e.g. Cassidy and Shaver 1999).

To take an example, Susan Goldberg's (2000) text *Attachment and Development* reviews and updates the field, reviewing the more recent assessment technologies of 'Q sorts' and 'the adult attachment interview' to supplement the 'strange situation', and so mark the further shift from psychoanalytic to psychological assessment. In a chapter entitled 'Beyond the Family', Japan figures as one of three contexts – alongside the kibbutz system in Israel ('representing' a collective system of child rearing – despite the limited ways in which this actually has occurred) and northern Germany (as an urban, Western industrialised context) – for the assessment of cultural variation in caregiving roles and attachment styles. Interestingly, the Japanese data prompt the most discussion, due to the need to interpret anomalous findings. After detailed discussion, Goldberg rather sensibly concludes that the problem may be the tool rather than what it has found, claiming that the strange situation appears to be so strange and distressing across all Japanese contexts that it generates a blanket response and fails to offer any useful discriminations:

> These cultural differences, and in particular the Japanese data, which not only failed to confirm the predictions but also failed to detect relationships between maternal care and attachment, gave rise to prolonged discussion regarding the cross-cultural validity of the strange situation. Just as some proponents argued that experiences of regular alternative care may render separations in the strange situation insufficiently stressful to activate attachment behaviour, it was suggested that the absence of separations between Japanese mothers and infants renders the separations of the strange situation excessively stressful (i.e. well beyond the moderate stress assumed by the classification scheme).
> (Goldberg 2000: 111)

Rather than eliciting wider reflection on the ethics as well as cultural presumptions structuring research relationships and paradigms, Goldberg prefers to emphasise a discourse of cultural specificity: 'Valid interpretations require intimate knowledge of child-rearing customs and goals' (2000: 112). Yet her textbook treatment belies an explosion of work alternately asserting and disputing the relevance of the concepts and methodological procedures of attachment research within a Japanese context (Takahashi 1990; Rothbaum *et al.* 2000, 2001; Chau 2001; Gjerde 2001; van Ijzenhoorn and Sagi 2001; Kondo-Ikemura 2001; Onishi and Gjerde 2002). Indeed, it is tempting to speculate about the broader cultural significance of the pre-occupation with questions of dependence, security and nurturance within the contemporary geopolitical situation, with the motif of the child, as ever (Steedman 1995), functioning as a key cultural-political index for preoccupations in an increasingly unstable and uncertain world (Duffield 2001; Pupavac 2002b, 2005).

Thus psychological study, in this case of attachment styles, within a specific culture works to bolster claims attesting to the generalisability of Western-defined psychological models, with emerging 'differences' functioning paradoxically to confirm this applicability. Japan as 'an example of a highly industrialised, urbanized non-Western country' (Goldberg 2000: 108) that, it should be noted, is therefore perceived by us as researchers as both legible and (through occupation/post-colonial relations) accessible, is mobilised rhetorically to support the cross-cultural project.

Significantly, Onishi and Gjerde's (2002) analysis in relation to cultural themes of 'marital asymmetry' as a feature of attachment histories (generated using the adult attachment interview) refuses cultural generalisations. Well aware of the cultural narratives in the West about the specificities of Japanese culture, which also circulate with popularity in Japan (see Burman 2007b), they take care to limit the claims they make for their sample and, correspondingly, for their interpretations:

> Our participants were young middle class Tokyo urbanites. We cannot exclude that quite different results might have emerged in samples of blue-collar workers. Small merchants, farmers, elderly, handicapped, or groups living on the margins of Japanese society, such as Ainus, Burakumins, Okinawans, Koreans, day workers, South East Asian female entertainers, Filipino women married to Japanese farmers, and Nikkeijin (i.e. individuals of Japanese descent who have returned, mostly from Brazil, after generations abroad), for whom the marital asymmetry may not be a significant theme.
>
> (Onishi and Gjerde 2002: 453)

Moreover, beyond culturally locating their sample, they also comment on the historical specificity of the research genre they are located within: 'to our knowledge, the asymmetry theme surfaced after World War II with the emergence of a new middle class. It should therefore not be reified as an enduring and ahistorical attribute of Japanese gender relations' (Onishi and Gjerde 2002: 453). There are clearly wider lessons here for the status of the preoccupations and assumptions informing the developmental psychological assessment of attachments.

Insensitive measures

Attachment research draws on a number of theoretical resources: ethology, systems theory and psychoanalysis. But the process of rendering psychoanalysis into terms that could be empirically investigated has produced an entirely different model. While for psychoanalysis the relation between psychical and external reality is complex, its investigation within developmental psychology has collapsed this subtle distinction into a single focal object, the mother. What we see played out in the history of 'attachment' is not only the uneasy coupling of developmental psychology and psychoanalysis. It is also, first, the productivity of a 'translation' process from theory to practice. (This is not to suggest that psychoanalysis did not already have its own 'practical' outlets, but that its introduction into developmental psychology called forth additional practices.) Second, the result of this (mis)rendering of psychoanalytic ideas within developmental psychology illustrates how the technology of research instruments not only produces the demand for measurement, but also thereby produces the object that is measured. 'Sensitive' and 'insensitive' mothers are produced by theories of maternal 'sensitivity', both through the incorporation of the theories within professional and policy structures and through women's consumption of those ideas. On both counts, then, the elision of phantasy and reality and the technologisation of empirical practice mean that the insertion of psychoanalysis within developmental psychological discourse as 'attachment' reinscribes the regulation of women as mothers.

Within conventional accounts, attachment is said to arise from mothers' rapid and appropriate responsiveness to children's demands of hunger, discomfort and boredom. Attractive as the concept is, it both fails to engage with the specificity and variability of caregiving, and (as we have already seen) in its attempts to identify optimal conditions for development it homogenises (treats as the same) normality and pathologises (treats as deviant) difference.

In the first instance, the myopic focus on mothers as the total environment for the child threatens to lead to a reification and abstraction of 'maternal sensitivity', and a corresponding failure to register how sensitivity varies according to situations and circumstances. Anne Woollett (1986) reported that mothers devote less attention to a younger child when other adults and older children are present and so in this context are correspondingly recorded as less 'sensitive'. Moreover, sensitivity exhibited by mothers and fathers has been differentially evaluated. Sensitivity 'is THE influential dimension of mothering in infancy: it not only fosters healthy psychological functioning during this developmental epoch, but it also lays the foundation on which future experience will be built' (Belsky 1981: 8). In contrast, as White and Woollett (1992) point out, fathers' lack of contingency and sensitivity is interpreted as fostering independence and problem solving by making greater communicative and cognitive demands on children (cf. Parke *et al.* 1989).

While what counts as sensitive and responsive mothering is graduated according to the age and development (Wachs and Gruen 1982), what remains constant is the onus on the mother. This measure of the quality of mothering is then linked to a wide range of later social, behavioural and intellectual qualities within the child (e.g. Light 1979). Moreover, class issues enter into the ascription of sensitivity. Many studies suggest that the patterns of interaction associated with 'sensitive mothering' are less likely to be exhibited by working-class than middle-class mothers (Newson and Newson 1968; Boulton 1983; Tizard and Hughes 1984; Fonagy 2003b). Valerie Walkerdine and Helen Lucey (1989) argue that the class-coded discourses of developmental psychology function to regulate both middle-class and working-class women, who from their different positions are either enjoined to produce active, autonomous children or stigmatised for failing to exhibit interactional patterns deemed to promote this. They identify these evaluations of mothering with the post-World War II preoccupation with creating self-governing citizens. Thus scrutiny and regulation of mothers became a matter central to the maintenance of a democratic society (see Chapter 13).

Basic instinct

The apparatus of attachment theory thus naturalises class and cultural privilege. In addition, as we have seen, it is also based on a biological model of mothering. Since Bowlby's project was to replace psychoanalysis by an approach more in line with dominant notions of 'science', he turned to ethology for what looked like empirical support from observational studies of animal behaviour. The comparisons between newborn animals following their mothers (or the first object they saw) and mother–infant relations, and the conclusions he drew, assumed a common focus on an instinctual basis of behaviour. While Anglo-US psychoanalysis has been dogged by the mistranslation of Freud's German term *Trieb* as *instinct* when it is better translated as 'impulse' or 'drive' (Bettelheim 1986), Bowlby's use of 'instinct' reflected his background in psychiatry and zoology as well as psychoanalysis. Indeed, his ideas were always the subject of controversy within the psychoanalytic establishment (Bowlby *et al.* 1986). Hence the newborn duck's imprinting on, or tendency to follow, its mother became transposed into the concept of a critical period by which the mother–child relationship had to be secured if maladjustment was to be avoided.

As Chapter 1 pointed out, evolutionary ideas are frequently employed to lend legitimacy to existing social relations of inequality, while Chapter 5 highlighted links between organisation of the family, family and racial harmony. As the title of Elena Lieven's (1981) essay 'If It's Natural We Can't Change It' makes clear, the appeal to biology serves to preserve the status quo. By designating gendered and racialised positions as 'natural', they can be treated as inevitable and even desirable. While the viability of extrapolating from animal behaviour to human (historically and culturally variable) practices is largely regarded as suspect, assumptions about 'maternal instincts' still circulate. Within attachment theory the fact that women bear children has been taken to mean that (only) biological mothers 'instinctually' want to, and know how to, care for their children, thereby pathologising those who do not.

If women who abuse their children are seen as deviant women, they are by definition deviant mothers. Concerns with abusing mothers may seem far from those of attachment, but the discourse of maternal sensitivity and maternal deprivation draws them together. Where this happens, all too often the context in which child survival and neglect takes place is ignored. What has been understood as 'maternal deprivation' in some circumstances has more to do with poverty than with women's 'mothering qualities'. Indeed Scheper-Hughes (1989b: 187) suggests that: 'In circumstances of extreme poverty and competition for resources, selective neglect is often a manifestation of parental interventions on behalf of family survival.' From her anthropological study of mothers in a shantytown in north-east Brazil where the infant mortality rate reaches 70 per cent, she argues:

> Within the shantytown, child death *a mingua* (accompanied by mater-nal indifference and neglect) is understood as an appropriate maternal response to a deficiency in the child. Part of learning how to mother on the Alto includes learning when to 'let go'.
>
> (Scheper-Hughes 1989b: 190)

It is not that the women in the shantytowns do not care for their children, but rather they have to find ways of dealing with their deaths through protective emotional distancing. Rather than blaming these women or their culture for the effects of poverty, we should recognise that 'infant and childhood mortality in the Third World is a problem of *political economy*, not of medical technology' (Scheper-Hughes 1989b: 187). In evaluating women's adequacy as mothers and the cultural mores that support mothering (as psychology does), we therefore need to distinguish between an infanticide-tolerant society (for economic reasons) and an abuse-tolerant society. (Here evolutionary psychology discussions of parental 'investment' miss the key point.) In modern affluent societies where child survival is not such a struggle (for so many), there has been a shift from promoting the quantity of children to the promotion of qualities within children. In this sense parents' involvement with their child replaces a concern with fertility rate such that: 'Children have become relatively worthless (economically) to their parents, but priceless in terms of their psychological worth: the pleasure and satisfaction they bring' (Scheper-Hughes 1989a: 12). There are risks to the child in terms of the heavy weight of expectation of achievement she now carries, along with the assumption – through the availability of contracep-tion – that all births are intentional. Scheper-Hughes (1989a) also suggests that the reported prevalence of malicious intentional child abuse in the West (and its rarity elsewhere) harks back to the days when children contributed to the productive economy, as seen in parental resentment of the greedy, consuming child.

Commenting on the context for discussions of mother love and child development (or lack of development) we should note that the psychic and political economy of mother love are not divorced from each other. When Winnicott (1958) outlined his 'Eighteen reasons why a mother hates her baby, even a boy' (with a whole history of the transcultural preference for boys and devaluation of girls slipped in here), he included (although he did not of course account for them in these ways) 'reasons' rooted in the competition and insecurity fostered between women. Such competition arises from the ways in which the behaviour of their child in familial and public arenas is deemed to reflect their competence and adequacy as mothers. Hence the discourse of 'maternal instinct' gives rise to that of pathological mothering: each requires the other as its converse to maintain it. Both are burdened by the weight of phantasy. Both impose equally impossible demands – of idealisation or devaluation – and with the terms cast in these ways it is difficult for women not to fall foul of these bipolar opposites that constitute each other, or at least not to feel that they do.

Development as the repudiation of femininity

Attachment is the prerequisite for separation, and failure of separation indicates insecure attachment. These developmental achievements are not neutral with respect to gender. The trajectory of development moves from *attachment*, a stereotypically feminine quality, to a culturally masculine *detachment*. Gendered assumptions enter into the very structure of developmental models, which, it can be argued, treat girls and women as intellectually inferior (Gilligan 1982). But not only is maturity measured as the masculine capacity to tolerate separation and absence, to go on to chart unknown territories, this exploration marks the differentiation from the first love object, from the mother (Dinnerstein 1978). There is thus a double repudiation of femininity, as both motor of developmental advance and aspect of personal experience, structured within the achievement of autonomy. This is not a casual by-product of the process, but rather is its delicately orchestrated objective:

> A key to the mental hygiene of early childhood lies in building up adequate self-dependence. Even in infancy this principle of self-dependence must be respected. Not only from the breast must the child be weaned. By slow gradations he must develop fortitudes which lie at the basis of detachment. He cannot always play in his mother's lap; he must in time begin to play in his pen; he must learn to play in an adjoining room, first for a few minutes, later for an hour at a time. If his mother must leave the house, he must be content to watch her through the window, even though it costs him a struggle. In time he must learn to go to bed alone, and later, to school alone.
>
> (Gesell 1950: 261)

So the process of acquiring self-reliance is seen as akin to weaning, requiring bravery, that is, a manly 'fortitude', and not achieved without a 'struggle'. Such conceptions are central to liberal individualism, linked to Euro-US masculinity. It is to psychoanalysis that we must turn for some understanding of the costs of 'maturity', but here too the cultural and gendered associations of detached rationality are rarely explored (Broughton 1988; Walkerdine 1988). This picture is now moderated by the rise of masculinity studies, which also address the diversely classed and racialised forms of masculinity (Mac an Ghaill 1994; Morgan 1996; Frosh *et al.* 2002). But this has typically been more concerned with male vulnerability than liberating women from their onerous responsibilities. Moreover, by a curious twist it seems that the attachments are asymmetrically 'sticky', since it is mothers who are portrayed as enthralled by their children, through the mandate to forgo their independence in order to foster their children's transition to autonomy.

Monkey business

In addition to ethological work, the set of animal studies closely associated with attachment theory are Harry Harlow's experiments with rhesus monkeys. Harlow's studies were conducted in the USA during the immediate post-World War II period, and shared concerns similar to those of Bowlby and others with the nature of mothering and the production of the normal child. Harlow's studies are generally regarded as providing empirical support for the theory of maternal deprivation with its associated sequelae of affectionless psychopathy and 'cycles' of abuse across generations, as the Stone *et al.* (1973) extract at the beginning of this chapter indicates. The report that infant monkeys separated from their mothers cling to a fluffy-covered object rather than the wire-coated dispenser of food is held to indicate that infants' needs extend beyond nutrition to comfort. The isolated monkeys were reported to mutilate themselves and they could not relate (or relate sexually) when older to other monkeys. These 'observations' are hailed as proof of the far-reaching and irreversible effects of early adversity. Yet the obsession with maternal responsibility for child (and adult) development precludes the formulation of other questions, such as the supposedly protective influence of rearing these 'maternally deprived' monkeys with other infant monkeys. In these ways mothering has become constituted as the single, absolute condition for normal psychological functioning.

As argued in Chapter 1, psychology played its part in social practices which functioned to maintain and naturalise the divisions between men and women, European and non-European, rich and poor, and humans and animals. Donna Haraway's (1989) analysis of the role of primatology in the history of science demonstrates that the study of apes has played a key role in structuring gender and racial inequalities into modern concepts of knowledge and civilisation. Drawing on Harlow's own writings, she elaborates the underlying themes of his work, arguing that Harlow's laboratory translated metaphorical fantasies about women, childbirth and sexuality into a grotesque, manufactured reality.

While, according to one of his accounts, he was inspired by Bowlby's ideas on attachment, Harlow, working in 1950s America, addressed a different social context where women were beginning to work outside the home. At an overt level, his project was humanistic, claiming to demonstrate that contact is more important than primary drive reduction (i.e. satisfying hunger) for the development of relationships, and his work was interpreted as a liberalising measure in reassuring working women that they could still be good mothers. But dispensing with women as mothers invited the possibility of men replacing them. Known as 'the father of the cloth mother', Harlow revelled in his absolute control of his surrogate mothers. Accompanying the realisation of the fantasy of male reproduction were misogynistic insults to women's bodies that were not only verbal (in Harlow's descriptions), but also structured into its procedures. For example, the early-isolated monkeys, as adults unable to conceive in the usual ways, were artificially impregnated by means of 'an apparatus affectionately termed the "rape rack", which we leave to the reader's imagination' (Harlow *et al.* 1971: 545). After this, the monkeys entered a new career as what he called 'motherless monkey mothers' within a range of Harlow-reared 'evil mothers'. These supposedly tested the hypothesis that maternal rejection caused psychopathology, and prompted the construction of surrogate 'evil mothers':

> designed to repel clinging infants. . . . One surrogate blasted its babies with compressed air, another tried to shake the infant off its chest, a third possessed an embedded catapult which periodically sent the infant flying, while the fourth carried concealed brass spikes beneath her ventral surface which would emerge on schedule or on demand.
>
> (Harlow *et al.* 1971: 543)

As Haraway notes, the sadism here is metaphorical rather than (or as well as) literal: the violence lies in the representation and interpretation of what is done, rather than (only) in the infliction of pain.

In Harlow's studies we see comparative psychology looking to the natural world to verify ideology, and thereby constructing the 'natural' in its own image. Nowhere is this more evident than in Harlow's 'nuclear family apparatus', a complex set of interlocking cages modelling what he held as the ideal living arrangements. He even claimed that offspring reared within this environment were intellectually advantaged, which, as Haraway comments, no doubt pleased his professional middle-class audience.

There can be nothing 'natural' about rearing animals in cages and warping their habits and reactions, and there can be no grounds from this for comparison with human dynamics and relationships. But I would argue that the frequency with which these studies are cited in popular as well as technical arenas not only arises from attraction to what Haraway (1989: 233) calls the 'heroic masculinistic narrative of self-birthing'. It also owes its power to its claims to scientific knowledge which legitimate, even mandate, the setting aside of moral qualms and squeamishness. If anything, these perhaps lead to an even greater investment in finding 'scientific' value and meaning within such work, setting up the chaining of meanings from women and human infants to the 'denaturalised' bodies of rhesus monkeys to enter as 'science' within the discourses of post-war sexual and repro- ductive politics. The malaise of gory fascination and disgust that these accounts inspire is part of what fuels the suppression of the huge leaps of reason, the collapsing together of cultural, historical and species specificity, to enable 'the production of the unmarked, abstract universal, man' (Haraway 1989: 233) from the study of tortured monkeys.

Love at first sight

If attachment refers to children's affectionate connection with their mothers, the term bonding has been applied to parents' (and specifically mothers') emotional ties to their children. Within both models, it is noticeable that the basic unit of analysis is the individual (mother or child) rather than the relationship. This reflects not only an asocial model which presumes and privileges preconstituted individuals, but also a preoccupation with identi- fying causes and thereby attributing blame. While the severity of Bowlby's pronouncements about critical periods has been moderated by subsequent accounts (e.g. Rutter 1982), Klaus and Kennell (1976) brought new life to the notion that early mother–child interaction determined later aspects of development; only for these later researchers the cut-off point was 36 hours. They claimed to be able to associate quality of relationship assessed when the infant was three days old with a wide variety of social, intellectual and behavioural outcomes, which ranged from permitting wide psychological distance to promoting physical abuse, failure to thrive and even aban- donment. Like attachment theory, this drew on ethology, drawing analogies with certain herd-living animals (such as goats) in which post-partum separation can lead to rejection of an offspring by the mother. Although no longer regarded as plausible within psychological research (White and Woollett 1992), their claims about the possible consequences of separation for mothers and babies due to particular hospital practices or admission to special care baby units have dramatically affected neonatal care.

The work has been criticised on a number of methodological grounds, and the original studies have not been replicated (Svejda *et al.* 1980). At one level there is an issue about whether this really matters, since the changes in practice, such as the greater involvement of parents, have been gener- ally welcomed. However, studies of early mother–child bonding fail to acknowledge that different mother–baby pairs might react to separation in a variety of ways, especially in circumstances where there is some question of developmental abnormality or even survival (Richards 1981). Moreover, they fail to consider the role of parental beliefs about separation before resorting to a biologically ordained sensitive or critical period. It should be recalled that a mother using 'natural childbirth' methods has a very different childbirth experience from that of a woman who has major technological intervention and drugs. In each case the perceived significance of separation might well be different. What we see here is that developmental psychology plays a part (albeit indirectly) in creating the phenomena it sets out to explain, and creating unnecessary anxiety for women who, for example because they have given birth via caesarian section, are unable to take advantage of the supposedly unique opportunities the first few hours of mother–child interaction offer.

To take another example, antenatal scans, conducted for medical purposes to check that a pregnancy is proceeding normally, have been noted to have generated additional effects – in terms of promoting the parents' relationship with their as yet unborn child. Currently 'three-dimensional' scans are being offered at private clinics to facilitate 'emotional bonding'. Yet all scans involve the possibility of identifying abnormality, but – like all truth claims – they are also only partial interpretations rather than the full picture. Concern has been expressed that parents seeking such services may not get quite the outcome they were looking for, and may even also be given false information.

Psychology both draws upon and contests medical authority. The significance attributed to early experience underlies the recent moves away from forms of childbirth dominated by medical technology. On the other hand, this emphasis on early experience can also bolster the legitimacy of the medical profession at a time of criticism of, and challenge to, the medicalisation of childbirth (Arney 1980). More importantly, it provides a pseudo-scientific basis to justify social policy. Arney (1980) discusses Frailberg's book *Every Child's Birthright* (1977) which identifies 'diseases of attachment', creating a panoply of (maternally) deprived individuals ('bondless', 'hollow' and with 'unbound aggression') on whom the social problems of violence and crime can be pinned. Bonding theory recalls and fulfils a familiar agenda.

> All the characteristics of the literature under review here were present in the IQ literature years ago – the claim that criminality and mental defectiveness result from one's early development or biological heritage, the claim that social dysfunctionality also results from it, the presumption that admittedly limited evidence is definitive and provides a ground for policy, the concern over 'cures' and the presumption that responsibility for treatment devolves onto the state or its agencies.
>
> (Arney 1980: 563)

Alongside the shift towards more 'natural' and child-centred approaches to childbirth ushered in through research on attachment and bonding, and extended further via 'new age' and complementary approaches, childbirth in the West is increasingly dominated by medical technology.

Early attachment and later developments

The account provided so far above engages with the classic textbook representation of attachment within developmental psychology. This, however, bears little resemblance both to the historical image of Bowlby and attachment theory within psychoanalysis and psychotherapy; nor does it address subsequent developments in attachment theory. In terms of research, Goldberg (2000) proposes that the extensive technical and conceptual work building on Bowlby's pioneering work can be seen as comprising three (overlapping) phases. The first was concerned with identifying predictors of infant behaviour in the strange situation; the second extended methods for assessing attachment beyond infancy (with, for example, the development of the adult attachment interview as an instrument to assess early relationships via analysis of retrospective accounts of relationship histories from adults) and took up Ainsworth's identification of a new mode of disorganised attachment and its clinical implications; third, as attachment research has moved beyond a focus on infancy, so it has moved to study *representations* of relationships, building on Bowlby's concept of 'internal working models' (see e.g. Prior and Glaser 2006).

Within psychoanalysis, attachment theory has until recently been treated with suspicion and often contempt for its scientific and biological interests, regarded by some as not psychoanalytic at all for its neglect of the unconscious and sexuality. Significantly, Fonagy's (2001) comprehensive and accessible account of attachment theory is addressed primarily to psychotherapists and psychoanalysts, rather than social scientists. This attempts to demonstrate the proximity of attachment theory concerns with those of various psychoanalytic traditions (for example, in showing how 'maternal sensitivity' is close to Bion's concept of 'containment' or Winnicott on 'mirroring'), as well as the clinical relevance of its claims. Green's (2003) collection attempts a similar task in connecting psychoanalytic theory with developments in neurophysiology. Currently, attachment work is enjoying a major upturn in reputation, for example, with the London-based Centre for Attachment Psychotherapy (CAP) associated with a dedicated therapy training (see Barrett 2006).

To make sense of this turn of events we need to consider broader cultural-social developments. These include: the demand for 'evidence-based' practice, and the crisis in psychoanalysis brought about by developments in genetics, and the more general cultural turn towards genetic explanations at a time when the project of mapping the human genome has ushered in the vista of extending the reach of biology into social policy. More parochially, the 'modernisation' agenda now preoccupying many states has given rise to increasingly stringent criteria for 'proof' of the efficacy of therapies, with psychoanalytic and other interpretive approaches badly hit by the problems of generating relevant 'evidence'.

While attachment theory espoused the project to make psychoanalysis 'scientific' from its outset, it has not since looked like a strong candidate to fit this bill, since its early claims about the devastating impact of early separations and the original predictions from the early theoretical formulations turned out to generate little empirical support (see Barrett 1998; Fonagy 2001). This may in part be because the concepts themselves translate badly into empirical formulations. Here Goldberg's comment that 'much of the existing research suffers from an inability to exploit fully the richness of these theoretical ideas' (2000: 254) would perhaps benefit from being read alongside her earlier point: 'The development of the strange situation and its potential for testing some of Bowlby's propositions appealed primarily to students of developmental psychology' (Goldberg 2000: 238). There were also criticisms of the self-confirming character of attachment theory's claims: 'The traditional attachment model is clearly circular. The response to separation is attributed to the disruption of a social bond, the existence of which is inferred from the presence of the separation response' (Fonagy 2003a: 118). These problems have prompted significant theoretical reconceptualisation, moving the domain of inquiry away from the presence or absence of security, or even exploration versus proximity seeking in relation to functional or felt security, to addressing the building of representations of one's own mental states through their being (more or less well) reflected by others:

> The mother's empathic emotion provides the infant with feedback on his [sic] emotional state. Thus the infant develops a secondary representation of his emotional state, with the mother's empathic face as the signifier and his own emotional arousal as the signified. The mother's expression tempers emotion to the extent that it is separate and different from the primary experience, although crucially it is not recognised as the mother's experience but as an organizer of a self-state. The inter-subjectivity is the bedrock of the intimate connection between attachment and self-regulation.
>
> (Fonagy 2003a: 115)

Hence this recent turn to studying emotional regulation returns to some of the same debates and criticisms that were discussed in relation to 'theory of mind' research in Chapter 3:

> In infancy the contingent responding of the attachment figure is thus far more than the provision of reassurance about a protective presence. It is the principal means by which we acquire understanding of our own

internal states, which is an intermediate step in the acquisition of the understanding of others as psychological entities.

(Fonagy 2003a: 115–116)

Thus in a recent reworking Fonagy and others (Fonagy 2001, 2003a, 2003b; Fonagy *et al.* 2004) claim that it is not the content of internal working models that is important but rather their presence and quality:

> The early relationship environment is crucial not because it shapes the quality of subsequent relationships (for which evidence is lacking, as we have seen) but because it serves to equip the individual with a mental processing system that will subsequently generate mental representations, including relationship representations.
>
> (Fonagy 2001: 31)

Attachment thus becomes a form of cognitive skill that is deemed to connect the biological with the interpersonal context of the family:

> The creation of this representational system is arguably the most important evolutionary function of attachment to a caregiver. Adopting this perspective helps to redress the prevailing bias against the centrality of the family as the major force in socialization, but it also shifts the emphasis from content of experience to psychological structure or mental mechanism and involves expanding on current ideas of the evolutionary function of attachment.
>
> (Fonagy 2001: 31)

We are returned, then, to the ambiguous status of attachment theory as a hybrid model between psychoanalysis, social psychology and sociobiology. These ambiguities structure current debates as to the best ways of assessing adult attachments and their antecedents: whether by self-report (through such instruments as the attachment style inventory) or through the less consciously presented indicators of narrative form, through the adult attachment interview (Bifulco 2002). Either way, however, major claims are put forward not only about the relationship between early experience and later mental health, but even – on the basis of retrospective measures of adult accounts of their early attachments – from women already identified as vulnerable – being able to predict prospective liability to significant mental health difficulties (Bifulco *et al.* 2006).

Minding the gap: through a scanner, darkly

Notwithstanding the fact that attachment theory is acknowledged to be a sociobiological model (Amin 2001; Green 2003: 3), rather than threatening to reduce the psychic to the biological, current accounts staunchly defend environmentalist/socialisation-focused work. They claim to acknowledge the role of early experience, including parenting:

> The role of genetics in personality development and psychopathology has been exaggerated. There are few examples where the conceptual journey between gene and behaviour is simple enough to be tracked. The assumptions of behaviour genetics are very substantial, and the interactions between genes and the polygenic nature of most attributes which are genetically determined make simple extrapolations from genomics to psychology risky and improbable.
>
> (Fonagy 2003a: 112)

Rather than refusing to engage with the attacks on developmental and psychoanalytic claims by behaviour geneticists 'triggered by the excitement of the human genome project and partly by research designs of increasing statistical sophistication' (Fonagy 2003a: 109), the strategy adopted by Fonagy and other attachment theorists has been to engage with the genetic research and try to turn its popularity to their own advantage. They draw upon, but critique, its terms by suggesting that 'behaviour geneticists study the "wrong" environment. The environment that triggers the expression of a gene is not the observable, objective environment. The child's experience of the environment is what counts. The manner in which the environment is experienced will act as a filter in the expression of genotype to phenotype' (Fonagy 2003a: 112). This is not to say that attachment researchers eschew comparative or neurophysiological research. Far from this, they mobilise similar claims and methodological devices. For example, Fonagy (2003a) claims that 'the Interpersonal Interpretive Mechanism . . . a genetically-defined capacity, probably localized in the medial pre-frontal cortex, is the mechanism of predictive significance' (p. 117). Elsewhere we get an even more detailed claim of neurophysiological links:

> Attachment may mark changes in neural organizations that are involved in later psychological disturbance. For example, it is possible that emotion regulation established in early childhood may substantially alter fear conditioning processes in the amygdala (LeDoux 1995) or connections between the prefrontal cortex and the limbic system (Schore 1997). There is evidence for elevated cortical secretion and delayed return to baseline in those with insecure disorganized attachment (Spangler and Schiede 1998). Systematically identifying the potential biological links that underpin attachment will be the task of the current decade.
>
> (Fonagy 2001: 46)

Or Green (2003), introducing her collection, claims: 'the emerging picture is of the mind as a multi-modular system designed to manage a wide variety of biopsychological motivations. Some of the working of these systems – memory systems, attachment/safety seeking through to emotional regulatory systems – is outlined here' (p. 9). So this new attachment research retains all the other political hallmarks of biologically oriented psychology in three ways. First, there is a continuing focus on mothers. For despite alternating between 'mothers' and 'caregivers' in their descriptions, it is specifically mothers who come under primary scrutiny: 'What is critical is the mother's capacity mentally to contain the baby and respond, in terms of physical care, in a manner that shows awareness of the child's mental state yet reflects coping (mirroring distress while communicating an incompatible affect)' (Fonagy 2001: 166). Indeed, Meins (1999), drawing on this work, posits a measure of maternal representations of the child's mental states (termed 'maternal mindedness', or 'MM') which specifies 'appropriate' and 'inappropriate' forms (see also Meins *et al.* 2003, 2006) and is increasingly being taken up by other researchers as a means of assessing the adequacy of mothering. For example, Lok and McMahon (2006) in a study which was – interestingly – funded by Financial Markets for Children investigate the relationship between 'MM' and an 'interaction measure' of affective congruence or 'emotional availability' (EA).

Second, in making the link between early assessment and developmental psychopathology, there is a focus on changing people rather than environments/social conditions (see also Rutter 2002). Indeed, this is even put forward as the easier, which of course will also turn out to be the cheaper, option:

> This has substantial significance for prevention, since the child's understanding of his environment is more readily modifiable than the environment itself, or the genes with which the environment interacts (Emde 1988). An attachment theory, intrapsychic perspective, may be helpful in considering not just what precipitates a disorder but also which processes influence the course of the disorder for better or worse.
>
> (Fonagy 2003a: 113)

Those 'worse options' include researching the affect regulation of teenage mothers, where – along the way – we also see how a neurological measure comes to figure within an evolutionarily embedded environmentalist claim:

> Mothers were asked to respond to sad or smiling faces of their babies while in an fMRI scanner. The striking result was that whereas the brains of teenage mothers hardly differentiated between these two emotions in their infants, the control women showed dramatic activation of the medial prefrontal cortex (mPFC) and cingulated cortex, areas involved in emotion recognition and processing. With the teen mothers, in response to sad infant faces, activation was limited to the caudate/ventral striatum and the fusiform face area and visual cortex,

whereas control women also showed activation in the region of the insula, which is associated with unpleasant emotions. Teenage mothers, perhaps one of the highest risks groups for the disorganization of attachment processes with their children, appear to show a dramatic lack of differentiation for emotional displays in their infants.

(Fonagy 2003b: 7)

So it is not even mothers but rather particular mothers who come in for particular attention within a paradigm that runs the risk of presuming and then enforcing the very pathologisation that they seek to minimise (see also Fonagy *et al.* 1991).

The comparative model characteristic of evolutionary biological models is also clearly in evidence, for Fonagy draws upon Suomi's (1991, 2000) 'biobehavioural' study of rhesus monkeys, extrapolating from these to the moderating effects of maternal responses for genetically endowed aggression, and its relation to serotonergic dysfunction. Other animal comparisons come into play, with the familiar appeal to nature once again enforcing traditional gender roles:

> Just as in rat pups the ontogenetic development of biological regulators crucially depends on the mother–infant unit, so in human development psychological interpretive capacity evolves in the context of repetitive interaction with the mother.
>
> (Fonagy 2003a: 118)

Third, notwithstanding its persuasive appeal, there remain significant interpretive tensions with psychoanalysis. Claims of accurate mirroring and being able to develop full understanding ('Secure attachment provides a relatively firm base for the acquisition of a full understanding of minds', Fonagy 2001: 46) conflict with psychoanalytic commitments to the inevitably distorted character of all communication, with all relationships – including research relationships – saturated with transferential meanings mobilised by all parties. Hence, as we shall see, in laying claim to science for psychoanalysis, this may actually work to undo psychoanalysis.

Emotions or cognitions?

Rather than being guilty of biological reductionism, the new current of attachment research is in more danger of rendering the emotions a mere subsystem of cognition. It is hard to read the following quotation as any different from a cognitive account:

> What is lost in 'loss' is not the bond but the opportunity to generate a higher-order regulatory mechanism: the mechanism for the appraisal and reorganisation of mental contexts. We conceptualise attachment as

a process which brings into being complex mental life from a complex behavioural system.

(Fonagy 2003a: 118)

This behavioural system is thus deemed to be measurable, and aided by fancy technologies that show bits of the brain lighting up. Certainly in an era where cognitive behavioural therapy is currently the only therapy deemed to be 'evidence based', owing to the difficulties of 'proving' the success of psychoanalytic interventions, the attraction of such empirical research is understandable. One reason for this may be because attachment theory has extended beyond infancy so its claims have become more general – and so insufficiently specific. But another effect of the generalisation of attachment-related research is that it is easy to lose sight of how attachment is only one aspect of the parent–child relationship, and parents are also 'playmates, disciplinarians, teachers, role models or sources of stimulation' (Goldberg 2000: 250). A further possibility is that it contributes to the broader cultural focus on emotions, as instanced by calls for the promotion of emotional literacy, which high profile therapists such as Susie Orbach (2001) have clearly espoused. As already noted (also Burman in press c), in their wider pedagogical and self-help forms these are clearly cognitive models.

Goldberg claims the contribution of attachment theory 'as a "lightening rod" to energize a dynamic centre of activity focused on developing and telling a "story" about parent–child relationships and their role in development' (2000: 237). But current political agendas invite a collapse of that narrative into biological precursors and technologies for early assessment. Green ends the introduction to her edited collection by claiming: 'Biological and clinical approaches present us with different but complementary ways of approaching emotional development . . . Bringing these two approaches under the same roof may also mean that the house beneath is neither a neat bungalow, two-up, two-down, nor a folly' (Green 2003: 19). Subverting Green's architectural metaphor, we might rather say that the realist claims to objective research threaten to deform psychoanalysis and its affirmation of the inevitability of engagement and misrepresentation, rendering it into that classic architectural compromise between traditional English empiricism and liberal individualism: the semi-detached.

(Preschool) lessons

Links between early experience and later development have been spectacularly difficult to establish. Criticisms focus on sample selection of atypical populations already labelled as deviant, whether prospectively, in following up children in care or who have suffered trauma (as in the early separation studies), or retrospectively, in looking backwards into the family history of convicted criminals or child abusers. Despite these methodological and theoretical inadequacies, concepts of bonding (and attachments) live on, and bonding is even thought to be conveniently assessable by means of retrospective questionnaires such as the Parental Bonding Instrument (e.g. Gamsa 1987), which earthshatteringly establishes 'care . . . as the major parental dimension' (Parker *et al.* 1979: 8). Addressing a conference on drugs on 17 November 1992, the late English Princess Diana ('the people's princess') advocated parental affection as a preventive factor in drug abuse. She drew on the theory that children 'deprived of affection' suffer a lack of stability that makes it more likely that they become vulnerable to drug addiction. She managed to portray 'hugging' within a medical model, with unforeseen medico-moral powers, saying: 'Hugging has no harmful side-effects. If we all play our part in making our children feel valued the result will be tremendous – there are potential huggers in every household.' The exhortation is to mobilise a hitherto unrecognised resource, but, whatever our feelings about the importance of affection for children, we should be wary of how this neglects state responsibility for the provision of resources. In these ways, ideologies of attachment and bonding both exonerate the state and provide scapegoats to account for the outcomes of seemingly thwarted affections in the form of socially inappropriate activity.

Moreover, enormous effort and resources go into early intervention programmes such as Head Start in the USA which claimed to 'compensate' for social deprivation and provide enriched environments, thereby proffering visions of greater equality and opportunity. Indeed in the UK Sure Start was explicitly informed by attachment theory. Disappointment over the effects of these projects has made subsequent interventions focus more explicitly on babies and toddlers and set out to make mothers more sensitive and responsive (see also Chapter 13). The problem with these projects is not only that, in identifying deprivation, the locus of the deficit tends to revolve around the child's mother, culture and class. Moreover, the evidence on long-term effects is unstable, with early indications of success more attributable to the optimism of the 1960s than to any specifically educationally enriching feature of the programme. We should be wary of a simplistic application of developmental psychological research in early intervention programmes:

> In the first place, it reinforces the political preference to urge single strategy and (relatively) inexpensive educational solutions to complex social and economic problems (Lazerson 1970). Second, it risks perpetuating the idea that the impact an educational intervention makes on an individual can be understood in isolation from the context in which it occurs. Thirdly, it fails to recognise that there may be features of experimental projects that it is difficult, even impossible to reproduce in a national social programme (including the fact of being experimental and by definition only being available to a particular group of children).
>
> (Woodhead 1988: 446)

Addressing child development programmes in poor, 'developing' countries, Penn (2005) extends this critique by pointing out how the emphasis on early intervention – based on US programmes such as Head Start – can be misleading. She points out not only that claims to the efficacy of such schemes are based on remarkably flimsy evidence, with very few longitudinal studies, but also that they presuppose a massive infrastructure of expensive services that may not be possible in most other countries. The rhetoric of early intervention may therefore be very far from its practice.

If there are difficulties in linking research with social policy, then the cultural practices on which research is based render general application even more problematic. Most research on the 'effects' of day care (Belsky 2006) has been conducted in the USA where there is no system of maternity or paternity leave, nearly all nursery and preschool provision is privately funded, there is heavy dependence on relatives for the care of young children and public provision is reserved for those deemed inadequate or especially in need. All this means that there are wide variations in quality of childcare and major inequalities in access to childcare (Hennessy *et al.* 1992). These may well be reflected in the character of the questions asked within day-care research, and in the kinds of results it produces. This body of work therefore has little relevance to countries with more flexible work and leave arrangements and where public provision of childcare is more extensive. Once again we have a clear instance of how the US domination of psychological research imposes an inappropriate agenda, which in this case presents the care of young children outside the home in an unnecessarily pessimistic light. Dahlberg *et al.* (1999) address this question of the elusive character of 'quality' childcare head on:

> What seems to underlie the 'problem with quality' is a sense and unease that what has been approached as an essentially technical issue of expert knowledge and measurement may, in fact, be a philosophical issue of value and dispute. Rather than discovering with it the truth, and with it certainty, we encounter multiple perspectives and ambivalence.
>
> (Dahlberg *et al.* 1999: 7)

Singer (1992: 14) claims that there are 'three themes, continually repeated during the history of child-care facilities: social innovation through interventions in family upbringing; the importance of the first years of childhood; and the (ambiguous) position of women'. In a period when more women than ever before are bringing up children alone, the scope for vulnerability to these themes is increasing rather than decreasing. But the increasing demand for female labour in industrialised countries through demographic changes in the age structure of populations and economic conditions has forced a re-evaluation of the organisation of childcare that has also brought fathers into the picture.

Further reading

Benjamin, J. (1988) *Bonds of Love*, London: Virago (connects the account here with more explicitly psychoanalytic analyses of power and gender in relationships, with particular reference to the significance of mother–child relations).

Scheper-Hughes, N. (ed.) (1989) *Child Survival: Anthropological Perspectives on the Treatment and Maltreatment of Children*, Dordrecht: Reidel (puts debates about child abuse within a cross-cultural context).

Singer, E. (1992) *Child-Care and the Psychology of Development*, London: Routledge (deals with the impact of child-centred approaches on women, in relation to theories of childcare and development).

For empirical re-evaluation of the notion of 'maternal deprivation', see:

Rutter, M. (1982) *Maternal Deprivation Reassessed*, Harmondsworth: Penguin.

For a very clear account of issues in childcare provision and research literature, see:

Dahlberg, G., Moss, P and Pence, A. (1999) *Beyond Quality in Early Childhood Education and Care: Postmodern Perspectives*, London: Falmer Press.

Hennessy, E., Martin, S., Moss, P. and Melhuish, E. (1992) *Children and Day Care: Lessons from Research*, London: Paul Chapman.

For a detailed and accessible review of developments in attachment theory, see:

Barrett, H. (2006) *Attachment and the Perils of Parenting: A Commentary and Critique*, London: National Family and Parenting Institute.

Fonagy, P. (2001) *Attachment and Psychoanalysis*, New York: The Other Press.

Suggested activities

Depending on the positions and interests of the group, it is often fruitful to discuss local resources for childcare provision, both currently and historically. This might involve finding out about the range of childcare options used by those who are currently parents of young children, and asking older relatives and friends. If difficulties are encountered in finding out about statutory provision, then this itself is a resource for discussion (as an issue about accessibility). In particular, questions such as the following could be addressed:

- What factors enter into a parent's decision in determining her childcare arrangements? What contemporary and historical variability emerges?
- If more than one person is involved in parenting a child, who takes responsibility for these arrangements?

- How accessible are available childcare services – in terms of location, price, hours covered? What theoretical frameworks are drawn upon to inform this structure?
- How do parents conceive of their relationships with those with whom they share the care of their children?
- How do non-parental carers of children talk about their relationships with the parents of the children they care for?
- To what extent are these accounts informed by developmental psychological concepts and theories (such as 'bonding' and 'attachment')?
- To what extent does developmental psychology address (as a research topic or as a theoretical issue) the affectional relationships non-parental carers develop with the children they care for?

8 Involving fathers

The recovery of some form of initiation is essential to the culture. The United States has undergone an unmistakeable decline since 1950, and I believe that if we do not find a third road besides the two mentioned here, the decline will continue. We have the grandiose road, taken by junk-bond dealers, high rollers and the owners of private jets; and we have the depressed road, taken by some long-term alcoholics, single mothers below the poverty line, crack addicts and fatherless men.

(Bly 1991: 53)

Alongside the child, developmental psychology constituted the woman as mother as its key *object* of concern and intervention. But its gaze has currently shifted to include men, men as fathers. This chapter explores why and how this has happened, and evaluates the adequacy of the models by which fatherhood is investigated. Moreover, irrespective of whether the 'new man' is old or new, real or fictional, the paradigms for studying him could certainly do with an overhaul and there are significant policy consequences of their conceptual and methodological occlusions. Further, the philosophical and methodological limitations of this work go beyond the study of fathers to throw into relief more general research assumptions and practices.

Meet the parents: mothers, fathers and children (and psychologists)

Fathers are a relatively recent addition to the developmental psychological literature. In part this derives from the dominance of attachment theory in Britain with its Kleinian psychoanalytic inflection. While attachment theory was a radical departure from Kleinian psychoanalysis, especially in abandoning the notion of unconscious phantasy, nevertheless both approaches shared a common tendency to eclipse the father figure and focus on early mother–child relations, rather than analysing the Oedipal triangle of mother, father and child (Riley 1983). Schaffer's (1971) synthesis of research in his *The Growth of Sociability* not only reflects these themes but also refers to the 'scientist' as male. The basic orienting question for the book is: 'How does the infant learn to distinguish among different human beings so that he [*sic*] is able to recognise his mother as familiar and strangers as unfamiliar?' (Schaffer 1971: 30).

Here we have the familiar situation where the mother is designated as the primary caregiver, with everyone else by implication falling into the category of stranger. The definition of mother extends beyond the biological childbearer to include any woman continuously involved in childcare (an ambiguous improvement). Correlatively, the child is specified as 'he', which can be interpreted in one of two ways: either as a reflection of stereotypical assumptions by which the mother–child couple is portrayed as reflecting the man–woman couple, or, when represented as the 'generic he', as offering an asocial model of child that implies gender is a detachable variable rather than a constitutive feature of subjectivity. While the latter alternative is simply inadequate, the former also clearly renders girl children invisible and, more than this, eclipses the significance of gender in childcare. For it is in relation to a woman that a child first experiences feelings of power, vulnerability and especially total helplessness – within prevailing childcare arrangements (Dinnerstein 1978). Clearly this observation holds different significance for the positions of boys and girls respectively in terms of the meanings gender holds.

The same point may also apply where men are the primary caregivers. It should be noted that the choice of terms in the extract above does not arise from the state of empirical findings at the time nor from the author's personal belief that only mothers 'mother' children. Schaffer was one of the first researchers to challenge the notion of 'monotropy', reporting that babies do form attachments to more than one person and can be equally attached to their fathers, and can even at times exhibit their most intense attachment to them (Schaffer and Emerson 1964).

By the mid-1970s, although there was more embarrassment and equivocation, the basic assumptions remained unchanged. Taking the Fontana 'Developing Child' series as an index, Daniel Stern in *The First Relationship* (1977) offers an apologetic footnote on the first page for retaining gender stereotypical terms (baby as 'he', caregiver as 'she') in the interests of 'easier and clearer reading'. Schaffer's (1977) book *Mothering* ties itself into some knots in trying to make 'mothering' a gender-neutral term: 'Our concern will primarily be with the description of mothering in the child's earliest years irrespective of who actually carries on this process . . . mother may be thought of as anyone with responsibility for the child's care over a prolonged period' (Schaffer 1977: 30). Nevertheless, the baby is still 'he'.

By the 1980s it was no longer possible to ignore the changes taking place in family organisation and childcare, and this was eventually reflected by the publication within the series of Alison Clarke-Stewart's *Day Care* (1982). By this stage the strategy of mere *inclusion* of fathers into child rearing (by generalising the term 'mother') has been surpassed by notions of *complementarity*: 'The parent's role includes being a dispenser of love and a disciplinarian, a verbal stimulator, a sensitive responder, a provider of materials and a choreographer of experiences for the child' (Clarke-Stewart 1982: 93). (Incidentally the child is still 'he'.) No prizes for guessing which parent provides which of these two main parental qualities, stimulation and responsiveness, identified as affecting children's development (p. 92). Clarke-Stewart goes on to welcome research now addressing the specificities of paternal contributions to childcare, arguing that:

> While his role in providing affection and discipline may parallel hers, the father is more likely to be a special playmate, who engages in exciting, physical games and active rough and tumble. This contributes to the child's sociability. He also provides psychological support to the mother and thus affects the child's development indirectly through her.
>
> (Clarke-Stewart 1982: 93–94)

The last comment could come straight from Bowlby, and, as we shall see, attention to the complementarity of parental roles works quite nicely to reassert traditional gender roles.

Finally responding to the popular interest in, and burgeoning popular literature about, fatherhood, the Fontana series published Ross Parke's *Fathering* in 1984. Parke's work has subsequently included cross-cultural study, which has been revealing not only of different gendered patternings of caregiving but also of norms about children and childhood. So Parke and Buriel (1998) pointed out not only that culture does moderate the claim that mothers and fathers play differently with their children, but also that an intervening cultural variable may be that some cultures simply devote less time to (or have less time to) play.

In Western contexts, as the baby emerged as the icon of the caring, green 1990s, it became glamorous, even mandatory, for men to be portrayed with children. Male fragrance advertisements portrayed beautiful men with equally beautiful babies and ambiguously gendered children to signify the emergence of a new image of vulnerable masculinity: the strong but sensitive man. At the inception of the new Ministry for Children in Norway, headed by a man (because it was considered that this would ensure it was taken more seriously), he posed for photos bare-chested and bearing (in his arms) *two* babies (*Guardian*, 21 May 1991)! While such ministries have arisen in response to the rising interest in children's rights, and in response to structures for monitoring and reporting required by signatories to the UN Convention on the Rights of the Child, they also exemplify the increasing surveillance of parents. As fathers have entered national social policies on the family, so too has the psychological literature been drawn upon as a key resource. Moreover, as fathers become increasingly subject to state regulation through the policy commitment to child rights, this reconfigures the relationship between state and family. Indeed the 'international child rights regime' has been put forward as indicative of the broader crisis in patriarchal authority in an era of political disaffection, increasing uncertainty and diminished subjectivity (Pupavac 2005).

Accounting for 'fathering': in the company of men

As discussed in Chapter 6, the earlier literature was more concerned with fathers' absence than with analysing the developmental consequences of active paternal contributions to child rearing. The single-parent family was stigmatised as necessarily having problems, and it was only from the mid-1980s that any more diverse or positive picture has emerged. Even this was within the popular rather than the psychological literature (e.g. Renvoize 1985; Shapiro 1987), and predominantly focused on middle-class women (cf. Campbell 1984; Phoenix 1991). In part this change of popular and academic focus arose from general social and structural changes in industrialised countries. Among the reasons put forward to account for the new preoccupation with fathering, Lorna McKee and Margaret O'Brien (1982) included the increase of women in paid employment, with corresponding consequences for men; the greater number of single-parent families, especially male-headed households; and the increase of (especially male) unemployment. Other factors include the development of a (small but vocal) male liberation movement (mainly in the USA), the continued privatisation of the nuclear family which locates childcare solely within the home, and cultural support for child-centred approaches which informs ideas about parental responsibilities and duties towards children. Above all, analysts of this period see this development as very much linked to the impact of the women's movement which, in calling for a redistribution of gender roles, has produced a general shift in women's conceptions of childcare and domestic labour. Denise Riley, reviewing the history of different feminist demands over childcare, comments on the difficulties of arriving at an adequate conception of the relationship between parents' and children's rights, and men's and women's:

> Adults' needs and children's needs are neither necessarily consonant nor necessarily incompatible; not everything can be accurately read off from the categories of men, women, and children. It is likely to be an increasingly sharp question, though, for feminism, since more 'rights' may be increasingly named and laid claim to by more contestants. Who and what is a 'parent', for instance; is there a genuine democracy of parents, inclined harmoniously over the child? Or instead are there only 'mothers' and 'fathers' who are, because of their different power, capacities and histories, always irreconcilable? Neither alternative, I think, is right.
>
> (Riley 1987: 184)

However, even from its inception there were two, contradictory, interpretations of men's increased interest and participation in childcare. On the one hand, it is hailed as a progressive move that men are taking a more equal share; on the other, these developments could be seen as reactionary in the sense that men are competing with women and taking over the one sphere where women have traditionally held some limited power and acknowledged expertise (albeit with the 'help' of the professionals). Indeed, this cultural development arose not only alongside the increasing participation of women in the labour force, but also coincided with a feminist reclaiming of mothering (Coward 1993; Benn 1998), accompanying the rise of cultural feminism and elaboration of a relational ethics of care more generally (Bowden 1997).

Sadly, developments in child custody legislation have meant that the inclusion of men is at the expense of women. Lynne Segal (1990) noted the contradictory character of anxieties about men, children and families, with the importance attributed to fatherhood at a time of unprecedented 'discoveries' of child sexual abuse and domestic violence (a point we will return to later in this chapter). Similarly, Suzanne Moore (1988), commenting on the general apparent erosion of gender boundaries within fashion and the media, coined the term 'gender tourism' to describe the asymmetrical 'exchange' of gender roles: while some men venture into culturally feminine spheres there seems to be little reciprocal movement towards secession of male privilege, thus leaving the patriarchal structure of power relations intact.

Yet patriarchy is as much a relationship between older and younger men, as it is between men and women. Traditional notions of patriarchy have therefore undergone considerable change with industrialisation and post-industrialisation – although they are far from disappearing.

Methodological inadequacies: guilt by association?

Fatherhood does of course have a history. Indeed we can re-read the history of child-rearing advice, with its increasing focus on mothers, as a tale of the exclusion of fathers. Demos (1983) discusses how Victorian models of fatherhood and their legacies – that are structured into the emerging advice literature – wiped out the pre-modern, pre-industrial narrative of the involved caring father (with positions for father as spiritual guide, advisor, guardian as well as disciplinarian). If men as fathers have become visible, there seems to have been little corresponding effort to develop new theoretical and methodological paradigms to theorise this. Developmental psychological studies have tended to research fathering as if it were just like mothering but with little reflection on how appropriate this may be, or indeed whether the fathering work presents any opportunity for more general theoretical reformulation or revision (e.g. Dubas and Gerris 2002). The research was blinkered in three ways (McKee and O'Brien 1982). First, it treats fathering as if it were a simple variety of mothering in terms of the tests and procedures used, for example, by investigating father–child instead of mother–child attachment in the 'strange situation' (e.g. Feldman 2003). Second, research issues were simply transferred from mothers to fathers. So, the preoccupation with the effects of separation was then applied to father–child relationships, and the work on women's experience of pregnancy and childbirth (e.g. Oakley 1980) paralleled by studies of men's experience of these, without considering that there may be other interesting questions to address, concerning, for example, the impact of a partner's pregnancy on other aspects of a man's life. Here more recent work has documented that men can suffer postnatal depression too (Edhborg *et al.* 2005), so finally underscoring the limits of genetic explanations.

Men are now at the sharp end of the inadequate models developed to evaluate women as mothers. Just as single mothers were constituted as a 'social problem', now lone fathers are classed as 'motherless' families. But, by contrast, gender identity and sex roles is one area where fathers as well as mothers have always been studied (e.g. Shinn 1978; Roberts *et al.* 1987), reflecting the homophobic worry that boys brought up by single mothers might be less masculine or become gay through lacking a male role model. Indeed fathers' roles in confirming the masculinity or femininity of their children is one of the longstanding contributions accorded to them in the psychological (and psychoanalytic) literature.

The third limitation structuring the research (McKee and O'Brien 1982) has been its cultural bias in the definition of family organisation. Within the burgeoning fathering literature, there was limited or little consideration of any family organisation outside the nuclear family, apart from one which is undergoing temporary change (separation, divorce). The research has tended to address only minor aberrations from the Western, nuclear blue-print, instead of engaging in wide cross-national study and multicultural research within the same country. For example, the Australian sample studied by Graeme Russell in *The Changing Role of Fathers?* (1983) was reflected on the book's cover where we see the child and father (both of whom are white) standing on the doorstep waving goodbye to executive attired mother, complete with that 1980s icon of the middle-class pro-fessional, the briefcase. The change under investigation here goes no further than a simple role exchange.

Now, in the era of the knowledge society and wireless access to the worldwide web where terms like 'flexible' work and 'family friendliness' populate policy discourse, it may seem that women are winning out over men, But far from the feminist project having been won, it is rather that under late capitalism men have perhaps come to share some aspects of women's positions – in relation to work at least, with a 'career' or 'job for life' transmuting into 'lifelong learning' and secure employment increasingly contingent on performance-related pay targets. While this has certainly benefited some women as well as some men, the erosion of gender-divided work has brought to many men as well as women the miseries and 'precarities' of low-paid, insecure and part-time work associated with the 'feminisation of poverty'.

More recently, developmental psychology's failure to provide a gendered analysis of family relations has been cited as contributing to a failure to attend to the role of gender relations within adult partnerships (in terms of their impacts on children). While psychologists take credit for informing twenty-first century British social policy on the family, Featherstone (2006) claims that New Labour's social policy has adopted an oversimplified version of this work. She reviews work that shows how Lamb's (1997) assertions about the absence of family hostility being a key index of child adjustment, and marital conflict a key corresponding index of maladjustment, have been taken up in the *National Service Framework for Children, Young People and Maternity Services* (Department of Health 2004) only in terms of 'bald statements . . . about father involvement per se improving outcomes to children' (Featherstone 2006: 303). Perhaps it is significant that the August 2006 special issue of *The Psychologist* (the professional publication sent to all members of the British Psychological Society) was devoted to 'Nipping Criminality in the Bud'. This reviews evidence on early intervention and parent programmes (Hutchings and Lane 2006; Sanders and Morawska 2006; Scott 2006; Sutton *et al.* 2006), and significantly resolves eventually the general gender neutrality of 'parent' to 'mother'. As Featherstone (2006: 300) comments: 'the uninterrogated and widespread use of the term parent is problematic because it can obscure the kinds of strategies needed to ensure that the differing and often complexly changing needs and desires of men and women are addressed'.

Interpreting the accounts

These problems could be regarded as part of the legacy of ethological observation as the main research method in developmental psychology (Lewis 1982). This approach is inappropriately tied to evolutionary and biological concepts through the ethological tradition, and specifically through attachment theory. This leads to a tendency to lapse into biological explanations of similarities (of e.g. gender-specific ways of relating to neonates) and differences. Observational research assumes that the act of observation does not change what it observes, a view even theoretical physics has revised, while human indeterminacy is of a different order still. In particular, the extent to which observations conducted in homes reflect typical circumstances is questionable.

A little reflection on Clarke-Stewart's (1982) widely cited account of complementary patterns and roles offered by mothers and fathers shows that a range of other possible interpretations can be put forward. In the first instance, it is difficult to sustain such global generalisations when the style and amount of parent (both mother and father) and child interaction varies according to the child's age and gender. Lewis (1982) reports work suggesting that what parents think the study is about affects how they interact with the child: if they think the research topic is play, they play more with the child. If they think it is investigating language they will talk more with her. In determining whether such observations constitute 'objective' measures of typical behaviour we have to consider how the parents construe the investigation.

Alternative readings of the finding that mothers interact less with their child when the father is at home might be that a mother sees it as an opportunity for him to be with the child, or that she knows that she will be observed by the researcher at some other time (during the day), or that she knows that the researcher is interested in father–infant interaction, or even that she is tired from looking after the child all day. This could also explain the report of different styles of play exhibited by mothers and fathers respectively. Mothers who have done, or know they are going to do, childcare all day may have less energy to engage in the 'rough and tumble' in which fathers are reported to indulge. While these multiple readings highlight the indeterminacy of infant action, and ambiguity of so-called 'observations' (Bradley 1989), there is some support for the last interpretation from Pedersen *et al.*'s (1982) study which reports that employed mothers played more with their children than mothers at home. This highlights how developmental psychological explanations can essentialise social differences arising from gender roles and inequalities through treating the knowledge-generating procedures of the discipline as neutral, context-free descriptions. Yet as we have seen, parents are now observed and assessed more than ever.

The poverty of the psychology of paternal care

To summarise so far, the limitations of theorising about mother care have correspondingly been exported to accounts of paternal involvement in childcare. There are three forms this has taken. First, there is the inclusion model which assimilates fathering to mothering. The second position asserts the 'equal but different' complementarity of maternal and paternal roles, an account which falls into biologically pre-given sexual divisions. The third approach investigates role reversals, circumstances where men stay at home and look after their children while women work. As we have seen, not only is this a rather restricted representation of departures from traditional childcare and family arrangements, but it also reasserts the normative status of the roles it deviates from, through the very discourse of role reversal which constitutes the reversed forms as an aberration.

As we have seen, the impoverished range and atheoretical quality of fathering research can be seen as arising from both the methods used and the motivations which prompted the research questions (Richards 1982). Research on fathers has developed in response to the feminist attack on psychology for both its exclusive preoccupation with mothers and its support for the idea that childcare is only women's concern, and it also reflects the increasing (attention to the) involvement of men in childcare. In addressing these challenges, developmental psychological work has simply extended mothering to include fathering in a wholesale way without engaging in theoretical adjustments, reflections or reformulations.

This review may seem all the more surprising given the current industry of publishing around men and masculinities. Thus it is not that men are absent, but rather that there is a divided model of fathering that accords fathers mothering qualities (Lewis and Lamb 2003) or else pathologises them as violent or abusive – another case of the research and representation dynamic of 'normalised absence/pathologised presence' identified by Phoenix (1987).

Involved fathers: media myth?

Whatever their role in developmental psychology, fathers have certainly come to figure more prominently in popular culture. But the extent to which this greater representation actually provides or supports changed roles for men as fathers is unclear. Betty Parsons' book *The Expectant Father* (1983) discusses the impact of a partner's pregnancy for men's lives in terms of learning to tolerate meals not being ready on time and surfaces not quite as polished as usual – scarcely indicating a more equitable division of domestic responsibilities. The fact that the UK magazine *Parents*, for example, addresses most of its articles to mothers casts doubt on the gender neutrality of its title, although this may well be a reflection of its readership. In the late 1980s childcare magazines started to include articles on or about fathers, but often in ways which confirmed men's peripheral role. While the September 1989 issue of *Parents* boasted a feature on fathers, this turns about to be a fashion spread of men and children who have been whisked off to a department store; the September 1989 issue of *Practical Parenting* carried an article on 'How to turn your man into a father' which is full of useful tips and tricks on luring him into the nursery, serving thereby to reaffirm both his reluctance and his marginal position, and constituting her as somehow already endowed with childcare knowledge. This is not to deride the positive aspects of acknowledging and supporting men's contributions, but the patronising tone often does more to emphasise traditional roles than to encourage change. Indeed the media predilection for depicting man with babies typically refers more to men's earning capacity or proprietorial relations over, rather than emotional involvement with, children by advertising cars or bank accounts (Burman 1991). Even that quintessential 1980s–1990s *Three Men and a Baby* series of Hollywood films (based on a French film of 1985, *Trois Hommes et un Couffin*) works to confirm men's ignorance and culturally sanctioned incompetence. At a more serious level, it is worth attending to how the resort to gender roles may be an important defensive response to the massive anxieties and uncertainties of caring for a new baby. Men may experience this as a threat to their rationality, with the loss of control over their lives damaging their masculinity, while their peripheral status is often confirmed by the promotion of breastfeeding as being best for babies:

> Gender differentiated discourses can be almost clung to at particular times of tension of anxiety but in the case of mothers can be also a major source of anxiety themselves. For example, the notion that 'mothers know best instinctively' can be a source of comfort for men faced with a crying baby and their inability to comfort it, but this can in turn be a major anxiety for the mother unable to quieten the crying baby.
>
> (Featherstone 2006: 308)

Moreover, despite the increasing attention to, and representation of, men with children, the extent to which this is actually reflected in changed childcare roles has been questioned. If the 'new man' is a media construction, it is now being accompanied by, or replaced by, the 'new lad', the militantly reconstructed male chauvinist (Kershaw 1991; O'Hagan 1991) or even the 'wild man' who seeks reconnection with powerful masculine mentors and models (Bly 1991). Even where 'role reversals' have been documented, the endurance of such arrangements is fragile. Russell's (1987) follow-up of his original (1983) study reports the families drifting back to the more conventional division of gender roles. Even where parental leave and benefits for infant and childcare are not gender specified, as is the case in Sweden, Sandkvist (1987) suggests that inertia and reluctance of both men and women to forgo traditional sources of identity (and privilege) mean that these measures are not widely taken up. Moreover, this trend has been confirmed nearly 20 years later (Haavind and Magnusson 2005a, 2005b). Further, studies of unemployed men in industrialised societies who are in a position to assume equal or even primary responsibility for childcare suggest that this rarely occurs. With work traditionally so central to cultural definitions of masculinity, both unemployed men and their wives seem to regard responsibility for childcare and housework as too great a threat to male gender identity (Morris 1987). Where women take on the role as primary wage earner in the event of their partner's unemployment, some recent work (Wheelock 1990) suggests that housework and childcare can be more equitably shared, but systems of state benefits combined with women's low rates of pay often make it uneconomical for women to engage in paid work. Even in dual-earner families when men do participate in, and express commitment to, equal household and childcare work, it is widely reported that women do the work of remembering and planning what there is to do, and women are more likely to take time off work when children are ill than their male partners (e.g. Horna and Lupri 1987; Lewis and Cooper 1991).

The early twenty-first century TV hit show *Wife Swap* puts gender and marital relations under scrutiny, perhaps even more than the panoply of *Supernanny* or *House of Tiny Tearaways* genre of programmes that succeeded it. But at the same time as it portrayed domestic labour and marital commitment as negotiable, it also (by its title) confirmed women as not only exchange objects but also as associated with the home. Moreover, this series reproduced dominant discourse on the family in at least four ways: first, in its heteronormativity – presuming a definition of the family as heterosexual and married (and with children). Second, in its portrayal of class and relative wealth as mere individual variations, this perpetuates strategies of individualisation, abstraction and exoneration of state responsibility. It thereby positioned the family as the site of (and therefore responsible for) social change. Third, it echoed contemporary neoliberalism: once class inequalities could be individualised, then money becomes something to manage, as a given – rather than a matter to object to or demand. Moreover, its personalised emphasis gave rise to dilemmas in imagining or prefiguring change. For how could it show that things can be different without getting into (victim-)blaming? A more radical approach might have engaged with the relationships between gender and feminisation, uncoupling gender from gender roles, to ask: is a 'wife' necessarily a woman?

Do families need fathers?

The psychological and social policy answer to this question is increasingly an emphatic 'yes', for current social policy agendas on active citizenship call for greater responsibility and involvement from fathers as well as mothers (although it seems that mothers may have little need for being accorded further responsibilities). There are however significant policy ambiguities, as indicated by the fact that the UK now provides paid paternity leave, but no longer supports men to accompany partners to antenatal clinics. It is easy to point to economic factors structuring such measures. Indeed, as Lister (2006) points out, flexibility seems to be required more of the family than of employers. British social policy has for some years attempted to enforce paternal involvement in financial terms, as indicated by the spectacularly unsuccessful and unpopular Child Support Agency (which tried to force men defaulting on maintenance arrangements to pay up). But this required separated mothers and fathers to engage in what were often unwanted negotiations, and so could work to pressurise and coerce mothers more, whilst in fact little extra income was gained from it.

Fathers' rights movements from the 1990s came to prominence over the 'memory wars', which not only concerned a backlash to certain institution-alised forms of feminisms enshrined in some (sometimes rather questionable) therapeutic practices (Haaken 1998). They also reflected increasingly contested discourses of paternal authority, as an effect of the historical exclusion of men from child rearing and childcaring. Some fathers' rights groups were clearly fronts for, or offered support to, fathers accused of having abused their daughters, and others explicitly appropriated a discourse of children's rights as an antifeminist strategy. So, for example, the Canadian Children's Rights Council, a fathers' rights group, usurped the acronym of the Canadian Coalition on the Rights of the Child. Yet this phenomenon cannot be dismissed as just this.

How can we understand this recent revival of parental interest in children? Featherstone (2006), drawing on Jenks's (1996) sociological analysis, suggests that children may now have come to represent love and certainty for fathers:

> Children, in a period where partners come and go, are seen not so much as promise but as primary and uncontested sources of love in 'the most fundamental, unchosen, unnegotiated form of relationship' (Jenks 1996: 107). . . . Fathers' increasingly vociferous calls for rights in relation to contact could partly be read in this context as a yearning for stability that cannot be attained easily elsewhere, or indeed may be fuelled by feelings of insecurity in relation to other areas of their lives.
>
> (Featherstone 2006: 309)

In the UK, fathers' rights groups have attempted to draw attention to their claims by demonstrating outside Parliament in September 2004 dressed in superhero costumes, interrupting the 2006 Wimbledon Tennis championships by streaking naked on to the pitch, and perhaps most bizarrely of all in December 2005 (at least being rumoured to have) plotted to abduct the son of the then British premier, Leo Blair. At the very least, what these antics indicate are the limited roles available to men to demonstrate their claims to involvement. It is certainly significant that their complaints concern government policy (on contact arrangements) as much as being directed towards feminist groups. Indeed current social policy analysts concur that there has been a divided focus on fathers that somehow distinguishes between men (as social problems) and fathers (as supportive and nurturing presences).

Men behaving badly

In their review, Scourfield and Drakeford (2002) note how British government policy currently works according to an affective and gender-stratified split. While the policy addresses women's employment outside the home optimistically, it deals pessimistically with women's role within the family. Conversely, while men's employment is treated pessimistically, their fathering role is presented positively. Each affective orientation structures a different approach to policy – optimism leads to facilitative policy, pessimism to authoritarian policy. But this positive view of involved fathers, with corresponding measures to promote the involvement of fathers, has been produced separately from policies addressing domestic violence:

It would appear that fathers should be engaged with and their involvement in families encouraged, whilst those who are involved in domestic violence are to be punished through the criminal justice system. There appears to be a failure to appreciate that the categories of father and domestic violence perpetrator may not be discrete.

(Featherstone 2006: 301)

Thus the raft of measures introduced to promote paternal involvement can in some cases endanger rather than support women and children. Contact arrangements have been identified as coercing women into unwanted communication with abusive partners, and presenting opportunities for the further abuse of both mother and children (and in some cases even abduction; Radford *et al.* 1999; Aitkenhead 2006). This divided thinking is reflected in the more general bifurcation of the representation of men: men as violent and men as vulnerable. But recent initiatives have highlighted these categories as connected, rather than mutually exclusive – showing the links between the destructive and self-destructive behaviour of men. Indeed the mental and physical health vulnerabilities of young men have come into policy focus – as most likely to be subject to physical attack in urban contexts and least likely to admit to being depressed or anxious. Yet once again the possible connections and consequences for young fathers remain less specified – especially since government policy on sex education in schools subscribes to an 'immaculate conception' model that all but removes the male and treats sexuality as equivalent to pregnancy, or rather how to avoid it (David *et al.* n.d.; Stronach *et al.* 2007). So, on a number of different fronts, the image of the indestructible, self-sufficient and violent man is shifting towards a more vulnerable, if ineffectual, model of masculinity.

Researching and interpreting paternal involvement

The difficulties in conducting and interpreting research on fathers' involvement in childcare provide important lessons that have a wider significance for developmental psychological practice. In a significant review, Lorna McKee (1982) criticised the widespread use of survey methods, highlighting the problems in analysing 'frequency data' based on standardised questions. These take as relevant only a narrow range of tasks, ignoring the permeation and interplay between childcare and housework. Second, different tasks are treated as if they are equivalent, thus rendering it impossible to assess whether, for example, one parent tends to change nappies more than another, or treating playing with the child as if it were of equal significance with bathing her. Studies often fail to take sufficient account of the age of the child when assessing extent of paternal involvement, not taking into account how differences within parental roles and contributions may be specific to a particular age range of the child, for example, if mothers are breastfeeding. Moreover, most research is based on mothers' accounts of their partners' involvement, thus posing a number of interpretational anomalies. Not only may what is said be different from what is done, but also class and 'race' differences enter into what is likely to be reported. While working-class men have traditionally played a much larger role in assuming childcare and household responsibilities (because their wives have had to work), they are much less likely to admit to this (Lumnis 1982). Similarly, working-class black women are documented as more likely to be employed than black men. Equally, Brannen and Moss (1987) suggest that women's uncritical and contradictory descriptions of their partners' roles may arise from ambivalence about gender and work roles which lead them to overestimate men's contributions.

Research on fathers can throw light on more far-reaching and often unquestioned research practices. Investigating parental practice has usually involved women being assessed, observed and interviewed by male researchers, or by female researchers authorised by male-dominated institutions. In their study of lone fathers, O'Brien and McKee (1983) inadvertently departed from the power relations structured within more typical research. They reported that the fathers seemed to have difficulty being placed in the subordinate position of being interviewed, and particularly being interviewed by women. The men employed various strategies to challenge the researchers' authority, ranging from refusing to address the questions, to treating the interview as a counselling session or even in some cases as an opportunity for sexual overtures and harassment. The disjunction between gender and research relations within this study provides insight, through their divergence, into the power dynamics within more typical developmental research (and the same dynamic emerged in a more recent study, Taylor 1995). Where power relations of gender and research roles converge (as when male interviewers interview women), the specificity of each may be obscured. Beyond highlighting interviewees' capacity to resist and define alternative agendas within the research, what this study illustrates, then, is that developmental psychology cannot treat the research relationship as having no impact on the research outcome, and that the gender of both researched and researcher plays a relevant structural role. When, as in this case, a study is set up in an unfamiliar way, we become aware of the factors influencing more familiar studies. If this study draws attention to power relations in research because the dynamics of power were no longer coincident, what implications does this have for other work in which the power of the researcher is so multiply structured as to have passed unexamined? In particular, the designation of the prototypical childcarer as female, the child as masculine and the psychological researcher as masculine can no longer be regarded as arbitrary or innocent.

Moreover, there are implications of this analysis for the dynamics of service provision. For while the gender-neutral terminology disguises how most welfare professionals are women and most child abusers are men, service providers' fears of violent men have undoubtedly contributed to their focus on women, even though this may stigmatise and problematise the women further (Daniel and Taylor 2006; Scourfield 2006). Moreover, there are gendered patterns of help seeking arising from the differential tolerance of fathers' and mothers' ambivalence. Indeed the increasingly sacred value accorded to childhood renders expressions of maternal ambivalence more problematic (Parker 1997), while gendered patterns of disclosure of 'worry' may well be further emphasised by prevailing gendered norms around the display of concern: 'In the interests of performing "good" motherhood, for example, women rather than men may have much more invested in worrying about their children, and in describing that concern to an interviewer' (Featherstone 2006: 308).

Engendering children, engendering parenthood

What issues of general significance emerge from the study of fatherhood? The critique of the reliance on observational methods can be taken further as conveniently reflecting a fantasy of researcher detachment that avoids having to address the emotional complexity of the researcher's own reactions and ambivalences around children and childcare (Richards 1982). The inadequacy of extrapolating a model of emotional attachment from mothers to fathers raises questions about its suitability as a general model to characterise the diversity of mothers' (as well as others') relationships with children. The attention to the power relations structured within, and sometimes infringed by, research relationships indicates the necessity for the researcher to be located clearly within the research enterprise, both in terms of the construction of the research material and its account.

Finally, the evaluation of parental roles and practice should promote a reconceptualisation of the definitions and relationships between mothers, fathers and children. Different parenting practices give rise to different children; definitions of childhood exist in relation to those of gender and gendered arrangements. Attention to the variability of these definitions invites a number of implications. The current focus on children's rights can work to further infantilise or confirm infantilisation of women by promoting children's rights over women's. The purported development of new forms of masculinity that emphasise caring and sensitivity can also reassert in new guise much more traditional patriarchal themes where men are portrayed as supplanting, rather than sharing with, women (Burman 1995a). From this it is clear we need to see definitions of children, mothering and fathering as interconnected. But it is also necessary to see these as separable so that the categories do not collapse into one another (see also Burman in press d). Such analysis of the diversity and relational character of childhoods contrasts with the universalised description of 'child' and 'children' that (as in the influential UK policy document *Every Child Matters*,

DfES 2003) continues to frame policy. Featherstone (2006) notes how the failure to attend to gender has led to gaps within both British social policy and service provision (see also Franklin 1999; Daniel *et al.* 2005).

However, with the rise of attention to children's rights, children's own views of their parents and parental relationship are now emerging within psychology. For example, Frosh *et al.*'s (2002) study of young schoolboys illuminates the hopes and disappointments about their fathers held by some boys, whilst also generating new methodological approaches to bring the emotional and gendered complexities of the researcher/researched relationship into analytic view. A new literature is now emphasising generative fathering, that demonstrates both overlapping and distinct positions for fathers (Hawkins and Dollahite 1997; Hobson 2002; Guishard-Pine 2006). Another recent study investigates men's fatherhood journeys, focusing on process and meaning (Henwood and Proctor 2003).

Separations and connections

The 1991 North American film *The Hand that Rocks the Cradle* (dir. Curtis) is more concerned with portraying the dire consequences that follow when a woman departs from her rightful role as full-time wife and mother (the central character almost loses the love of both her baby and husband) than with addressing the real changes in the distribution of affectional relations that accompany shared childcare and more equal forms of parenting. The film is about the disasters that befall a family who employ a nanny to look after their two children. The woman whom they choose (who turns out to hold this family responsible for the loss of her own) is consumed by such obsessional jealousy that she attempts to murder the wife and replace her in both the husband's and children's affections. The popularity of the film indicates its expression of widespread fears and phantasies set in circulation at a time when more women than ever are seeking to change traditional childcare arrangements through crèches, childminders, nannies (i.e. primarily through the employment of women) or shared childcare between men and women. Indeed a 2006 Children Survey of Great Britain listed a catalogue of complaints about the expense and lack of flexibility of the interface between employment and childcare, while 75 per cent of mothers employing nannies report that 86 per cent worry that their child is closer to the nanny than they are (Attewill and Butt 2006).

While increased paternal participation in childcare indicates a challenge to the psychic patterning of traditional parenting relationships, the cultural representation of this, as exemplified in this film, is in terms of the very traditional theme of women competing for the love of men and children, rather than in terms of the changed responsibilities of men. In terms of the film genre, all that is new about this is the addition of 'tug of love' over children within the more typical narrative of seduction and (in)fidelity. But the anxiety generated by sharing childcare and the emotional investments made by *all* the carers (i.e. not just the parents) are clearly very current preoccupations. These more complex issues have been rarely considered within the developmental psychological literature.

Similarly, the (1992) film *Falling Down* (dir. Schumacher) plots the disintegration of a white working-class man from family man to gun-crazed maniac, as the structures that comprise his life and livelihood successively disappear. Without job, wife and friends – even without his car – he is an alienated subject in an uncaring world. All that remains is his rage, racism and misogyny. The man thwarted from coming home to his daughter's birthday celebration ends up in a bloodbath of his own making. The challenge posed by this iconic 1990s film is to resist merely dismissing this character as inherently evil or flawed. Rather we can see this film as depicting a crisis in white, working-class US masculinity which connects themes of fatherhood with other societal challenges in the form of unemployment and challenge to his self-esteem predicated on subscription to white supremacy. One lesson from this film is that citizenship does not guarantee inclusion. The ruthless and alienating urban post-industrial culture that made him and has disposed of him finally triggers the unravelling of a particular form of white masculinity with tragic results (while the relationship between exclusionary forms of citizenship, militarised masculinity and the evacuation of an ethic of care is taken up vividly in Cuarón's 2006 dystopic film *Children of Men*).

Fiction became political scandal in the UK with the demise of David Blunkett, first in November 2004 as Home Secretary, then in October 2005 as Minister for Work and Pensions. With his tabloid-style soundbite 'What I was prepared to sacrifice, for that little boy' (quoted in *Guardian*, 16 December 2004), Blunkett joined the ranks of other (male) cabinet ministers who resigned supposedly to 'devote quality time' to their families (only to return a few years later to greater – if not long-term – power, as with his successor Charles Clarke). Blunkett's passion for paternal commitment was, however, generated by the termination of his relationship with his putative son's mother. It was a matter of some irony that the legal measures he took to claim this child was 'his' (via DNA test) in fact established that he was not the boy's biological father. This case was not only revealing of how an appeal to emotions could now be legitimate rhetorical tactics in British politics, but was also indicative of a new discourse of involved fatherhood that could be invoked to exonerate dereliction of (political) duty. But his appeal was compelling: 'What sort of human being, what sort of politician do people want? [Someone] who would actually put their career, put their public persona before actually doing what a decent human being would want to do?' (*Guardian*, 16 December 2004).

The last three chapters have explored the representation of contexts and caring relationships within developmental psychology. Not only has the 'discipline' been shown to promote and inform popular and professional practice in families and childcare, but its research practices also both reproduce and obscure social inequalities within the deep structure of its knowledge production processes. Five key themes have emerged from our story so far, and will arise again in slightly different forms in later parts of this book. The first of these concerns the way in which the investigation of action and interaction in developmental psychology has been structured by the technology – of testing, of observation, of measurement in general. The demand to provide standardised, quantifiable measures produces or constructs the research object as abstracted from social relations.

Second, the primary focal object of developmental psychological intervention (and its associated panoply of practices) has historically been not children, but mothers – or rather 'the mother'. Here we can note that it is significant that the limitations of the paradigms investigating adult–child relations are attaining recognition only when they are being applied to men. Just as *The Hand that Rocks the Cradle* displaced a struggle between men and women for the love of children into a competition between women (primarily over a man), and *Wife Swap* conflates gendered models of domestic labour with mothering, so we can see how the evaluation and objectification of women through the regulation of mothering produces women as subjects as well as objects.

Third, as earlier chapters have argued, these discourses of regulation rely upon assumptions about the relevance of evolutionary theory to human populations in more or less overt ways.

Fourth, as was discussed in more detail in Chapter 7, behind the scientific objectivity that structures developmental psychological research lies a set of phantasies of control that betray legacies of fear and insecurity at the same time as derogating women's designated powers of mothering. Here psychoanalytic theorising has something to offer in excavating what is passed over, or absent, within psychology: in this sense psychoanalysis is the repressed other of psychology.

Fifth, the abstraction of 'the child' and 'the family' as the units of analysis within developmental psychology reflects a failure to theorise the conditions that give rise to the psychology of the context that they inhabit, and in particular makes possible victim-blaming explanations where mothers are treated as responsible, for example, for the outcome of the distress caused by poverty.

So far in this book we have been dealing with accounts of children's early development and relationships. But contexts of care are, within current developmental discourses, inseparable from those of communication and education. The rest of this book takes up these issues to focus on areas generally characterised as language and cognitive development.

Further reading

Cabrera, N., Tamis-LeMonda, C., Bradley, R., Hofferth, S. and Lamb, M. (2000) 'Fatherhood in the twenty-first century', *Child Development*, *71*, *1*: 127–136.

Featherstone, B. (2006) 'Why gender matters in child welfare and protection', *Critical Social Policy*, 26, 2: 294–314.

Frosh, S., Phoenix, A. and Pattman, R. (2002) *Young Masculinities*, London: Palgrave.

Henwood, K. and Proctor, J. (2003) 'The "good father": reading men's accounts of paternal involvement during the transition to first-time fatherhood', *British Journal of Social Psychology*, 42: 337–355.

Hobson, B. (ed.) (2002) *Making Men into Fathers: Men, Masculinities and the Social Politics of Fatherhood*, Cambridge: Cambridge University Press.

Robb, M. (2004) 'Exploring fatherhood: masculinity and intersubjectivity in the research process', *Journal of Social Work Practice*, 18, 3: 395–406.

Suggested activities

Collect together a selection of contemporary images of men from magazines, advertisements, newspaper articles and childcare literature, and consider:

- what gender-relevant qualities they reflect
- the extent to which the current focus on men constitutes a reiteration of or a transition from traditional gender themes
- what relation is being posited between the model of child and the model of man
- what tensions and contradictions does the current imagery betray?

Part III

Developing communication

A concern with methodological issues combines with conceptual and political problems in discussions of language development, with Chapter 9 focusing on the theoretical burden carried by accounts of language, Chapter 10 investigating claims for a specific language code that promotes language learning and Chapter 11 moving beyond the discussion of difference and variability to draw attention to power as a structural dimension of developmental psychological research.

9   Language talk

[L]inguistic diversity is an asset. It provides an opportunity for pupils to gain firsthand experience, knowledge and understanding of other cultures and perspectives. It also helps to prepare pupils for life in a multicultural society by promoting respect for all forms of language. Variety of language is a rich resource which schools should use as they implement the National Curriculum.

> (*Linguistic Diversity and the National Curriculum*, circular 11, National Curriculum Council, March 1991)

David Pascal, the [National Curriculum] council chairman has signalled that he not only expects teachers to correct children who fail to use Standard English in any lesson or in the playground, but also that they should use Standard English when talking to each other.

> (*Guardian*, 1 April 1993)

We need to know much more about the skills and knowledge of bilingual teachers, in order to contribute to defining the 'new agenda' which is presently being written about equal opportunities and 'multicultural education' in twenty-first century Britain. Such knowledge will not only be valuable in multilingual classrooms, it will help to prevent the new ideologies of 'cohesion' and 'inclusion' and citizenship', with their possibly dangerous assimilationist tendencies, from becoming the new racisms of the education system.

> (Conteh with Hussain and Rehman 2004: 14)

Research on language is one of the most vibrant and theoretically dynamic areas in developmental psychology. The process of children learning to talk, of entering language, poses in miniature the wider questions of social development. Moreover, some critical psychologists (and those in other disciplines) look to these developmental psychological accounts as the route to elaborate a socially and materially based theory of mind. As we shall see, the research does not always live up to this expectation. In failing to do justice to the variety and complexity of what it means to talk, not only does the research reproduce the familiar division between individual and social that it sets out to transcend, but it also maintains social and educational inequalities. This chapter reviews the forms which research on early language development has taken, focusing particularly on current functional approaches, and raises problems with these traditions. As we shall see, the same themes identified in Parts I and II about the relations between the structuring of developmental psychology and the regulation of families arise in particular ways within child language research.

Turning to language

The 'turn to language' within the social and human sciences brought about an attention to issues of interpretation. Social constructionists such as Harré, Shotter and Gergen challenged positivist psychology to recognise the constructed basis of its 'data' by focusing on the accounting procedures of both psychologists and their research 'subjects' (Harré 1983). But, paradoxically, while these developments precipitated a 'crisis' in social psychology (Parker 1989), they have brought new credibility and invigoration to developmental psychology: social psychology's 'crisis' has boosted developmental psychology's status and profile. Now, as a new variant of the developmental myth (which sees what comes earlier as causally related to later events), psychology looks to parent–child communication in the hope of finding a solid grounding for social relations. As we shall see, in a bizarre way, in portraying adult–child interaction as the prototypical forum from which to elaborate psychological theories of social relations, social constructionism has thus brought about a new respect for empirical developmental psychology, with little reflection on the contexts and assumptions of its production. While this pretends to provide a socially and materially based model of psychology, it actually legitimates inadequate and oppressive psychological theories.

At the outset we should note that typical textbook accounts of developmental psychological child language research have not reflected the preoccupations of the recent research literature. They describe the sequence from babbling to the emergence of the first words, to the use of single word and gesture combinations to convey sentence-like meaning ('holophrases') and the emergence of condensed word combinations that display a rudimentary or 'telegraphic' grammatical structure. However, a restricted analysis of the role of language emerges from these accounts. If acquisition of language is taken to mark the graduation from infancy into early childhood, the role of language as the constitutive medium for the rest of development is ignored, or at best underplayed. As a topic, therefore, language appears within textbook chapters or subsections on early childhood as if, once they have 'cracked the linguistic code', children's language learning consists of a simple accumulation of grammar and vocabulary. Seen in this way, the significance of language is limited and static. This view suppresses attention to language development (after all what is it that develops?), and divorces language from its contexts of use. It also fails to theorise qualitative shifts in the structure and use of language in later childhood (such as those arising from becoming literate), and it ignores variations in use arising from social positions and relations. Variation therefore becomes identified with departures from a standard, a standard which is itself a false construction.

Foundations and formalities

In part the preoccupation with acquisition derives from the legacy of both biological and structuralist approaches to language. In many respects the difficulty of locating language development research in relation to other disciplines instantiates the general problem of the place of developmental psychology. Explanations put forward for language and its course of development draw upon neurology, biology, linguistics, history, sociology and anthropology – to name a few. Rather than choose between competing explanations, as in most of the language debates, a more appropriate question is to resolve what it is developmental psychological accounts of language seek to explain. If we are interested in the specific patterns individual children exhibit in learning to talk, then no single theory or disciplinary model will suffice, nor can they simply be combined in an additive way.

Chomsky's structural analysis of language emphasised the creativity and generativity of (children's) language use which, he argued, could not arise from mere imitation of linguistic role models. Chomsky distinguished between the surface structure of the grammatical features of specific languages and (what he called) the deep structure of what he regarded as a universal grammar that underlies and is presupposed by all languages. It is this deep structure that, according to Chomsky, makes possible the acquisition of specific languages through transforming or realising the universal deep structure into a specific linguistic form. But Chomsky treated the child as a separate, isolated symbol manipulator, making it so difficult to envisage how the momentous achievements of language could occur that he invoked an innate mechanism (a Language Acquisition Device) to account for it. His claims that this was biologically pre-programmed and was specific to language have been challenged on both counts (see below). Most developmental psychology textbooks (including those reviewed in Chapter 4) outline Chomsky's (1959) critique of Skinner as the specific form in which the heredity and environment debate over language development has been played out.

What Chomsky offered was a formal model of the structure of language. He was not, however, suggesting that this could be taken as a psychological account of how children learn to talk. This conceptual confusion, made within much developmental psycholinguistic research, is tantamount to a

variety of psychological essentialism, whereby form is treated as (an empirically investigable) property of mind. As Michael Silverstein (1991) notes:

> Noam Chomsky has himself frequently been at pains to point out the
> incoherence of assuming that the formalist 'linguistic organ', to repeat
> his metaphor, has anything to do, in realtime psychological processual
> terms, with language production/comprehension as studiable by
> empirical means of observational and laboratory psychology. Yet, of
> course many others have . . . attempted to study linguistic competence,
> or its development in children, by direct means without understanding
> the cluster of commitments that place such competence, as a conceptual
> construct, beyond the realm of the normal evidentiary modalities of
> psychology.
>
> (Silverstein 1991: 151–152)

His argument is therefore that formal models of language structure have no
direct bearing on the understanding of how children develop and exhibit
these features, and the attempt to base a psychological investigation on this
conceptual foundation appears misconceived (see also Sinha 1989).

Increasing awareness of the limitations of formal, structural models of
language has prompted the emergence of approaches which focus on the
functions of language in context. But before we join the rush from structural to functional approaches (which themselves retain elements of these
problems), we should recall that the problem is not formalism in itself but
rather it is psychologists' failure to appreciate the limits of its applicability.
What structuralist accounts do offer is an analysis of the specificity of
language as a representational system which goes beyond mere substitution
for, or reference to, objects to set up new possible domains of meanings.
They pave the way for according language a privileged status as a conventionally agreed, public, symbolic system which not only represents but
also communicates (and, social constructionists would add, constitutes)
meaning. Moreover, regularities noted in the structure of language learning
across cultures may be due to communicative universals rather than biology. Specific and less helpful legacies of Chomsky's work include a focus
on structure rather than context and the separation of language from
general communicative processes.

Actions speak louder than words: from structure to function

Critics of the formal, structural models of language and their associated
claims of innateness treat the emergence of language as having continuities
with non-linguistic developments, also highlighting prelinguistic precursors
to language. By these accounts, meaning is not uniquely linguistic but arises
from action. This seems a more promising route for a more socially based
theory of individual language development. These so-called 'functional'

approaches, called functional because they focus on language use (rather than structure), draw on a number of theoretical resources which include aspects of the work of Piaget, Vygotsky and some influence of 'ordinary language' philosophy.

First, they refer to Piaget's (1953) account of sensorimotor cognition which relates communicative abilities to the development of more general cognitive structures and changes. This draws attention to how language is a process of representation – that is, of symbolising or re-presenting something that is no longer present. Children's abilities to engage in purposive behaviour, understanding of cause–effect relations and means–end relations are all required for language (to want to communicate, to appreciate that words can produce effects and to use words as the tool to produce those effects, respectively). Hence it is argued that the entry into language draws on other representational abilities, such as deferred imitation (reproducing a behaviour in another context – which is required for the learning of words) and object permanence (maintaining a representation of an object without external stimulus – necessary for remembering the word label).

Second, accounts highlight how in learning to talk a child needs not only to use a particular label to refer to a particular object, but also to use conventional labels or words in order to participate in a language community. Language is, after all, not only a symbolic system, but, in order to function communicatively, its signs have to be shared and understood. Work like Carter's (1978) documents the route by which children initially exhibit variable vocalisations which are linked to specific gestures, and later come to use the same vocalisation no longer tied to a particular action. This conventionalisation of sounds relies on their increasing decontextualisation.

In tracing the specific continuities between activity and the emergence of language, Lock's (1978) analysis of the changing meaning and use of sounds and gestures suggests how they come to be increasingly separated from the action or event they initially accompanied, thus paving the way for their use as symbols. He illustrates this through the example of a child raising its arms. As a response that was once a simple association elicited by a wide variety of cues, this comes to function as a gesture which has some detachment from the immediate context of its exhibition, and ultimately functions not in simple anticipation of being, but as a *request* to be, picked up. In these terms, the developmental path is correspondingly seen as a move from intention to convention via the transition from action, to gesture, to symbol.

Third, accounts which highlight the emergence of language as arising within and from action emphasise how language is used to do things. The 'ordinary language' philosophy of Austin (1962) and Searle (1972) points out that language is not only used to name or label things, but also has non-descriptive functions (such as excusing or commanding) which constitute events, or 'speech acts', in themselves. When we speak we not only utter words, but in so doing our words constitute 'speech acts' and as such produce particular effects within the person(s) addressed, such as feeling pleased when being complimented (Austin 1962). Applied to early language development, this has been used to suggest that a complex social as well as linguistic knowledge is involved in learning to communicate. Learning to speak is also learning how to *mean* (Halliday 1975), with all the semantic and pragmatic, as well as syntactic, understanding this involves. In particular, Bates *et al.* (1979) suggested that this speech act model can inform the exhibition and interpretation of children's early language. Like their gestures, children's utterances are initially *treated* as intentional, that is, as intended to produce effects. By this kind of model, it is only later that children understand the use of vocalisation to affect the behaviour of others.

Useful as these functional approaches have been in moving away from idealised or context-free models of language, they nevertheless retain some of the latter's guiding assumptions which they simply supplement rather than revise. In particular, the mapping of linguistic form on to psycho-linguistic function and the failure to analyse the context of the production of the linguistic material under study invite the criticisms that they simply lapse into the same problems as exclusively formal models but in an inadvertent way. Moreover, the very term 'functionalist' harks back to an evolutionary framework that invokes biological (and social) adaptation and instrumentalism that is at odds with the ethos of most of this work. Concluding his critique of contemporary forms of 'functionalist developmentalism', Silverstein (1991) warns against the incoherence of a 'developmentalist "functionalism" mixed with non-developmental formalism' (Silverstein 1991: 152). He comments:

> The irony may be that, in contrast to the mysterious pre-experiential, *sui generis* formal structure of committed formalist developmentalism, 'functionalism' of this sort always seems to appeal to mysterious, pre-experimental formal-functional transparency, commonsense naturalness, and analogy.
>
> (Silverstein 1991: 179)

Hearing voices?

Emphasis on the emergence of language through activity, continuity of linguistic and prelinguistic development and the general character of the prerequisites for language as common to all representational processes sets the stage for broader discussions of the relationship between language and thought. This issue also connects with questions about the individual–society relation and the social construction of subjectivity. In particular, textbook coverage presents this in terms of the debate between Piaget and Vygotsky over the status of 'egocentric speech'.

Despite his tendencies towards formalism in other areas (which is itself a source of other problems, see Chapter 13; Rotman 1978), Piaget is called upon by functionalist child language researchers seeking to locate language within the context of child action and interaction. While his views on the status of language shifted over time and were sometimes contradictory (Flavell 1963), Piaget is generally seen as having regarded language as reflecting (rather than more actively constituting) more general cognitive and representational processes. In this his views differ from those of Chomsky: while for Chomsky language and thought are independent, Piaget's ideas are used to treat cognitive development as the precondition for language development. Development consists of individual action on the world which gives rise to cognitive structures and thus representation, including language. Language is therefore simply one of various representational systems.

In contrast, Vygotsky saw language as fundamentally communicative (rather than solely action oriented) and therefore social. Although importantly Piaget was an interactional as well as functional theorist, Vygotsky went beyond interactionism to put forward a dialectical model. Whereas Piaget privileged adaptation, Vygotsky emphasised transformation. Vygotsky theorised language and thinking as originating separately but as coming to control each other. Vygotsky focused on the cultural mediation of action that thus makes actions inherently and inevitably social, rather than simply influenced by society as in Piaget's account. So, rather than thought constituting language (an individualist, cognitive model), or language constituting cognition (a social determinist model), speech completes thinking:

> The structure of speech is not simply the mirror image of the structure of thought. It cannot, therefore, be placed on thought like clothes off a rack. Speech does not merely serve as the expression of developed thought. Thought is restructured as it is transformed into speech. It is not expressed but completed in the word. Therefore, precisely because of the contrasting directions of movement, the development of the internal and external aspects of speech forms a new unity.
>
> (Vygotsky 1987: 251, cited in Holzman 2006: 115)

As Cole and Cole put it in their Vygotskyan-informed textbook:

> In Vygotsky's framework, language allows thought to be individual and social at the same time. It is the medium through which individual thought is communicated to others while at the same time it allows social reality to be converted into the idiosyncratic thought of the individual. This conversion from the social to the individual is never complete, even in the adult, whose individual thought processes continue to be shaped in part by the conventional meanings present in the lexicon and speech habits of the culture.
>
> (Cole and Cole 1989: 296)

The two theorists offer correspondingly divergent interpretations of young children's speech. Piaget regarded young children's speech as egocentric, or unadapted to the communicative context. His model of the egocentric character of young children's thinking was based on his analysis of children's speech (Piaget 1926), and he treated egocentrism as an inability to take into account the perspective of, or interests of, others, which in turn confirmed his view of the unsocialised character of the child. By contrast, Vygotsky understood 'egocentric' (or self-directed) speech as functioning as an intermediary between activity and thought, as an external aid or prop to problem solving, that helps children to plan and direct their actions. In one celebrated example, a child who was drawing a picture of a car when the pencil broke commented 'It's broken' and went on to draw a broken car. Vygotsky interpreted this as indicating that egocentric speech had modified the course of the activity and therefore plays a more integral role: 'The child's accidentally provoked egocentric utterance so manifestly affected his activity that it is impossible to mistake it for a mere by-product, an accompaniment to interfering with the melody' (Vygotsky 1962: 17). Thought, far from existing separately from speech, is rather a development from it as 'inner speech':

> The older children in our experiments behaved differently from the younger ones when faced with obstacles. Often the child examined the situation in silence, then found a solution. When asked what he was thinking about, he gave answers that were quite close to the thinking-aloud operation of the pre-schooler. This would indicate that the same mental operations that the pre-schooler carries out through egocentric speech are already relegated to soundless inner speech in the schoolchild.
>
> (Vygotsky 1962: 17–18)

Bridges and byways

Vygotsky has been taken up by developmental psychologists largely due to increasing recognition of the abstracted and asocial character of Piaget's model. Indeed Vygotsky's ideas have also been claimed as part of a set of 'bridging disciplines' (along with social constructionism, cultural psychology and narrative approaches) connecting feminist thinking with developmental psychology (Miller and Kofsky Scholnick 2000a: 10). In some senses, the functions played by Vygotsky's work to warrant more 'social' accounts of development are not unlike those played by that of G.H. Mead. Put (over)simply, for Piaget development is from the 'inside out' – a movement away from non-verbal (what he called 'autistic') thinking, first to egocentrism and then to inner speech (as thought). In contrast, for Vygotsky development is from the 'outside in', that is, from the social to the individual. The individual is therefore the end rather than the starting point of the process of development. Thus for Vygotsky, thought and action are connected or mediated via language as an interactional and cultural tool. We will return to some of the educational implications arising from these differing views of the social. The key point for now is that they give rise to different conceptions of development: 'for Piaget, what develops is the individual child acting in the environment (other people not excluded), whereas for many of today's Vygotskian approaches what develops is the community and the patterns of participation in it or the mother–child dyad' (Vianna and Stetsenko 2006: 89).

As a Soviet developmental psychologist, albeit one very much in touch with and influenced by European psychology (Valsiner 1988), Vygotsky was working within a theoretical framework which challenged the individualism of Western psychology, and treated the individual as constructed through the social. Vygotsky's cultural-historical perspective emphasises the differential meanings and values of both biological and environmental factors according to the specific context, and here context is understood as including the historical development of culture (Vygotsky 1978a). This conception of culture as a 'living continuous flow of practices that stretch throughout history and are enacted by each generation of people' (Vianna and Stetsenko 2006: 89) is what connects Vygotsky to the Soviet tradition of Marxist psychology, and these ideas were developed further by Leontiev and Luria.

This emphasis on the socially mediated character of development contributes to Vygotsky's popularity with early social constructionists such as Harré and Shotter (e.g. Shotter 1973; Harré 1986; Cole and Cole 1989), and more recent postmodern commentators (Holzman 2006). The Vygotskyan notion of development as participation within 'communities of practice' has inspired much developmental and social psychological research, attending to specific cultural (including professional) settings (Rogoff 1990, 2003; Lave and Wenger 1991). Holzman (2006) highlights the radical potential of Vygotsky's approach for the transformation of the model of the thought–language relationship:

> Vygotsky's language completing thought ('thought completed in the word') presents an alternative to the dominant Western philosophical-linguistic-psychological paradigm, which rests on the assumption that language expresses thought. Vygotsky is not reversing the order of their relationship; he is rejecting the bifurcated interactionist view of language and thought and therefore doing away with the necessity of 'reconnecting' them, that is, he rejects the overdetermined and over-determining conception that language, denotes, names, represents and expresses. Language completing thought identifies language as socio-cultural relational activity.
>
> (Holzman 2006: 115–116)

Yet despite hopes of building a thoroughly social model of the individual, the full implications of Vygotsky's ideas have still not been reflected in developmental psychological theories (see also Daniels 2006). This is primarily due to the conservative readings of Vygotsky's work within English language psychology, which has tended to treat it largely as an educational technology. The Vygotskyan notion of 'zone of proximal development' (what a child can do with help as indicative of what she will shortly be able to do unaided) is typically interpreted in a narrow sense to inform theories of instruction (e.g. Newman *et al.* 1989; Crain 2005). Although it can be used in more radical ways (Newman and Holzman 1993), in part this exacerbates already existing trends within Vygotsky's work, due to the tendency to reduce the social world to the inter-individual, with its focus on small group, or dyadic, interaction. As James Wertsch (1991) comments: 'What is somewhat ironic for someone interested in formulating a Marxist psychology, he made precious little mention of broader historical, institutional, or cultural processes such as class struggle, alienation and the rise of commodity fetishism' (Wertsch 1991: 46). However, subsequent developments of his work, in activity theory, do take up this wider cultural-political perspective (e.g. Engestrom *et al.* 1999) to take up the study of development beyond contexts of early development and focus on the performative character and transformative possibilities of action and interaction (Holzman 1999; Holzman 2006).

The arguments about the limitations of infancy research made in Chapters 2 and 3 are just as relevant to discussions of child language research. As we shall see, theorists – whether philosophers, psychoanalysts or social constructionists – who see the roots of social life in the selective analysis of early caregiver–child interaction currently on offer therefore risk screening out some of the most important aspects of its contemporary organisation.

Game playing and routines

Together with the influence of Vygotsky, the work on precursors has led to a focus on the characteristics of action in which children are seen as embedded in that action as well as exhibiting it. The particular focus here has been on how adults support children's language learning. This includes the role of specific contexts in the promotion and support for children's early communication. The influence of these ideas is mainly felt in developmental psychology through Margaret Donaldson's (1978) notion of embedded thinking and 'human sense' and (explicitly drawing on Vygotsky's ideas) through Jerome Bruner's notion of 'scaffolding'. Bruner's work is the one which is best known in developmental psychology in the USA as well as Europe.

According to Bruner's conceptual framework, the scaffolding of early adult–child interaction originates in adults' attribution of communicative intention to the child, such that even young infants are treated as if they are conversational partners (Snow 1977). In addition, the structure of conversation is seen to be prefigured by the structure of rhythmic games many adults play with infants. These set up contingent patterns of inter-action which are held to involve, frame and structure the children's actions: from initially simply reacting to the game, the child begins to show antici-pation of, for example, being tickled, and finally starts initiating turns. The turn taking that Kaye (1982) saw within infant feeding (see Chapter 3) now takes on a key role in setting up the pragmatic structure of dialogue through the reciprocal roles set up by the alternation between speaker and hearer (Bruner 1975/6). This reversibility of roles is regarded as prerequisite to the use of deictic terms, that is those aspects of language that can be interpreted only in terms of the context of the speaker, such as 'this/that', 'here/there' and (especially important for communication) the pronouns 'I/you'. Joint activity, as the context in which early communicative inter-actions take place, forms the basis for joint reference or attention. This is indicated by mutual gaze, and from an early age the following and directing of gaze seems to be a reciprocal system (Scaife and Bruner 1975). Joint attention and action are said to pave the way for, and are mirrored by, the topic-comment structure that characterises children's earliest words, and this structure forms the building block for the subject-predicate structure of linguistic propositions (Bruner 1983). That these conventions are so firmly installed is illustrated by the recent youth culture insult 'Talk to the hand, 'cos the face ain't listening!': for it works as an insult precisely by virtue of its reversal of the norms of communication, in denying the attribution of subjectivity and intentionality – marked by mutual gaze and attention – to the addressee.

Functional continuities are therefore traced between the structure of adult–child activities and the conceptual demands presupposed by lan-guage. But not only are these continuities subject to the claims of implicitly harking back to formalism (as already reviewed), they are also rooted in the assumption that language learning lies in dyadic interaction. As Lieven (1994) points out, the idea that all language learning is a dyadic process is a very particular cultural construction that reflects the Eurocentric and class biases of child language research. While most children learn to talk in polyadic situations (interacting with more than one adult, and with other children), and this may play a much more active role in the process by which children pair utterances with meaning, child language research routinely screens out all language partners other than the mother and child (see, for example, the Hoff-Ginsberg quotation below). While there is little research on the effects of siblings on children's language, young chil-dren's language is more complex when their environment includes mother and an older sibling than when they are with mothers alone (Barton and Tomasello 1994).

Bruner uses terms like 'routines', 'formats' and 'scaffolding' to describe the regular and rule-bound patterns of caregiver–child interaction which, he claims, enable adults to mark important features of the action gesturally or vocally and eventually to induct children into doing so too. These forms establish familiar contexts within which children first exhibit initial babbling sounds, then more differentiated vocalisations and then standard lexical words. Within this account, play is central to language development, since games provide the context for joint activity with others and 'tension-free' opportunities for the exercise and exploration of abilities. Routines set up shared action formats with clear sets of expectations and actions. These in turn set up a restricted and shared set of meanings that can help to provide references to which more advanced communicative signals are attached.

The context of book reading has attracted particular attention as a valuable context for the teaching of vocabulary. Pictures in early reading books, as two-dimensional representations of three-dimensional objects, are regarded as aids to decontextualisation, and the instructional pattern of query, answer and feedback plus label exhibited by mother–child pairs is seen as a prototypical instructional process (Ninio and Bruner 1978). The value accorded to this activity has been extended to include not only other aspects of language development but also success in schooling (Tittnich *et al.* 1990; Rogoff 2003). But here we need to step back to reflect on the terms and claims being elaborated.

Labelling and name calling

Despite the widespread focus on reading as instantiating the principal properties for language teaching, there are difficulties in treating it as the ideal-typical model. In the first place, it is a highly specific activity which has a structure that is not characteristic of adult–child interaction elsewhere. Indeed it was selected *because* of its idealised presentation of labels. It seems that different caregiving contexts (feeding, bathing, playing with toys, reading) all give rise to different patterning of adult–child talk (Hoff-Ginsberg 1991). As Durkin (1987: 116) comments: 'Since language acquisition is universal and picture-book reading is culture specific, the causal potential of this situation is uncertain.'

Second, the priority accorded to play divorces language learning from other everyday caregiving contexts, and presents a sanitised and idealised picture of women at home with no commitments other than to devote themselves to extending their child's vocabulary. While child language research follows in the footsteps of the developmental tradition of observation, most work is based on intensive analysis of relatively few 'case' studies, in fact often taking the form of diary studies of the researchers' own children. But far from simply recording what happens in homes, early studies isolated the objects of study from their everyday contexts by excluding all parties other than mother and 'target' child, failing to document situations representative even of the participants. For example: 'Because the children in this study were too young and because the mothers did not work outside the home, their spending several hours together at home was not a contrived situation except for the occasional exclusion of an infant sibling who would otherwise have been present' (Hoff-Ginsberg 1991: 786).

Third, learning to talk is not the same as learning labels, for it has been suggested that children learn words and only later realise that words are names through the insight that actions name objects (McShane 1980). This therefore calls into question the exclusive importance accorded both to labelling and to the promotion of adult–child interaction around contexts said to aid label learning. This links up with the regulation of women through the extension of criteria for adequate childcare into educational provision (Walkerdine and Lucey 1989), exporting the discourse of 'sensitive mothering' from affective to educative domains (see also Chapter 12 for further examples). Rather, we should see the equation of language with naming as a reflection of the formalist emphasis on words as object names and on language as a referential activity, mapping concepts on to objects. What this does is to set up precisely the dualist division between language and thought that it aimed to resolve. Theoretically then this assumption harks back to the priority accorded to thinking by the philosopher Descartes, treating thought as private and divorced from language and social relations. It also presumes that language represents truths, rather than produces its own realities. In this sense the model of language on offer is profoundly and naively realist – unlike the constructionist and discourse analytic work emerging in social psychology (Parker 1992a; Burman and Parker 1993; Parker 1998; Nightingale and Crombie 1999; Parker 2002). Politically, the fetishism within child language research on language as object rather than relationship can be connected to broader analyses of commodity fetishism within capitalism. Communicative processes are reduced to words which are treated as utterances by individuals, abstracted from their relations of production. These words acquire value as indices not only of children's competence but also of caring and teaching mothers (see Chapter 10). Practically, this research pressurises children by treating vocabulary as the primary index of language development and oppresses families, and especially mothers, by demanding that they should devote themselves to accelerating this.

Fourth, the reduction of language development to labelling bleaches all emotions out of contexts of meaning construction. To the extent that developmental psychology subscribes to a representational theory of language, it imagines that emotions are irrelevant, and, where it does admit their importance, it allows only the 'nice' emotions through. In particular, accounts present an overharmonious view of parent–child interaction. Subtle mismatches are a routine and perhaps necessary feature of adult–child interaction. Mention has already been made in Chapter 8 of the differential evaluation of maternal and paternal communicational demands on children. Durkin (1987) cautions against the tendency of research to produce an idealised, sanitised representation of parent–child interaction. In a similar vein, Ben Bradley (Sylvester Bradley 1983; Bradley 1989, 1993) provides examples of the ways in which infant negativity and aggression are screened out of observational studies only to reappear as originating from the mothers. Using a Lacanian psychoanalytic framework, Urwin (1982, 1984) demonstrates how contexts of adult–infant play involve negotiations over and attributions of assertion and pleasure as well as identification:

> These playful interactions also provide the adult with occasions for playing with power and control, producing the baby as all-powerful one minute, and perhaps undercutting this the next, through breaking the baby's expectations, for example. In some instances the interactions may be highly erotic or sexualized. Here one would anticipate that the sex of parent and infant would produce differences, though not altogether predictable ones. The mother, for example, may conjure in fantasy the potential lover who controls or entices her, or project herself as the passive recipient of the desires of another, or as active and potent, a positioning which may not be available elsewhere. As for the baby in the mirror stage, these kinds of interactions act as a support to the adult's own narcissism. This is one of the reasons why relating to babies can be so pleasurable.
>
> (Urwin 1984: 294)

The variety of fantasies and positionings available within adult–infant interaction make it unlikely that this would be as consistent and stable as current formulations of functionalist-constructivist work assume:

> Much has been made of mothers 'interpreting' their baby's actions as if they signalled specific intentions or carried a particular meaning as an explanation for related changes in the babies' communications. . . . But by itself interpretation carries no magical properties. First . . . posing the problem in terms of meaning outside getting inside by-passes the issue of the infant's contribution. Second . . . one would anticipate that adults would normally show more inconsistency, more ambivalence, or contradiction than these studies seem to presume. For example, competing demands on the mother, her conscious and unconscious desires, will affect her subjective positioning and hence the particular discourse through which she reads the baby's behaviour at any one time.
>
> (Urwin 1984: 298)

Finally, this focus on play moves away from a functional to a competence model since it treats the child rather than the interaction as the unit of analysis, thus illustrating a tendency for socially mediated models to collapse into more traditional socio-cultural evaluation. The focus on conventionalisation and labelling can lead to a suppression of the multiple forms of variation. While class variation in child language and caregiver–child language is measured against norms which are themselves based on samples of white, middle-class mothers (Lieven 1994), nowhere is the selective and regulatory structure of research more evident than in its treatment of multilingualism.

Native tongues: making multilingualism puzzling

The linguist Suzette Elgin's (1985) science fiction novel *Native Tongue* draws attention to the relationship between language, embodiment, subjectivity and intersubjectivity. She explores these questions through the challenges posed for cross-species communication, challenges of the kind precisely foreclosed by mainstream cultural representations – such as the computer programmed 'universal translator' in *Star Trek* – which take language as a transparent medium and translation as providing a perfect match across languages, so erasing cultural differences. Yet these issues are recapitulated in different form via the study of multilingualism. Moreover, so assumed are the relationships between language, personal history and identity, as well as cultural assumptions about the gendered patterning of caregiving relationships, that it is easy not to notice how they are structured into such notions as 'mother tongue', and equally that one's 'native tongue' is not only the language one is most familiar with but is also often tied up with one's earliest relationships (connecting nature with nation) and closest to one's sense of 'self'.

There are two main questions thrown up by an attention to multilingual issues: the first is why it has been so absent from mainstream accounts and the second is why it has not been treated as a topic of interest rather than as a problem. In contrast to sociolinguistic work (e.g. Chaika 1982), there has been until recently an almost overwhelming assumption within accounts of early language development not only that this is unilinear, but also that children learn a single language. Books with titles like *A First Language* (Brown 1973) or the journal title *First Language* suggest that children learn to talk one language, or at least one language at a time. While accounts of language learning rarely now omit all mention of bilingualism or, especially, multilingualism, it typically appears as an extra chapter or 'issue' in a text. The editors of a volume on bilingual development comment on how little crossover there is between researchers with a particular interest in bilingualism and those working on language development (Homel *et al.* 1987). Bilingualism is effectively excluded from research as if it were a confounding variable, with studies littered with comments in sample sections or footnotes such as 'All of the participants were white, native speakers of English; all the families were monolingual' (Hoff-Ginsberg 1991: 785), and 'All were white, British-born two parent families' (McGuire 1991: 147), with no explanation about why or how the cultural background or family composition was relevant to the research aims. Moreover, multilingual issues often do not figure even in books specifically designed for an applied professional audience (e.g. Tittnich *et al.* 1990).

From this we might suppose that speaking more than one language is unusual. However, whatever the multiple forms and definitions of being multilingual (Baetens Beardsmore 1982), the majority of the world's population are bilingual or multilingual. Once again we see the Anglocentric samples of white, middle-class monolinguals – majorities within their own countries, but a fraction of the world's population – which form the basis of research coming to function as the typical measure of development.

Not only has coverage of multilingualism been conspicuous by its absence, but where it has been discussed this is often in a negative light. Indeed, current research on multilingualism is combating a tradition which treated it as a cognitive and educational handicap (cf. Hakuta 1986). This is no surprise considering the methodological procedures by which these 'findings' emerged. Early twentieth-century studies attempted to correlate bilingualism and IQ (itself a culturally biased test) by comparing monolingual and bilingual performance on verbal tests in the bilingual child's *second* language. Even now, multilingual children are disadvantaged in assessment contexts which rely exclusively on verbal tests rather than also using non-verbal tests (McLaughlin 1984; Demie *et al.* 2003; Gravelle 2003).

The negative view of bilingualism arises from the investigation of linguistic minorities within a dominant culture, in which poverty and racism often confound the language issues. As Skutnabb Kangas (1981) makes clear, the linguistic and educational tasks facing those whose home language is that of the majority or minority group are very different, and language-teaching programmes correspondingly should reflect this. For a native speaker of a high-status majority language (e.g. English in the UK), learning a second language is an optional extra that current theories consider is best done through immersion programmes. For children whose home language is that of a cultural or national minority, they have to learn the dominant language in order to have access to educational and employment opportunities. It is not surprising that children who are not yet proficient in the language in which they are learning curriculum subjects fail to achieve to the level of their native speaker counterparts. Moreover, as well as the historical treatment of bilingualism as a remedial educational issue, language difficulties are often confused with communicational problems by teachers (conversely also creating problems in identifying genuine learning disabilities). These factors have contributed to bilingualism being seen as a 'special educational' issue, which – interacting also with dynamics of institutional racism – is reflected in the overrepresentation of cultural minorities in education sectors associated with low academic achievement (CRE 1992; Demie *et al.* 2003). In turn this both draws attention away from the problem of an irrelevant curriculum as responsible for minority children's educational difficulties and reinstates cultural dominance:

Developing from the notion of cultural deprivation, the immigrant children's special needs in education soon became the acceptable approach to cope with their alleged cultural and linguistic deficiencies. Gradually public attention was diverted away from the content of the curriculum and its dubious relevance to non-English children and directed towards evidence for their presumed cultural limitations and linguistic handicaps. The assumption was that the discontinuity between these children and their school was the result of the mal-functioning of the children themselves, not the school.

(Tosi 1988: 82–83)

Current theories take the position that disadvantaged cultural minorities should be taught through the medium of their home language, thus sup-porting and maintaining their cultural background, as well as facilitating the transfer of linguistic and reasoning skills from one language to the other. (The resources to make this theory a practical pedagogical reality are, however, rarely forthcoming.) But, as the tensions between theory, policy and practice in the quotes at the beginning of this chapter suggest, even now multilingualism is often portrayed within assimilationist and compensatory models as a necessary evil to facilitate transition to the majority language. (For early critiques and opportunities of the National Curriculum see Savva 1990; Conteh 1992. For more recent accounts see Gammon 2003.) Here we see how the status of bilingual teachers interacts with that accorded the culture and language of their pupils (Conteh *et al.* 2004). It is in this context that Anglo-US developmental psychology text-books continue to discuss bilingualism in terms of the educational dis-advantage of minority children, with specific concern expressed at levels of provision for, and low rates of success of, English language programmes.

The complexity of the issues raised by multilingualism is rarely acknowledged. There are grave methodological and conceptual problems with the prevalent assumptions structuring linguistic and psychological research that being bilingual is equivalent to being monolingual in two languages (Grosjean 1989, 1998). Discussions are often just in terms of bilingualism, yet rarely if ever is one an absolutely 'balanced' bilingual, or 'balanced' in all spheres (and what assumptions underlie this drive towards equilibrium?), since factors such as frequency and contexts of use, as well as cultural and familial identifications, enter the definition. As Pavlenko (2005) points out:

The scholarship to date has focused predominantly on childhood and immigrant bilingualism, where adults move from one country to another. In reality, however, in the contemporary world of transcul-tural migration, individuals and groups of people often make multiple linguistic and cultural transitions that affect their linguistic repertoires. Russian Jews living in the Ukraine, for instance, grow up speaking

Russian and may have some knowledge of Ukrainian, Yiddish, and a foreign language, most commonly English, French or German. Upon emigration to Israel, their linguistic repertoire is transformed – they learn Hebrew, improve their English and also pick up some Arabic. Some may continue the immigrant journey out of Israel and into the United States, where their repertoire changes once again – they work in English and speak Russian to friends and family members, while Hebrew, Ukrainian, Yiddish and Arabic undergo the process of attrition. What happens in the lives of many individuals, then, is the ongoing change in dominance, competence and proficiency in all languages in question.

(Pavlenko 2005: 9)

The relationship between methods of instruction and status of the speaker as part of a linguistic minority or majority has already been mentioned. But in some circumstances the meanings and relative importance accorded to bilingualism are not connected with majority or minority status. This is a key but often overlooked problem in educational and mental health assessments, where the instruments may already be structured by Eurocentric cultural assumptions and where translation and backtranslation may pose as many problems as they solve. Thus Drennan *et al.* (1991), in their study of the production of a Xhosa version of the Beck Depression Inventory (BDI), highlight how translation has to be understood as an interactional and conflictual enterprise – that recognised procedures such as backtranslation and consensus decision making may merely mask. Further, as an urbanised elite, translators may themselves no longer be fully fluent in the varieties of the languages they are translating and may also feel under pressure to avoid conflict and gloss over translation problems.

Treatments of multilingualism should be seen in their historical and class contexts. While currently most discussions of multilingual issues in Europe and the USA are cast within a political framework of assimilation of minority groups (in terms of aiming either to promote or to prevent this), historically it has been cultural élites who have been multilingual while the colonised or subordinate groups have been denied access to other languages as a means of social control (as was the case under apartheid in South Africa; see Pludderman 1999 for an update). To take a European example, as an expression of rise of federalism, in the 1990s the Catalunya (the regional state administration) repudiated Spanish as their first language and promoted Catalan, which was seen as expressing resistance to rule from Madrid (Torres 1992). In general, questions of power are integrally linked with those of rights to language. The largely undisputed view that children from cultural minorities should be supported to be schooled in the medium of the majority language has also been paralleled by the rise of supplementary schools for purposes of cultural maintenance (sometimes focused around religion, sometimes around national heritage). However, here too questions of language and power remain inescapable, reinforcing how national or religious communities cannot be taken as 'essential' or homogeneous. For example, Issa (2005) reviews some of the political complexities and sensitivities involved in Turkish language supplementary provision in the UK, where the fact that Turkish Cypriot departs from the standard (Istanbul) Turkish taught in the schools, and is looked upon less favourably by teachers, poses the question of which Turkish should be taught (which in turn requires reconsideration of why it is being taught).

Thus the fact that Anglo-US-dominated psychological research has assumed a monolingual language learner itself speaks volumes about legacies of colonialism and imperialism – of both the territorial and the cultural varieties. Given the association between language and cultural identity, and the history of colonialism (in which erosion of indigenous languages played a role crucial to the maintenance of political control), there is clearly an obligation on language researchers in general to dissociate themselves from that tradition and address proper, theoretically informed questions which the study of multilingualism demands. Surpassing a grudgingly corrective model, positive views are emerging of the role and importance of being bilingual, in terms of more flexible cognitive and problem-solving skills and more general benefits of being less tied to a particular world view (Skutnabb Kangas and Cummins 1988). Far from treating bilingualism as a problem, some researchers have subjected *mono*lingualism to scrutiny: 'Monolingualism is a psychological island. It is an ideological cramp. It is an illness, a disease which should be eradicated as soon as possible because it is dangerous for world peace' (Skutnabb Kangas 1988: 13).

This disease metaphor has been taken up by the Instituto Central America to promote language schools with the slogan 'El monolingualismo es curable' ('Monolingualism can be cured'). Interestingly, this carries different implications for different audiences. While it functions as an invitation to Europeans and North Americans to learn (Latin-American) Spanish, it is also an exhortation to speakers of indigenous languages to learn international languages so that they can participate in the world scene directly. More generally, the rise of translation studies (e.g. Venuti 2000) outside psychology has built on models of language that treat it as doing more than simply reflecting what it describes. This has highlighted the impossibility of perfect matching or translation across languages, so that it always involves some ambiguities and negotiation of a range of possibilities which may be resolved by personal preference, performance of particular allegiances and other social as well as cultural-linguistic factors (as in the case of the Drennan *et al.* 1991 study mentioned earlier). Hence this work has focused attention on the interpretive and interpersonal complexities involved in moving between languages. Just as code switching presents many possibilities for marking affiliation and negotiating status, so multilingual speakers not only have a wider available array of conceptual nuances, but also readymade resources to reflect upon their socio-cultural form. In this sense multilingual speakers have access to a vital methodology for the analysis of the relationship between speaking and thinking, since their movement between languages demands this. Rather than being the exception within accounts of language learning, and philosophical discussions of the relationship between speaking and thinking, we might do better to think of it as the paradigm research tool (Zavos 2005). Here, as Pavlenko (2005) points out, the position of the researcher, as mono-, bi- or multilingual, with a particular language history and degrees of fluency, becomes a matter of methodological significance.

Speaking with feeling

Consideration of multilingual language development therefore illustrates a set of general issues relevant to, but tending also to be eclipsed by, accounts of language development. Recognising language as a source of cultural or national identification invested with great emotional significance may, and should, inform the analysis of the origins and functions of individual differences in children's speech. Moreover, in spite of Bruner's benign notions of 'scaffolding', the initial context for learning language can also involve emotionally highly charged and conflictual situations. Roger Brown (1973) reports from his pioneering longitudinal study of the language development of a child, Eve, that she first used the time adverbials 'after', 'then' and 'first' after they were explicitly directed towards her in negotiating her request that she be allowed to drink milk from her baby sister's bottle. Further, it was only a considerable time later that she used these words in other contexts. Lieven (1982) discusses this account as highlighting how language learning takes place in particular contexts and that early language use displays that history. The conclusions she draws are that there is no single route to learning language, and that it is a continuous process. Children differ in the ways they construct speech and what they use speech for.

Related to this, it is also clear that the cultural context in which the child lives enters into the structure and style of, as well as the actual, language she speaks. Urwin (1984) too argues that descriptions of language development are so focused on whether or when a child has achieved possession of a particular linguistic or grammatical structure that they fail to attend to the emotional significance of the development under consideration. The cognitivist interpretation of a child's extension of her linguistic repertoire is assumed to be determined by the salience of the objects or actions they name. But, more than this, common first words like 'more' or 'gone' 'are precisely those which are particularly likely to mark the child's own control within predictable practices' (Urwin 1984: 312). Salience here necessarily takes on emotional meanings that remain untheorised within current accounts.

Here we might connect with Freud's (1922/1981) understanding of the origins of language as lying in the infant's efforts to bring back (or to 'hallucinate' the presence of) the lost object (usually the mother or key caregiver). This is the origin of the 'repetition compulsion' discussed by Freud in relation to the 'fort–da' ('gone–here') game played by the little boy, of throwing away and retrieving a cotton reel, according to which (in Freud's analysis) he gained some control over the separation from his mother (thereby also prompting a psychoanalytic theory of play – see Chapter 13). This view would position emotions, or rather – in psycho-analytic terms – drives, as the key spur to psychic structuring, but significantly it denies a conception of developmental progress. Moreover, it intimates a rather different conception of the role and achievement of the rationality that is positioned as the pinnacle of mental development. It would also suggest a whole different way of looking at what is at stake in development. Indeed it is worth pointing out to the reader why there is no separate chapter in this book on 'emotional development'. For, in the other textbooks that this one aims to comment upon, apart from dealing with questions of attachment and separation (which we have already discussed in Chapter 7), 'emotions' are addressed largely in terms of 'emotional aware-ness'. Not only does this effectively reduce emotions to a form of cognitive ability, but – within prevailing models – this usually means that psycho-social development reduces to discussions of individual (and worse still sometimes maternal) mental health. Hence normalisation and pathologisa-tion are close bedfellows, and the focus on dyadic communication can acquire multiple political valencies. It is clear, then, that a more differ-entiated approach to language development is necessary: one that attends to contexts of language use as well as structure. To this end we now turn to the research investigating talk addressed to, as well as exhibited by, children.

Further reading

Bruner, J. (1983) *Child's Talk: Learning to Use Language*, Oxford: Oxford University Press (a very readable exposition of Bruner's ideas).

Cummins, J. (2001) *Negotiating Identities: Education for Empowerment in a Diverse Society*, 2nd edn, Los Angeles: California Association for Bilingual Education (takes up the debates about language and cultural dominance to education in a varied and useful collection).

Daniels, H. (ed.) (1996) *An Introduction to Vygotsky*, London and New York: Routledge.

Gillen, J. (2000) 'Listening to young children talking on the telephone: a reassess-ment of Vygotsky's notion of egocentric speech', *Contemporary Issues in Early Childhood*, 1, 2: 171–184.

Pavlenko, A. (2005) *Emotions and Multilingualism*, New York: Cambridge University Press (specifically addresses the complex relations between language and affectivity).

Suggested activities

1   Taking the 'anti-linguicism manifesto' elaborated in Chapter 1 of Skutnabb Kangas and Cummins (1988), develop a structured series of questions to be addressed as individuals or in small groups:

- To what extent are or were language issues addressed in courses you are taking or have taken?
- What is the effect of the presence or absence of these issues? Whose language is the medium of instruction?
- What is the relationship between the language of instruction and cultural assumptions permeating the theory?
- What is the relationship between language use and structural positions of disadvantage?

2   Generate an audio or video record of a 15-minute period of adult–infant or adult–child interaction, to:

(a) consider how you create a representation of that record; i.e. what form of transcription and what assumptions this expresses about your research questions, and how this enters into the forms of interpretations you might make (see Ochs 1979)

(b) having addressed this, focus on three examples from which to consider the consequences of the different models of language addressed in this chapter: structural, functional and performative.

10 Discourses of caregiving talk

When you give your child a bath, bathe him in language.

(Bullock 1974: 58)

This chapter reviews the research literature that investigates the role of the contexts in which children learn to talk. As we shall see, this domain provides a key arena in which the main themes structuring language research are played out. First, the obsession with the speed of development at the expense of theory: it is an unexamined assumption that the earlier a child speaks or exhibits a particular construction the better (which, as we have seen, is part of what structures the negative view of bilingualism). The second theme to be considered at some length in this chapter is the privileging of particular language styles which imports the structure of evaluation and regulation of families, and especially women, we encountered in the literature on 'attachment' (Chapter 7) into the arena of child language development. Third, related to this, we see a polarisation set up between those adult caregivers (until recently almost exclusively defined as mothers) who are considered to promote child language development either adequately or inadequately (again subject to this dubious assumption about rate of development) and with the corresponding pillorying of the latter category of (deemed 'insensitive') mothers.

It is a commonly held view that children benefit from the speech they are exposed to within the course of caregiving. The fact that many adults in many places modify their speech to children has given rise to the pervasive assumption that this must aid language learning. However, research has produced no clear answer to the question of what it is about the speech directed to children that is helpful. Methodological and interpretational limitations of research give rise to an account of language development that is oversimplified and insensitive to analysing the precise role that specific features of the linguistic environment play in the promotion of language. These absences not only obscure an understanding of how the speech directed to children relates to how they acquire and develop language, but the research also sets up an unwarranted negative stereotype of caregivers who are routinely designated as deficient in their supposedly language-promoting qualities. This negative evaluation extends beyond individuals to the rating of class and cultural language variation. As we shall see, this insensitivity to variation and its significance has conceptual implications for an adequate study of language, as well as major educational and political effects. In this chapter I present a critical review of this research, taking issue with the assumption that there is a single model of how to talk with children. Issues of difference, discourse and practice necessarily enter into the evaluation of appropriate communication.

Babytalk

Research from the 1960s onwards has documented systematic differences between speech directed to children and speech between adults. This takes the form of shorter sentences, simplified syntactic forms, well-formed utterances, use of higher pitch, exaggerated intonation and slower speed. This talk addressed to children is also characterised by redundancy, with frequent entire or partial repetitions (Snow 1972), is closely tied to the immediate context (Snow 1977) and exhibits particular features that have been interpreted as functioning to engage children in, and support their, talk. In particular, they are regarded as helping the segmentation and learning of words, through repetition and familiar word frames identifying word boundaries, and mapping ideas on to language by talking about what is accessible and elaborating on what the child says (Cross 1977).

Indicative of ideological presumptions about who looks after children and who is responsible for their development, this child-directed speech style was dubbed 'motherese', a term which figured in textbooks until the 1990s despite increasing recognition that mothers are not necessarily children's sole or major caregivers and that these modifications are not confined to mothers, or even adults, since older children use them towards younger ones (Dunn and Kendrick 1982). Even when accounts shift to the less loaded term 'infant-' or 'child-directed speech', research is based almost exclusively on mothers' speech to children; the change in terminology has not reflected any fundamental reorganisation of research procedures or questions.

As an adaptation to children's limited linguistic proficiency, this speech style appeared to offer an alternative account for language learning that dispensed with the need for Chomsky's innate language acquisition device. This was because the designation of babytalk as a simplified speech register appeared to challenge his claim that the linguistic models to which children were exposed were too degenerate to enable language development. However, the mere prevalence of speech modifications to children does not in itself imply that these are helpful, or why they are (if they are). There are problems in demonstrating the value of child-directed speech in teaching grammar, not least because this model collapses into a more radical form of nativism, only this time locating the competence within the mother rather than the child. Instead of postulating an innate facility to learn language within the child, mothers are invested with an 'omniscient' (Shatz 1982) facility to promote language learning with no explanation as to how this arises. This produces both a fundamentally asocial account of the origins of language development and a consensual and unitary model of social relations:

> The conjecture that the caregiver is innately attuned to the emergent abilities of the infant, and equipped to accommodate her or his beha- viour so as to frame input at just the right level of complexity suggests not only omniscience but X-ray vision: since not all linguistic activity and knowledge is overt, the adult must be making skilful intuitive inferences from limited and potentially ambiguous data and elabor- ating these at just the right time and in just the right way. . . . Such a theory is 'social' only in the limited sense that it represents one party as acting and the other as reacting instinctively: the outcome is operation in unison, and arrival at like-mindedness.
>
> (Durkin 1987: 109–110)

In addition to these conceptual problems, researchers have tended only to describe features of child-directed speech rather than analyse what it is about the specific features that is helpful. Where this has been addressed, attempting to link frequencies of features of maternal and child speech has confused rather than informed the picture.

'Input and output'

Notwithstanding the initial investment in demonstrating the facilitating effects of child-directed speech and some clear ideas about how this pro- motes word *meaning*, it has become apparent that the research into child- directed speech can say little about how this aids the teaching of specific aspects of language. Most research has focused on grammar, rather than on the broad spectrum of linguistic, pragmatic, metalinguistic and discursive involved in language use. Even within this restricted domain, the clear picture painted by early studies has been clouded by reports that speech to children is sometimes more, rather than less, grammatically complex than speech between adults. As Durkin (1987: 128) notes, 'simplification as a strategy is not equivalent to simplification as an effect'. This observation casts doubt on the status of child-directed speech as a simplified speech register.

Moreover, despite Bruner's claims that maternal speech varies in relation to and graduates with the child's language level, studies have also failed to demonstrate such 'fine-tuning'. A conceptual problem with Bruner's 'close- coupled feedback system' (Ninio and Bruner 1978) is that according fixed knowledge to parents ignores how parental beliefs inform the language addressed to, and therefore the language models available to, children. Furthermore, 'fine-tuning' turns out to be rather complicated to research since global measures relating characteristics of the mother's and the child's speech by calculating the average length of (mothers') utterances (MLU) can be mediated by the feedback mothers receive about their communicative successes or failures with their children (Bohannen and Marquis 1977). Such broad measures can therefore mask, rather than illuminate, subtle changes in the complexity of speech mothers address to children (Pine 1992a).

Since such speech is also addressed to foreigners and animals (Ferguson 1977), it has even been suggested that this style may reflect the effort to communicate with a designated non-competent speaker rather than a desire to teach language. By this account, these speech modifications may be a by-product of a restricted set of semantic relations associated with, but not specifically concerned with, syntax. Indeed, speech directed to children arises within activity and from the desire to communicate, rather than for the sole purpose of language teaching.

'Effects'

The attempt to explore the effects of adult speech modifications on children has produced an inconclusive and inconsistent literature. In part this arises from a set of methodological difficulties that express more far-reaching limitations in the way in which language development has been conceptualised. In the first place, there may be no basis for inferring causal relations from correlations between particular features of adult speech and particular aspects of language development. After all, the adult could be *responding* to advances in the child's language, rather than solely promoting those advances. The use of simple correlational models is also inadequate, since this does not take into account how specificities of speech addressed to children may no longer be relevant once children have progressed beyond particular linguistic stages. Moreover, there is no reason to suppose, as correlational models do, that adult speech modifications should have a linear relationship to language development (Bohannen and Hush-Pasek 1984). Even if an effect is found, this may arise from features that are only indirectly associated with the input, such as other changes over time that are then reflected within talk to children.

It is in this context that we should be wary of moral panics generated around media targeting child audiences, such as that generated by the late 1990s children's TV series, *Teletubbies*. The outrage principally concerned the degenerate language model provided to children, which supposedly imitated very young children's early language use (as in 'eh-oh' for 'hello'), rather than presenting the ideal type they learn to speak from. However, children's programmers heralded it as a welcome move away from adult-centred to child-centred formats. Claims to knowledge about language development and age appropriateness figured on both sides. While the *Teletubbies* controversy broke at the peak of debates around the supposed 'dumbing down' of British culture and educational standards, with discussion focusing on the inarticulacy and 'dumbness' of the characters (Buckingham 1999), probably this was partly precisely why they became taken up as a style icon within youth culture (alongside their obvious consumer-friendly characteristics, psychedelic associations and ambiguous sexuality). Notwithstanding these problems, by 1998 the series had been sold to more than 59 broadcasters around the world and had generated a massive revenue for BBC Worldwide from the merchandising articles alone. At issue, then, were the competing values of instruction versus imaginative appeal and entertainment, both of which enter into child-centred educational approaches but whose tensions emerge periodically. It is worth noting that the wider popularity of the series fits with the general celebration of babylike or infantile attributes (as indicated by young women wearing dummies in nightclubs as style accessories?), that connects with wider themes of infantilisation of subjectivity discussed earlier (see also Gordo Lopez and Burman 2004).

A further set of issues highlights the connection between methodological procedures and the status of available models. The theories to account for adult speech modifications are post hoc, working back from correlation between maternal and child speech features to speculation about what function the maternal characteristics play, and while this does not render the research meaningless, it does mean that it should be interpreted with caution. The models also presume that any effects of child-directed speech on child language will remain constant with the child's level of linguistic ability. Clearly, there may be constraints on when a child can make use of available linguistic resources and support (through their frequency or salience). Reflecting the general move towards acknowledging children as contributors to the structure of the context in which they grow up, research has shifted to exploring how this context is used by the child within the process of acquiring and developing language.

'Uses'

A further general problem in interpreting how children use the language they are exposed to is that the relationships reported between talk addressed to, and exhibited by, children can be explained in a number of ways. So while maternal expansions are regarded as beneficial to child language development in terms of repeating what has just been said (by mother or child) and thus reducing the processing load for the child (e.g. Cross 1977; Wells and Robinson 1982), it is unclear exactly what it is about such 'recasts' that is helpful. Possible ways that 'recasts' could promote language include: following on from what the child says; maintaining the topic of what the child has been talking about; expanding the utterance using words the child has used; reformulating the child's utterance by adding to or correcting it; or it may simply be a specific indication of a more general conversation-eliciting style of maternal speech. Furthermore, these functions are not mutually exclusive, since they may be determined by more general changes in relationships between mothers and children whereby mothers modify the way they talk in accordance with children's language growth. While Farrar (1990) was able to demonstrate specific relations between how mothers adjust their speech to children and the children's acquisition of grammatical elements, he suggests that this effect is specific to a particular point in the child's linguistic development and only relates to the acquisition of particular grammatical structures rather than being generally facilitative. The broader issue this kind of study raises, therefore, is the need to refine both theoretical models and methodological procedures in order to analyse both the features of adult speech considered predictive of linguistic growth and the structure of that developmental process.

Concluding his review of caregiver talk research, Pine (1994) calls for a more sophisticated approach to research analysing the relationship between child-directed speech and language acquisition that moves beyond the documentation of general frequency effects to more detailed analyses of what it is that individual children hear and say, and how each child's linguistic system changes within the period under investigation. This demands a more qualitative and fine-grained approach to the study of maternal speech effects. It also requires examination of the assumptions behind what makes a good language learning environment, and why (see also Theakston *et al.* 2001, 2004). In particular, while the models have offered some suggestions about how child-directed speech may involve children in talk while reducing communicative and processing demands (Snow 1977), it is unclear whether these characteristics of child-directed speech arise from specifically communicative pressures or rather whether they reflect a particular culture-blind model of the language-learning child.

Styles and stereotypes

Since the research on child-directed speech is based on mothers' speech to children, it should come as no surprise that this latches into the wider discourse of 'sensitive mothering'. In terms of language development, maternal insensitivity has been equated with directiveness and intrusiveness. In a classic study, Nelson (1973: 69) distinguishes an 'object-oriented, question-asking, relatively concise style' (seen as 'sensitive') with a 'behaviour-oriented, intrusive, discursive style' (seen as insensitive). In a similar vein, McDonald and Pien (1982) contrast a conversationally oriented style with a behaviourally regulatory style. Julian Pine (1992a, 1992b) takes issue with these simple positive/negative classifications, arguing that they do nothing to inform the understanding of children's language learning, and that moreover they reflect what is no more than a stereotype of 'good mothering'. Three particular problems can be noted.

First, they confuse 'child centredness' with a particular language-oriented style of interaction. But since there is no reason why asking questions should be a necessary index of maternal sensitivity, this gives rise to some rather bizarre contradictions: 'Thus a mother who "orders her child around" (Nelson 1973: 68) is seen as being "intrusive", whereas a mother who insists on her child answering a long series of "What's that?" questions is not' (Pine 1992a: 5).

It is clear that both question asking and behaviour controlling can be done in a more or a less 'sensitive' way. This means there is no necessary relationship between 'maternal sensitivity' and 'directiveness'. Therefore: 'the tendency to view question-asking positively and directiveness negatively would seem to reflect the value placed in our culture on particular kinds of language-oriented, as opposed to behaviour-oriented, forms of activity and to have little to do with the child-centredness or otherwise of the mothers concerned' (Pine 1992a: 6).

Second, as Pine points out, the way in which the notion of 'maternal sensitivity' is operationalised implies stability in the structure and significance of mothers' interactional behaviour irrespective of the age or stage of the child. Diverse aspects of mothers' speech, such as directives, imperatives and conversational redirections, are collapsed together within the category 'maternal directiveness', thus treating as equivalent devices which direct children's attention and those which regulate their behaviour. It would seem unlikely that asking questions would serve the same (mal)functions for a one-year-old as for a three-year-old child. Questions directed to 13-month-old babies might well act as prompts and aids to structure children's responses rather than as 'real' questions. Based on his study of children at the one-word stage of language development, Pine (1992b) suggests that a more appropriate reformulation of McDonald and Pien's (1982) classification might be between behavioural directives and tutorial prompts or test questions.

Third, as well as definitional incoherence and homogenisation over time and culture, there are additional methodological and conceptual difficulties in relating child language characteristics to 'maternal sensitivity'. Nelson (1973) introduced a classification of 'referential' and 'expressive' mothers which she regards as arising from differences in functional characteristics of mother–child interaction, specifically between maternal direction and children's referential vocabulary (knowledge of word labels) when they have a repertoire of 50 words. The differential valuation of children who use more object words ('referential') and those who use a larger number of phrases ('expressive') betrays a cognitivist orientation which equates language with labelling (see Chapter 9). Moreover, claims made for referentiality as an index of language development are now being disputed. Lieven and Pine (1990) and Pine and Lieven (1990) argue that such claims arise as an artefact of studies which use cross-sectional designs (comparing different aged groups at the same time) rather than longitudinal designs and use age rather than linguistic level as the yardstick of comparison. If we recall that so-called referential-nominal children overwhelmingly come from the upper-middle classes of Western industrialised societies, then it becomes apparent that class and cultural assumptions are structured into a seemingly disinterested developmental measure.

More than this, the dimension of 'maternal sensitivity' which was originally supposed to determine the child's level of *emotional* security (or 'attachment') has now been rendered into a measure of *linguistic* adequacy. The regulation of mothering has extended beyond the domain of caring for children into promoting their linguistic and educational progress. Yet nowhere has it been established that *rate* of language development bears any relation to later linguistic or educational competence. This is simply an unanalysed assumption that is overdetermined by the technologisation of development and the drive to maximise and accelerate it (Rose 1990). The well-known joke 'why do mothers take their children to supermarkets to smack them?' implicitly addresses how settings like supermarkets are deliberately structured to incite children to make demands on their parents to buy them goods, such as the sweets placed by the check-out where parents have to wait or forfeit their place in the queue, and are thus both trapped and maximally open to and embarrassed by the scrutiny of others. Of course, stereotypically, it is the authoritarian mother (who is – stereotypically – working class) who smacks her child. So the problematisation of the mother in this joke wilfully overlooks the structural arrangements and (in cultural-historical terms) the environmental affordances that create the conditions for and provoke such acts, to personalise these as the responsibility of the individual mother instead.

The child-centred approach (both within language teaching and pedagogical practices more generally) thus sets up further means for the regulation of women, as mothers and as teachers (since the overwhelming majority of teachers and nursery workers are women). Collapsing the distinction between play and work as the child-centred approach does (see Chapter 12 for further elaboration) and making all play potentially educative has given rise to the requirement that women convert their household labour into educational opportunities for their children (Walkerdine and Lucey 1989). This takes to ridiculous lengths the principle of learning through 'direct' experience which keeps women constantly busy constructing interesting and 'stimulating' activities, as well as caring for their offspring. An article on 'Tips for talking to toddlers' suggests:

> Sing songs and say rhymes.
> Introduce books as early as possible – home-made scrap-books and magazines as well as picture books. Look at the pictures and ask questions.

Talk as you work and give a running commentary at least some of the time you are pushing the pram.

Visit railway stations, ferries, markets, rivers, airports so that vocabulary is extended.

Just talking is not enough, particularly if the parent is just pontificating.

(*Independent on Sunday*, 19 May 1991)

Language as cultural practice

In some ways the research on syntactic development illustrates clearly the inappropriateness of attempts to formulate general models of language learning. Such evidence that does relate forms of speech addressed to children with the emergence of particular forms is highly qualified and specific to the particular language being learnt by the child. To take an example, there is a debate over exactly what it is about binary choice questions (questions to which the answer is either yes or no) that contributes to the emergence of auxiliary verb forms in children's speech. Newport *et al.* (1977), who first reported this association, suggested that these questions may be helpful by making auxiliary verb forms more salient because they are placed initially within questions (such as 'Can you?' 'Do you?'). This, however, can scarcely be relevant to languages that do not place auxiliaries at the beginning of questions or have no auxiliaries at all. Similarly, the practices held to best induct children into language reflect culturally specific ideas about what it means to learn to talk.

Bambi Schieffelin and Elinor Ochs (1986) draw on anthropological and socio-historical (Vygotskyan) approaches to challenge the abstraction of language development from general cultural practices, and to explore how cross-cultural perspectives inform the understanding of language learning as itself constituting, as well as encoding, cultural practice:

> [A]ll societies do not rely on the very same set of language-socialising procedures. Indeed although prompting a child what to say appears widespread, expanding children's utterances, using leading questions, announcing activities/events for a child, and using a simplified lexicon and grammar to do so are cross-culturally variable.
>
> (Ochs 1986: 6)

Those studies which highlight the prevalence of child-directed speech even across cultures (e.g. in Japanese, Korean, Israeli, Mandarin Chinese, as well as US and European cultures) are almost exclusively of academic or middle-class backgrounds. As Lieven notes: 'This raises the question of whether we are dealing with the effects of higher education or of some ideological homogenization of the upper middle classes in advanced industrial societies' (Lieven 1994: 67). Even where adult speech modifications are found or reported, they do not always take the phonetic or prosodic form identified in the 1970s literature (such as Snow and Ferguson 1977).

Ochs (1983) reports from her study of language socialisation in Western Samoa, where children have a variety of caregivers and siblings provide the most active direct care, that mothers tend to address older siblings in order to direct the care rather than addressing the children who receive it. Hence Samoan children do not expect a direct maternal response to their indication of need. Moreover, the organisation of status hierarchies determines speech adaptations, so that adults, as higher status people, do not adapt their speech to their children. There is little opportunity here for the supposedly universal babytalk register to occur, and instead children are given explicit instruction and direction about how to speak. What this highlights is how the notions of sensitivity and responsiveness so prevalent within the developmental psychological and psycholinguistic literature are themselves cultural practices. Even the tendency to accord personality, individuality and intentionality to young babies also emerges as specific to Western cultural beliefs: 'It is important to realize that when an American mother responds to her infant in a particular way, she is doing so not because of *innate biological* patterning, but because she is acting on cultural assumptions about qualities and capacities of young children' (Ochs 1983: 188). In a similar vein, Bambi Schieffelin's (1983, 1990) study of Kaluli children in Papua New Guinea highlights how their explicitly instructional style of language induction follows from cultural beliefs about the entry into language marking the boundary between inhabiting the world of animals and spirits and that of humans. Sound play is discouraged because it is seen as animal-like, and this is taboo. Learning to speak is regarded as marking the child's departure from the land of spirits to join human society. Accordingly, children are prompted into language through explicit demands to imitate model utterances, and since high cultural value is placed on being able to produce well-formed speech, immature forms are devalued as 'soft' and socially inappropriate, rather than interpreted as steps towards linguistic competence.

This should make us cautious of the strong claims made for the value of a topic-expanding style since so many children learn to talk in its absence or with a more directive style. Lieven (1994) argues that the variation in cultural practices and corresponding child strategies for language learning may offer important insights for approaches to language delay and disorders. Although they may not display the features that figure within the literature, she points out that these cultural practices do all provide some support and scaffolding, whether through talk or activity, through which children can construct semantic and syntactic relations. She suggests that specific cultural practices may provide the equivalent of those features attributed to the (supposedly) child-directed speech code.

Taking the example of the Kaluli practice (reported by Schieffelin) of holding a baby up facing away and 'speaking for them' in a high-pitched voice, she argues that this apparently instructional mode may nevertheless provide a strategy for promoting the segmentation of the stream of language and attribution of meaning by drawing children's attention to segments of speech that they can identify and memorise, and, ultimately, reproduce. She also comments on Schieffelin's report that, although mothers do not display child-directed speech, they do exhibit adaptation to their children's communicative status, but by organising the children's focus of attention rather than responding to it (as in the topic-expanding style). The repetition and exhortation to imitate 'may well give the child the same sort of segmental and syntactic information which, it has been argued, sequences of child topics and their expansions by adults provide' (Lieven 1994: 68).

The lesson here is that, when investigations go beyond being fixated on measuring the prevalence of a style to the analysis of what functions it is held to play in language development, it emerges that similar functions can be identified in other, more common, forms of speech to children. It also demonstrates just how ludicrous and unjust is the negative evaluation of class and cultural practices structured within child language research.

Moreover, cultural practices enter into not only the rate but also the nature of the language spoken. Indeed, what counts as using language is itself culturally variable (Schieffelin 1979):

> The important generalization is that although children the world over will ultimately assume the basic communicative roles (speaker, addressee, referent audience), societies differ in the developmental point at which and the situations in which it is appropriate for children to assume particular roles, these differences being linked to their attitudes about children and their communicative competence.
>
> (Ochs 1986: 8)

In Shirley Brice Heath's (1983) ethnography of three different English-language communities in mid-America, within the African-American community she calls 'Trackton', children are rarely addressed until they can speak, their babbles or first words are rarely noted or encouraged, but they are continuously surrounded by an intensely verbal culture of talk, activity and storytelling. This corresponds to the community's cultural beliefs that children cannot be taught, but have to learn for themselves. These children 'break into' language, first by imitating the ends of words, and then they vary and repeat these oral 'chunks', adding other parts and playing with the sounds. These children go on to exhibit an analogical and imaginative approach to language use, in contrast to the nearby white 'Roadville' children who are taught to talk with an emphasis on accuracy and labelling. While the 'Roadville' children had a better grasp of narrative sequence, they lacked the 'Trackton' children's imaginative ways with language. Not only is the process of language development therefore not unitary, but language use is itself diverse.

Cultural practice through language

Language learning is not divorced from other socio-cultural meanings of growing up. It is not only integral to participation within social life, but is also a major tool for conveying cultural knowledge about social relations. While much research has been devoted to the process and promotion of children's language learning, the issue of what else children learn through language has been eclipsed. Yet the very forms and variety of the language children learn to talk encode structural meanings about the world they (will) inhabit. Analyses of caregiver talk in playgroup and nursery settings, even those with an explicit commitment to gender equality, indicate the pervasive asymmetrical use of gender-specified descriptions. Browne and France (1985) report that, in a British nursery, girls gained approval for their appearance and behaviour (as 'pretty', 'sweet natured', 'neat and tidy'), while boys were praised for their activity ('tough', 'brave', 'big', 'strong'). When girls exhibited the assertive behaviours deemed appropriate for boys who could stick up for themselves, they were called 'proper little madams'. While such double standards are probably so familiar to us as to sound banal, we cannot ignore how children absorb social as well as linguistic categories from what we say to them. Moreover, teaching girls to be good rather than clever (as the gender-divided language suggests) has been identified within processes of devaluing girls' educational achievements (Licht and Dweck 1987; Walkerdine and Lucey 1989).

At more general methodological as well as theoretical levels, it is important to attend to the particular forms of language to which children are exposed and the particular practices within which children are reared. Schieffelin (1990) notes in her research with the Kaluli that it is not surprising to find a marked absence of the forms associated with men and with public, formal speech in the children's utterances, since it is women who are primarily involved in childcare. An equivalent lesson for the US and European research is that close attention to the structure of adult–child interaction suggests that some deviant characteristics of child speech, which have been treated as evidence of immaturity, arise as a reflection of the speech addressed to them through parental efforts to present simplified linguistic forms (Durkin 1987).

The cross-linguistic research presents a catalogue of misinterpretations and misattributions of deficit to children or adult language teachers and cultures owing to the failure to analyse the language that the child actually hears (rather than a formal grammar of the language). This is especially important given the different structural demands of different languages. For example, Gopnik and Choi's (1990) claim that Korean children learn labelling later than English children due to a greater emphasis in the

Korean language on verbs is now being disputed as arising instead from the differing practices of English and Korean mothers who place differential emphasis on naming objects rather than the social routines involved in playing with them.

A further example of the consequences of the cultural and linguistic insensitivity that can enter into cross-linguistic research arises from work which attempts to relate language acquisition to cognitive development. In Clancy's (1989) study of Korean children she reports that 'wh'-questions (that is, why, what, where interrogatives) did not appear in the order that would be predicted according to their supposed cognitive complexity; and by contrast the children seemed to be using 'how' much earlier than would be expected. However, attending to the language that the children actually heard (the 'input') indicated that Korean mothers were using the word translated as 'how' in English in ways that would suggest it should actually be translated as 'what' (both the above examples cited in Lieven 1994). Once again we see features of social and linguistic context have been mistaken for properties of child development.

Diversity, deficiency and dominance

Basil Bernstein's terminology of 'restricted' and 'elaborated' codes to describe class-related language variations still circulates as a theory of linguistic and cultural deficit, despite his protestations in popular as well as academic publications (e.g. Bernstein 1970) that the deprivations contributing to educational inequalities are social and not linguistic. Even in introducing a volume of Bernstein's research, Michael Halliday (1973) was compelled to dispel this misreading. Similarly, even where it is resisted, the ethnographic and anthropological work discussed above is transposed into a deficit or disadvantage model. While Brice Heath (1986) grapples with the tricky issue of how cultural differences in language practices relate to children's educational progress, her account is concerned with the failure of current schooling practices to recognise, support and differentially engage with the variety and diversity of linguistic styles. As well as addressing the relative strengths and weaknesses of subcultural languages, she therefore problematises the culture of the school rather than that of the children. The fact that references to her work in textbooks (Bukatko and Daehler 1992) and professional handbooks (Tittnich *et al.* 1990) fail to appreciate this point indicates not only the productivity of the process of popularising research but also the intransigence of normative assumptions that underlie developmental psychological practice.

Until recently, diversity of patterns of language use and development therefore get a bad press within developmental psycholinguistic research. Both academic and popular accounts subscribe to a variety of the 'cycle of deprivation' theory which relates the child's lexical style to the mother's interactional style. Variation tends to be analysed only in terms of the negative evaluation of particular maternal practices. Despite the fact that this classification of maternal practices is erroneous and unhelpful, the devaluation and derision of working-class and minority women for their communicative and interactional styles continues. Mothers have been encouraged to talk to their children in particular, culturally sanctioned ways, castigated for their failure to do so spontaneously, and educational policies and aid have been transfixed by mother–child interaction as *the* route to educational improvement (and national development).

The quotation at the beginning of this chapter is from the Bullock Report, *A Language For Life*, a policy document commissioned by the British Department of Education and Science (Bullock 1974). This suggests that the 'gap' between home and school can be filled by maternal talk to children, and by this structural inequalities become simply a matter of deficient linguistic style. The resonances of medical and racial hygiene within the metaphor of bathing and cleansing hint at the longer history of the preoccupation (reviewed in Chapters 1 and 4) with surveying the homes and habits of working-class and disadvantaged groups. To a greater or lesser extent the research on maternal style therefore both mirrors and contributes to conceptions of cultural deficiency which, wittingly or unwittingly, fail to recognise that the forms celebrated as superior are those associated with the already privileged middle-class culture which is then reproduced in schooling (Bernstein 1973). Culturally mediated differences are postulated without analysing what the nature of the deficiency is supposed to be, without recognising that a deficiency can be defined only in relation to the demands of a particular context. Since contexts and meanings vary, according to a particular style a fixed status as deficient or lacking in some way not only homogenises culturally diverse practices, it also posits middle-class white language norms as universally superior while naturalising the cultural hierarchy.

Macdonald (2006) provides a South African-based version of Brice Heath's (1983) analysis of her three distinct speech and literacy contexts within a single national context (which was discussed above). She uses a Vygotskyan cultural-historical framework, focusing on the variety of mediational forms and processes, to draw attention to the ways in which historically racialised divisions and their current legacies in terms of poverty and access to schooling interact with linguistic and cultural differences. The South African context is one of rapid political change (since democratisation) which also includes curriculum reform in schools and a high cultural value placed on education and educational achievement. The three communities she discusses include 'Maintown' which are the white, largely native English speaking, equivalent to the Western, urban, industrialised and technologically enriched families recognisable in elite middle-class contexts the world over; 'Roadville' who are the black middle class – not as affluent and with their own cultural and linguistic traditions that demarcate school and home; and 'Ntesha Tsela' (literally meaning 'beating a path for yourself' – reflecting the struggle to get to school and stay there). Here it is important to consider the effect of English as the medium of educational instruction, in a country which has 22 recognised national languages, as also interacting with a range of other cultural-historical 'mediational' factors.

Macdonald's analysis applies the Vygotskyan notion of 'situation definition', whereby the context is understood to be defined by those who are operating in it – in this case the macro-context of context-specific meanings of being an adult or a child, which create quite radical disjunctions for these South African children in how they are expected to be at home and at school: 'At home they are expected to be highly reliable and take on responsibility; at schools, teachers assume they are "blank slates"' (p. 53). The teachers as agents in the mediation are shown to bring different resources to the contexts (in terms of levels of training and models of education, for example). This interacts with 'the materiality of mediational means' – i.e. the physical state of resources in the classroom, the teacher–pupil ratio (as a function of class privilege), and even of being able to afford the school fees to maintain continuous attendance (which is what gives rise to so much failure and repeating of years). As an illustration of 'multiple goals of action', Macdonald discusses the classic I-R-E sequence described by Wertsch (1998) and assumed to be general, in which the teacher asks an inauthentic question (i.e. the answer to which she already knows), a child offers a response, and the teacher then evaluates this answer, in relation to the educational task of creating joint meaning. This fulfils the role of maintaining control and regulating the children's attention rather than teaching:

> This most time-honoured form of teaching may proceed without any real understanding on the part of most of the class – it has the form of teaching, but a competing goal of controlling the class, ensuring that real understanding on the part of all the children is unlikely to ensue. Insofar as the I-R-E sequence is embedded within a familiar knowledge domain for the learners, meaning will be created; however, in a situation such as Ntesha Tsela, if the knowledge domain is 'experience-far', and the language of the I-R-E is not well mastered by the children, very little meaning will be created.
>
> (Macdonald 2006: 65)

This example highlights the contribution of ethnographic analysis of a specific local context, as an exemplification of wider developmental principles. Overall, it demonstrates how a cultural-historical frame addresses how current systems of disadvantage interact with cultural norms and (more longstanding and wide-ranging) structures of exclusion to create specific educational trajectories, that cannot be said to lie within the culture or the individual, but rather their combined interaction with the dominant cultural practices structured within educational policy and practice.

Social relations influence what is said to and by children, and enter into the standards by which it is interpreted. It seems that there can be no *one* model of language learning, and that we must attend to *difference*. However, the emphasis on differences can be only half the story, and we must move on to the analysis of how this difference is structured. Hence, for an adequate analysis of language development, questions of power necessarily arise. Yet, with the exception of Urwin's (1984) analysis discussed in Chapter 8, the notion of 'context' employed within developmental psycholinguistic research typically includes no notion of power. While 'conversational control' does arise as a topic, and asymmetrical patterning of adult–child discourse is explored (e.g. Camaioni 1979; French and MacLure 1981), this is discussed only in terms of the facilitating features of caregiver speech to set up shared meanings. That this 'facilitation' is also a form of social control is either taken for granted or assumed to be desirable. Just because power relationships, within parenting and within research, are so pervasive as to be taken for granted does not mean that they do not inform both accounts of what children know and how we know what they know. In the next chapter we move from a focus on difference to one on power.

Further reading

For the classic elaboration of 'motherese', see chapters in:

Snow, C. and Ferguson, C. (eds) (1977) *Talking to Children*, Cambridge: Cambridge University Press.

For updates on this work, see:

Cameron-Falkner, T., Lieven, E. and Tomasello, M. (2003) 'A construction based analysis of child directed speech', *Cognitive Science, 27*: 843–873.
Theakston, A., Lieven, E., Pine, J. and Rowland, C. (2004) 'Semantic generality, input frequency and the acquisition of syntax', *Journal of Child Language, 31*: 61–99.

For a review taking account of the literature on cultural variation in language structure in relation to acquisition, see:

Lieven, E. (1994) 'Crosslinguistic and crosscultural aspects of language addressed to children', in C. Gallaway and B. Richards (eds) *Input and Interaction in Language Acquisition*, Cambridge: Cambridge University Press.
Pine, J. (1994) 'The language of primary caretakers', in C. Gallaway and B. Richards (eds) *Input and Interaction in Language Acquisition*, Cambridge: Cambridge University Press.

On cultural practices and language socialisation, the classic text remains:

Schieffelin, B. and Ochs, E. (eds) (1986) *Language Socialisation across Cultures*, Cambridge: Cambridge University Press.

On applications of Vygotskyan perspectives to language and educational contexts, see:

MacDonald, C. (2006) 'The properties of mediated action in three different literacy contexts in South Africa', *Theory and Psychology*, *16*, *1*: 51–80.

Suggested activities

Taking accounts such as Snow (1972) and more popular variants such as the 'Tips for talking to toddlers' discussed above, explore these in relation to assumptions about gender, class and culture, such as:

- Who are they addressed to?
- How do they address their audience?
- Is the promotion of language linked to later developmental achievements and, if so, of what kind?
- To what extent is having children at home considered an educational rather than a caring activity?
- What demands does this pose? How necessary is this?

11 Language and power in developmental research

Speak roughly to your little boy
And beat him if he sneezes
He only does it to annoy
Because he knows it teases.
  (Lewis Carroll, *Alice's Adventures in Wonderland*)

Those have most power to hurt us, that we love.
  (Francis Beaumont, 1584–1616, *The Maid's Tragedy*)

In this chapter I address the consequences of taking power relations as central to developmental psychological and psycholinguistic research, and focus on five examples of research. These illustrate not only different approaches to the study of children's language use and functioning but will also be used to advocate the following five claims. First, we need to understand the power relationships in which children are *positioned* in order to interpret appropriately what children say within developmental psychological studies. Second, children *express* their developing understanding of relationships through language. Third, children *use* alternative positionings made available to them through language to contest and change their social position. Fourth, *analysing the power* relations that underpin developmental psychological research can, when acknowledged, work to aid rather than obscure the interpretation of children's actions and interactions. Fifth, institutional power relations are not only recapitulated within research and service intervention, but have *material effects* on children's and families' lives.

This attention to the contexts in which developmental psychological research is constructed shows how the study of children's knowledge or 'abilities' is not separate from issues of language and power, but turns out to be inextricably intertwined with them. The conception of power here is not as a property to be possessed or exercised by one individual over another, but is a position set out within relationships; in this case relationships structured by the history of psychology and the positions elaborated (of professional surveillance) within discourses of scientific research. These are reinscribed within the current material practices of intervention that developmental psychology informs and legitimates, including educational and clinical psychology, health visiting, social work (see Henriques *et al.* 1984; Parker 1992a). Attending to power is not to treat it as a by-product of specific instances or utterances. Rather, discourses structure what can and cannot be spoken. Discourses construct the objects they discuss, and produce varieties of subjectivities that inhabit the frameworks of meaning they delineate (Foucault 1972). So far this book has been concerned with the ways in which developmental psychology participates in institutional discourses that elaborate specific positions (of expert professional, recipient of service), and that in particular produce children and families as its subjects. In applying this perspective to the study of child language, we have seen in Chapters 9 and 10 how discourses of maternal sensitivity regulate women. In this chapter it will be argued that the power with which discourse is invested is not only a matter of the way language is used, but rather, as we shall see, how power structures the selection, production and investigation of language.

Beyond the sentence

In exploring how children learn, use language and are positioned within power relations intimated by language, we have to move beyond definitions of language in terms of syntactic and even semantic structures, to address the broader structuring of meanings that language plays a key role in expressing and maintaining. In other words, we have to extend the unit of study beyond the traditional domain of linguistics, the sentence, to wider linguistic and textual practices, that is to discourse.

Developmental psycholinguistic researchers have come to recognise that more than grammatical knowledge is required for competent language use. Moreover, meanings do not arise from sentences in isolation, but through referential systems that are connected both to each other and to the social practices which they describe and constitute. Part of what it means to learn to talk is to know the rules by which talk is organised. Children therefore need to know more than linguistic rules to participate in the negotiation of meanings. Since language use is connected to the performance of roles and relationships, and talk is the forum in which these are mediated, resisted, played out, children require some awareness of the rules by which social relationships are regulated. All this means that we need to see language as more than simply reflecting the world, or transparently representing it, but rather as a means by which we engage with, and sometimes transform, relationships with institutions.

The focus of this chapter is on approaches to the study of children and childhood that take the relationship between language and power as the tool of analysis as well as topic. So while the studies reviewed in this chapter arise from distinct and contrasting theoretical and methodological perspectives, there are three assumptions that the range of perspectives concerned with varieties of 'discourse analysis' or discursive approaches share. First, meaning is viewed as determined by particular contexts, circumstances and relationships that hold at the moment of utterance, rather than as specified according to pre-existing and context-free rules. Second, the notion of power that informs these studies is one that does not accord children and their interlocutors a fixed or unique position. Power is not an absolute attribute or possession wielded by one party (for example, an adult) over another (the child). Rather, one's status or power position exists only in relation to others, indeed some would argue it constitutes that relationship. Third, it follows from this *relative* notion of power that one is not uniquely positioned within relationships, but that multiple positions are made available through varieties of discursive practices. Hence, while part of being an adult is, within some discourses, to be accorded a (relatively) more powerful position than that of a child, children can draw upon discourses of, for example, parental duty and responsibility to exercise considerable control over others.

Discursive approaches, connected with social constructionist approaches generally, are now having some impact across psychology. The five examples addressed in this chapter indicate the contribution of a range of perspectives within this approach.

Restricted rights to talk: the silence of the lambs?

In the first place, an adequate analysis of children's talk demands an understanding of power for the interpretation of what children say. Harvey Sacks (1972), using conversation analysis, discusses a piece of child's talk in terms of what its form indicates about the structuring of social interaction and the speaker's position within this. He uses conversation analysis to draw attention to the shared social knowledge we bring to bear in interpreting social behaviour, highlighting the work of interpretation done by competent communicators. Within this framework the selection of a particular linguistic form can be seen as the product or realisation of social meanings and categories.

As an approach, conversation analysis derives from ethnomethodological work in sociology which explores how we come to understand, account for and make comprehensible particular pieces of social interaction. An ethnomethodologist focuses on the ways language is used to conduct and correspondingly constitute forms of social organisation. A conversation analyst explores how conversation is organised in turns, how particular choices of linguistic form constrain the turn-taking sequence and what the particular pattern of openings, closings, conclusions, hesitations and repair devices indicates about the nature of the relationship between interactants. In other words, this is a sociolinguistic approach to language, but one which is not tied simply to documenting frequencies of occurrence or variation of linguistic forms. Rather, conversation analysts take a piece of text and attempt to tease out generalisations or rules that describe how the talk is organised (often producing a description that is much longer than the texts they investigate).

One text that Sacks (1972) uses to explore adult–child relations is this: 'The baby cried. The mommy picked it up', said by a 2-year-9-month-old little girl. Sacks sets out to show that not only are the two sentences connected, but that they qualify as a story. He argues that shared knowledge about social organisation enters into the 'topic frames' according to which talk is interpreted, so that mention of a baby invokes the expectation of a mommy. It would therefore be redundant for the child to have said 'Its mommy'. Moreover, Sacks argues that when taken in the context of children's restricted rights to talk, this reduced fragment of conversation can qualify as a story and, further, that the elliptical nature of the story is itself an index of the child's limited access to what he calls the 'conversational floor'. Rather than adopting conventional story markers such as 'once upon a time', she introduces her story by 'announcing a problem', a conversational device that allows parties to commence talking in circumstances where they would otherwise be flouting social norms. (Consider 'It looks like rain' said at a bus stop to initiate talk.) Announcing the 'problem' of the baby crying therefore constitutes an appropriate 'ticket' to start talking. From opening the story with the problem, the mommy picking up the baby is an appropriate end or resolution to the 'problem', given current norms about the role of women and their capacities to satisfy babies' needs. In this context of limited space to talk, Sacks argues it would therefore be superfluous to add 'and then the baby went to sleep', which would have been a more explicit story ending. Hence the recognition of the power asymmetries within which children are positioned brings about a revaluation of the status and function of what they say. Furthermore, the structural forms of power relations themselves arise from generalised frameworks of meaning and organisation such as familial discourses.

While it may seem far-fetched to invest so much interpretation in such a little text, the overall significance of this example lies in the attention to speakers' rights to talk, the opportunities available for taking the conversational floor and the implications these have for the psychological evaluation of the quality and quantity of what children say. As a further illustration, Sacks discusses the characteristic opening question used by children: 'You know what?' This is one of a curious class of questions that properly invites another question ('What?') as its answer. Moreover, it is the initial answerer rather than the questioner who has the 'reserved right' to speak again after the other speaks. This may seem a paradoxical device for children to use to promote their access to the conversational floor. However, not only does the child speak again through the obligation to reply to the 'What?' question, but she is also answering an 'open' question, in the sense that the asker does not know, but the child *does know* the answer. The child can then go on to talk about whatever she deems to be an appropriate answer through meeting the obligation of replying to a question. (Consider the rise of the 'opener' 'what it is, is . . .' – often used at the beginning of unsolicited phone calls – that functions as such precisely because it implies that the interlocutor has asked the question 'What is it?', and so accords the speaker the right to 'reply' to the question they position the other as having posed.)

Sacks takes the prevalence of 'You know what?' questions in children's talk as indicative of children's restricted speaking rights: by using this device they can ensure that they will be allowed to speak again (through the obligation to answer the question 'What?'). What this pattern of turn taking suggests is that children have rights to *begin* to talk but they may continue only if requested. This device guarantees them some space to talk within the conventions of the structure of conversation. Hence the structure of language is used to secure, albeit limited, conversational access by children. An understanding of children's status and speaking rights therefore enters into the form and structure of what they say.

Conversational analysis has since developed into a wide discipline concerned with the fine grain of talk (see e.g. Wooffitt 2005). It elucidates the covert rules of interaction and their negotiation, focusing on the detail of the conversation, mainly via elaborate transcription schemes that document paralinguistic features such as hesitations and rising intonational contours, on the basis of which interpretations can be made regarding the speaker's intentions. Sometimes this can even allow interpretation of what is not said. So in Silverman *et al.*'s (1998) analysis of the conversation between a parent and teacher at a school parents' evening, the authors argue that the child's silence in this interaction works as a strategy to avoid being enlisted into a discourse of moral improvement.

Learning one's place

Children also indicate through the language they use their developing *awareness* of the power relationships within which they (and others) are positioned. Children's sociolinguistic skills of interpreting and adapting their talk to particular contexts have been used to assess their social as well as linguistic understanding, as in Elizabeth Slosberg Andersen's (1990) research with children who were invited to display their understanding of gender, professional and caregiving linguistic registers through playing out scenarios with puppets. Much work in this area has focused on children' s use of markers of politeness (itself a huge area of cross-linguistic study). Ervin Tripp *et al.*'s (1984) year-long observational study of four families with two or more children aged between two and eight years investigated children's developing understanding of power relations within their families through the analysis of what they call 'linguistic control acts'. In analysing the structure of talk addressed to parents, siblings, child visitors and researchers, they noted that children's 'effective power', or the ability to get compliance from their addressee, was dependent on many factors. Although typically accorded a low-status position, within the familial context children could exert some power, particularly in securing compliance from caregivers when requesting goods and services constructed as due to them by virtue of discourses of parental obligation to care for children.

Ervin Tripp *et al.* (1984) also analysed how the form of requests reflected both the esteem with which the addressee is endowed by the speaker and the speaker's evaluation of the 'costliness' of the request. A developmental pattern was documented of increasing variety of forms in which to express deference, ranging from overt forms (such as 'Please'), to justifications (where the speaker attempts to present a rationale for their request or bases it on common-sense norms rather than naked assertion of power), to more indirect forms of allusion or hinting, where the goal of the request is not made explicit (as where 'It's very cold in here' functions as an indirect request to turn the heating on). This covert form expresses the greatest esteem for the speaker by according him or her the choice of ignoring the implicit request. Ervin Tripp *et al.* also analyse examples of children rapidly moving from more to less explicit forms of request as they are forced to revalue its 'cost' to the addressee. The authors report the following inter-action in which Patty, an adult female researcher, was addressed by Saul, a three-year-old boy:

S: Hey, I'm hungry
P: Didn't you eat your breakfast?
S: No, I didn't. I just go to bed, and I want to eat. I'm hungry
P: You're hungry
S: Could you get me something to eat?
P: No I can't. You have to ask your Mom
S: Well, Momma won't give me something
P: (laughing) Well, why not?
S: Because he he [sic] won't fix me anything
P: Doesn't she usually?
S: No. Do you have a lot of cake at your house?

(Ervin Tripp *et al.* 1984: 133)

In this extract the differing formulations used by Saul reflect his changing evaluations of the 'cost' of his request. Initially this was expressed as a direct demand ('I'm hungry'), then it became clear that this was a request which Patty was not going to comply with immediately. Saul moved then to justification ('I want to eat. I'm hungry'), and then to a polite formulation ('Could you get me something to eat?') and finally resorted to a very indirect hint ('Do you have a lot of cake in your house?'). Once again issues of power are central not only in the use of deferential forms, but in the expectation that Patty as a female researcher would respond to demands cast in terms of need and nurturance.

As the example above illustrates, in the display of flexibility in the forms and strategies used in relation to the cost of their requests, young children also demonstrate their awareness of gender-specific roles and responsibilities through the differential forms of their requests to their parents. Less polite imperatives were directed to mothers and more appeasing explanations to fathers. This reflects culturally sanctioned expectations that mothers function to meet the demands of children, especially if these are expressed as 'needs'. Children correspondingly used assertions of want and helplessness to make their mothers comply. The authors comment on the utterance of a seven-year-old boy who said 'If you don't give [me] some now, I won't want any later.' In order for this to function as a threat, we must presume that mothers have some investment in their caregiving role, at least in the form of being seen to fulfil their role as proper mothers. Correlatively, mothers were noted as being more co-operative to the requests of girls than boys. Moreover, it seemed that girls used a greater range of strategies in dealing with demands made of them while not complying any more frequently than boys; girls ignored requests as much as they refused or complied with them. What this study indicates is, first, that gender issues are highly salient within routine parent–child interaction (to both parent and child) and, second, that gender enters into the forms of language expressed by and directed to children. This awareness of discourses of gender can be regarded as a specific example of the ways social meanings, including those which mark power asymmetries, inform the contexts and the products of children's talk even in a language such as English, that does not readily (lexically or grammatically) 'mark' these relationships between gender, age and power (see Baxter 2002 for an example applied to educational contexts).

Changing places?

Not only do children express their awareness of asymmetries and roles through the forms of language they use, but they also draw on alternative discourses to change their positioning. Walkerdine (1981) analyses some astonishing material where two three-year-old boys verbally sexually harass their female nursery school teacher in response to her criticism of their behaviour towards another (girl) child. Walkerdine discusses this in terms of the boys assuming the position of men within language in relation to which the teacher, as a sexually objectified woman, is positioned as inferior. They therefore counter their relatively powerless position as pupils in relation to her authority as a teacher by using a discourse of cultural masculinity which positions women as passive and powerless. What this illustrates is that not only is there a range of possible positions made available by alternative discourses structuring social relations, but also that these positions are competing and contradictory. In this example the multiplicity of positionings functions as a resource by which the inferior status arising from the configuration of one discourse can be resisted.

In Burman (1992a) I describe how I set up a role play within interviews I was conducting with children by which I asked them to interview me. Intended as an attempt to create a more egalitarian structure within my research by according them more authority as 'interviewers', at one point I found myself constrained by the very discursive structure I had set up to answer questions that demanded a degree of personal disclosure I found most uncomfortable. (It should also be noted that this was a situation in which I, like many other researchers, routinely placed children.) When 'Anna' asked me if I had a 'boyfriend', not only was I unable to avoid answering the question without challenging her conversational control and thereby departing from the fragile 'role play' I had set up, but I was also unable to define my own terms to talk about relationships and friendships. The pressure for my compliance arose from my own presentation of the interview encounter as voluntary and collaborative. Not only was I forced to position myself within the discourse of compulsory heterosexuality (Rich 1983), but the requirement to speak arose from those immediate and wider discursive structures of the role play and the research interview that had authorised me to set up the research encounter in the first place.

Even though this arose during an interviewing relationship within which I was positioned as more powerful, within adult–child and experimenter–subject relations, I could not therefore depart from the structure of talk which positioned me as subordinate and under obligation to respond. My child 'interviewer' was able to use the discursive structure of the interview encounter to assert control over conversational topic as well as turn.

In *The Mastery of Reason* (1988), Valerie Walkerdine discusses how casting a psychological assessment within the framework of a task or game (as developmental psychologists often do) presents a misleading represen-tation of the structural power relations of experimenter and child. In particular, the kinds of questions typically asked of children within such investigations draw upon pedagogical discursive practices, such as asking children pseudo-questions, that is, questions where they know that we know the answers (consider the I-R-E sequence discussed in Chapter 10). She argues:

> What is a game, and how are the roles of the participants defined? How far does a device designed to lessen the effects of a powerful experi-menter, by 'putting the child at ease', also serve to render the power invisible, by disclaiming its presence, while making the child an object of an evaluative reading from a different discourse? It could be argued that, rather than helping, it is dishonest and disingenuous.
>
> (Walkerdine 1988: 54)

In the instance reported above I was required to adhere to the subject position of 'respondent' which I had assumed through my obligation to respect the rules of the pseudo-egalitarian structure I had set up. This is an interesting example precisely because it demonstrates how the partial but not complete coexistence of experimental and 'game' ('playing interviews') discursive practices can give rise to contradictions and divergences of subject positions of the kind analysed above. But this exceptional instance, itself brought about by a particularly assertive little girl, highlights the much more pervasive situation where the teaching/experimental discourse so invades and informs pseudo-collaborative psychologist–child interaction that, in the terms typically formulated, we cannot determine by which rules and roles the children are playing. This raises questions not only about the ways children read or understand the more covert manipulations of psychologist–child assessment, and the delusions of democracy that psychologists playing games with children may harbour (see also Chapter 13 for a critique of notions of democracy in education), but also links in with the fantasy of non-intervention and untainted scholarly purity with which observational work is often invested:

> It is important to note the positive effectivity of the experimental discourse in positioning me as 'experimenter' and the children as 'subjects'. This provides a set of rules, of regulations of practice, the interpretation of the practice, the interaction itself, in which certain things are done, said and then read. . . . Like the classroom, the experiment produces a discursive practice in which evidence is read, and a regime of truth produced; in that sense, then, the dichotomies objective/subjective take on a different significance. Similarly, those criticisms of experiments which treat observational data as more 'natural' or 'ecologically valid' fall into a trap, which fails to engage with the positive effectivity of the discursive practice in which any performance is produced.
>
> (Walkerdine 1988: 51)

Fixing interpretation

In addition to being a means of expression of, and intervention within, social relations, language is also the forum in which linguistic understanding is investigated. We have already seen how gender and cultural assumptions are reproduced both within language and the study of language. It is time to look more generally at the intersection between contexts of talk and the constitution of children's talk as a research object.

The analysis of 'discourse' both as method and as theoretical 'perspective' has had considerable impact within social psychology (Billig *et al.* 1988; Middleton and Edwards 1990; Parker and Shotter 1990; Parker

1992a; Parker *et al.* 1999; Willig 1999; Parker 2002), and offers useful critiques of developmental psychology (see e.g. Henriques *et al.* 1984; Davies and Harré 1990; Billington 2000; MacLure 2003). The recognition that social meanings are inscribed within language means that language is productive, as well as reflective, of meaning. While language constitutes meaning, this meaning is not only a free-floating linguistic array but is also irreducibly tied to material-political structures. Indeed the very concept of discourse disrupts the idea of 'language', since it is not reducible to the merely linguistic (Jaworksi and Coupland 1999; Haworth 2000; Fairclough 2003). Requests from teachers to have dreams interpreted, to have their labelling of a child as 'damaged' ratified, anxious questions from mothers after their children have taken part in some developmental psychological study of 'Did she do all right?' – all these are routine indications of, and elements of, the contradictory but privileged discourses, or sets of expert knowledge, with which developmental psychological researchers are credited. This book has already described the discourses that structured the emergence of developmental psychological practice and the consequences of these for its terms of enquiry, in particular in constituting 'the child', 'the family' and women (as mothers) as focal objects. The positions these (clinical, scientific) discourses delineate overdetermine and structure current developmental psychological practice. As the above examples illustrate, they structure the ways in which developmental psychological researchers are perceived when they go into schools or homes. They fuel the power of evaluation and regulation with which researchers are invested.

Issues of power correspondingly enter into the discursive structure by which developmental psychological research is constituted and interpreted. They inform the production as well as the interpretation of what children say. As discussed in earlier chapters in this book, some current critiques of developmental psychology have highlighted how the dominant discourses which portray children as inherently benign and mothers as facilitative of development thereby suppress or fail to see the ambiguity and indeterminacy of, especially, infant action and interaction (Urwin 1984; Bradley 1989). The power of the discourses therefore works not only at the level of determining the agenda for research questions, but also in selectively structuring the 'evidence'. One kind of strategy to explore the ways in which power has entered into the structure of developmental psychological research is to recover the multiple meanings that have been obscured. On the other hand, an analysis which attends to the diversity and ambiguity of interpretations of children's talk and activity can simply work to celebrate the multiplicity of interpretations without clearly theorising the constitutive effects of power.

Within the role-play part of the study from which the example above was drawn, another child, (whom I will call) 'Ravi', moved from asking me questions (about how I arrived at the school and where my bicycle was) to make the comment 'Sometimes bicycles get stolen.' I interpreted this statement as an offer of an issue he wanted to talk about, and the lexical indeterminacy of the statement not only as indicating his awareness that he was deviating from the role-play structure, but also as constituting an indirect request to abandon it. In this context the role play was dispensable, or at least positioned as enframed within, or constituted by, a set of broader structural power relations which accorded me the right to accept or reject his offer. The important point to note about this is that in terms of my original, quite typical, developmental psychological research question the indeterminacy of Ravi's statement could be taken to indicate a failure of understanding rather than comprising a specific discursive negotiation. 'Sometimes bicycles get stolen' is a syntactically and semantically anomalous statement, with maximum lexical markers of uncertainty – of time, person and number. On a purely linguistic reading it can generate at least three possible sets of interpretations, as friendly advice, as a veiled threat, and as a request to narrate a specific past experience. But the ambiguity it expresses qualifies not the certainty of what has happened or might happen, but the tentativeness of the request. The uncertainty does not concern whether or not a bicycle has been stolen, or whose bicycle has been stolen, but rather whether it was permissible for him to talk about his. Questions of power have here entered the linguistic structure of what is said as well as how it is interpreted (see Burman 1992a, 1993).

While this example harks back in some ways to Sacks' analysis, described earlier, of the fruitful ambiguity of seemingly indeterminate syntactic forms (such as 'D'you know what?') as a means to gain permission to speak, its significance can be developed in two ways. First, taking such issues seriously demands a careful scrutiny and revaluation of the contexts in which received wisdom about children's knowledge and abilities is arrived at. Second, despite the multiple readings and referents that can be drawn from Ravi's statement, an attention to the structural effects of power relations within the adult–child, experimenter–child encounter can work to disambiguate, or fix, interpretation. Discourses, including those constituting developmental psychology, are more than linguistic. Language may constitute the material world, and may even comprise the totality of our understanding of it, but the discursive arrangement of meaning arises from material-political structures. There may be no unadulterated 'truth' of what children are 'really' like or 'really' know, but rather our task is to be better able to interpret and recognise how the context of investigation structures that which we 'discover' or document.

Between the lines/beyond words

We have already encountered an example that attempted to interpret the significance of not speaking, as well as of what is said (see the discussion of Silverman *et al.* 1998), while in Chapter 6 we also considered how the project to 'give voice' to children could work in disempowering, as well as empowering, ways – by inciting accounts of personal experience that could in some circumstances work to make the speaker feel exposed and vulnerable. At a more general level the practice of consulting with children and young people, 'giving them voice' to comment on policies and practices, whilst important, can not only function tokenistically but also at a cynical level the elicitation of individualised opinions (which 'user consultations' generally provide) can work to legitimate the construction of a limited programme for change.

The fifth example to be considered in this chapter concerns multidisciplinary case conferences, or review meetings, of the kind routinely convened around children and families. Case conferences are decision-making arenas, with the decisions made having considerable impact on the lives of those who are its focal topic (in relation to schooling provision or custody, for example). They are convened in schools to determine causes of action in relation to specific children's education provision. It is a significant reflection on the complex relations between matters of language and power that participants in such case conferences – including the high status professionals – typically report dissatisfaction with such meetings and a sense of mystification about how the decisions made were arrived at. An action research project set up to analyse their process (Marks 1993a, 1993b; Marks *et al.* 1995) further highlighted how participants were drawing on competing discursive frameworks that at times converged or overlapped and so were indistinguishable, but at other points in the conversation they diverged considerably. These sudden shifts between agreement and apparent gaps in mutual understanding often marked significant disruption to, or alternatively a turning point in, the decision-making process.

Here we need to invoke a model of discourse that goes beyond the words or particular conversational roles structuring the record of a particular interaction, to connect these to broader institutional frames. Throughout this book we have been dealing with how developmental psychology informs particular understandings of the meanings and positions of 'parent', 'mother', 'father', 'child', 'youth', 'teacher', etc. and we have been exploring the consequences of these for how parents and teachers and children may experience themselves and their relationships with each other. Discourses, or frameworks of meaning, not only constitute the objects of which they speak, but these objects are also subjects (Parker 2002). Put another way, we are both subjected to, and subjects of, discourse. So in order to understand what is going on in educational case conferences we have to go beyond the precise words spoken and their turn-taking sequence (though these may well offer useful clues) to consider how these also bring institutional relationships and structures into play.

To be specific, it is clear that how we describe a child's schooling difficulties is indicative of our evaluation of, or explanation for, those difficulties. To talk of a 'problem child' labels the child *as* the problem, while a 'child with problems' can open up for discussion the contexts and relationships in which such problems occur: that is, positioning the 'problem' as residing in interactions or physical circumstances. In our case conference research, we could identify several competing discourses, each of which portrayed the child and the problem differently, with correspondingly different proposed outcomes identified. A key context for the research was the longstanding (see Coard 1971) concern at national and regional levels with the number of African-Caribbean boys who were labelled as having behavioural and moderate learning difficulties, and this trend continues today, although the labels have shifted slightly (Sewell 1997).

To return to the discourses surrounding the child in education case conferences, throughout the 30 or so such conferences that were analysed, several key discourses emerged. First, what we called 'the school management' discourse focused on the child as a discipline problem, and therefore as a *problem for* the school. The desirable outcome, according to this discourse, was to have the child removed from the school. A second discourse that was just as prevalent was 'developmental', in the sense that it interpreted problem behaviour in terms of developmental life stages such as 'adolescence' and associated age/stage-related concerns such as 'showing off to peers' and 'testing out boundaries'. Extract One shows these discourses at work (with transcription conventions following the scheme suggested by Potter and Wetherell 1987).

Extract One: from adolescent image-making to response to specific contextualisation

Education Welfare Officer (EW): Is he creating a status?
Head of Year (HY): He certainly is doing that (.) in that these situations occur when there is an audience . . .
EW: Withdrawing him is perhaps the best thing to do for Mike (.) because that stops the situation escalating (.) you know (.) play to an audience (.) mm because he is very different in (. . .) isn't he?
. . .
Educational Psychologist (EP): He's feeding into that image again isn't he?
HY: Yeah
EP: With respect to the intimidation (.) that will (.) or the (assertion) of power (.) are there particular pupils where he does this more than others (.) is there a pattern to it or could it happen to anyone?

Yet this framework around special developmental 'needs' could also give rise to a similar outcome to the first: removing the child from the mainstream school to a specialist educational resource where he would receive more attention and 'have more space to be himself'. A third discourse which, as we will see, was rather harder to specify concerned gender and 'race' issues, and their impact on the child as an explanatory framework for the problematic behaviour under discussion at a particular case conference. The area for action and intervention arising from this discourse was not the child, but the *contexts* in which the child's actions occurred: to support the school in dealing with the gendered and racialised contexts in which his problematic behaviour happened, and to open up the question of whether the actions were causes of, or alternatively responses to, provocation. Significantly, this 'contextual' discourse shared a key term or discursive element with the 'developmental/child-centred' discourse: identity.

Extract Two: racism, identity and adolescence – tensions and temporary convergence

EP: He needs to find an arena he can really get his positive image from/
EW: /That's right yes/
EP: /In a non-aggressive way
EW: And would that group allow (.) give him a permission (.) to be himself?
(.)
EP: Is there any work done in school about identity and sort of (.) particularly (.) a perspective on racism and problems they've . . .

Finally, in this case conference the educational psychologist tries to mobilise a rather different explanatory framework: one which positions the child as a victim rather than a perpetrator, and his actions as a response rather than a cause. Here we might draw upon some conversational analytic techniques to interpret the remarkable hesitancy and indirectness of the formulation below, with its multiple reformulations, as indicative of her anticipation that she is putting forward a 'minority' or unpopular view that is likely to encounter some hostility. Notice here that the remedial approach implied would be one of *supporting the school* to address the home and school circumstances of the child, rather than removing him from the school.

Extract Three: articulating racism?

EP: and certainly (.) talking to him as (.) as I have about life outside school (.) and so on (.) I mean that's very much a part of it (.) the reality (.) maybe that's been brought into the school (.) and looking at the (.) the dimension of skin colour (.) again I suppose (.) I don't know whether you'd agree with me (.) but I'd like to say that (.) that very often it seems that (. . .) black boys (.) where they feel that power's taken away from them (.) in more ways than one (.) and perhaps that the future is possibly bleak (.) that they can assert some

power in this way (.) by intimidating people (.) that's their only way
of feeling good (.) I mean that's one way of looking at it

(Burman 1996a: 2–18)

A further significant feature is that this model does not only concern 'race'
and the possible response to experiences of racism, but also gender – or
rather their intersection. For circulating in this interaction is an unspoken
but still indisputably present wider discourse that combines gender and
racialisation to constitute a young African-Caribbean man as a threat. In
relation to our previous discussions of rights to talk, and the multiple
meanings of silence, it is worth noting that at this particular case conference
the child's mother was present, but the child who was at the centre of its
proceedings was not. Moreover, we have seen how these different discourses give rise to quite different outcomes, in terms of recommendations
for intervention, with the child and his family.

It is important to emphasise that the process of subscribing to these
discourses was not conscious or intentional but rather indicative of the
ways we are spoken to by language as much as speaking it – in the sense of
cultural frameworks inevitably entering into our ways of thinking and
acting. In this sense, a discursive framework moves the analytic focus away
from the individual or their talk, to the historical conditions that create the
conditions in which this talk can occur. It therefore marks discursive
frameworks as challenging traditional psychological models which portray
thoughts or 'attributions' only in individual terms (Potter and Wetherell
1987) and which treat identities as properties of oneself rather than interactional performances (Parker 2002). Since this research was generated in
response to concern from educational professionals, we were able to use
this material to develop training materials. These helped staff explore
dominant meaning frameworks that enter their everyday professional
interactions, from a perspective that explored the cultural resources they
inadvertently mobilised, rather than the oppressive ideas they somehow
'possessed' (see Marks *et al.* 1995).

This avenue of research has opened up new vistas of developmental and
educational research that have had fruitful consequences and, more
importantly perhaps, significant consequences for professional practice. It
also connects with developments in modes of therapeutic intervention (see
Parker 1999) and the rise of 'narrative psychology' (Squire 2000). For
example, Billington (2000) uses discourse analysis to trace through the
shifts in construction and deconstruction of a child's 'educational needs' for
a local educational authority statement (the legal document which generates
the resources for provision). He documents how phrases are transposed or
alternatively omitted from the cumulative reports written by different
professionals, which give rise to quite different representations, and corresponding recommendations for the child's education provision. Similarly,
Moss and Petrie (2002) analyse a key British educational policy document

to highlight the model of childhood underlying the programme for 'children's services' being outlined, and are thereby able to illuminate the shortcomings of its model – since children are portrayed as passive and in need of protection and segregation. MacNaughton (2005) proposes strategies for 'affirming and attending to the "other"' in discourse, which include attending to which meanings are set in circulation, and which are silenced or (pre)supposed. These include: highlighting forms of binary analysis; exposing those meanings that are erased; 'wondering' other meanings; and generating descriptive metaphors as tactics for deforming and contradicting meanings. Further, to help 'map' meanings, she recommends seeking multiple meanings, meaning traces and the limits to such meaning. Finally, she describes the uses of an 'epistemological shudder' as an aid to envisaging alternative possibilities, rather than those foreclosed by current discursive surroundings, that is, 'seeking the otherwise'.

In the past three chapters I have described moves to set up more socially based accounts of language development and use (which have largely failed within more traditional approaches). I have drawn attention to the importance of issues of difference which are usually suppressed or devalued within mainstream models, but which actually demonstrate the impossibility of a single model of the language learner or language teacher. Finally, this chapter has focused on power relations, as structuring differences between children, parents and researchers, differences that are mediated by gender, class and cultural-racialised positions. Drawing attention to these power relations is not (only) a matter of highlighting the ways children are oppressed and how they manoeuvre within these unequal relationships. For these are not simply local aberrations or abuses, but form the material and discursive structures within which, and in relation to which, developmental psychology functions. Indeed this is exactly the charge formulated by child rights advocates and the 'new' sociologists of childhood: that developmental psychology function with a deficit model of childhood that, as we shall see in Chapter 12, always risks mistaking the limits imposed by the structural and interpersonal context for the 'competence' of the child. The realms of signification that developmental psychology elaborates, of 'sensitive' mothers, of 'damaged' or even 'whole' children (see later), of scientific research and clinical evaluation (read disinterested façade masking manipulation and exploitation?), are firmly connected to the historical and current professional-political practice of developmental psychology.

Further reading

The following texts specifically address adult–child, and in some cases specifically psychologist–child, relationships:

Burman, E. (1992a) 'Feminism and discourse in developmental psychology: power, subjectivity and interpretation', *Feminism and Psychology*, 2, 1: 450.

Davies, B. and Harré, R. (1990) 'Positioning: the discursive production of selves', *Journal for the Theory of Social Behaviour, 20, 1*: 433.

Walkerdine, V. (1981) 'Sex, power and pedagogy', *Screen Education, 38*: 14–21, reprinted in *Schoolgirl Fictions*, London: Verso, 1990.

Other key texts for analysing discourses in educational and developmental research:

Billington, T. (2000) *Separating, Losing and Excluding Children*, London: Falmer Press.

MacNaughton, G. (2005) *Doing Foucault in Early Childhood Studies: Applying Poststructural Ideas*, Abingdon and New York: RoutledgeFalmer.

MacLure, M. (2003) *Discourse in Educational and Social Research*, Maidenhead: Open University Press.

Suggested activities

Generate (ensuring informed consent) a record of some adult–child talk, of the sort that happens at teatime. Use this as a resource for:

(a) engaging with the issues posed by determining 'informed consent' – how can this be distinguished from 'compliance'?

(b) engaging with the issues raised by doing transcription, of which those raised by child language pose in miniature the wider questions about selectivity and interpretation in the transforming of an auditory representation into a written one. For material on this, see:

(c) discussing the variety and complexity of the power relationships being elaborated, in terms of what broader sets of meanings (of e.g. gender or parental or child responsibilities) they instantiate.

If the taping is not being conducted in the home of the person who is taping and he or she is present:

- How is he or she addressed or included within encounter?
- If they are not present, then why not (and what fantasies of non-contamination of data are being maintained)?
- Does this remove the process of interpretation?
- How is the purpose of the enterprise discussed, and what does this indicate about the position of the psychologist/student/researcher?

Part IV

Cognitive development: the making of rationality

This final part analyses the significance of Piaget's and Vygotsky's contributions as major intellectual figures and resources for developmental psychology. Chapter 12 explores how cultural issues mingle with those of method in how and why and in what ways their ideas were taken up. Chapter 13 considers the impact of the educational applications associated with their ideas. Chapter 14 moves from the cognitive developmental account of moral development to reflect on the moral status of developmental psychological practice, and this book within it.

12 Piaget, Vygotsky and developmental psychology

He's researching surface texture, differentiating between colours, and developing his audiosensory perception. He thinks he's playing with a rattle.

(for Duplo, *Parents* magazine, December 1984)

The name most associated with developmental psychology, indeed in popular accounts almost synonymous with it, is still that of Jean Piaget. This is notwithstanding the rise of interest in Vygotskyan approaches within the discipline, and various subsequent syntheses and reformulations. This focus of this chapter, therefore, will be on why and how Piaget's work has come to occupy this position, with some contrasts and connections made to the position accorded to Vygotsky. We follow through some of the classic debates and criticisms, attending to key theorists and commentators.

It is fair to say that no nurse, social worker, counsellor or teacher will complete her training without learning about Piaget's stage model of cognitive development. Not only is this somewhat surprising when we consider that Piaget's primary interest was neither in psychology nor in education, but it also marks something of the particular construction and reception of Piaget's ideas both within the discipline of developmental psychology and the applied practices it informs. It is this process of selective uptake and distribution of ideas, structured by the particular work the model was invoked for, that forms the topic of this chapter.

Filtered knowledge/disciplinary effects

It is useful when reflecting on perceptions of the contribution of Piaget's work to recall the variety of disciplines he worked within, and across. So, while his role in education, psychology and philosophy of science is well known, the fact that he also held professorships in sociology from 1939–1952, and before that from 1925–1929 jointly in psychology and philosophy of science, is largely forgotten. He was also a member of the International Psycho-Analytic Association, was in analysis for some time and even wrote on developmental psychology and psychoanalysis (Piaget 1919), but most Anglo-US psychologists are unaware of this.

Similarly, as we have already seen (in Chapters 9 and 10), Vygotsky appears in developmental textbooks in relation to his dispute with Piaget over his different interpretation of 'egocentric speech' (a term which in fact derives from Piaget's engagement with psychoanalysis), and as the originator of educational strategies that engage the child through their 'zone of proximal development' (ZPD). Yet Vygotsky was also a polymath, as interested in literature and art as he was in neurology and psychology. Indeed in both cases, while as individuals they were both visionary and original, their work was more than individual. As we will see, Piaget's Centre for Genetic Epistemology evolved its own school and perspective that remained at odds with the dominant reception of Piagetian work in Anglo-US psychology.

Even more significantly perhaps, mainstream accounts of Vygotsky focus on the man himself, subscribing to the romantic Western story of the misunderstood Soviet genius, who died of tuberculosis at the tender age of 37 offering only a sketch of a theory of culture and consciousness whose implications subsequent scholars are still exploring. Accounts vary over just how committed Vygotsky was to the project of developing a Marxist psychology, preferring to emphasise his liminal position as deeply knowledgeable about but also able to critically evaluate debates in Western psychology. 'Vygotsky's writings provide a special perspective – that of a 'stranger' who – without belonging to the mainstream of Western psychology – was its astute observer and commentator' (Kozulin 1990: 3).

Indeed the popularity of his work was affected by the political turbulence of post-revolutionary Russia – from running a major institute in the 1920s to being banned after his death during the Stalinist era – but its reception has been structured according to currents in Western psychology:

> It is not surprising, therefore, that when Vygotsky's ideas began to percolate through to the West in the 1960s, only the most 'compatible' were immediately accepted. Among these were the notions of the unity of cognition and behavior, and the social origin of individual behavior. What for Vygotsky early on became a starting point for psychological inquiry, for his western followers, like Jerome Bruner, was the result of years of struggle with and within neobehaviorism. Next came recognition of different modes of speech in child development. This time an appreciation for Vygotsky came on the wave of popularity for his former opponent, Jean Piaget. Later on a surge of interest in cross-cultural and literacy studies and once again Vygotsky's works proved to be relevant. Taking into account this step-by-step rediscovery of Vygotsky's works, it becomes clear that they should not be treated as an artifact of the past, but rather as still incompletely understood blueprints for the future of psychology.
>
> (Kozulin 1990: 5–6)

Further, it has been suggested that the collaborative character of Vygotsky's work has been underestimated to suit the Western, bourgeois model of research and scholarship as an individual activity. Stetsenko and Arievitch (2004), while admitting the shifts in popularity and state support for the approach, argue that the ideas associated with Vygotsky should be considered as part of a more collective and collaborative group project. They draw on letters and records highlighting how Vygotsky himself saw this work as joint, as well as pointing to the shifting authorship of some of his books.

Yet notwithstanding the rise of interest in cultural-historical (Vygotsk-yan) approaches within the discipline, Piaget remains the dominant psychological resource for professionals who want to know how children think. This is in contrast to the current academic climate that largely downplays Piaget's importance although, as we have seen, continuities remain within the current trend for 'theory of mind' research (discussed in Chapter 3). However, features of both the model and his questions live on. It could be argued that it is precisely because Piaget's influence on developmental psychology has been so profound in structuring the form of the discipline that it is largely invisible.

Impressive as Piaget's work was, its popularity (and subsequent fluctuations in popularity) is not simply a response to its intrinsic worth. This chapter explores the role and impact of Piaget's work, treating this not (only) in terms of the achievements of an individual man. Rather, his work provides a case study in evaluating steps in the process of formulating, taking up and interpreting a set of ideas. The movement from theorist to inscription in practice is complex. Piaget's guiding preoccupations reflected the cultural and historical contexts that his work also came to inform. Especially within Anglo-US readings of his work, aspects incongruent with the dominant empiricist culture are ignored or treated as flaws. As we shall see, some of these selections and suppressions provide useful indications of themes and functions that structure contemporary developmental psychology.

Of molluscs and men: Piaget and developmental psychology

Piaget has been held responsible for a number of specific contributions to developmental psychology. He is credited with the recognition that children's thinking is qualitatively different from that of adults, that different ways of thinking predominate at different ages and that these correspond with progressively more adequate ways of organising knowledge – hence his status as a stage theorist, and the association of his name in education and welfare practices with the apparatus of ages and stages (e.g. Burns 1986), despite the fact that notions of stage sequences were in wide circulation by the beginning of the twentieth century. His work is generally portrayed as humanist, countering the mechanistic accounts of child learning and training put forward by behaviourism, and emphasising children's active involvement in, and construction of, their learning environment (Ginsberg and Opper 1979; Gardner 1982). Piaget's focus on the organisation of knowledge and the elaboration of rules governing this organisation places him firmly as the exponent of the wider intellectual movement of structuralism within developmental psychology (Broughton 1981a).

His emphasis on adaptation reflects the backcloth of evolutionary theory, and he was instrumental in importing this theory into psychology. As the celebrated story goes, he started out working on environmental adaptations in molluscs (publishing a paper on this at the age of 11) and went on to apply the same concepts of assimilation, accommodation and adaptation to the development of logical thinking. Not only did he combine the disciplines through the transitions in his working life, but he also set out to link biology and philosophy through the study of the development of the child. Piaget was the creator and architect of 'genetic epistemology' (the study of the origins and growth of knowledge) as an expression of his interest in the developmental construction and organisation of thought. The overarching questions that prompted this model arose within the same late nineteenth and early twentieth century concern to uncover 'truths' about the nature of thinking which informed the development of social anthropology, psychiatry and criminology.

A further factor in the popularity of Piaget's model was that it presented a model of development in interactionist terms at a time of dissatisfaction with the 'empty vessel' environmental determinism of behaviourism as well as the rationalism and innatism of genetic determinism. Offering a model that drives development from the concrete to the abstract, he traced a trajectory from early reaction patterns to primitive habits to rational, logical thought. Piaget's work also paved the way for the cognitive approach that has come to dominate psychology for the past five decades, with his influence seen most particularly in cognitive science and artificial intelligence (Boden 1979; Papert 1980; Rutkowska 1993). In terms of methodology, Piaget attempted to counter some of the spurious assumptions of empiricism that guided standardised testing methods through his 'clinical' or 'critical' interviewing procedures, although this aspect has been eclipsed within the selective incorporation of Piaget's work within Anglo-US developmental psychology.

Piaget's questions

Although the consequences of this are rarely understood, Piaget's project of genetic epistemology meant that he was interested in children only insofar as they instantiated, and provided a forum for investigating, general epistemological questions about the origins and growth of thought. There are several implications of this. First, his preoccupation with the general knower or 'epistemic subject' rather than individual children means that he was not primarily a 'psychologist'. Irrespective of whether there is a specific domain of the psychological, Piaget intended to work in psychology for only a brief period before returning to biology or philosophy. His interest lay in providing a general account of the emergence of knowledge, rather than a specific analysis of how and when individual children exhibited this. Interestingly, despite holding many professorships in psychology and education within his lifetime (including in experimental psychology) in France and Switzerland, he had no formal qualifications in psychology. When in 1976 he wanted to present his book on the equilibration of cognitive structures to the University of Geneva (where he had worked since 1929) as a thesis for a doctorate in psychology, the university officials refused on the grounds that his work could not be contained within one discipline (Gruber and Vonèche 1977: xiii).

Many of the debates around the status of Piagetian research arise from the failure to appreciate that Piaget was not a psychologist nor primarily interested in the psychological implications of his work (see also Lourenco and Machado 1996). Nevertheless, genuine difficulties do arise in determining how to turn the Piagetian epistemological project into a psychological one. Through his exclusive focus on the abstracted epistemic knower, Piaget blurred the distinction between individual and socio-cultural context. As Venn and Walkerdine (1978) put it:

> For Piaget, the individual subject is an exemplar, the typical representative of the species. He subscribes to the Lamarckian idea of cumulative assimilation, whereby the characteristics of individuals over time are resorbed into a single intellectual organism. Thus the processes, including those of cognitive development are the same in all single individuals, so that one need only study any exemplar and generalise.
>
> (Venn and Walkerdine 1978: 79)

The Piagetian model is therefore unable to theorise cultural and historical change in relation to the development of knowledge. Moreover, since the content of thought is accorded less importance than its (generalisable) structure, the emphasis on action is eroded in favour of a tendency towards increasing abstraction and idealisation:

> For Piaget the development of thought becomes 'indifferent to' the actual content of thought and the material base, although constructed out of it. He speaks of action on the concrete as being the basis out of which the operational structures are constructed, but his account is in the end unsatisfactory because he is more concerned with the results of abstraction as indicators of the way the mind works. . . . He is not dealing with scientific knowledge as such.
>
> (Venn and Walkerdine 1978: 87)

Hence Piaget depicted a subject who is irrevocably isolated and positioned outside history and society (Riegel 1976; Broughton 1981b).

Having introduced some of the key aspects of Piaget's project and preoccupations, we can now turn to the ways these have been taken up and drawn upon to warrant particular psychological and educational practices. The popular equation of Piaget with developmental psychology threatens to ignore the conditions under which Piaget's work became so well known, and in particular its continuities with other bodies of theory which facilitated its assimilation into Anglo-US psychology. The child-centred approach with which his work is so heavily identified pre-dates his appearance on the British and US intellectual 'scene' (Walkerdine 1984). Moreover, Piaget's association with the current practice of developmental psychology, with a repertoire of conservation tasks cast as standardised assessments, seriously misrepresents his own methodological approach, ignores the debates about method that dogged Anglo-American debates with Geneva-based researchers and does not adequately account for the processes which transformed single case studies into experimentally administered tests (Burman 1996b). This selective incorporation is not so much a misreading as an opportunistic utilisation of techniques to fit into the already burgeoning 'technologies of the social' to which developmental psychology contributed.

Terms of the debates: continents and conflicts

Clashes over methods have played a major part in debates about the status of Piagetian theory, disputes that have been overdetermined by broader cultural and geographically informed differences in aims and epistemological framework. Put briefly, Piaget's investigations with children took place as the social sciences were moving from informal observation and experimentation to developing standardised forms of assessment, a tendency that Piaget, in general, vigorously opposed. His 'clinical method' or, as he later called it, 'critical examination' is a flexible semi-structured interviewing technique (which is still in use in Geneva today), involving several investigations across a variety of problems that is designed to provide a profile of each child's thinking. While Piaget's early investigations relied primarily on interpreting children's reports and opinions, with an early interest in the structure and coherence of their narratives, his investigations increasingly became based on children's actions as well as what they said about the result of their actions. This approach contrasts strongly with standardised experimental techniques in its emphasis on treating each encounter with a child in its own terms to 'take account of the whole mental context' (Piaget 1929: 19).

It is significant that Vygotsky, while critical of Piaget for his neglect of attention to language and culture, regarded Piaget's method as his most important contribution. From their very different perspectives, what they shared was an understanding of the participation of the researcher within the experimental task. Vygotsky depicted developmental research as indistinguishable from teaching and instruction contexts. In other words, the context for discovering what children know is inseparable from teaching them. This is what Newman and Holzman (1993) describe as his 'tool and result' approach. He saw empirical research as linked to the practical promotion of children's psychological functioning in future situations. The experimenter is therefore an active participant in the context of a study aiming to help children construct new means to solve the problems posed to them (Vygotsky 1978b). As with Piaget, the 'dependent variable' within Vygotsky's method is the experimenter's observation of the process by which the solution is reached. This model of the research process is a far cry from mainstream British and US developmental work in which the variables under investigation are located firmly within the child (rather than constructed in relation to the child) and the context of investigation is seen as neutral or invisible.

Hence a number of false oppositions have structured and polarised the Anglo-US interpretation of Piaget and Geneva-based Piagetian research. One issue that fuelled the industry of Piaget critique was based on a misrendering of the conservation task to sever the children's judgements from their explanations, with dispute over which of these was the more accurate index of children's knowledge (e.g. Brainerd 1973). A similar literature was devoted to splitting action from account (that is, what children said from what they did), giving rise to debates about whether verbal or non-verbal measures are the most appropriate (Miller 1976; Siegel 1978; Wheldall and Poborca 1980). Inadequate as these treatments were, what they did correctly highlight was the ambiguous role of language and neglect of social relations within Piagetian research. Whatever their insensitivities to the subtleties of Piaget's theoretical edifice, the debates about 'décalage' (which for Piaget has a complex theoretical meaning, but which is interpreted by Anglo-US researchers simply in terms of within-subject and between-subject variation) do question the structural character of the model. Studies which demonstrated that children (e.g. Donaldson 1978) and adults (McCabe 1987) performed inconsistently, or that their performance could vary dramatically according to slight modifications of task characteristics, challenged the idea of the successive emergence of distinct and coherent structures of thinking.

Broad differences of interpretation that are focused around methodological issues are also reflected in contrasting approaches to the concept of development. While Piaget was committed to a qualitative model of development in which stages came to play a key role, the preoccupations that motivated, in particular, the US research concerned the acceleration of development, as typified in the 'training studies' which try to teach children to do Piagetian-type problems at ever earlier ages. Piaget scornfully termed this the 'American question'. This development also challenges the qualitative and structural features of the model, replacing Piaget's temporally ordered sequence of development with a much more malleable motion of learning (although accounts varied according to whether they proposed that the period of time between stages was compressed or called for stages to be disposed of altogether). However, later on there were indications of rapprochement on this issue (e.g. Karmiloff Smith 1979).

A final area of misconception that spans both theory and method concerns the aims of Piagetian investigation. Piaget's ideas and research are often treated as investigating and determining whether or not a child 'has' a particular concept. Critiques of Piaget largely set out to show that under different circumstances children can demonstrate possession of the qualities associated with the concept at ages earlier than those indicated by Piaget – the so-called 'early successes' Donaldson (1978) and others describe. However, Piaget was less concerned with what children knew, and more interested in the status of their knowledge (Piaget 1929). His interest in mapping the growth of logic on to children's thinking led him to develop a taxonomy of children's responses to explore whether they regarded their opinions as necessary or contingent. This is an interest more in 'propositional attitude' (Russell 1982), or the status children accord their judgements as knowledge, or belief, or opinion, than in concept acquisition.

Missing links: Piaget and Vygotsky

Having reviewed some of the forms and agendas structuring the selective incorporation of Piagetian ideas, and indicated how this also exemplifies the issues posed in interpreting the impact of Vygotsky's work, it is now time to reflect a little more on their connections and what is missing from the dominant story we are told about them. In part this story works to undermine the reification of accounts of theory construction, since we see the fragility and arbitrary character of connections, encounters and their contingency on political events. In this case, there is a further suppressed story to tell regarding the covert connections between Piaget and Vygotsky through psychoanalysis. What in turn this illustrates is the ways dominant (political and cultural) agendas have selectively structured the renderings of the relationship between emotion-cognition, including as structured within their work too.

As indicated at the beginning of this chapter, Piaget's engagement with psychoanalysis has been little recognised or attended to in Anglo-US developmental psychology. Still less known is the fact that he had a daily training analysis for eight months, and presented a paper at the International Psycho-Analytic Congress in Berlin in 1922 at which Freud himself was present (indeed Piaget himself was rather insulted that the audience only looked at Freud throughout his reading of the paper, to gauge how to react to it). Our lack of knowledge in this area arises in part because Piaget was himself reluctant to discuss it, and even offered variable accounts about whether or not he completed his training analysis and, if not, who terminated it. But more recently further documentary material has come to light that has generated a psychodynamically oriented analysis of the themes and forms of Piaget's work (Schepeler 1993) and which also offers new connections with and interpretive insights into the development of Vygotsky's theorisings.

The key figure between them is Sabina Spielrein, herself a key psycho-analyst who was credited by Freud for inspiring the idea of the 'death impulse' (or death drive), and who played a key role in the translation of Freud's work and dissemination of psychoanalysis. It was Spielrein who was Piaget's psychoanalyst. Russian-born, but completing her studies in Switzerland, as a teenager Spielrein entered analysis with Jung (a fact that Schepeler claims Piaget did not know, since he was very dismissive of Jung's work), played a significant role within the later Jung–Freud split and returned to Russia in 1923. Significantly, Santiago-Delefosse and Oderic Delefosse (2002) note that she gave lectures at the newly founded Russian Psychoanalytic Society that were attended by Vygotsky and Luria, as well as holding a research position at the State Institute of Psychoanalysis, as a paedologist at the Village of the Third International, and the position of Director of the Child Psychology Section of the First University of Moscow.

Although psychoanalytic ideas were denounced and banned at the inception of Stalinism, and Vygotsky's ideas also suffered during this period, we should not allow this to occlude the fruitfulness of this early period of engagement with psychoanalytic ideas in the new Soviet Russia. However that context is relevant in interpreting the later reluctance of Vygotsky to explicitly associate with psychoanalytic ideas. As for Spielrein herself, her father and brother were arrested in the mid-1930s, and her brother was subsequently executed as a 'Trotskyist' agent. Psychology and paedology, the disciplines in which Spielrein worked, were denounced as 'deleterious' and the institutions closed. She worked as a school physician in Rostov for some years until 1941 when she was shot dead by occupying German troops in front of the town synagogue.

While Schepeler's (1993) account offers some psychoanalytic inter-pretations of Piaget's accounts of his analysis with Spielrein (as concerned with unresolved maternal transferences), Santiago-Delefosse and Oderic Delefosse (2002) provide a detailed analysis and comparison of the models of language and of thought across Piaget, Vygotsky and Spielrein's work – insofar as can be determined from the few of the latter's writings that have survived. Both accounts, however, emphasise the unique and specific influ-ence of Spielrein on both Piaget and Vygotsky, whilst also highlighting some differences, and the remarkable prescience and creativity of her ideas. It is from her influence that we see the psychoanalytic inflection of Piaget's early books, and in Vygotsky's proximity to psychoanalytic ideas. Indeed Piaget did acknowledge Spielrein's influence and inspiration as a colleague and co-researcher, rather than a psychoanalyst (it was she who had brought him to the Berlin conference in 1922 and they planned various research projects on child development together). With current interests in attachment theory now focusing on the analysis of the coherence and organisation of children's narratives (e.g. Oppenheim 2006), there are possibilities for forging further reconnections.

So for very different reasons both Piaget and Vygotsky disavowed the psychoanalytic connections in their models – Vygotsky for political reasons, Piaget for largely personal ones – with his lifelong preference for cognitive approaches derived from his difficulties with his mother. Indeed, according to Piaget's sister, herself a psychoanalyst, it seems that Piaget's difficulties in undertaking the rather unorthodox project of psycho-analysing his mother were responsible for his decision not to proceed further as a psychoanalyst: 'According to Madame Piaget-Burger, Piaget's effort at psycho-analysis ended rather abruptly when his mother refused to accept her son's interpretations. Piaget, his sister recalled, was strongly affected by this failure ("il aurait vivement ressenti cet echec", Vidal 1987: 189)' (Schepeler 1993: 269). However, despite their different origins we see as a joint result the suppression of the influence of psychoanalysis, and along with that a suppression of its joint influence on (and therefore a key aspect informing the commonalities between) two major developmental psychological approaches.

Continuities and resources: modernity, science and gender

My account so far may seem to imply that Piaget's concerns were far removed from those who have taken up his work, especially in Britain and the USA. As for Vygotsky, while it is clear that he was committed to generating a dialectical psychology to support the development of a post-revolutionary state, the relative recency with which his writings have become available – alongside their rather narrow interpretation in relation to specifically educational applications – tells an equivalent tale of selective incorporation. I have focused so far on points of tension to highlight the process and problems of this selective take-up of Piaget's work. However, there are also important points of convergence that clarify how and why these particular readings of Piaget and Vygotsky came to occupy so important a position within Anglo-US developmental psychology and their associated educational and welfare practices. In particular, the amenability of his ideas for incorporation within apparatuses of social regulation together with a common commitment to science and progress brought together these diverse traditions in the name of modern improvement.

In general, developmental psychology is a paradigmatically *modern* dis-cipline, arising at a time of commitment to narratives of truth, objectivity, science and reason. It shares its origins with psychology and the modern social sciences generally in the late nineteenth century, when scientific discoveries and developments were revolutionising Western Europe at every level from sanitation to railways, to factory production, to the triumph of science over religion. As already discussed in Chapter 1, developmental psychology participated in the post-Darwinian theorising which linked individual change and growth with evolutionary outcomes (Riley 1983). It was in this context that Piaget became the exemplar of developmental psychology, formulating his project of 'genetic epistemology', attempting to apply biological concepts of adaptation, environmental pressure and change to humans, which he specifically identified within the development of the child. However, it is important to note that Vygotsky too had a broader project in view, to facilitate transformational development at individual and societal levels, although this is generally less known about (or perhaps attended to) in Anglo-US psychology.

From the previous section we have seen that biographical factors enter into Piaget's repudiation of the affective sphere, as associated with femininity. Clearly such personal factors could only arise from, and certainly acquire such wide circulation through, much wider cultural resonances. The originator of modern science, Francis Bacon (1561–1626) inscribed the scientific project with gendered and racialised hierarchy, with his thesis 'The Masculine Birth of Time' (translated by Farrington in 1951) heralding a new model of scientific knowledge that would dominate and control nature, as a precursor to its harnessing for industrial capital (Merchant 1980). As Indian eco-feminist Vandana Shiva puts it:

> Science as a male venture, based on the subjugation of female nature and female sex, provided support for the polarization of gender. Patriarchy as the new scientific and technological power was a political need of emerging industrial capitalism. While on the one hand the ideology of science sanctioned the denudation of nature, on the other it legitimised the dependency of women and the authority of men. Science and masculinity were associated in domination over nature and femininity . . . The de-mothering of nature through modern science and the marriage of knowledge with power was simultaneously a source of subjugating women as well as non-European peoples.
>
> (Shiva 1997: 164–165)

Piaget's commitment to the modern project can be seen in his depiction of the developing child as a budding scientist systematically encountering problems in the material world, developing hypotheses and learning by discovery and activity (Piaget 1957). Here the individual is the unit of development, rationally resolving obstacles presented by, and within, the material world. Logic, epitomised within 'the scientific method', is cast as the pinnacle of intellectual development. This produces a model of thinking that treats the individual as prior and separate, and celebrates activity and discovery – qualities which also carry colonial and gendered nuances. As the quotation at the beginning of this chapter indicates, science, itself a gendered practice, becomes imported into representations of children such that the quintessential developing child was a boy (see also Walkerdine 1988; Walkerdine and Lucey 1989; Burman 1995a). Such assumptions are made and remade manifest in current advertising for 'educational' toys, where, until recent calls for greater gender neutrality in representations of children, as well as depicting the learner as a scientist 'he' [sic] is also depicted as an astronaut: 'His space top's heading for Venus (it's just to the left of the fridge). It's countdown time for intrepid astronauts' (*Under Five*, December 1990); and as a construction engineer:

> Fisher-Price understand that no major construction job is complete without a chicken on top. Even the simple act of picking up one of the blocks helps a baby learn how to grip. Once he's mastered that he'll try stacking them up. This is good too – it develops his eye/hand co-ordination. And even if he knocks the whole lot down, it's still edu-cational. (It shows a baby he's in control and gives him his first feelings of independence.)
>
> (for Fisher Price in *Practical Parenting*, September 1988)

Notice how being destructive or making a mess is sanitised ('if he knocks the whole lot down, it's still educational') so that any protesting mother is positioned as impairing motor ('developing eye/hand co-ordination') and emotional development ('shows a baby he's in control and gives him his first feelings of independence'). Texts such as these combine cognitive (problem-solving) with affective ('mastery') developmental imperatives, enjoining both indulgence and a requirement to bolster a fragile (male) ego. (Gender-specified) parent and child mirror the heterosexual and gender roles of woman and man through the positioning of woman as carer and the devel-oping child as masculine pioneer, or at least woman providing the beneficent gaze by which the illusion of the male(child)'s power and autonomy is maintained. (In Burman 1995a and 2003 I also explore other investments in the portrayal of mother and child as a heterosexual couple.)

Similarly, modern preoccupations not only permeate the identification of the subject of Piagetian developmental psychology, but also structure the model itself. In Piaget's account, the goal of development is greater adaptation to changing and ever more complex environmental demands. The developmental trajectory of children's thinking follows the 'up the hill' model of science and progress (Rorty 1980): a hierarchical model of 'cog-nitive structures' emerges whereby a more mature logic arises from and supersedes earlier and less adequate structures. The developmental path this produces is depicted as common to all, irrespective of culture and history. As such it is thoroughly normative (and Vygotsky's model also suffers from some of the same problems). The clash between Piaget, with his commit-ment to internal processes of 'equilibration' determining the pace of development, and the social reforming tendencies of 'compensatory education' (associated particularly with the USA and the work of Bruner) plays out the contradiction between naturalism and cultural intervention that pervades the modern project generally (Burman 1992b). The specific shape that these debates take within child-centred education forms the focus of the next chapter, while here we might note that Piaget's original preoccupations with children's theories about scientific and astronomical phenomena remain current research topics (Nobes *et al.* 2005; Panagiotaki *et al.* 2006).

Science and morality

Two further strands associated with modernity are exemplified within the Piagetian model (and not only the Anglo-US misreading of his work). The model is committed to the project of human emancipation (improving the condition of human life). As argued in the last section, the modern commitment to progress imposes an enclosed, self-sufficient, autonomous individual.

Second, as well as treating scientific rationality as the pinnacle of psychological development, Piaget follows the modern project in his faith in science as promoting well-being and peaceful coexistence as opposed to Social Darwinism, war, competition and so on. In common with others of his time, Piaget, developing his ideas in Europe between two world wars, was deeply concerned to envisage how morality and reason could prevail over what he saw as biological doom and destruction (Piaget 1918a, 1933):

> Science is one of the finest examples of the adaptation of the human mind. It is the victory of mind over matter. But how has this success been achieved? Not merely by accumulating knowledge and experience. Far from it. Rather by constructing an intellectual co-ordinating tool by means of which the mind is able to connect one fact with another. This is what we need socially . . . a new mental instrument at once intellectual and moral, for in such a sphere the two things are one.
>
> (Piaget 1933: 7)

In addition to his commitment to science, Piaget's religious background within liberal protestantism and active involvement within the student Christian activity testify to a lifelong preoccupation with (and commitment to) reconciling faith with religion and finding a rational basis for morality (Vandenberg 1993). Many of his earliest writings were on this theme, including his semi-autobiographical novel (Piaget 1918b). Vidal (1987) argues that Piaget's motivation to find the roots of morality in social coexistence derive as much from his early rejection of metaphysics and his search for a rational and objective basis for religion as from a desire to refute innatism in developmental psychobiology. Moreover, this was explicitly associated with accounts of disorder and upheaval in the political sphere (as a state of affairs to be avoided, rather than – as in Vygotsky's model – the conditions for the emergence of new forms of social life). While this rhetoric does not appear explicitly in Piaget's accounts of children's thinking, Vidal argues that they formed part of the motivation for his investigation of children's thinking, along with the general project to psychologise metaphysics.

Liberal paradoxes

In these ways, Piaget's model of individual development is deeply imbued with liberalism. The transition from egocentric to socially adapted thinking is explicitly formulated in anti-authoritarian terms: 'Every progress made in the different moral and social domains results from the fact that we have freed ourselves from egocentrism and from intellectual and moral coercion' (Piaget 1933: 22). In advocating 'new', 'child-centred' educational approaches, Piaget subscribed to the liberal view of education as the key to greater co-operation, and cautioned against the dangers of imposing a particular set of values or political philosophy, unable to acknowledge the imposition of the particular politics he advocated. As for other social reformers, childhood for Piaget became a topic of interest as the site of intervention for a particular social project, namely the promotion of peace and harmony. The challenge of educating children involved recognising adult faults of self-centredness and subjection to social coercion, as well as children's condition:

> Childhood, I believe, will furnish an explanation of our difficulties and failings. At the same time, however, it will teach us how to do better than we have done, showing us the reserves of energy that exist in human beings and the sort of education that will enable us to rise above our present level of development.
>
> (Piaget 1933: 13)

In these sentiments Piaget subscribed to Enlightenment philosophical beliefs that children can teach us what society can be like, can testify to the potential which participation in society has drummed out of us, harking back to the romantic notion of the child as 'father to the man'. While children testify to the malleability of human nature, to the violence of coercive society, they also demonstrate the achievement of modern Western society in relation to 'other' cultures who are seen as closer to nature. In this sense there is a paradoxical conception of childhood at work, whereby experience, culture and action both mitigate and afford biological forces. If war is natural, for example, then we need society to protect us from destruction. While Piaget's view was more sophisticated than this, his only recourse was still simply to invoke reason and love as equally inherent in human society (Piaget 1918a).

Other traces: cultural chauvinism

Like most other modern accounts Piaget's theoretical framework privileges masculine and Western forms of reasoning, stigmatising and dubbing as inferior the irrational. Piaget himself invited comparison across history and cultures to illustrate the value of Western 'progress':

> If we begin to lose faith in humanity, in the possibilities of progress of which mankind is capable, there is nothing that will so reassure us as to look back at the past and compare society today with those so-called primitive peoples. . . . Such a comparison is enough to show us not only how plastic mankind is, and how easily human nature can be transformed by its social environment, but also how this transformation is essentially the result of education. We will realise in fact that the primitive is intellectually and morally even more the slave of selfcentredness and social coercion than we are liable to be.
>
> (Piaget 1933: 21)

Indeed his model of scientific progress remains a serious companion to the model of scientific 'revolutions' put forward by Kuhn (1962; Tsou 2006). As already noted in earlier chapters, such child-primitive comparisons were commonplace in nineteenth-century anthropological, psychoanalytical and psychological theorising. What they indicate is that in its single-minded march to true maturity such a model is unaware of, and resistant to, recognising the cultural and historical origins and specificities of its own project. Even the term 'progress' has origins which lie in the secularisation of the life project, from divinity to social improvement, which (as we have seen) characterised Piaget's commitments, as well as recapitulating the themes of his era:

> A portentous faith built on progress is the real spiritual foundation of modern man, the tradition he stands on. The idea has been the most influential and ubiquitous notion in the formation of modern thought, merging the power of the model world with the speck of a chimerical metamorphosis of Christian faith. Progress possesses the brightness derived from its close link with the sacred – even where as here, the scared is not presented as such. It has the lustre of transcendence. Consequently, it has to be enshrined nowadays in achievement that would seem to confirm that man, the terminator of the gods, is indeed supplanting them through the conquest of the heavens in space and time. But its proper home remains the First World. There it reveals that man no longer needs a creator, but constantly re-fashions himself . . .

> Progress explains current phenomena inconsistent with its promise by reference to future perfection.
>
> (Sbert 1992: 195)

Thus sanctioned, the programme of 'progress' can be imposed on the rest of the world:

> Once the causes of the wealth of nations had been properly assigned to the novel Western way of subordinating society to the market and technological innovation, the idea of progress provided the new justification for inequality at home and Western self-assertion abroad. It was progress which had permitted Europeans to 'discover' the whole world, and progress which would explain their growing hegemony over the global horizon.
>
> (Sbert 1992: 197)

Chapter 14 takes up further the consequences of the resonances between the terms of individual and international economic development, whilst also indicating how psychologists have responded to criticisms of cross-cultural psychology. Here we can simply note that, at least at the level of common terminology, such resonances exist between the two domains, and have been used in the service of maintaining cultural chauvinisms. We should also note how frameworks have since emerged that formulate models of learning in context, focusing on notions of apprenticeship and situated learning. In particular the works of Rogoff (1990), Lave and Wenger (1991) and Wenger (1998) have been influential in shifting the unit of analysis away from the individual to portray knowledge as generated from and in relation to 'communities of practice'. But even if current comparisons between Western and non-Western societies were not intended by Piaget, his ideas and educational innovations were certainly taken up and interpreted in these ways, as in this popular post-World War II account for training teachers:

> One of the great changes in American life is that we are struggling to be decent to children [. . .] This is a new idea. In many parts of the world children are [. . .] children. Like sticks. Or lower class. Or second class. But gradually, in America particularly, but elsewhere too, our conscience is being heard: Citizens are people . . . women are people . . . natives are people . . . workers are people . . . Our country has been one of the first to take the next step: Children are people. This is a step to feel proud of. We have begun to ask ourselves: 'What is a child after?' The question complicates life, but it is a sign of our decency that we have begun to ask it. You have every right to feel good about what you do.
>
> (Hymes 1955: 138–139, punctuation in original)

Piaget was a prolific and original theorist, but his guiding preoccupations were also very much rooted in the modern celebration of science and reason as the panacea for social inequalities. Vygotsky too, as a Marxist, was committed to the modern project of social improvement via science and technology. Now in an era where science and industrialisation have brought pollution rather than sanitation, unemployment rather than work, new industrial disease and exploitation of labour rather than health and leisure, and small- and large-scale destruction of the planet, it is less clear that science has so much to offer. This chapter has indicated something of the cultural and intellectual context of Piaget's and Vygotsky's work, focusing on the selective interpretation of their work. In particular, in line with the wider cultural impact of his work, we have focused on Piaget's theories and their wider cultural resonances, and shown how differences in accounts of his methodology reinscribe pre-existing agendas in fulfilling social demands to classify and test children. Unless we have a clear understanding of Piaget's ideas we will be unable to tackle the real problems in his work. Some indications of the misconceived gender and cultural assumptions underlying this model have also been mentioned, and they will be taken up further in the next chapter, which specifically addresses the educational impact of such ideas.

Further reading

For a coherent analysis of the assumptions underlying Piagetian theory, the earlier literature remains the best, see:

Broughton, J. (1981a) 'Piaget's structural developmental psychology I: Piaget and structuralism', *Human Development*, 24: 78–109.
—— (1981b) 'Piaget's structural developmental psychology III: logic and psychology', *Human Development*, 24: 195–224.

For a radical critique of the contemporary forms of cognitive developmental psychology (which remains as relevant as when it was first published), see:

Riegel, K. (1976) 'The dialectics of human development', *American Psychologist*, 698–700.

For more detail on the selective appropriation of Piaget's methodological approach, see:

Burman, E. (1996b) 'Continuities and discontinuities in interpretive and textual approaches to developmental psychology', *Human Development*, 39: 330–349.

On Piaget's less known sociological writings, see:

Smith, L. (ed.) (1965/1995) *Jean Piaget: Sociological Studies*, London; Routledge.

258   *Deconstructing developmental psychology*

For a sense of the breadth of Piaget's work, see:

Gruber, H. and Vonèche, J. (1977) *The Essential Piaget: An Interpretive Reference and Guide*, London: Routledge & Kegan Paul (a key compilation and synthesis of Piaget's work).

For more (critical) biographical analysis, see:

Schepeler, E. (1993) 'Jean Piaget's experiences on the couch: some clues to a mystery', *International Journal of Psycho-Analysis, 74*: 255–273.
Vidal, F. (1987) 'Jean Piaget and the liberal protestant tradition', in M. Ash and M. Woodward (eds) *Psychology in Twentieth Century Thought and Society*, Cambridge: Cambridge University Press.

On Vygotsky, see:

Joravsky, D. (1987) 'L.S. Vygotskii: muffled deity of Soviet psychology', pp. 189–213 in M. Ash and M. Woodward (eds) *Psychology in Twentieth Century Thought and Society*, Cambridge: Cambridge University Press.
Kozulin, A. (1990) *Vygotsky's Psychology: A Biography of Ideas*, Hemel Hempstead: Harvester Wheatsheaf.

On the relations between their models of language and thought, see:

Santiago-Delefosse, M. and Oderic Delefosse, J. (2002) 'Spielrein, Piaget and Vygotsky: three positions on child thought and language', *Theory and Psychology, 12, 6*: 723–747.

On 'communities of practice' see:

Lave, J. and Wenger, E. (1991) *Situated Learning: Legitimate Peripheral Participation*, Cambridge: Cambridge University Press.
Wenger, E. (1998) *Communities of Practice. Learning, Meaning and Identity.* Cambridge: Cambridge University Press.

Suggested activities

1   On Piaget and the issue of accelerating development, read and discuss: H. Clarizio (1981) 'Natural vs. accelerated readiness', in H. Clarizio, R. Craig and W. Mehrens (eds) *Contemporary Issues in Educational Psychology*, Boston: Allyn and Bacon. On the consequences of orienting instruction to the individual child's 'learning needs', see K. Kepler and J. Randall (1981) 'Individualization: the subversion of elementary schooling', in Clarizio *et al.* (1981).
2   Drawing on the extracts reproduced in Gruber and Vonèche (1977) from Piaget's novel *Recherche*, his other early writings about the relation between science and moral issues, and

including 'Biology and war', explore the relations (and tensions) between science and social emancipation, through such questions as:

- What role does reason play in Piaget's view of society?
- What incompatibilities does Piaget struggle with in his analysis of the relations between science and emotions? Between science and humanism? And between science and religion?
- What model of society does Piaget elaborate, and what are its consequences? How adequate is a model that takes as its unit separate individuals? What scope is there for the analysis of structural power relations and differences? How does this model relate to models of market forces and relations?
- Next, use the same questions to interrogate one of the early articles Piaget published in English for a popular audience elaborating his ideas, 'The child and modern physics', *Scientific American*, *197*: 46–51.

13 Child-centred education: shifts and continuities

You will make mistakes sometimes, but gearing your effort to the needs and interests of children is worthwhile. No matter how you keep score you can know in your heart: Yours is a democratic, a reasonable effort. Your children will increasingly feel right; each day as they live will be more satisfying. You can hardly ask for more than that.

(Hymes 1955: 139)

The one thing we have to avoid then, even while we carry on our old process of education, is this development of the powers of so-called self-expression in a child. Let us beware of artificially stimulating his [sic] self-consciousness and his so-called imagination. All that we do is to pervert the child into a ghastly state of self-consciousness, making him affectedly try to show off as we wish him to show off. The moment the least trace of self-consciousness enters into a child, goodbye to everything except falsity. . . . The top and bottom of it is, that it is a crime to teach a child anything at all, schoolwise.

(D.H. Lawrence 1973: 194–196)

The new flexible, independent, autonomous, responsible and problem-solving child/parent/citizen of the turn of the twenty-first century illustrates the ways in which the governing of the soul has shifted, and a globalized cultural and economic future; however, this shift is not a natural progression towards freedom but a continuation of internments, enclosures, and inclusions/exclusions. These effects of power require a continual critical vigilance.

(Popkewitz and Bloch 2001: 109)

This chapter takes up themes conventionally associated with Piaget's work to explore their inscription and development within 'child-centred' approaches to education. Child-centred pedagogy plays out the conflicts and internal contradictions of both emancipatory and normative tendencies. These tendencies are prevalent in, but by no means exclusive to, Piaget. This child-centred pedagogy subscribes to a naturalised, individualised model of childhood which confirms social privileges and pathologises those who are already socially disadvantaged.

'Child-centred' education enjoyed its heyday in terms of explicit inscription within educational policies in the post-World War II period, reaching its apotheosis in Britain with the Plowden Report (1967). It continues to be influential in approaches to infant and primary (elementary) education. However, as time goes on, conceptual incoherence as well as failure to challenge social inequalities have brought about criticisms from both sides of the political spectrum (for different reasons), the effects of which are now seen in the return towards more structured approaches to education.

'Progressive' education

Although Piaget came to be the key theorist cited in the development of the new 'progressive' education of 1960s and 1970s Britain and America, its conceptual roots lie in the work of various European eighteenth- and nineteenth-century philosophers and educationalists such as Jean-Jacques Rousseau, Johann Pestalozzi, Friedrich Froebel and, in the early part of this century, Maria Montessori and the psychoanalysts Susan Isaacs and Margaret Lowenfeld (Singer 1992). The philosopher John Dewey has also been an important resource, particularly in the USA. While there are clearly major differences of approach between the different theorists, broadly speaking all subscribed to a 'child-centred' approach in the sense of advocating that education should be oriented towards children's interests, needs and developmental growth and informed by an understanding of child development. This approach contrasts with an educational approach emphasising performance in terms of the achievement of standard forms of accreditation, with a fixed curriculum divided into specific disciplines, and with formal teaching methods. While these are the theorists commonly cited to account for its origins, it was the set of technologies it gave rise to and its associated practices that make it important, and important to developmental psychology and the whole landscape of education.

In part, the emergence of 'progressive' education was a response to the 'payment by results' schemes of the first elementary schools of the 1870s onwards. In these, funding for the school depended on the achievement of pupils (thereby setting up a disincentive to have less able pupils within the school), with a corresponding instrumental and vocational model of education as the (measurable – thanks to psychologists) acquisition of skills. A second factor in the emergence of child-centred pedagogy was the reaction to rote methods of teaching, such as repetitive drills. A third reflection of this development was the rejection of a (behaviourist) model of the child as an empty vessel simply absorbing and reacting according to external contingencies. Associated with this was also the emphasis on 'love' and 'nature', which also coincided with the introduction of women into teaching (see Walkerdine 1984). As we shall see, the above three factors position the emergence of 'progressive education' as a key expression of individualism. Moreover, within the post-World War II period the call for educational provision oriented to a child's needs and interests became synonymous with the creation and maintenance of a democratic, 'free' and open society which could foster independence of thought and action.

Central tenets of the child-centred approach are indicated by five key terms: readiness, choice, needs, play and discovery. 'Readiness' means that the child must be ready to learn, with learning concerned with social and emotional, as well as cognitive, development. 'Choice' highlights how learning should be directed towards the individual interests of the child, and that the child should dictate the timing and content of the learning process. In terms of 'needs', children are seen to have fundamental needs, with the failure to meet these giving rise to later (both individual and social) problems. (In this sense child-centred approaches have continuities with mental hygienists in laying claim to a rhetoric of 'prevention' of different types of ill health.) The focus on 'play' suggests that learning should be voluntary, enjoyable, self-directed, non-goal oriented, functional for emotional well-being and that the general opposition between work and play should be broken down. The promotion of autonomy was seen as central to fostering curiosity, confidence and competence, in which play functioned as the guarantor of freedom and independence. Finally, the role of 'discovery' highlights that learning takes place through individual, personal experience.

In this model, education was conceptualised as the external realisation of an inner potential, with the emphasis on the uniqueness of each child giving rise to a demand that learning should be 'relevant' to her needs and interests. The process of learning was valued over the topic or content of what was learned, and the commitment to learning by doing rather than being told meant that the teacher's active role was defined as structuring the environment provided for the child. The extract below takes Piaget as the originator of child-centred education to arrive at the following definitions of a teacher's role:

1   The teacher is an analyst in the sense that he [sic] analyses the unit to be presented in terms of what will provide for optimal intellectual, social and emotional (including attitudinal) development.
2   He manipulates the environment in that he selects certain material and plans certain experiences which he believes will promote the outcomes desired.
3   The teacher becomes more a guide, expert, advisor and group leader, in the broad sense, in what is essentially a flexible and fluid teaching-learning environment.

(McNally 1974: 127–128)

While the first of these points reflects the child-centred approach's claim to deal with the 'whole child', the second and third highlight how the teacher's intervention occurs in the form of provision of context rather than instruction or regulation of the child.

Dilemmas and ambiguities of practice

As a statement of teachers' commitments to the educational development of their charges, the child-centred approach expresses some important sentiments. However, some difficulties have emerged in translating them into practice. In the first place, a teacher attempting to conform to these precepts encounters an untenable conflict between the mandate for non-interference to promote independence, and her institutional position as responsible for children's learning. How can she oversee the individual development of a class of 30 children? Various studies of accounts of, and implementation of, 'progressive' education (Sharp and Green 1975; Billig *et al.* 1988) have highlighted how teachers positioned themselves as responsible for, but helpless in, moulding children's development, thereby inducing great guilt (Walkerdine 1988). The designation of intervention as tantamount to authoritarian repression meant that teachers could not criticise or regulate children's behaviour. In her analysis of a situation where a teacher was verbally abused by her three-year-old male pupils using sexist language (also mentioned in Chapter 11), Walkerdine (1981) argues that the teacher's subscription to a romantic, child-centred model of children's needs meant that she treated the expression of aggression as natural. By this designation, not only could she not blame the children, but she could assert her authority only at the expense of inciting later personality and social maladjustment. As Lowenfeld, the influential psychotherapist and educationalist, put it:

> The forces of destruction, aggression and hostile emotion which form so powerful an element for good or evil in the human character, can display themselves fully in the play of childhood, and become through this expression integrated in the controlled and conscious personality. Forces unrealised in childhood remain as an inner drive, forever seeking outlets, and lead men to express them not any longer in play, since this is regarded as an activity in childhood, but in industrial competition, anarchy and war.
>
> (Lowenfeld 1935: 324–325)

A second set of problems arises from conceptual incoherence within child-centred approaches. Apart from the general uncertainty about how to recognise when a child is 'ready', and how to determine a child's 'needs', it would seem that middle-class children are more 'ready' than working-class children since they are more prepared and familiar with the skills needed to engage with schooling. The uncritical commitment to 'readiness' therefore maintains unequal treatment of children, since teachers devote most of their time to the 'ready' and most able children, that is, those they define as most able to benefit (Sharp and Green 1975). In terms of the claim to dissolve the play–work opposition, this opposition is nevertheless reinstated within the distinction between time-wasting versus therapeutic and 'productive' play, with children directed accordingly. Moreover, the glorification of play as functional, voluntary and co-operative soon turns out to be idealised, since this ignores the coercive, cruel and dangerous aspects of many forms of 'play', in the form of personal hobbies, children's games or institutional school activities (Sutton Smith and Kelly Byrne 1984; Sutton-Smith 1997). Both on analysis and in practice, therefore, the child-centred approach dissolves into intuitions, ad hoc judgements that advocate the meting out of educational provision in unequal ways, and undermines the authority and efficacy of the teacher as structuring and responsible for what children learn.

Not only is the pedagogy difficult to apply, but it is also worse than unhelpful. In the first place it denies the teacher's power relation with the child (Edwards and Mercer 1987). Moreover, subscription to a child-centred philosophy sometimes acts as a mask behind which teachers mark their professional distance from parents and disguise a firm control that holds in practice (Sharp and Green 1975). Second, it strips the child of the aid of the teacher through the teacher's efforts to foster autonomy – in this sense reproducing one of the differences between Piagetian and Vygotskyan informed educational approaches (Moll 1990; Vianna and Stetsenko 2006). Third, concern has been generated about how children can be isolated through the attempts to promote learning tied to individual need (Kepler and Randall 1981). The rest of this chapter draws out the origins and significance of these limitations.

Autonomy and individualism: free thinkers?

Child-centred approaches perpetuate a model of learning that accords with a liberal model of society – as composed of rational, freely choosing, isolated, equal individuals (Sullivan 1977). With its connotations of separation and detachment, so close is autonomy perceived to be to the maintenance of a liberal, 'free' society (seen as best promoted by home care) that proposals in the USA for day-care provision set out in the Child Development Act 1971 were vetoed by the then President Nixon on the grounds that this threatened the traditional (North) American family and (North) America's tradition of individualism. This claim motivated Carol Speekmann Klass's (1985) case study of a day-care centre, from which she concluded that, far from encouraging children to be more collectively oriented, day care seems to produce autonomous children capable of self-directed activity who are not dependent on adult authority.

There are tensions between the priority accorded to individual development and the egalitarian impulses of US individualism. In its positive hue, individualism carries connotations of self-reliance, self-improvement, independence of thought and non-conformity. But it is also associated with self-interest, competition and abdication of personal responsibilities in favour of economic forces, specifically the vagaries of the market. The progressive strands of individualism within modern Western societies, such as equal rights and social reform movements, coexist with, and are rooted within, the development and expansion of capitalist free-market economies. Popkewitz and Bloch (2001) discuss the convergence of Taylorist efficiency imperatives with kindergarten philosophy:

> One of the tasks of teaching was to develop a uniform, calculable rational cosmopolitan self who could act and develop naturally as self-responsible as a universal citizen that, at the same time, had prescribed boundaries and tasks to seemingly preserve social harmony and order . . . what has often been lost in social histories of the curriculum is that both the social efficiency movements in schooling and industrialisation as well as child development orientations were possible to consider only in the broader conjecture that tied the registers of social administration with freedom. Taylor, social efficiency, and child development-oriented educators thought that the new efficiency or the new freedom of, for example, child-centered play would free the worker/child in the realization of a liberal democracy . . . The psychologies of childhood were viewed as a form of preventative medicine to counteract the problems of the parent, particularly to offset the problem mother who appeared to produce the problem child.
>
> (Popkewitz and Bloch 2001: 97)

Treating the individual as the unit of social, educational and economic activity perpetuates rather than challenges social inequalities. The focus on individual children masks patterns of difference based on gender, class or culture. Indeed, it is noteworthy that in Sally Lubeck's (1986) comparative study of two nurseries (one a predominantly white preschool, the other a Head Start centre with black children and teachers), the latter exhibited greater group and community orientation. This could be taken to suggest that the pattern noted by Speekmann Klass is yet another reflection of culture-bound research masquerading as 'culture free'. In addition, Lubeck observed different patterns of interaction between the teachers and children which she maps on to different family (nuclear versus extended) patterns of interaction. She makes some claims about how the preschool's 'centrifugal' patterning of time and space, with children working away from the group, and activity structured around 'choice', treats children as uniquely different, linking the promotion of individuality and autonomy with receptiveness to change. In contrast, the 'centripetal' force she identifies in the Head Start centre encouraged children to cohere and be part of a group. We should note here that she links collectivity to conformity in a way that reflects Western individualism, and further devalues the cultural group designated as exhibiting these patterns of behaviour: 'By structuring time, space and activity so that children do what others do, while also conforming to the directives of the teachers, the teachers thus seem to socialize children to adapt to the reality they themselves experience' (Lubeck 1986: 138). However, on closer inspection this reality is not a culturally specific pattern of relating, but a response to circumstances of both disadvantage and intrusive monitoring by educational authorities. The institutional pressures she notes as structuring the functioning of the Head Start centre – with officials and inspectors dropping in unannounced at any time, as well as greater administrative demands in the running of a social service programme – could easily account for the teachers' tendency to work with each other, and apart from the children. Minority cultural patterns exist in relation to those of the majority and should be interpreted correspondingly. Otherwise responses to disadvantage are mistakenly treated as intrinsic properties of a static culture. As already noted, such trends have become more entrenched in recent times, with more rigid testing regimes and further emphasis on individualised, flexible learning to be adaptable and useful in an increasingly competitive job market (Fendler 2001).

Democracy: the self-governing child

Along with autonomy, democracy is a key term within the child-centred discourse, which, in the post-war period, functioned as the guarantor of anti-authoritarianism. It is interesting to revisit these debates of a half a century ago, now as new imperialist wars are being waged in the name of spreading 'democracy'. Child rearing attracted attention as the arena in which the foundations of a democratic society could be laid. In the USA the White House held conferences on 'Children in a Democratic Society'. Advice to parents and educators spelt out the social merits and benefits of the 'new' approaches. But this celebration of egalitarianism all too often could also take the form of self-righteous cultural chauvinism, with choice and economic freedom equated with democratic participation:

> Little children – preschoolers still at home – get a lot of backing in their urge to grow. In America we like independent little fellows. We admire gumption and an up-at-them quality. We are all for independence [. . .] We don't put long dresses on our babies. We don't bind their feet . . . Boy or girl, the Five is in jeans, free to run and dig [. . .] From an early age we give youngsters an allowance, 'This is your money; spend it as you wish . . .' We listen when children talk, as if they really were people. We give them reasons when we talk, just as if they were human [. . .] In this country you don't have to be twenty one to vote . . . in families. Children cast their votes from eighteen *months* on, and their vote is counted too.
>
> (Hymes 1955: 108–110, punctuation in original)

Children are treated not 'as', but 'just as if they were', human. There is something disingenuous and deceptive about these claims to equality, with explicit contrasts with those who do (or did) not equivalently subscribe to equal treatment irrespective of gender and age.

Moreover, child-centred education becomes a compensatory measure that can offset material inequalities, and, further, is located as critical in the production of self-disciplining citizens. Concluding her book *The Self-Respecting Child*, written just as child-centred education was beginning to structure primary schooling in Britain, Allison Stallibrass (1974: 259) emphasised how encouraging children to become 'competent and self-governing' at an early age would make them more likely to be like this even if their environment is 'inappropriate and stultifying'. So it seems an early inculcation of child-centredness forestalls not only later alienation, but also pre-empts less savoury influences: here the threat of coercion (with its connotations of authoritarianism) looms large:

> Even if the school to which a child proceeds at the age of five or eight turns out to be a barrack-square type, he [sic] will be no more unhappy there if he has developed an inner core of individuality through making choices and decisions for himself, than if he has become a soft piece of clay, pliant in the hands of anyone wanting to try to cast him in a common or prematurely adult mould. . . . In any case, State infant schools are rapidly becoming places where such qualities as self-reliance, initiative and spontaneity are welcomed, and a sheep-like conformity discouraged.
>
> (Stallibrass 1974: 259–260)

What is left unspecified is precisely what it is that children may be moulded towards (although the reference above to 'common' should alert us to the devaluation and pathologisation of working-class values). This allows us to leave unexamined the assumptions about the nature of individuals and their relations with society that the child-centred pedagogy maintains. Moreover, while democracy is celebrated as central to child as well as societal development, this shifts away from state structures and policies to become less a feature of social structures and more an evaluation of family life (see also Popkewitz and Bloch 2001; Dahlberg and Moss 2005). The following quotation from Gesell emphasises the longstanding character of this presupposition:

> Throughout the preschool years there is an intimate interaction between the psychologies of the child and of the parent. Democracy is a way of life which demands attitudes of tolerance and fair play. If we wish to lay the basis of such attitudes in young children we must begin with the education of adults. The adults in their own behavior must furnish

the models and intimations of the democratic way. . . . Democracy is a mature virtue, a product of gradual growth, which embodies obedience, self-control, self-direction.

(Gesell 1950: 310)

While self-control and self-direction are central to the child-centred pedagogy, it becomes apparent that obedience is a covert outcome of it, since children are considered to be more willing to obey rules if these appear to arise out of their own deliberations and choices. While the overt exertion of authority would smack of totalitarianism, its covert application in the name of the betterment and protection of society is seen as laudable. Moreover, the emphasis on participation, on the child's active engagement in the production of their own knowledge, can also function as a tactic of recruitment that both renders the child more subject to regulation and makes it harder for them to escape surveillance (see Cooke and Kothari 2001). Hence, notwithstanding the cultural value placed on freedom, it becomes clear that the child-centred pedagogy is just as coercive as traditional approaches but in more subtle ways, and that underlying the model of the romantic, natural, innocent child lies an image of children as destructive, asocial and therefore threatening to the social order (Walkerdine and Lucey 1989; MacNaughton 2005).

The home and the school

Not only can groups be stigmatised but child-centredness can lead to individualised interpretations of what are really socially structured inequalities. The commitment to an optimistic and meritocratic view of education as self-realisation and as the key to social mobility renders invisible the role of the school in perpetuating inequality. Since it fails to accord any importance to the role of teacher and school as agents, the focus is on the home background. The only available explanation to account for pupil failure or underachievement is therefore in terms of individual or cultural deficit – blaming the child or the family (Fuchs 1973; Sharp and Green 1975). Indeed, so influential were the ideas about educational achievement as the outcome of a maturing inner potential that it was only relatively recently that research demonstrated that features of school organisation and functioning do have an impact on children's educational achievement in them (Rutter *et al.* 1979; Smith and Tomlinson 1989).

Child-centred approaches therefore tend to subscribe to notions of compensatory education and cultural disadvantage or deprivation by assuming that there is something wrong or missing in the child's background. They link easily with a social pathology view of the background from which the child is drawn. Correspondingly, pupil success is seen as due to appropriateness of the pedagogy but pupil failure is attributed to home background.

Despite a rhetoric of parent participation, parents are disparaged for failing to uphold 'progressive' educational ideals if they demand more structured approaches. This liberal model also assumes children come to school with equal access to educational opportunities. It ignores the role of the school as perpetuating middle-class norms and values which therefore advantage middle-class children.

While the shift to neoliberalism that characterises the late twentieth and early twenty-first century has only intensified this individualisation of structural inequalities (see Hultqvist and Dahlberg 2001), it is still useful to see how this came about through building on pre-existing themes. As we saw in Chapter 10, through discussion of the studies of Brice Heath (1983) and Macdonald (2006), this occlusion of the cultural modes privileged by models of schooling only exacerbates existing exclusions and deprivations. By being blind to cultural differences, and treating all children as the same, it thereby denies and perpetuates the inequality of their starting positions. In his review of (and plea for) child-development programmes within Third World countries, Robert Myers (1992) cautions against this dominant model, which within a Third World context all too often means the devaluation of indigenous cultures and values in favour of Western-based educational ideas:

> Conceptualising the entry into school as a 'transition' *from* home *to* school puts undue emphasis on school and tends to devalue the home as a place for learning: Our concern, therefore, should be centred on the ability of a child to learn in various environments rather than on learning as if it only occurred in schools.
>
> (Myers 1992: 211, original emphasis)

Furthermore, the goal of democracy and the identification of democratic styles of child rearing and education were explicitly linked to longstanding fears about working-class family life:

> Underprivileged children suffer not only in a physical sense. They suffer psychologically. They feel mental insecurity. In crowded and shiftless homes they develop anxieties and perplexities. They see sights and experience shocks from which more fortunate children are in decency spared. Innumerable households still use methods of harsh discipline, chronic scolding, shouting, terrifying threats, slapping, beating. Needless to say, such inconsiderate disregard for the dignity of the individual is inconsistent with the spirit of democracy. In fact, misguided and crude forms of child management are so widespread as to constitute a public health problem, a task of preventive mental hygiene.
>
> (Gesell 1950: 310)

In the above account it is clear that 'decency' is code for class, and that working-class cultural patterns are pathologised. This is not to condone the mistreatment of children but rather to point out that, notwithstanding the commitment to democracy, measures for promotion of tolerance do not extend to a willingness to see value in diversity (Walkerdine and Lucey 1989).

From the above formulations it is easy to see how the discourse of child-centredness slips into social regulation. Indeed, Gesell went on to urge three main areas of 'social control' for the welfare of the preschool child: first, medical supervision of child development; second, parental and pre-parental education in which 'adult education has come into increasing prominence as a means of social control' (Gesell 1950: 311); third, readaptation of the kindergarten and nursery school. He justified his calls to attend less to the achievement of skills such as reading than to differences between children in terms of the preschool's role in what he termed 'supervisory hygiene' (Gesell 1950: 313).

In a similar vein, the frontispiece to Strang's (1959) *Introduction to Child Study* depicts a mother holding a baby and taking two children (girl and boy) into a church-like building. The caption reads: 'The whole family goes to school. Thus schools contribute intimately and intensively to child development.' Education became the route to intervene in and reform family life – although we could note that only the mother is shown in the picture, thus reiterating how it is primarily mothers who are the site of intervention and evaluation. A focus on the child abstracted from context therefore moves to an evaluation of family life that is divorced from an understanding of social inequalities. Hence education is positioned as the central apparatus of social regulation in the production of the fiction of the democratic citizen.

Even where attempts have been made to recognise social disadvantage, all too often these read as indictments of families instead of social structures (or social services). The influential 1970s National Children's Bureau report on educational inequality in Britain, *Born to Fail?* (Wedge and Prosser 1973), struggles to avoid blaming parents for their poverty and unemployment while at the same time treating lack of parental involvement in children's schooling as an index of parental interest in, or aspiration for, their children (rather than an indication of how schooling fails to engage with child and family). But so powerful is the discourse of familial responsibility that child-centredness, with its failure to theorise social relations, could scarcely avoid being incorporated into it. A reminder of the continuity and potency of these themes was the leader of a teachers' union's comments dismissing children of lone parents as 'no hopers' in his address to a union annual conference: 'Peter Dawson, general secretary of Professional Association of Teachers, said that teachers faced the appalling consequences of a million lone-parent families. Schools were being turned into first-aid posts for psychologically crippled children' (*Independent*, 2 August 1991).

The whole child?

Mearns's (1961) National Children's Home lecture epitomises how normative and punitive moral assumptions enter into a seemingly naturalistic child-centred approach. Written as advice for professionals working with children, his book *The Whole Child* was intended especially for those working in residential settings. In this sense the need to deal with 'the whole child' arose from the demands of total institutional (rather than specifically educational) care. Far from being 'whole', Mearns's 'child' literally breaks down into constituent components. 'CHILD' is an acronym, where C stands for 'care and companionship', H for 'home and habits', I for 'independence and interests', L for 'love and laughter' and D for 'discipline and direction'. Each letter therefore moves explicitly from a seemingly benign discourse of child-centredness to one of overt social regulation: in the name of 'the whole child' the apparatus of moral evaluation is maintained. What this demonstrates is how child-centredness is, albeit in different forms, social regulation, that is, the surveillance par excellence of children since it presents itself as 'freely' undertaken. Correspondingly, the model of the 'whole child' exists only in relation to that of the 'damaged' or 'disadvantaged child' (whom we encountered in Chapter 11) that it thereby both produces and regulates.

Familiar themes emerge. Homes are to blame: 'In almost every case of maladjustment the defect has its origin in a home which has failed in some respect' (Mearns 1961: 28–29). Play and laughter, so central to the lexicon of child-centredness, become literal metaphors of mental hygiene: 'It [laughter] is, moreover a potent disinfectant to destroy the twin germs of jealousy and envy' (Mearns 1961: 29). Moreover, the channelling of ability and affection comes in for particular concern, demonstrating how the individualism of child-centredness leads to resignation rather than support. The account of 'the school years' takes two issues as the focus of interest. Intelligence is seen as fixed, as:

> an hereditary characteristic. Poor environment can retard, even prevent, its proper flowering; but not even the most elaborate education can make any significant improvement in the IQ. The moral here is that parents must accept a child's intelligence for what it is and expend their efforts not in trying to improve it.
>
> (Mearns 1961: 35)

The second key issue for 'the school years' is 'homosexuality', presented within a general section on 'The Handicapped Child'. This is treated as relevant only to men, since 'female homosexuality is not a community problem in this country' (Mearns 1961: 36). Sexual orientation is cast within a disease model:

In fairness to those who are themselves the helpless victims of the homosexual abnormality, it should be said that many have resisted their impulses and have adjusted themselves to their disability. They remain instinctively and psychologically homosexual, but boys are safe from them, since they are able to canalize their urges in artistic and similar pursuits. These facts do not however lessen the general risk.

(Mearns 1961: 36–37)

These sentiments are not only homophobic, but they also reflect naturalised and essentialised views of male and female sexuality. It seems that 'the whole child' is endowed with gender and sexual orientation from the beginning, with gender-differentiated sexual drives. Moreover, these exist only as problems to be managed:

Matters are perhaps rather simpler for girls because they are less readily aroused and in most cases have a deeper sense of moral responsibility. Be that as it may, the position is never plain-sailing if the circumstances of temptation are created. Boys are more inflammable, sexually speaking, and they are from the psychological viewpoint, egocentric, self-seeking and demanding. Boys take; girls give.

(Mearns 1961: 75–76)

The failure to see child development as socially constructed rather than biologically unfolding leads to an ignorance of the ways the models reinscribe particular moral values. Far from being 'whole', with pedagogy 'centred' around her or him, the child of the child-centred approaches is a carefully orchestrated social production with 'needs' and (gender, class, cultural, sexual) qualities designated to mesh with normative conceptions of social arrangements.

Writing at a key moment when child-centredness had become official education policy in Britain, Garland and White (1980), in their review of the theory and practice of nursery care, distinguished between those nurseries guided by an underlying assumption that the child should ultimately determine what will satisfy her needs (seen as child-centred) and those which positioned the adult in that role (seen as authoritarian). The 'predominant goals' of the former were, in their analysis, the social and emotional development of the children, while in the latter the focus was on cognitive growth and the acquisition of skills. The authors trace continuities in philosophy to the differing traditions from which preschool care developed. They saw the more authoritarian, skills-based style as having its roots in institutions concerned with the care of children of poor and working women, in which the dominant theme was (as discussed also in Chapter 1) one of rehabilitation. They suggest:

Looking back at some of the day nurseries we visited, it is hard not to feel that there existed a continuity of tradition between the dame schools, in which the emphasis was on keeping children out of mischief, and those we saw in which, as we have described, the children were felt to be primitive and irrational creatures to be kept carefully and constantly controlled by the adult world.

(Garland and White 1980: 112)

It has been the argument of this chapter that, notwithstanding its rhetoric of emancipation and empowerment, child-centred approaches are still associated with those preoccupations with social control and regulation, only with self-regulation regarded as more effective than overt coercion precisely because it gives the impression of freedom and choice. Underlying the playing, autonomous child lurks a model of an aggressive and primitive being whose instinctual impulses need to be indulged in order to ward off later emotional complexes (and social problems) – hence the theoretical basis for the opposition between the two philosophies becomes tenuous. Even the distinction between the focus on building social relations rather than cognitive skills collapses so that the social orientation becomes a means of maximising the cognitive: 'those nurseries who place social and emotional goals first do so because they feel that in terms of the child's longterm success as a cognitive being, a sound emotional being is essential' (Garland and White 1980: 111).

Emotions in the classroom?

More recently there has been a surge of attention to features of emotional expression in schools in the form of 'emotional literacy' and 'emotional intelligence', which are claimed to be as or even more important than cognitive skills. Goleman (1996) promotes 'emotional intelligence' as an index or measure that, he claims, matters more for individual success and social harmony than received measures of intelligence. Indeed the whole notion of 'emotional intelligence' – and its success – harks back to the (tainted but still discursively available) notion of IQ, in the sense of confirming its legitimacy at the same time as claiming to surpass or supplement it. Both notions involve the positing of an individual (stable) personality trait that is assumed to be unevenly distributed across a population (thereby available for various forms of manipulation and trade within a capitalist economy):

Emotional intelligence serves capitalism at several levels. If workers and schoolchildren are conversational in emotional literacy, the labor system profits. Simultaneously, the 'self-help' industry profits from information commodified and consumed by our own obsession with ourselves. The increasing authority of cognitive science fuels our popular and scholarly fascination with the self as a cybernetic system rather than simply a functionalist organism. Neurological science is systematically attempting to tame emotions, one of the most resistant sites of human and social life.

(Boler 1999: 76)

In fact cognitive psychologists, who have come to take this notion seriously because of the public attention it has generated, largely see it as a collection of cognitive skills, rather than as anything specifically emotional (Matthews *et al.* 2002). Boler (1999) goes on to discuss how the moral panic around childhood functions as a way of blaming individuals and neglecting the social origins of problems, arguing:

As with the mental hygiene movement early in this century, individual children are blamed for 'poor skills and impulse-control'. The pervasiveness of the individualism is startling: Even communication, which, of all skills seems most obviously to occur in a social context, is portrayed as rooted solely in the individual.

(Boler 1999: 94)

As an indication of the increasing circulation and legitimacy of this concept the February 2006 issue of *The Psychologist* (magazine of the British Psychological Society, the sole professional psychology organisation in the UK) contained no less than five advertisements for emotional literacy related courses and materials, while the August 2006 issue offers a training course that will show how 'new norms for the EQ-i:S can now help identity high risk students' (p. 499). Notwithstanding the claims to social and organisational applications, the discourse of skills and competence returns political analysis to the level of individual acquisition and expression, and action to a matter of training:

To teach young people to police themselves is more cost-efficient than outfitting an urban school with police and safety monitors. . . . It is cost-effective to teach students to internalise appropriate control of their emotions by teaching them to take 'responsibility' and learn 'self-control'. Thus the social, economic, and political forces that underlie these youth crises are masked, and the individuals are blamed for lack of self-control.

(Boler 1999: 86)

But while the uptake of emotional intelligence may have been rapid, and nakedly commercial, emotional literacy initially seemed to offer educators and therapists a new role within the project of challenging social exclusion. For example, social agendas are accorded as much weight as individual ones in Peter Sharp's (2001) *Nurturing Emotional Literacy – A Practical*

Guide for Teachers, Parents and those in the Caring Professions. Sharp's account is noteworthy for its humanist, personal growth flavour (note the 'nurturing' of the title), whilst still retaining many of the same claims. The opening sentence of the book offers a definition that focuses on 'success': 'Emotional literacy may be defined as the ability to recognise, understand, handle, and appropriately express emotions. Put more simply, it means using your emotions to help yourself and others succeed' (p. 1). But this presupposes particular measures of success that bring in norms of adaptation and economic productivity. Like Goleman, emotional literacy is equated with mental health, with both these portrayed as features produced by and around the individual (p. 15 and Figure 2.1), while it is also presented as a set of skills, competencies and elements (p. 25) reiterating (on p. 103) the link between emotional literacy and self-esteem. As a training text, the assumptions are laid out loud and clear, including the public order and prosperity priority: 'Failure to pursue the goal of nurturing emotional literacy will result ultimately in poorer productivity and social exclusion' (2001: 4). Links are made with a social agenda, with Table 4.1 (p. 46) titled 'Emotional literacy encompasses' listing such individual concerns as 'learning and achievement' and 'spiritual, moral, social and cultural development' alongside 'equal opportunities, health promotion, citizenship, behaviour and discipline, social inclusion and crime and disorder'. Sharp's account is also noteworthy for the way – even more than Goleman – all references to gender, race and class are washed away. What remains is the classical humanist subject, devoid of any such attributes. The testing technology of emotional intelligence is modulated, in this treatment, into a set of personally growthful maxims and exercises for self-awareness, with personal trajectories being elaborated. He even includes his own (second) version of the 'Life Map: my journey along life's journey' (p. 21), presumably to inspire the reader to complete the blank version helpfully provided in the appendix. But, expressed as an individual, linear, progressive journey, the models of individual–social relations, and indeed the available explanations for the social problems encountered by individuals, are even more restricted.

So a more psychotherapeutic agenda is no less signed up to capitalising on emotions than a cognitivist one, while both Sharp and Antidote – the British emotional literacy movement (see www.antidote.org) – claim to inform management and local government. But as a tool to promote social inclusion there are the usual sequelae of psychologisation, in the form of stripping the context away from the subject and the contexts in which people act, with all the usual risks of victim blaming. So having been left out of the picture, state support and intervention are allowed to re-enter only as and how they like, and 'negative' affect is decontextualised into disorder:

> There is no discussion of the fact that rules of middle-class politeness
> may not serve the cultural context of inner-city children's material lives

– not only that, to use middle-class skills of politeness in some contexts could conceivably put one at risk. Children develop survival skills that make sense within their social environment. This is not to say that violence is the only answer, but rather that the social development programmes offer no analysis of how and why children have *intelligently* developed the particular strategies they have.

(Boler 1999: 94, original emphasis)

Moreover, talking of 'risk,' what we can see are the classic hallmarks of the risk society – with individuals bearing its markers, not only now on their bodies but also in their minds, with the societal imperative to assess and clean up errant interiorities.

If we are really to become interested in children's emotional experiences, rather than in trying to manage them or make uncomfortable emotions disappear, then we have to engage with them, and with our own responses to them. Salzberger-Wittenberg *et al.* (1983) offer a classic account of how anxiety and fear enter into the schooling process. They discuss their work with training teachers, helping them to acknowledge the continuing influence of their own schooling memories and to draw upon them to work better with children's emotional responses. From this perspective, all learning involves emotions such as fear, insecurity and anxiety – the denial of which will only make the learner less able to learn. Such work also requires the teacher or parent to be able to identify with the child. Given the ways parents and teachers are increasingly made to feel responsible for children's actions, this is not always easy. Dorothy Rowe's (2005) analysis of attention deficit hyperactivity disorder (ADHD) as 'adults' fear of frightened children' highlights how caretakers' own anxieties of being seen as inadequate or culpable can get in the way of being able to engage with a child, and so render their actions literally incomprehensible. Such approaches are far away from the technology of EQ, but there may be no easy short cuts to human engagement.

From progress to backlash?

Corresponding to the contradictions within the liberatory direction of child-centred approaches and the return to themes of reforming a pre-social, anti-social child, there are problems with confining the educational goal to the promotion of individual development. Contemplating how the apparently radical, empowering tendencies of the 1960s 'progressive education' could have transmuted into the instrumentalism and atomistic skills-oriented vocationalism of the 1990s 'conservative revolution in education' (Jones 1989), James Avis (1991) identifies as the source of continuity its thorough-going individualism:

Each child and student is categorized atomistically and expected to pursue their own separate and autonomous development. The difficulty here is that there is no grasp of the collective processes or indeed the formation of collective ways of appropriating and using educational forms and knowledge. Education is reduced to the pursuit of individual development. The social processes involved in the production of knowledge are ignored and knowledge is rid of its social uses.

(Avis 1991: 117)

The fact that 'progressive education' operates with a concept of knowledge devoid of social differences means that not only does it fail to address how knowledge can be used to dismantle structures of oppression, but it thereby also exacerbates those social divisions by naturalising them. As such, from a focus on process it has been reduced to a set of teaching techniques that intensify structures of individualisation.

What Piaget and the other theorists who inspired 'child-centred' approaches to education share is a commitment to this view of knowledge as arising outside social structures and relations. In some senses the fact that Piaget is taken as the primary source of these ideas (rather than the psychoanalysts) confirms this even further, given his focus on the abstract epistemic subject and his model of the problem-solving scientist. It is this model of learning, as a separate, isolated activity, that sets up the continuities with the current instrumentalist orientations through a conceptual transition from knowledge as process to knowledge as the exercise of techniques:

We can point to the rash of strategies of curriculum development which are premised on the notion of skills, of the separation of form from content, of, therefore, a crude positivism that enshrines the reification of knowledge in educational practices. The extent to which such an abstraction is consistent with the abstraction of labour as commodity is revealing.

(Venn and Walkerdine 1978: 71)

Beyond child-centredness? Vygotsky and activity theory

Vygotsky has a variable press in relation to child-centred approaches. Crain (2005) claims that his model is not child-centred because of its focus on what the child can do with help, and its orientation towards what she will be able to do in the future. While this may well reflect the dominant reception of Vygotsky's work, as an educational technology, it does not do justice to its guiding philosophical framework. For in order to distinguish learning and development, and to construct appropriate zones of proximal development, there has to be detailed analysis of the multiple actors and contexts that will support the new activity. Indeed the attention to the analysis of the context and its specificities has given rise to the whole new post-Vygotskyan paradigm of 'activity theory'. It is true that Vygotsky's anti-individualism challenges a traditional child-centred account, with its tendency to abstract the child from social context. So instead, activity theory perhaps offers one route away from some of the impasses that the child-centred pedagogy seemed to impose.

Currently there are efforts to synthesise Piagetian and Vygotskyan insights, without ignoring the tensions between them (over the Piagetian notion of interaction, for example, as opposed to the Vygotskyan notion of dialectics). This involves taking seriously the cultural status of our mental instruments, and how these can be taught and learnt through collaborative activity (Vianna and Stetsenko 2006). Other approaches highlight the importance of moving away from static conceptions of ability or competence to focus on situated performance as a more empowering and affirmative model of exploration and learning (Holzman 2006). While these advocates are keen to ward off a conception of Vygotskyan approaches as neglecting individual-specific features, they also uphold the political gains and critiques of his vision. As such – notwithstanding the success and impact of cultural psychology (Stigler *et al.* 1990), and some vital contributions from Rogoff (1990, 2003) and others – these perspectives remain relatively marginal within mainstream developmental and educational accounts, which seek to strip them of their wider historical-political perspective and turn a project of social transformation into one of adaptation. Indeed Vygotsky was as signed up to the 'scientific' project of problem solving as was Piaget, to the detriment of attending to social and emotional developmental issues. Joravsky (1987) contrasts the controversy surrounding literary figures with the respectability accorded to psychologists in Soviet Russia:

> I am groping for the reason why the boldest psychologists in the most liberal periods of Russian history – pre- as well as postrevolutionary – have been quite tame politically, have provoked only a little ideological controversy compared to the most creative imaginative writers. If one may indulge in antique language, the writers challenge the politicians to struggle for our souls, while scientific psychologists turn away, striving to extricate themselves from any entanglement with the soul, the essence of a human being. The determined phenomenalism of modern science helps to win it acceptance – or toleration, or indifference – while the essentialism of imaginative writers keeps many people intensely interested, sometimes in awe, sometimes in anger.
>
> (Joravsky 1987: 207)

The new educational crisis: 'overachieving' girls?

If the prototypical child of Piaget's little problem-solving scientist was a boy, then it seems that the current prototypical educational subject is a girl.

For it is girls who appear to be succeeding in schools and in higher education across the 'developed' world. This poses some interesting questions, not least in relation to the models of science and mastery that were put forward (in Chapter 12) as inherent to the modernist project, and reinscribed within developmental psychological models. Thus, coinciding with the increasing policy focus on men and masculinity, as well as concerns about unruly boys (Timimi 2005; see Chapters 5 and 8), current educational debates now address the problem of 'overachieving girls/ underachieving boys' ('Boys seven years behind girls as GCSE results gap remains' *Guardian*, 20 October 2006)

We have seen how twenty-first century culture and political economy has broken down the traditional binary between rationality and emotion by instrumentalising affective life and bringing it even more under the remit of capital. This happens not only in the targeting of consumers, but – in the context of post-industrial economy which relies on the service sector – also in demanding of workers that we show we really enjoy serving our customers (Hochschild 1983, 2003). The rise of 'emotional intelligence' discussed earlier in this chapter is only one indication of this cultural shift, and as we have seen it accompanies a skills-based model that carves up the learner and the process of learning into competencies and certifiable qualities. One effect of this move within schools towards portfolio-based work and continuous assessment is that it appears to help girls' performance. Whereas girls were thought to be disadvantaged in multiple choice tests, especially when the test scores and items were manipulated because girls originally outstripped boys in the early version of school assessments such as the British '11+' (Goldstein 1987), now they are achieving highly.

That this is occurring at a time of claims of falling standards, and anxieties about the falling status of professions in which women predominate (including psychology), is perhaps worthy of some reflection. It also accompanies general rise of anxieties about the success of women in business, as more companies have come to value 'people skills' as a way of managing conflict between staff better. Could it be that we now inhabit a less masculinist world, in which women are the prototypical learning, developing and earning (economically productive) subjects?

However, it should be noted that this gender 'effect' may be less reliable and stable than is frequently assumed. Once 'race' and class are factored in, the gender-specific effect in school achievement largely 'washes out' (Lucey 2001). What does seem to be the case, though, is that girls – as conscientious and continuous workers – do seem now to benefit from the current systems, while boys – whose inconsistency and spontaneity were taken as 'natural talent' by teachers (Walkerdine *et al.* 1990) – are less willing to demonstrate their subordination to an educational apparatus that demands increasing self-regulation. The danger of mistaking media myth for fact in this discussion is that we overlook the other effects mobilised by the new feminised subject at play, in particular that the new, feminised neoliberal subject may just be a cosier and just as exploitative version of the old culturally masculine one (Burman 2005a, 2007a).

Popkewitz and Bloch's (2001) review of a century of conceptions of child, parent and school relations concludes that the pedagogical subject of the twenty-first century is 'cosmopolitan': 'Today's cosmopolitan self is constructivist, active, entrepreneurial, and works for the self's capacity and potentialities through a perpetual intervention in one's life' (p. 109). This subject gives rise to new configurations of experts surrounding the child and family to generate the kind of flexible, lifelong learning individual that creates self-sufficient individuals prepared for uncertain economic futures:

> The new conceptions of child, parent and community are ruled by an expertism that governs communication systems through which desire and striving for self-actualising and individual personal responsibility are constructed. A new form of expertise is a partnership that the professional investigates, maps, classifies, and works on the territories of individuality for a lifelong learning. The enabling professional empowers the individual for self-management of choice and the autonomous conduct of their life. These new territories of the individual make resistance and revolt, as we have argued, more distant and less plausible.
>
> (Popkewitz and Bloch 2001: 109)

Moreover, the implied universality of the discourse of the cosmopolitan subject does, of course, mask its thoroughly exclusionary and privileged character. So we can see how for too long the debates about education have floundered on a set of false oppositions between child-centredness and vocationalism, in which the learning needs of individual children are pitted against the industrial needs of society. Being child-centred meant that the child was abstracted from social relations, fuelling the charge that whims of children were being indulged without due reference to the society in which they lived. Yet beneath the rhetoric of child-centredness we have seen the older themes of social pathology and regulation resurging. As Singer (2005) reflects on the lessons of the history of early child care and education:

> Liberation of the child always goes hand in hand with new forms of discipline . . . Secondly, childcare centres are special, designed child's worlds, that have to be filled up. Childcare centres are cultural inventions, as are images of the child that inspire curricula and educational methods . . . Thirdly, all new forms of progressive education that put the child's activity and creativity in the centre imply new forms of disciplining of the child. All methods can turn into orthodoxy and silence discussions with opponents; all methods can be translated into practice in a mechanical and child-silencing way.
>
> (Singer 2005: 618)

The liberalism that child-centredness was supposed to express celebrates freedom and choice, but existing social inequalities structure differential access to choice. Increasingly, parents and children are expected to shoulder more responsibilities in the name of greater participation and democracy, but are actually accorded fewer means to fulfil these. I have explored the role of developmental psychology in legitimising the translation of individualism into normative conceptions of development. Its moral status, conceptions of morality and implications for moral-political intervention remain to be addressed in the next and last chapter.

Further reading

Dahlberg, G. and Moss, P. (2005) 'The preschool as a site for democratic politics', in G. Dahlberg and P. Moss (eds) *Ethics and Politics in Early Childhood Education*, London: RoutledgeFalmer.

Hultqvist, K. and Dahlberg, G. (eds) (2001) *Governing the Child in the New Millennium*, New York and London: RoutledgeFalmer.

Singer, E. (1992) *Child Care and the Psychology of Development*, London: Routledge (describes the origins and impact of child-centred practices).

Walkerdine, V. (1984; 1998) 'Developmental psychology and the child-centred pedagogy: the insertion of Piaget in primary education', in J. Henriques, W. Hollway, C. Urwin, C. Venn and V. Walkerdine, *Changing the Subject: Psychology, Social Regulation and Subjectivity*, London: Routledge.

Walkerdine, V. and Lucey, H. (1989) *Democracy in the Kitchen: Regulating Mothers and Socialising Daughters*, London: Virago.

Suggested activities

1   Analyse interviews with teachers, either by recording teachers' accounts in local schools or training colleges, or drawing on available extracts from such texts as Billig *et al.* (1988) or Sharp and Green (1975). What are the tensions between a commitment to the needs and interests of children and the statutory requirement to teach skills such as reading and numbers?

2   Explore how the child-centred approach moves from a focus on the child as having needs or problems to the child as being a problem. Here structural legacies of developmental psychology's role and function (see Chapter 1) are currently played out within the domain of educational psychology. Read Marks (1993a, 1996) and Ford (1982) for accounts of the relationships between coexistent and competing frameworks of meaning. In particular, consider professional and parental perceptions of the purpose of a case conference in relation to the following questions:

- What is the problem?
- Who is the problem?
- What agendas or professional interests are being played out/ maintained?
- What is the relationship between a discourse of developmental needs and a school management discourse of removing a 'difficult' child from a school?
- To what extent are ideological or common-sense notions about social conformity and adaptation replayed within 'expert' reports?
- What structural constraints overdetermine the decision-making process?

14 Morality and the goals of development

Developmentalism is a beguiling creed, to be a developer of backward lands an attractive vocation. We all want to see ourselves as bearers of aid, rectifiers of past injustice. To be sent among a distant nation as a conveyer of progress can only make one feel good. . . . It boosts self esteem. It is to regain certainty and purpose, to cast away the ennui and despair of decaying industrial society and to restore bracing faith in the goodness and charity of one's fellow men and women.

(Morris 1992: 1)

It has been clear that an underlying project of developmental psychology has been to produce moral citizens appropriate to the maintenance of bourgeois democracy, but it has been less clear what notion of morality it subscribes to. This chapter addresses the treatment of morality in developmental psychology. The debates and criticisms generated in this area can be regarded as encapsulating in a microcosm the limitations of current developmental models. While the moral assumptions permeating models of moral development have attracted some critical attention, their exhibition within this arena should be understood as only one particular instance of what is a general problem. In this chapter the moral status of models of moral development is located within the broader cultural and political landscape within which developmental psychology functions. The remaining questions about whether developmental psychology can outgrow rather than simply process, mature and recycle the conservative and culture-bound presentations of early twentieth-century privileged men are complex. But a prerequisite for this is to understand what these theories are and do.

Piaget's rules on children's games

In *The Moral Judgement of the Child* (1932) Piaget describes his investigations of children's developing appreciation of morality. He conceived of morality as systems of rules, and his aim was to understand how we acquire these rules. In line with his paradoxical model of the child both as asocial and party to insights that civilisation has knocked out of us, Piaget held that most of the moral rules we learn are imposed and enforced on us ready-made by adults. However, he saw in the 'social games' played by children the opportunity to see how these rules are constructed and interpreted by them. By asking children to teach him how to play the game of marbles and asking questions about who had won the game and why, Piaget built up a picture of characteristic ways in which children of different ages both practised and accounted for the rules.

Piaget traced a development in children's play from regularities or rituals that an individual child devises to amuse herself which are full of idiosyncratic habits and symbols, to an imitation of some aspects of what others are doing in terms of rules she has devised but assumes hold generally. At this point, he argued, children may believe themselves to be playing together, but may in fact be playing entirely different games in parallel, without seeing the need for a shared set of rules. This clearly ties in with Piaget's ideas about childhood egocentrism. By about seven or eight years of age, he claimed, children began to see the game of marbles as a competitive game structured by rules. The success of the game depends on mutual co-operation between players according to collectively upheld rules. By 11 or 12 years (in what he later termed formal operational thinking) Piaget argued that children are interested not only in rules governing the particular game or version of the game they are playing, but in reflecting upon the total set of possible variations that might be called upon in a given case – in other words a hypothetico-deductive approach characteristic of formal reasoning. At this point we should note that, for Piaget, it is the appreciation and engagement with *competition* that is taken as the indicator of sociality.

This work formed the basis for a wide-ranging exploration of children's moral understanding. He explored children's awareness of rules by asking them such questions as 'Can rules be changed?', 'Have rules always been the same as they are today?' and 'How did rules begin?'. At the second stage (which would be called 'preoperational' in his later work), children's imitation of rules was based on a perception of rules as sacred and unalterable, despite violating these rules in their own play. Once again childhood egocentrism is used to account for this paradox. Piaget identified a developmental progression from *heteronomy*, where the self is undifferentiated from the (social, moral, physical) context, to *autonomy*, where the individual chooses to engage in particular social contracts. He traced a change in approach towards rules from an initial *unilateral respect* (where rules are obeyed due to adult constraint) to *mutual respect* (where rules are social conventions operating to maintain fairness). He went on to pose stories involving minor misdeeds to children, investigating their ideas about responsibility in terms of moral questions he considered relevant to children, such as stealing and lying. The outcome of his 'clinical' interviews with children was that he claimed that, in contrast to older children and adults, young children judged the naughtiness of an action by its results rather than by the agent's intentions, that is, the magnitude of the damage is treated as the index of the scale of the misdeed.

Kohlberg on Piaget

Laurence Kohlberg (1969a, 1969b, 1976), a US developmental psychologist, elaborated on and developed Piaget's work on moral reasoning to put forward a series of six stages and three levels in the development and articulation of moral judgement from childhood to adulthood. He based his work on the classification of the kinds of moral reasoning displayed by individuals of different ages when they were confronted with hypothetical dilemmas. The most celebrated 'dilemma' used to elicit the underlying structure of people's moral reasoning was about a penniless man, Heinz, who urgently needs an expensive medicine to save his wife's life, and which the pharmacist refuses to give or supply on credit. Should he steal the drug? Here there is a conflict between the values of property and life. We should pause to note that, in the transition from Geneva to the USA and from the 1930s to the 1960s, a process of methodological and taxonomic rigidity has taken place. The ascription of moral level has become a question of classification according to age or stage; from premoralism, to conformism, to individual principled morality.

A number of claims underlie the framework. First, the stages are said to be universal and fixed. Second, the sequence is invariant, with variation only in rate of progression or fixation at a particular stage. And, third, each stage is a structured whole, with characteristics of reasoning associated with a stage related together into a total world view. All this is reminiscent of Piaget's model of the relations that hold between the organisation of cognitive operations. In terms of evidence used to support this model, there is apparently fairly widespread support for the claim that the stages occur in a fixed order (Colby *et al.* 1983). There is also cross-sectional support, in that higher stages are reported among older subjects. In addition, some longitudinal studies suggest that over a period of years individuals tend to advance to higher stages (Walker 1989). Even some cross-cultural work lent support, with Kohlberg (1969b) identifying the same sequence of stages (with the stories slightly adapted) in the USA, Britain, Taiwan, Mexico and Turkey, and the stages and sequences confirmed in other societies by Edwards (1981). So it seemed as though the arena of moral development had been pretty well sorted out. Or had it?

Kohlberg's dilemmas

From the 1970s some critical voices emerged which suggested that the sorting process was on a less than equitable basis. It seemed that the ascription of the moral highground was of uncertain validity, of contested value and unfair distribution.

In terms of methodological criticisms, a first problem arises from basing a classification of moral level on verbal reports. Unlike Piaget's early work, Kohlberg's model relies exclusively on what people say about what (other) people should do, based on hypothetical situations. But being more thoughtful, circumspect, taking more factors into consideration does not necessarily mean that people behave more morally. Further, the practice of investigating moral reasoning via hypothetical situations makes the moral problems posed even more detached and distanced. In this context Carol Gilligan's (1982) work on women's reasoning about the real-life dilemma of whether or not to terminate a pregnancy provides a particularly striking contrast.

Second, corresponding to the work challenging what is seen as Piaget's rather pessimistic view of children's abilities, there has been some work which seeks to analyse and minimise the linguistic and narrative demands of the task. Stein *et al.* (1979) reformulated Heinz's dilemma into a story about a lady who had a sick husband and had to steal some cat's whiskers in order to make the only medicine that would save his life. Despite the fairy tale genre and simplicity of the story, they report young children as having difficulties understanding it. They suggest that the children do not draw the obvious inference that the medicine will save the man's life since they cannot maintain the major goal in mind while trying to pursue the subgoals of securing the whiskers and making the medicine. In order to engage with the dilemma, the task presupposes the ability to understand a complex narrative and to think through alternative courses of action, both of which may be more complicated than the process of making moral judgements alone.

Criticisms addressed to the theory rather than the procedures by which it was arrived at also take a number of forms. In the first place, it is claimed that it addresses only a very restricted notion of morality. While this is not the place to go into alternative (such as behavioural or psychoanalytic) models of morality, the Kohlbergian model of morality as moral reasoning cannot engage with issues of moral commitment, individual priorities or differences of moral salience of particular issues. Nor does it address the subjective experience of feelings of guilt and shame which, as Kagan (1984) notes, children exhibit from an early age. Once again we see that a cognitive developmental model which prioritises rationality cannot theorise its relation with emotions except insofar as emotions are regarded as subordinate to, or at best by-products of, cognition.

The rigidity of representation of morality also fails to deal with domain specificity, familiarity and, further, the reality of the conflicting moral codes and priorities we are subject to (Turiel 1983; Song *et al.* 1987). Moreover, not only is this a model which treats talk about moral behaviour as equivalent to moral activity, it also fails to address how accounting for the morality of one's behaviour tends to follow rather than precede the actions. Hence these accounts measure moral rationalisation rather than reasoning (Hogen 1975). Subsequent research has continued the trend towards treating morality in cognitive terms. Dodge's (2006) review applies the whole gambit of ethological and neurophysiological as well as social psychological approaches to the study of antisocial behaviour, taking attributional processes as the primary analytical device responsible for young people's 'externalising' (i.e. aggressive or hostile) behaviour. Determinants of moral (or immoral) actions thus become a subset of other decision-making and reasoning processes (see also Griffifth Fontaine *et al.* 2002) or – in full circle – bring us back to assessments of the 'quality' of parenting (e.g. Lansford *et al.* 2003).

Double standards: gender-differentiating rights and responsibilities

One of the most influential criticisms of the model is that the stages do not fit female development. Carol Gilligan (1982) points out that both Piaget and Kohlberg derived their stage norms from studying boys and men. She questions the capacity of the model to express women's psychological development. She reinterprets boys' and girls' accounts of Heinz's dilemma, where in terms of Kohlbergian criteria the girls would be scored as reasoning at a lower moral stage of development. Instead she points out that the girls' and women's reservations about stealing the drug were based on additional considerations arising from an engagement with the context, such as the effect on the wife if the man was imprisoned for the crime and the worry about who would care for her if she fell ill again.

Although it is unclear whether she is advocating improving or abandoning it, Gilligan therefore throws the model of moral development that Kohlberg proposes into question. In tracing a linear progression from undifferentiation or attachment to autonomy, she argues that it subscribes to a model of morality based on individual rights and freedoms of the kind enshrined in Western legal systems, whereas, she holds, women's moral development is characterised by a much more contextualised morality concerned with conflicting responsibilities and care – that is, concerned with responsibilities and relationships rather than rights and rules. She argues that Kohlberg's model emphasises separation rather than connection by taking the individual rather than the relationship as the primary unit of analysis.

Gilligan ties these different conceptions of morality to the different roles traditionally accorded to men and women. Since typically women define their identity through relationships of intimacy and care, the moral issues that women face are to do with learning to assert their own needs without seeing this as 'selfish'. For both sexes, she argues, the issues that we face are to do with the conflict between integrity (separateness) and care (attachment), but that men and women approach these issues with different moral orientations. For men the emphasis is on 'equality', based on an understanding of fairness, equal respect, balancing the claims of other and self. In contrast, women's morality, she claims, is more oriented to issues of responsibility, with recognition of differences in need that an equal rights approach cannot address – an ethic of compassion and care and not wanting to hurt. Gilligan calls for the necessity for these contrasting moral orientations to be seen as complementary rather than one being systematically downgraded, and ultimately for them to be integrated into a more adequate vision of moral maturity. While there are problems with the idealisation of women's qualities within this account (see Spelman 1990; Elam 1994), the value of this work lies in demonstrating the limited application to and far-reaching devaluation of women structured within the cognitive developmental model.

Culture and the goals of development

A further serious difficulty with Kohlberg's model lies in the status of the sixth stage, which represents individual moral conviction as the most advanced morality beyond the respect for democratically arrived at and contractually maintained rules (Stage Five). First, few people are designated as attaining the higher points on the developmental ladder (with Jesus Christ, Mahatma Gandhi and Martin Luther King named by Kohlberg as among the lucky few – he also includes himself!). This raises questions about the theoretical status of the highest point of development. Second, some cultures are recorded as not reaching even beyond the second stage. There are clearly methodological difficulties involved in the study of people from one culture by those of another. These are issues that anthropologists routinely address, although some have been known to rely on psychology with disastrous results (see e.g. Hallpike 1979). The suggestion that Kohlberg's stages can be related to the 'complexity' of societies (Edwards 1981) sets up a hierarchy from 'primitive' to 'complex' which simply reflects a Western cultural bias. It may, however, be more accurate to make a distinction between rural and urban societies, with Stage Five reported much less frequently in the former (Snarey 1985). But this calls for an analysis that connects cognitive/moral development with culture and context.

However, a further issue comes into play when researchers measure indigenous people's abilities and interests by means of a test devised outside their own culture. Here developmental psychology reproduces and bolsters the dynamic of imperialism by offering tools that produce a picture of inferiority and moral underdevelopment through the ethnocentric and culturally chauvinist assumptions that inform both theory and tool (Joseph *et al.* 1990). Kohlberg later reformulated some of his claims about Stage Six so that it is now seen as an ideal, rather than a necessary endpoint of development (Levine *et al.* 1985). This, however, seems to offer a rather cosmetic change which leaves the methodological, and moral-political, problems intact.

In this we can see played out problems common to all developmental psychological theories that claim to hold generally. The postulation of a starting state and an endstate involves the prescription of the endpoint, the goal, of development. We talk in terms of 'progressing', 'advancing' from one stage to the next. But the norms by which we evaluate that development may be far from universal. In particular, as we have seen, the individual autonomy of conscience of Stage Six fits well with the modern, Western ideology of individualism. But this is not the highest point of moral development for all cultures, many of which have traditionally valued obedience and respect for elders and tradition over personal conviction. Kagan (1984) notes that in Japan the guiding principle of social interaction is to avoid conflict and maintain harmonious relationships. While we should beware of the dangers of essentialising cultural-political practices (i.e. treating these as if they are static, unchanging and somewhere 'inherent' properties) and overestimating the coherence of national identities (which are, of course, always fractured by, for example, class and gender relations), we can at least note that with such a different value system and contrasting view of the relationship between individuals, we could expect that a Kohlbergian Stage Six person would be considered aberrant and amoral in according personal principles more importance than societal expectations, as outlined by Doi (1973, 1986).

Further, the model of 'man' prescribed in Kohlberg's (and by implication Piaget's) model derives from particular social interests, based on a liberal model of society seen as functioning by means of social contractual arrangements between people (Simpson 1974; Sampson 1989). The rationality that is so highly valued in the cognitive developmental model ties in with a bourgeois conception of the individual which either accepts class divisions or denies their existence (Buck-Morss 1975; Sullivan 1977). In its celebration of autonomy, Kohlbergian theory therefore partakes of a liberal view that sees society as composed of independent units who co-operate only when the terms of co-operation are such as to further the ends of each of the parties. This also clearly recalls Piaget's definition of social interaction in game playing through competition. Not only does this lead to an asocial view of the individual, in terms of the ascription of pre-social interests, but it also sets up a form of conceptual imperialism in its application to cultures which do not share this underlying model. Sullivan treats this model as a case example of the political and conceptual problems wrought by an inadequate theory of the social: thought is severed from action, form from content, the abstract from the concrete and, ultimately, emotion from intellect. More recent work has drawn on other theoretical resources to offer a more nuanced and social account. For example, Woods (2004) draws on post-Vygotskyan frameworks emphasising the performativity of utterances and interactions, through the work of Bakhtin and Volosinov, to inform her ethnographic research investigating moral accounts provided by schoolchildren in relation to their setting and the relationships they are embedded within. Singer and Doorenebal (2006) have applied Vygotskyan perspectives to analyse children's narratives of being betrayed by a friend, while Mitlenburg and Singer (2000) have used these principles to inform a therapeutic approach to the analysis of the moral development of survivors of child abuse.

These questions about gender, emotions and the interrelations between models return us to the key themes of this book, and the key strategies mobilised to 'deconstruct' developmental psychology. In particular, we have seen how developmental psychological models abstract the individual from social context, to render class, culture and gendered positions as merely supplementary attributes to, rather than as constitutive of, the developing subject. Not only is the social reduced to the individual, then, but – as we have seen – the development of the individual (child) is increasingly targeted as a site of intervention and manipulation for the production of flexible, autonomous and especially economically self-sufficient citizens (Fendler 2001; Lister 2006). Thus conceptions of the developing child connect with models of national development. This 'development' works as a key term in policy links made to connect the individual child to national and international change. As we shall see, developmental models also foster particular contemporary understandings of the relations between the 'First' and 'Third' worlds, as well as having historical links with colonialism (see Chapter 1). While these issues are elaborated upon more extensively in the companion book to this, *Developments: Child, Image, Nation* (Burman in press a), the last part of this chapter moves to consider such questions.

Developmental psychology and the developing world

Some of the methodological and moral difficulties described above have been reflected in the failure of the project of cross-cultural psychology (Burman, 2007 b). On practical grounds researchers have been forced to recognise that the cultural assumptions held by research 'subjects' about the nature of the task demanded of them did not always correspond with that intended by the researchers. In a telling study, Cole *et al.* (1971) found that the African Kpelle consistently failed Piagetian classification tasks when asked 'how a wise man' would organise piles of foods and household items together. It was only when in despair the researcher asked how 'a fool would do it' that they exhibited the typical Western classification based on type (sorting similar items together) that had been defined as task success, rather than functional relations that reflected the ways the items were used. Such findings paved the way for the generation of alternative, more contextually attuned models focusing on cultural specificities and communities of practice (see Lave and Wenger 1991; Nelson *et al.* 2000; Rogoff 2003).

Such examples highlight that the problems are more than mere practical or technical difficulties, and cast doubt on the entire project of developmental psychology. The presentation of a general model that depicts development as unitary irrespective of culture, class, gender and history means that difference can be recognised only in terms of aberrations, deviations – that is, in terms of relative progress on a linear scale. The developmental psychology we know is tied to the culture which produced it. While such insights have had some impact within academic psychology, they are maintained in policy and in popular representations of childhood and child development.

The image of the active, natural, innocent child functions within the economy of cultural representations of children in so-called developing countries in ways which castigate poor people for their poverty, lapse into racist assumptions about child neglect and penalise the children of the poor rather than promote their welfare. Claire Cassidy (1989) discusses how, when poverty and ignorance lead to malnutrition in Third World countries, this is sometimes treated by welfare workers as an example of parental neglect. There is a failure to distinguish between culturally normative and deviant forms in evaluating child development in 'other' cultures. In purveying what is advertised as a general, universal model of development, developmental psychology is a vital ingredient in what Jo Boyden (1990) termed the 'globalization of childhood'. While Western sentimentalised representations of children are rooted in the attempt to deny children's agency (notwithstanding the claims of child-centredness) and prevent social unrest, the key dimensions that have come to structure Western organisation of childhood are being inappropriately imposed in 'developing' countries. The division between public and private has been central to Western industrialisation, but it should be recalled that poor people have less privacy, and street children may have none at all (although many children *of* the street are not actually children living *on* the streets (Glauser 1990; Burr 2006). But Western conceptions of children as unknowing, helpless and in need of protection from the public sphere may actually disable and criminalise children who are coping as best they can (see e.g. Kleeberg-Niepage 2005). All too often, policies and practices developed in the West function more in punitive than protective ways for Third World children – even in literal ways by being dispensed by the police, who in some Third World countries have also been responsible for the murder of children in their custody.

Similarly, as discussed in Chapter 5 (and more extensively in Burman 2006), while the regulation of child labour is clearly important, attempts to abolish this in line with supposed Western practice frequently ignore the extent to which families (and children) are dependent on the incomes children generate, and would therefore need to be compensated in order to let their children attend school. Further, the schooling which is on offer is often of varying quality, and may take the form of enforced assimilation to a colonial language. The schooling experience may therefore be one which fails rather than enables children. The Western priority accorded to education may be misplaced in the sense that this is unlikely to be organised around principles of personal development or enlightenment.

The undifferentiated, globalised model of childhood not only fails to address the varying cultural value and position of children (Zelizer 1985), but also ignores gender as a structural issue in development (in both the senses of individual and economic development). Aid agencies are now being forced to recognise that specific priorities need to be set up for girls and women (e.g. Wallace and March 1991), while the role of gendered meanings in structuring not only entirely different subjectivities and livelihoods, but also actual nutrition and survival, is gradually emerging through the efforts of women's organisations (Scheper-Hughes 1989b; Batou 1991).

In general, the concept of childhood on offer is a Western construction that is now being incorporated, as though it were universal, into aid and development policies (Burman 1994a, 1994b, 1994c). Associations between the development of the child and the development of the nation or state are familiar. Indeed many aid policy documents present their rationale for promoting child survival and development in terms of the future benefit to the state (e.g. Myers 1992). But there are other resonances I want to mobilise here. Tim Morris opens his account of his experiences as an aid worker in the Middle East (in the extract I have positioned at the beginning of this chapter) with a critique of the cultural chauvinism, complacency and personal investments set up within aid work. Just as he is exposing the problems inherent in defining goals for societal development, so too do the same problems arise within the determination of the direction and endpoint of individual development. The notion of 'progress', whether attached to societies or 'the lifespan', implies linear movement across history and between cultures. Comparison within these terms is now being recognised as increasingly untenable. In particular, the implication that there is a detached, disinterested set of devices or techniques for this purpose, such as developmental psychology purports to provide, illustrates the extent to which we have come to believe in the abstract disembodied psychological subject, and dismiss all it fails to address as merely either supplementary or inappropriate. In this regard, it should be noted that the focus within this book on literature and interpretations produced by researchers in Britain and especially the USA is not, or not merely, a reflection of my own parochialism. Anglo-US psychology extends its influence much further than its own linguistic and cultural domains through the dynamic of imperialism. Developmental psychology therefore functions as a tool of cultural imperialism through the reproduction of Western values and models within post-colonial societies.

Assumptions about child development and adjustment also play a key role in psychosocial interventions provided by international agencies following humanitarian emergencies, with the very distinction between 'natural' and 'humanitarian' disasters itself an artificial construction

(Middleton and O'Keefe 1998; Duffield 2001). Rodriguez Mora's (2003) analysis of the UNICEF-led response to the humanitarian emergency caused by the massive mudslides in Caracas, Venezuela, in 1999 is a case in point. This was a participatory study in the sense that she and the other psychologists in Caracas worked alongside the international agencies in delivering aid and support. Her study generates questions and reflections relevant to the project of aid as a mode of international governance that not only consolidates pre-existing inter- and intra-state power inequalities but also obscures their analysis in structural terms.

Three areas are of particular relevance here. First the expectation that the population would be traumatised, alongside particular ideas of what behaviours this should involve, led the aid workers to be particularly shocked and disapproving when some people were found to be having sex in the temporary shelter accommodation (a commandeered former barracks – itself marking the continuity of militarisation, and the connections between military and humanitarian intervention in these people's lives). Second, the international aid organisations approached their interventions with the erroneous expectation that their work would be to deal with children who were abandoned, whereas in fact children were multiply claimed by families – thus illustrating the inappropriateness of Western representations of children as burdens rather than of value to families. Third, Rodriguez Mora discusses the use of the 'knapsack of dreams', a play therapy tool for children developed in Guatemala and incorporated into UNICEF practice, which worked to impose a particular understanding of what children were supposed to be like and how they should react to disaster and disruption in their lives but did not reflect the experiences and responses of these children.

Needless to say, although such effects have arisen despite the good intentions of individuals and organisations, they still demand critical reflection and response. In particular, the focus on trauma can work to prescribe how people should react to disasters in their lives (Summerfield 2001). Moreover, it can work within neoliberal politics as a rationale to limit aid to short-term interventions (such as psychosocial support or training) rather than investment in rebuilding infrastructure or capacity building (Palmary 2006), while the general assumption of damage and vulnerability can diminish the credibility of political claims (Pupavac 2002a, 2002b, 2004).

Developmental psychology and the production of childhood

Closer to home, these issues arise in analogous ways within discussions of child abuse, in particular the recognition of child sexual abuse. Part of the reason why this issue commands such media attention lies in the challenge to the image of the safe, happy and protected child. As we saw in Chapters 5 and 8, not only do the family, or trusted parental figures, no longer necessarily provide a safe, caring environment for children and so warrant greater scrutiny and intervention from the state, but the model of the child as innocent can render the 'knowing' child as somehow culpable within her own abuse (Kitzinger 1990). Issues of power that constitute the abuse are eclipsed within the effort to ward off children's agency and sexuality and maintain a romantic sentimental image of the passive, innocent child (Stainton Rogers and Stainton Rogers 1992).

Once constituted in such ways, children's assertion or aggression becomes very hard to acknowledge or deal with except in pathological terms. The British case of the two Liverpool boys who murdered a three-year-old boy in 1993 was remarkable not only because the perpetrators were regarded as legally responsible for their actions despite being minors, but also for the general vilification directed towards their familial, class, community and regional backgrounds. The fact that they were given 'new identities' on their release from prison some ten years later further underscores how their actions were seen as so uniquely personal and their personal responsibility such that their societal readmittance could only be predicated on the surrender of who they previously were. Here we can see at work a key effect of the abstraction of childhood from socio-political conditions: it seems that they can be excised from the body politic at will. That this was not the only possible response to such events was illustrated by the legal and social response to an equivalent case of child murder happening at a similar time in Trondheim, Norway, where the specific community and the state in general saw this as a matter of general responsibility, with the focus of intervention on rehabilitation rather than punishment (see BBC world service 'When children kill children', www.bbc. co.uk/worldservice/people/highlights/001109_child.shtml).

While developmental psychology plays a key role in the legitimation and perpetuation of these dangerously limited and sometimes plainly false conceptions of childhood, they mesh with dominant cultural imagery which glorifies and markets childhood as a commodity. In the green and caring 1990s, children signified as icons of simplicity and naturalness, the necessary accessory for any soap or shampoo advertisement and caring (especially male) figure. But according intrinsic, natural qualities to children gives rise to representations of gender and sexual orientation as somehow essential and inherent, as where child models are portrayed engaging in heterosexual dating postures as a means of selling clothes that are simply scaled down versions of their parents' (Burman 1991).

The twenty-first century appears to be acquiring a rather more ambivalent view of children's aggression and sexuality. Children's knowingness attracts complex responses, as children have to teach their parents how to use their electronic gadgets, and increasingly embrace the position of societal participation through consumption that the market offers them. This includes children's own relation to their sexuality. In a culture that eroticises little girls (and sometimes little boys), the strength of the demonisation of paedophiles surely betrays how their crimes merely take a culturally-incited theme to a particular, but problematic, conclusion. Although we should take care to read such texts as indices of social anxieties rather than reflections of actual children's understandings or actions, films such as *Hard Candy* (2006) express the complex possibilities and interrelations of adult–child, male–female relationships. Not only as in *Lolita* (the film of Nabokov's novel, made in 1962 and remade in 1997), can the little girl mobilise the knowledge of her attractiveness seductively, but in *Hard Candy* she can use it to entrap and exact revenge.

Ethics and politics

Similar problems attend discussions of ethics in psychological research with children, where the larger question of consultation over the nature of the investigation, and its relevance to the lives and interests of children, gets scaled down into a set of bureaucratic procedures for ensuring 'informed consent'. In general, as Moss *et al.* (2000) and other accounts point out, we are better at protecting children than facilitating their participation in constructing our models about them. Since the question of which factors ensure or are relevant to 'informed consent' effectively restates the whole project of developmental psychology, the reduction of such key issues to a procedure for ensuring compliance is surely an example of how defensive practice obscures the formulation of genuine psychological inquiry. Perhaps more than anywhere else, such practices justify dismissal of developmental psychology by the new sociologists of childhood as working with a deficiency model of what children can do and know.

Discussions of the impact of developmental psychological knowledge often flounder on the issue of whether it reflects or produces the practices it describes. While it would be naive to accord too much significance to a relatively minor arena of academic and popular culture, nevertheless the act of reproduction of both common-sense and technical-political understandings within the seemingly objective arena of scientific research functions to recycle existing historically and culturally specific ideas as legitimised, eternal knowledge. Models about children and child rearing achieve a reality in part because they comprise the fabric of both professional and everyday knowledge about ourselves and our relationships. We cannot easily get outside them since they have constituted our very subjectivities, and in that sense notions of 'reflection' and even 'production' fail to convey their reality within our lives.

Baker and Freebody (1987) discuss how a particular cultural form, in this case, children's first reading books, acts to 'constitute the child' by presenting a particular, school-endorsed set of representations of child, family, school and social relations within the materials. While purporting to reflect the children's development, these function to organise it. They map out their school and personal careers and ambitions as pupils, boys and girls, with class positions (see also Rose 1985), and relay sets of ideas about the positions and rights of adults and children. The consequences of this may even enter into the children's abilities to engage with educational processes. As they put it:

> Young readers, whose identities as children differ from the images embedded in the texts, may have particular difficulties in relating to these books. For all children there may exist the practical problems of knowing how to treat these images while taking part in a reading instruction based on them, in such a way as to appear to be concurring with school-endorsed portraits in the texts.
>
> (Baker and Freebody 1987: 57)

Morality and change

We have moved very fast in this chapter from a discussion of Piaget's work on morality to the role that developmental psychology plays in the new world, and now the new world order. What developmental psychology all too often neglects, even when it studies morality, is its own moral status as a moral science, and its moral positions in the world. We have seen how developmental psychology has functioned as an instrument of classification and evaluation, as a tool for 'mental hygiene', a euphemism for the control and surveillance of populations deemed likely to be troublesome or burdensome – working-class children, single parents, minority groups and poor people the world over. Clothed in the rhetoric of scientific rigour and detachment, it has worked in very partial ways. The denial of moral-political assumptions underlying developmental psychology has merely worked to maintain reactionary practices. Now it is time to recognise that the 'science' of development is not separate from concerns of 'truth', and therefore of morality, politics and government.

This book started with an account of how developmental psychology arose, and the moral-political agendas it served and expressed. From the constitution of the isolated, individual 'child' as its unit of study, to an equivalent focus on families, mothers, and now fathers, developmental psychology functions as a key resource for legislating upon and distributing welfare interventions. Parts I and II of this book demonstrated how development is portrayed as either divorced from social and material circumstances, or within so oversimplified and sanitised a conception of the 'social' that it diverts and proscribes critical evaluation and colludes in the pathologisation of individuals and groups on the basis of their failure to reflect the Western, middle-class norms that have structured developmental psychological research. In Parts II and III we saw how these assumptions structure not only the explicit accounts of how to care for, and who should care for, children, but also enter in less direct but equally evaluative ways into accounts of language and learning. 'Sensitive' mothers are not only better mothers in the ways that they respond to and look after their charges, but they also maximalise (Rose 1990) their children's learning. We may claim, as the theories of cognitive development and education discussed in Part IV do, to deal with the 'whole child', but this child is endowed with a false unity conferred by its abstraction from social relations. These last chapters have argued that the rationality and individualism that 'he' is accorded construct an image of mental life which privileges cultural masculinity and mirrors market demands for skills and efficient functioning. The costs of accounting for 'mastery' and development in these ways are that, beneath the facade of the whole, adjusted and integrated self, the subject of developmental psychology is fragmented, alienated and split.

In over 20 years of teaching a wide range of undergraduate and professional groups, within each group I have encountered two sorts of reactions to developmental psychology. One is that it is mystificatory and jargon ridden, which creates some hostility on the grounds of its exclusivity and inaccessibility; the other is to dismiss it as simply common sense. Significantly, both reactions are correct. What should be clear from this book is that dressed up in its claims to present some particular expertise (of which it devotes considerable energy to maintaining sole control), developmental psychology (like the rest of psychology) imports ideological understandings into its theories that are incorporated into 'science'. As I have shown, the methodologies as well as the theories reflect these assumptions, but coded at a deeper level through the relation between science and modern states, advanced capitalism demands more elaborate and specialised modes of individualisation.

Disciplinary tensions

In contrast to developmental psychology's model of the child development as stable, regular and uniform, the new discipline of childhood studies, devoted to the understanding of children and childhoods, subscribes to a model of the child as competent social actor (e.g. James *et al.* 1998). Informed by sociological, anthropological and historical approaches (among others), it challenges what is seen as developmental psychology's deficit or inferiority model, that focuses on what children cannot do relative to adults, and positions children as passive (Alderson 2002). While developmental psychological work makes claims for children's needs, childhood studies typically talk in terms of children's rights. The latter stands as a useful corrective to and commentary upon psychological models, challenging the naturalisation and abstraction of children and notions of childhood by emphasising children's active engagement in and transformation of social practices.

In this sense we can see something of the division of labour between these two approaches, as each appears to address a different, but equally significant, area of social policy. Developmental psychology has been accorded (or rather, as we have seen, managed to wrest away from medicine) the role of arbiter of normality, while other disciplines have addressed the cultural context of children's activities, including the situated character of the evaluation these attract. Both function politically, and none are innocent in terms of the broader agendas they contribute to. For example, both sets of models can mobilise instrumental accounts of children and childhoods (i.e. to inform social policy on national development). Both are implicated within current economically instrumentalising discourses of investment and citizenship. Moreover, however justified such critiques may be, and however valuable it may be to see children's lives as cultures (rather than as abstracted from culture and engaged in some quasi-biological natural process, as Clark *et al.* 2005 also point out), there remains a problem to conceptualise just what it is that makes children different from adults – other than social status (although this clearly is very important). This is not to say that sociologists and historians are naive about developmental changes associated with age; rather it has been a key analytical strategy to 'bracket' out such notions, to allow room for other considerations to emerge. In this sense, however, the two approaches remain deeply connected, if only by virtue of their structural antagonism. While of course developmental psychology does not, and should not, have the franchise on models of change and development, it remains our task to engage with and reformulate these models in the light of critiques from elsewhere; and vice versa.

My text here should be read as a preliminary effort to bring these perspectives into closer dialogue. Given the circulation and permeation of psychological culture under the 'psy complex', at the level of public policy as well as 'personal' lifestyle (i.e. consumer 'choice') and popular culture, I consider it invidious to maintain disciplinary distinctions as absolute. Indeed psychologistic assumptions can lurk in models that are not explicitly psychological, just as psychologists are also as much consumers as producers of psychology – with developmental psychology probably a key culprit in this area. Normative ideas about children, families and relationships cannot simply be expunged or dispensed with. We cannot suspend or wish them away. Rather we have to interrogate them and reassess them, as we encounter their ambiguities. Nor can we substitute one set of certainties (critical or otherwise) for another. Instead we have to deal with the inevitably insufficient and underspecified character of our theories (whether in the form of assessment of psychological capacities or application of child rights policies) and consciously address the interpretive activity we engage in to make those theories applicable. As many commentators have noted (e.g. Rustin 2004; Cooper 2005), policy responses to failures of state responsibilities towards children have typically taken the form of imposing further bureaucratic structures of regulation. But these cannot in themselves guarantee appropriate practice; they only specify minimum standards. The human qualities required for work with children and families cannot be legislated for, even if such legislation must document the consequences of their absence.

My primary aim in this book is to support those practitioners inside and outside psychology, many of whom have already generated their own suspicions of the partiality and inadequacy of current psychological models by making more accessible a range of critical tools and analyses. Thus the critiques of developmental psychology put forward here have emerged from within psychology (through what has became known as discursive and critical psychology), as well as from outside. Together, they offer a wide-ranging and coherent set of resources to challenge the prevailing ways in which assumptions about children and development are mobilised in national and international policies. They also, hopefully, can support alternative pedagogical practices (see Carolan and Zeedyk 2006). Perhaps we could reclaim the multidisciplinary focus of 'child development' to trouble the narrower concerns of developmental psychology. At any rate, we can insist on the privilege and partiality of mainstream developmental psychology, and so better contest its insertions within, or 'application' to, social policy as offering only one version of the truth, rather than 'the' truth. Claims about what children are like have far-reaching effects, so that the basis of such claims – often currently rooted in supposedly scientific developmental psychology – demands particular vigilance. The project of prefiguring minds and bodies capable of revolutionary social change and the transformation of structures and relations of oppression remains as pressing as ever. But we will not find the answers in developmental psychology, now or ever.

Constructing and deconstructing

This book has attempted to identify and evaluate the central themes that structure contemporary developmental psychology. In part the journey has been a historical one, in aiming to understand the specific conditions that prompted the emergence of, and agenda for, what has come to be a central agency for the regulation and control of individual and family life. In other ways we have had to look beyond the theories to understand the cultural and political role that the academic practice of developmental psychology fulfils. Both home and school are informed by developmental psychology, and it enters into the ways we talk and reflect upon our feelings and intellect and, more than this, produces 'us' in its image.

The process of delineating and commenting on these discourses is part of the process of deconstructing, of dismantling the power of this apparatus for the construction of subjects by which we are disciplined and constituted. We have seen how inequality and differential treatment on the basis of class, culture, gender, age and sexuality permeate the deep structure of developmental psychological practice. Both in its terms of formulation and via its insertions in social policy, developmental psychology therefore contributes to the maintenance of the social formation which gave rise to it.

These problems are increasingly acknowledged within, as well as outside, the discipline. The range of proposals put forward includes the need for a greater diversity of theoretical resources, and for espousing a set of moral-political commitments that lie outside the discipline with which to reinterpret grandiose (universalist, ahistorical) developmental claims (both as formulated from within developmental psychology and as 'applied' within social policies). It is important to note that this does not necessarily mean jettisoning all the models and methods of developmental psychology, but it certainly means tempering the claims we make for them and understanding better which perspectives they privilege and which they exclude. For some commentators, perhaps the same kind of developmental questions remain, but we should expect to get multiple answers; while for others, such as Woodhead *et al.* (1999), cultural psychology offers a key alternative resource. Nelson *et al.* (2000) produce one such reformulation of the project as follows:

> To state that we must understand a particular child's developmental history and specific life experiences does not mean to deny commonality in the developmental process and product. Rather, the expectation is that particular applications of a common process may result in different pathways toward understanding and different constructions of a general model. Commonalities in psychological understanding arise because people, including children at all ages, are engaged in *making sense* of their worlds, and in particular of making sense of self and others in the social milieu in which they find themselves. The job of the researcher is to articulate this process of making sense and apply it to the problems of psychological understanding.
>
> (Nelson *et al.* 2000: 77)

This project of weighing up the generality of claims in relation to the specificities of local contexts and conventions surrounding childhood is also just as much an issue in the application of child rights legislation, where equivalent problems of cultural imperialism in the imposition (or equally withholding!) of particular understandings of children and childhoods come to the fore. There is now a significant literature addressing this set of problems (see e.g. Burman 1996c; Franklin 2002b; Ansell 2005; Burr 2006). Overall the project of decolonising psychology has a long way to go and there are particular problems – to do with psychology's deep implication in the Anglo-Eurocentric order – that make this a complex and perhaps impossible endeavour (Strauble 2005).

I have been using the term deconstruction as a mode of analysis which invites scrutiny of the limits and presuppositions that have guided research. While deconstruction threatens to disallow absolute justification of any position (Burman 1990, 1993) – including mine here – nevertheless there can be no fully practising deconstructor. In this sense Woodhead *et al.*'s (1999) depiction of a relativist constructionism that refuses to take a moral-political stance is not a necessary consequence. In his words: 'A point must be established where diversity becomes deprivation, where variation becomes violation, plurality becomes pathology, by any standards' (p. 16). Rather, the deconstructionist project aims to bring to light, to acknowledge, the investment and hidden subjectivity that lie beneath the claims to disinterested, true knowledge. To move too swiftly from deconstruction to reconstruction may foreclose the emergence of other interpretive and political possibilities that could come from a more sustained interrogation of hidden presuppositions of developmental reasoning. Beyond this, it inevitably risks replacing one exclusionary disciplinary apparatus with another – for there is no innocent or neutral position. Hence the impetus behind this book reflects Gayatri Chakravorty Spivak's (1990) character-isation of the 'corrective and critical' role of deconstruction:

> In one way or another academics are in the business of ideological production. . . . Our institutional responsibility is of course to offer a responsible critique of the structure of production of the knowledge we teach even as we teach it, but, in addition, we must go public as often as we can.
>
> (Spivak 1990: 103)

What is achieved by such a process of deconstruction? I would like to hope that at the very least some caution about the indiscriminate application of general models should follow, and in particular how these are 'applied' or interpreted to inform policies and models of service provision. Ideas are tools for change, and they are certainly used to prevent change. The pur-pose of this deconstruction is to lay bare, to make public, the parameters by which our own change and development has been structured. The domain of developmental psychology is a modern, Western construction, which is itself contested and under revision, though currently often continually reinvented. Taking apart, challenging its scientific certainty and grip on common sense, may help us to recognise other ways of talking about those issues that currently are dealt with within the terms of developmental psychology, and perhaps other developmental psychologies to formulate. Exploitation and oppression suffuse the structure of developmental psy-chology. Our task is to deconstruct it.

Further reading

Burman, E. (in press a) *Developments: Child, Image, Nation*, London: Routledge.
Dahlberg, G. and Moss, P. (2005) *Ethics and Politics in Early Childhood Education*, London: RoutledgeFalmer.

Morss, J. (1996) 'Writing against development', in J. Morss (ed.) *Growing Critical: Alternatives to Developmental Psychology*, London: Routledge.

Penn, H. (2005) *Unequal Childhoods: Young Children's Lives in Poor Countries*, London: RoutledgeFalmer.

Suggested activities

1   Take any developmental psychology test or assessment task (whether of infant development scales, conservation tasks or child-rearing styles) and consider:

- its claims to generality
- the extent to which the categorisation of behaviours reflects or refers to specific cultural practices
- the extent to which the definition of positive parenting behaviours addresses culturally specific understandings of children's qualities and corresponding models of caregiving activities.

2   Explore Boyden's (1990) notion of the 'globalization of child-hood'. What are the dominant cultural images of childhood? Whose childhood do they reflect? Collect a corpus of images of children from all over the world and explore:

- whether the children are used to express the same or different sets of qualities
- to what extent the children are represented within or as separate from their cultural and familial context. What implications can be drawn from this about (a) models of development and (b) the symbolic functions played by images of children?

References

Abbott, P. (1989) 'Family lifestyles and structures', pp. 79–87 in W. Stainton Rogers, D. Hevey, J. Roche and E. Ash (eds) *Child Abuse and Neglect: Facing the Challenge*, London: Batsford.

Abramovitch, R., Freedman, J.L., Thoden, K. and Nikolich, C. (1991) 'Children's capacity to consent to participation in psychological research: empirical findings', *Child Development*, 62: 1100–1109.

Ainsworth, M. (1967) *Infancy in Uganda: Infant Care and the Growth of Love*. Baltimore: Johns Hopkins University Press.

Ainsworth, M.D.S., Bell, S.M. and Stayton, D.J. (1974) 'Infant–mother attachment and social development: "socialisation" as a product of reciprocal responsiveness to signals', pp. 99–136 in M.P.M. Richards (ed.) *The Integration of the Child into a Social World*, Cambridge: Cambridge University Press.

Aitkenhead, D. (2006) 'The sins of the fathers', *Guardian*, 8 May: 6–11.

Alderson, P. (2002) 'Young children's health care rights and consent', pp. 155–167 in B. Franklin (ed.) *The New Handbook of Children's Rights*, Abingdon: Routledge.

Alldred, P. (1996) 'Whose expertise? Conceptualising resistance to advice about child-rearing', pp. 133–151 in E. Burman, G. Aitken, P. Alldred, R. Allwood, T. Billington, A. Gordo-Lopez, C. Heenan, D. Marks and S. Warner (eds) *Psychology, Discourse Practice: From Regulation to Resistance*, London: Taylor & Francis.

Alldred, P. and Burman, E. (2005) 'Hearing and interpreting children's voices: discourse analytic contributions', pp. 175–198 in S. Greene and D. Hogan (eds) *Researching Children's Experience: Approaches and Methods*, London: Sage.

Alldred, P. and Gillies, V. (2002) 'Eliciting research accounts: re/producing modern subjects?', pp. 146–165 in M. Mauthner, M. Birch and T. Miller (eds) *Ethics in Qualitative Research*, London: Sage.

Amin, T. (2001) 'Evolutionary psychology returns to its Bowlbian roots', *Behavior and Philosophy*, 29: 79–93.

Andenaes, A. (in press) 'Development through daily routines'.

Anderssen, N., Amlie, C. and Ytterøy, E.A. (2001) 'A critical look at psychological research on the children of lesbian or gay parents', *International Journal of Critical Psychology*, 1, 3: 173–181.

—— (2002) 'Outcomes for children with lesbian or gay parents. A review of studies from 1978 to 2000', *Scandinavian Journal of Psychology*, 43: 335–351.

Ansell, N. (2005) *Children, Youth and Development*, Abingdon: Routledge.

Ariès, P. (1962) *Centuries of Childhood*, Cape: London.

Arney, W.R. (1980) 'Maternal–infant bonding: the politics of falling in love with your child', *Feminist Studies*, *6*, *3*: 547–570.

Attewill, F. and Butt, R. (2006) 'One in 3 working mothers unhappy with nurseries', *Guardian*, 16 October (http://education.guardian.co.uk/earlyyears/story/0,,1923494,00.html).

Austin, J.L. (1962) *How to Do Things with Words*, Oxford: Oxford University Press.

Avis, J. (1991) 'The strange fate of progressive education', in Education Group II, Cultural Studies University of Birmingham, *Education Limited: Schooling and Training and the New Right since 1979*, London: Unwin Hyman.

Baetens Beardsmore, H. (1982) *Bilingualism: Basic Principles*, Clevedon: Multilingual Matters.

Baker, C.D. and Freebody, P. (1987) '"Constituting the child" in beginning school reading books', *British Journal of Sociology of Education*, *8*, *1*: 55–76.

Baltes, P.B., Reese, H.W. and Lipsett, L.P. (1980) 'Life-span developmental psychology', *Annual Review of Psychology*, *23*: 611–626.

Barkham, P. (2006a) '"It's all about reputation"', *Guardian*, 4 August.

—— (2006b) 'Stuck on the "mummy track" – why having a baby means lower pay and prospects', *Guardian*, 20 January.

Baron-Cohen, S. (1995) *Mindblindness: An Essay on Autism and Theory of Mind*, Cambridge: MIT Press.

Baron-Cohen, S., Leslie, A. and Frith, U. (1985) 'Does the autistic child have a "theory of mind"?', *Cognition*, *21*: 37–46.

Barrett, H. (1998) 'Protest-despair-detachment: questioning the myth', pp. 64–84 in I. Hutchby and J. Moran-Ellis (eds) *Children and Social Competence: Arenas of Action*, London: Falmer Press.

—— (2006) *Attachment and the Perils of Parenting: A Commentary and Critique*, London: National Family and Parenting Institute.

Barton, M. and Tomasello, M. (1994) 'The rest of the family: the role of father and siblings in early language development', pp. 109–134 in C. Gallaway and B. Richards (eds) *Input and Interaction in Language Acquisition*, Cambridge: Cambridge University Press.

Bates, E., Camaioni, L. and Volyera, V. (1979) 'The acquisition of performatives prior to speech', in E. Ochs and B. Schieffelin (eds) *Developmental Pragmatics*, New York: Academic Press.

Batou, J. (1991) '100 million women are missing', *International Viewpoint*, *206*: 26–28.

Baxter, J. (2002) 'Competing discourses in the classroom: a post-structuralist discourse analysis of girls' and boys' speech in public contexts', *Discourse and Society*, *13*, *6*: 827–842.

BBC (2000) 'When children kill children', http://www.bbc.co.uk/worldservice/people/highlights/001109_child.shtml (accessed 07/09/2006).

Bee, H. and Boyd, D. (2007) *The Developing Child*, 11th edn, Boston: Pearson.

Beekman, D. (1979) *The Mechanical Baby: A Popular History of the Theory and Practice of Childraising*, London: Dobson.

Beinart, J. (1992) 'Darkly through a lens: changing perceptions of the African child in sickness and in health, 1900–1945', pp. 220–243 in R. Cooter (ed.) *In the Name of the Child*, London and New York: Routledge.

Bell, R. and Harper, L. (1977) *Child Effects on Adults*, Hillsdale, NJ: Lawrence Erlbaum Associates, Inc.

Belsky, J. (1981) 'Early human experience: a family perspective', *Developmental Psychology*, *17*: 3–23.

—— (2006) 'Early child care and early child development: major findings of the NICDH Study of Early Child Care', *European Journal of Developmental Psychology*, *3*: 95–110.

Belsky, J. and Rovine, M.J. (1988) 'Nonmaternal care in the first year of life and the security of infant–parent attachment', *Child Development*, *59*: 1577.

Benjamin, J. (1988) *Bonds of Love*, London: Virago.

Benn, M. (1998) *Madonna and Child: Towards a New Politics of Motherhood*, London: Jonathan Cape.

Berk, L. (2007) *Development Through the Lifespan*, 4th edn, Boston: Pearson.

Bernstein, B. (1970) 'Education cannot compensate for society', *New Society*, *26*: 344–347.

—— (ed.) (1973) *Class, Codes and Control, Vol. 2*, London: Routledge & Kegan Paul.

Bettelheim, B. (1986) *Freud and Man's Soul*, Harmondsworth: Flamingo.

Bhavnani, K. (1990) 'What's power got to do with it? Empowerment and social research', pp. 41–152 in I. Parker and J. Shotter (eds) *Deconstructing Social Psychology*, London: Routledge.

Bifulco, A. (2002) 'Attachment style measurement – a clinical and epidemiological perspective', *Attachment and Human Development*, *4*: 180–188.

Bifulco, A., Kwon, J., Jacobs, C., Moran, P., Bunn, A. and Beer, N. (2006) 'Adult attachment style as mediatory between childhood neglect/abuse and adult depression and anxiety', *Social Psychiatry Psychiatric Epidemiology*, *41*, *10*: 796–805.

Billig, M., Condor, S., Edwards, D., Gane, M., Middleton, D. and Radley, A. (1988) *Ideological Dilemmas*, London: Sage.

Billington, T. (1996) 'Pathologising children: psychology in education and acts of government', pp. 37–54 in E. Burman, G. Aitken, P. Alldred, R. Allwood, T. Billington, A. Gordo-Lopez, C. Heenan, D. Marks and S. Warner (eds) *Psychology, Discourse Practice: From Regulation to Resistance*, London: Taylor & Francis.

—— (2000) *Separating, Losing and Excluding Children*, London: Falmer Press.

—— (2006) *Working with Children: Assessment, Intervention and Representation*, London: Sage.

Billington, T. and Pomerantz, M. (eds) (2003) *Children at the Margins: Supporting Children, Supporting Schools*, Stoke: Trentham Books.

Black, A. (2003) 'Medicating normality: the psychiatric colonization of childhood', Academy for the Study of the Psychoanalytic Arts, http://www.AcademyAnalyticArts.org/black2.html (accessed 10/09/2006).

Blakemore, C. and Cooper, G.F. (1970) 'Development of the brain depends on the visual environment', *Nature*, *228*: 477–478.

Blurton Jones, N. (1972) *Ethological Studies of Child Behaviour*, Cambridge: Cambridge University Press.

Bly, R. (1991) *Iron John: A Book about Men*, Shaftesbury: Element.

Boden, M. (1979) *Piaget*, London: Fontana.

Bohannen, J. and Hush-Pasek, K. (1984) 'Do children say as they're told? A new perspective on motherese', in L. Feagans, C. Garvey and R. Golinkoff (eds) *The Origins and Growth of Communication*, Norwood, NJ: Ablex.

Bohannen, J. and Marquis, A. (1977) 'Children's control of adult speech', *Child Development*, 48: 1002–1008.

Boler, M. (1999) *Feeling Power: Emotions and Education*, New York and London: Routledge.

Borger, J. (2006) 'Gunned down: the teenager who dared to walk across his neighbour's prized lawn', *Guardian*, 22 March: 3.

Borstelmann, L. (1983) 'Children before psychology: ideas about children from antiquity to the late 1800s', pp. 1–40 in W. Kessen (ed.) *Handbook of Child Psychology, Vol. 1: History, Theory and Method*, New York: Wiley.

Boulton, M.G. (1983) *On Being a Mother: A Study of Women with Pre-school Children*, London: Tavistock.

Bowden, P. (1997) *Caring: Gender-sensitive Ethics*, London: Routledge.

Bower, T. (1966) 'The visual world of infants', *Scientific American*, 215, 6: 180–193.

—— (1977) 'Blind babies see with their ears', *New Scientist*, 73: 255–257.

Bower, T., Broughton, J. and Moore, M. (1970) 'Infant responses to approaching objects: an indication of response to distal variables', *Perception and Psychophysics*, 8: 51–53.

Bowers, J. (1990) 'All hail the great abstraction: star wars and the politics of cognitive psychology', pp. 127–140 in I. Parker and J. Shotter (eds) *Deconstructing Social Psychology*, London: Routledge.

Bowlby, J. (1951) *Maternal Care and Mental Health*, Geneva: World Health Organization.

Bowlby, J., Figlio, K. and Young, R. (1986) 'An interview with John Bowlby on the origins and reception of his work', *Free Associations*, 6: 364.

Boyd, S. (1989) 'From gender specificity to gender neutrality? Ideologies in Canadian child custody law', in C. Smart and S. Sevenhuijsen (eds) *Child Custody and the Politics of Gender*, London: Routledge.

Boyden, J. (1990) 'Childhood and the policy makers: a comparative perspective on the globalization of childhood', pp. 184–215 in A. James and A. Prout (eds) *Constructing and Reconstructing Childhood: Contemporary Issues in the Sociological Study of Childhood*, Basingstoke: Falmer Press.

Boyden, J. with Holden, P. (1991) *Children of the Cities*, London: Zed Books.

Boyden, J. and Hudson, A. (1985) *Children: Rights and Responsibilities*, London: Minority Rights Group.

Bradley, B. (1989) *Visions of Infancy*, Oxford: Blackwell.

—— (1991) 'Infancy as paradise', *Human Development*, 34: 35–54.

—— (1993) 'A serpent's guide to children's "theories of mind"', *Theory and Psychology*, 3, 4: 497–521.

Brah, A. (1996) *Cartographies of Diaspora*, London: Routledge.

Brainerd, C. (1973) 'Judgements and explanations as criteria for the process of cognitive structures', *Psychological Bulletin*, 79, 3: 172–179.

Brannen, J. and Moss, P. (1987) 'Fathers in dual-earner households – through mothers' eyes', pp. 126–143 in C. Lewis and M. O'Brien (eds) *Reassessing Fatherhood: New Observations on Fatherhood and the Modern Family*, London: Sage.

Brannen, J. and Wilson, G. (eds) (1987) *Give and Take in Families: Studies in Resource Distribution*, London: Allen & Unwin.

Brazelton, T.B., Koslowski, B. and Main, M. (1974) 'The origins of reciprocity', in M. Lewis and L. Rosenblum (eds) *The Effect of the Infant on its Caregiver*, New York: Wiley.

Bremner, J.G. (1988) *Infancy*, Oxford: Blackwell.

Brice Heath, S. (1983) *Ways with Words*, Cambridge: Cambridge University Press.

—— (1986) 'What no bedtime story means: narrative skills at home and at school', in B. Schieffelin and E. Ochs (eds) *Language Socialisation across Cultures*, Cambridge: Cambridge University Press.

Bronfenbrenner, U. (1979) *The Ecology of Human Development*, Cambridge, MA: Harvard University Press.

Bronfenbrenner, U., Kessel, F., Kessen, W. and White, S. (1986) 'Toward a critical social history of developmental psychology: a propaeduetic discussion', *American Psychologist, 41, 11*: 1218–1230.

Broughton, J. (1981a) 'Piaget's structural developmental psychology I: Piaget and structuralism', *Human Development, 24*: 78–109.

—— (1981b) 'Piaget's structural developmental psychology III: logic and psychology', *Human Development, 24*: 195–224.

—— (1987) 'Introduction', in J. Broughton (ed.) *Critical Theories of Psychological Development*, New York: Plenum Press.

—— (1988) 'The masculine authority of the cognitive', in B. Infielder (ed.) *Piaget Today*, Hove, UK: Lawrence Erlbaum Associates Ltd.

Brown, R. (1973) *A First Language*, Harmondsworth: Penguin.

Browne, N. and France, P. (1985) '"Only cissies wear dresses": a look at sexist talk in the nursery', in G. Weiner (ed.) *Just a Bunch of Girls: Feminist Approaches to Schooling*, Milton Keynes: Open University Press.

Bruner, J. (1975/6) 'From communication to language', *Cognition, 3*: 355–387.

—— (1978) 'Learning how to do things with words', in J. Bruner and A. Garten (eds) *Human Growth and Development*, Oxford: Clarendon Press.

—— (1983) *Child's Talk: Learning to Use Language*, Oxford: Oxford University Press.

Buckingham, D. (1999) 'Blurring the boundaries: Teletubbies and children's media today', *Televizion, 12, 2*: 8–12.

Buck-Morss, S. (1975) 'Socio-economic bias in Piaget's theory and its implications for cross-cultural studies', *Human Development, 18*: 3515.

Bukatko, D. and Daehler, M. (1992) *Child Development: A Topical Approach*, Boston, MA: Houghton Mifflin.

Bullock, A. (1974) *A Language for Life: Report of the Committee of Enquiry Appointed by the Secretary of State for Education under the chairmanship of Sir Alan Bullock*, London: HMSO.

Burman, E. (1990) 'Differing with deconstruction: a feminist critique', pp. 208–220 in I. Parker and J. Shotter (eds) *Deconstructing Social Psychology*, London: Routledge.

—— (1991) 'Power, gender and developmental psychology', *Feminism and Psychology, 1, 1*: 141–153.

—— (1992a) 'Feminism and discourse in developmental psychology: power, subjectivity and interpretation', *Feminism & Psychology, 2, 1*: 45–60.

—— (1992b) 'Developmental psychology and the postmodern child', pp. 95–110 in J. Doherty, E. Graham and M. Malek (eds) *Postmodernism and the Social Sciences*, London: Macmillan.

—— (1993) 'Beyond discursive relativism: power and subjectivity in developmental psychology', pp. 433–442 in H. Stam, L. Moss, W. Thorngate and B. Caplan (eds) *Recent Trends in Theoretical Psychology*, Vol. 3, New York: Springer Verlag.

—— (1994a) 'Innocents abroad: projecting western fantasies of childhood onto the iconography of emergencies', *Disasters: Journal of Disaster Studies and Management, 18, 3*: 238–253.

—— (1994b) 'Developmental phallacies: psychology, gender and childhood', *Agenda: A Journal about Women and Gender, 22*: 11–20.

—— (1994c) 'Poor children: charity appeals and ideologies of childhood', *Changes: An International Journal of Psychology and Psychotherapy, 12, 1*: 29–36.

—— (1995a) 'What is it? Masculinity and femininity and the cultural representation of childhood', pp. 49–67 in S. Wilkinson and C. Kitzinger (eds) *Feminism and Discourse*, London: Sage.

—— (1995b) 'Developing differences: childhood and economic development', *Children and Society, 9, 3*: 121–141.

—— (1995c) 'The abnormal distribution of development: child development and policies for southern women', *Gender, Place and Culture, 2, 1*: 21–36.

—— (1996a) 'Deconstructing developmental psychology: a feminist approach', *Nordiske Udkast, 2*: 2–18.

—— (1996b) 'Continuities and discontinuities in interpretive and textual approaches to developmental psychology', *Human Development, 39*: 330–349.

—— (1996c) 'Local, global or globalized: child development and international child rights legislation', *Childhood: A Global Journal of Child Research, 3, 1*: 45–66.

—— (1997a) 'False memories, true hopes: revenge of the postmodern on therapy', *New Formations, 30*: 122–134.

—— (1997b) 'Psychology: market, metaphor and metamorphosis', *Culture and Psychology, 3, 2*: 143–152.

—— (1998a) 'Children, false memories and disciplinary alliances: tensions between developmental psychology and psychoanalysis', *Psychoanalysis and Contemporary Thought, 21, 3*: 307–333.

—— (1998b) 'The child, the woman and the cyborg: (im)possibilities of a feminist developmental psychology', pp. 210–232 in C. Griffin, K. Henwood and A. Phoenix (eds) *Standpoints and Differences: Feminist Perspectives on Psychology*, London and Thousand Oaks: Sage.

—— (1998c) *La Deconstruccion de la Psicologia Evolutiva*, Madrid: Visor Apredizaje.

—— (1999) 'The child and the cyborg: metaphors of abjection and subjection', in A. Gordo Lopez and I. Parker (eds) *Cyberpsychology*, London: Macmillan.

—— (2003) 'Beyond the baby and the bathwater: postdualistic developmental psychologies for diverse childhoods', Academy for the Study of the Psychoanalytic Arts (www.AcademyAnalyticArts.org), http://www.academyanalyticarts.org/burman.html (accessed 07/09/2006).

—— (2005a) 'Childhood, neoliberalism and the feminization of education', *Gender and Education, 17, 4*: 351–368.

—— (2005b) 'Engendering culture in psychology', *Theory and Psychology, 15, 4*: 527–548.

—— (2006) 'Engendering development: some methodological perspectives on child labour', *Forum for Qualitative Social Research*, 7, 1 (http://www.qualitative-research/net/fqs-texte/1-06/06-1-1-e.pdf).

—— (in press a) *Developments: Child, Image, Nation*, London: Routledge.

—— (in press b) 'Developmental psychology', in W. Stainton Rogers and C. Willig (eds) *Handbook of Qualitative Psychology*, London and Thousand Oaks: Sage.

—— (in press c) 'Beyond emotional literacy in feminised educational research', *British Education Research Journal*.

—— (in press d) 'Beyond "womenandchildren" and "women vs. children": engendering childhood and reformulating motherhood', *International Journal of Child Rights*.

—— (2007a) 'Pedagogies and politics: shifting agendas within the gendering of childhood', pp. 642–650 in J. Kincheloe and R. Horn (eds) *Praeger Handbook of Education and Psychology* (Vol. 3), Westport, CT: Greenwood Press.

—— (2007b) 'Between orientalism and normalization: cross-cultural lessons from Japan for a critical history of psychology', *History of Psychology*, 10 2: 179–198.

Burman, E. and MacLure, M. (2005) 'Deconstruction as a method of research: stories from the field', pp. 284–293 in B. Somekh and C. Lewin (eds) *Research Methods in the Social Sciences*, London: Sage.

Burman, E. and Parker, I. (eds) (1993) *Discourse Analytic Research: Repertoires and Readings of Texts in Action*, London: Routledge (full text available on www.discourseunit.com).

Burman, E., Aitken, G., Alldred, A., Allwood, R., Billington, T., Goldberg, B., Gordo Lopez, A.J., Heenan, C., Marks, D. and Warner, S. (1996) *Psychology Discourse Practice: From Regulation to Resistance*, London: Taylor & Francis.

Burman, E., Smailes, S. and Chantler, K. (2004) '"Culture" as a barrier to domestic violence services for minoritised women', *Critical Social Policy*, 24, 3: 332–357.

Burns, D. (2000) 'Feminism, psychology and social policy: constructing political boundaries at the grassroots', *Feminism and Psychology*, 10, 3: 367–380.

Burns, R. (1986) *Child Development: A Text for the Caring Professions*, Kent: Croom Helm.

Burr, R. (2006) *Vietnam's Children in a Changing World*, New Brunswick, Jersey and London: Rutgers University Press.

Buss, D. and Reeve, H. (2003) 'Evolutionary psychology and developmental dynamics: comment on Lickliter and Honeycutt (2003)', *Psychological Bulletin*, 129, 6: 848–853.

Butler, J. (1997) *The Psychic Life of Power*, New York: Routledge.

Butterworth, G. (ed.) (1980) *Infancy and Epistemology: An Evaluation of Piaget's Theory*, Brighton: Harvester.

Cabrera, N., Tamis-LeMonda, C., Bradley, R., Hofferth, S. and Lamb, M. (2000) 'Fatherhood in the twenty-first century', *Child Development*, 71, 1: 127–136.

Cairns, R. (1983) 'The emergence of developmental psychology', pp. 40–101 in W. Kessen (ed.) *Handbook of Child Psychology, Vol. 1: History, Theory and Method*, New York: Wiley.

Calder, J. (2005) 'Histories of child abuse', *Journal of Critical Psychology, Counselling and Psychotherapy*, 5, 3: 111–123.

Camaioni, L. (1979) 'Child–adult and child–child conversations: an interactional approach', in E. Ochs and B. Schieffelin (eds) *Developmental Pragmatics*, New York: Academic Press.

Cameron-Falkner, T., Lieven, E. and Tomasello, M. (2003) 'A construction based analysis of child directed speech', *Cognitive Science, 27*: 843–873.

Campbell, B. (1984) 'Women on the rock and roll', in B. Campbell (ed.) *Wigan Pier Revisited*, London: Virago.

Canella, G. and Viruru, R. (2004) *Childhood and Postcolonization*, New York and London: RoutledgeFalmer.

Caplan, P. (1985) 'Mother-blaming in major clinical journals', *American Journal of Orthopsychiatry, 55, 3*: 345–353.

Carolan, L. and Zeedyk, M.S. (2006) 'Feminist teaching on scientific epistemology, objectivity and truth: a student's perspective and an instructor's response', *Psychology of Women Section Review, 8, 1*: 12–30.

Carter, A. (1978) 'From sensorimotor vocalizations to words: a case study in the evolution of attention-directing communication in the second year', in A. Lock (ed.) *Action, Gesture and Symbol*, London: Academic Press.

Carvel, J. (2003) 'Child poverty adverts banned', *Guardian*, 10 December.

Cassidy, C. (1989) 'Worldview conflict and toddler malnutrition: change agent dilemmas', in N. Scheper-Hughes (ed.) *Child Survival and Neglect*, Dordrecht: Reidel.

Cassidy, J. and Shaver, P. (eds) (1999) *Handbook of Attachment*, New York: Guilford Press.

Chaika, E. (1982) *Language: The Social Mirror*, Rowley, MA: Newbury House.

Chau, R. (2001) 'Integrating culture and attachment', *American Psychologist, 56*: 822–823.

Chomsky, N. (1959) 'A review of B.F. Skinner's *Verbal Behaviour*', *Language, 35*: 26–58.

Clancy, P. (1989) 'Form and function in the acquisition of Korean wh- questions', *Journal of Child Language, 6*: 323–347.

Clarizio, H., (1981) 'Nature vs. accelerated readiness', in H. Clarizio, R. Craig and W. Mehrens (eds) *Contemporary Issues in Educational Psychology*, Boston: Allyn & Bacon.

Clarizio, H., Craig, R. and Mehrens, W. (eds) *Contemporary Issues in Educational Psychology*, Boston, MA: Allyn & Bacon.

Clark, A., Kjorhold, A. and Moss, P. (eds) (2005) *Beyond Listening: Children's Perspectives on Early Children's Services*. Bristol: The Policy Press.

Clarke, A.M. and Clarke, A.D. (1976) *Early Experience: Myth and Evidence*, London: Open Books.

Clarke-Stewart, A. (1982) *Day Care*, London: Fontana.

Clarke-Stewart, K.A. (1988) 'The "effects" of infant day care reconsidered', *Early Childhood Research Quarterly, 3*: 293–318.

Coard, B. (1971) *How the West Indian Child is made Educationally Subnormal in the British School System*, London: New Beacon Books.

Cohen, C.B., Deloache, J.S. and Rissman, M.W. (1979) 'The effect of stimulus complexity on infant visual attention and habituation', *Child Development, 46*: 611–617.

Cohen, G. (ed.) (1987) *Social Change and the Life Course*, London: Tavistock.

Colby, A., Kohlberg, L., Gibbs, J. and Lieberman, M. (1983) 'A longitudinal study of moral judgement', *Monographs of the Society for Research in Child Development, 48, 1–2*.

Cole, M. and Cole, S. (1989) *The Development of Children*, New York: Scientific American Books/Freeman.

Cole, M., Gay, J., Glick, J. and Sharp, D.W. (1971) *The Cultural Context of Learning and Thinking*, New York: Basic Books.

Condon, W. (1977) 'A primary phase in the organisation of infant responding behaviour', in H. Schaffer (ed.) *Studies in Mother–Infant Interaction*, London: Academic Press.

Conteh, J. (1992) 'Monolingual children and diversity: the space in the centre', *Multicultural Teaching*, *11*, *1*: 27–31.

Conteh, J. with Hussain, S. and Rehman, R. (2004) 'More than just a "rich resource"? – the knowledge and skills of bilingual teachers', *Race Equality Teaching*, *23*, *1*: 11–14.

Cooke, B. and Kothari, U. (eds) (2001) *Participation: The New Tyranny*, London: Zed Books.

Cooper, A. (2005) 'Surface and depth in the Victoria Climbié inquiry report', *Child and Family Social Work*, *10*: 1–9.

Cooter, R. (ed.) (1992) *In the Name of the Child: Health and Welfare 1880–1940*, London: Routledge.

Costall, A. and Leudar, I. (2004) 'Where is the "theory" in theory of mind?', *Theory and Psychology*, *14*, *5*: 623–626.

Costall, A., Leudar, I. and Reddy, V. (2006) 'Failing to see the irony in "mind-reading"', *Theory and Psychology*, *16*, *2*: 163–168.

Council for Racial Equality (CRE) (1992) *Set to Fail*, Oxford: Council for Racial Equality.

Coward, R. (1993) *Our Treacherous Hearts*, London: Faber and Faber.

Cradock, G. (2006) 'Distributing children's rights and responsibilities: children and the neoliberal state', paper presented at the Child and Youth Rights Conference; Investment and Citizenship: Towards a Transdisciplinary Dialogue on Child and Youth Rights, Brock University, Canada, July.

—— (2007) 'The responsibility dance: creating neo-liberal children', *Childhood*, *14*, *2*: 153–172.

Craig, G. (2004) Mother knows best: gastrostomy feeding and disabled children', unpublished PhD dissertation, University College, London.

—— (2005) 'Mother knows best: gastrostomy feeding and disabled children', *Psychology of Women Section Review*, *7*, *1*: 44–48.

Crain, W. (2005) *Theories of Development: Concepts and Applications*, 5th edn, Upper-Saddle River, NJ: Pearson/Prentice Hall.

Cross, T. (1977) 'Mothers' speech adjustments: the contribution of selected child listener variables', in C. Snow and C. Ferguson (eds) *Talking to Children*, Cambridge: Cambridge University Press.

Cullingford, C. (1991) *The Inner World of the Child: Children's Ideas about School*, London: Cassell.

Cummins, J. (2001) *Negotiating Identities: Education for Empowerment in a Diverse Society*, 2nd edn, Los Angeles: California Association for Bilingual Education.

Cushman, P. (1991) 'Ideology obscured: political uses of the self in Daniel Stern's infant', *American Psychologist*, *46*: 206–219.

Dahlberg, G. and Moss, P. (2005) *Ethics and Politics in Early Childhood Education*, London and New York: RoutledgeFalmer.

Dahlberg, G., Moss, P. and Pence, A. (1999) *Beyond Quality in Early Childhood*

Education and Care: Postmodern Perspectives, London and New York: RoutledgeFalmer.

Dalley, G. (1988) *Ideologies of Caring: Re-thinking Community and Collectivism*, Basingstoke: Macmillan.

Daniel, B. and Taylor, J. (2006) 'Gender and child neglect: theory, research and policy', *Critical Social Policy*, *26*, *2*: 426–439.

Daniel, B., Featherstone, B., Hooper, C.-A. and Scourfield, J. (2005) 'Why gender matters for *Every Child Matters*', *British Journal of Social Work*, *35*: 1343–1355.

Daniels, H. (ed.) (1996) *An Introduction to Vygotsky*, London and New York: Routledge.

—— (2006) 'The "social" in post-Vygotskyan theory', *Theory and Psychology*, *16*, *1*: 37–50.

Daniels, D. and Plomin, R. (1985) 'Differential experience of siblings in the same family', *Developmental Psychology*, *21*, *5*: 747–760.

David, M., Alldred, P. and Smith, P. (no date) 'Briefing paper for head teachers and PSHE co-ordinators: "Get Real About Sex": linking sex and relationship education to the achievement agenda' – a report of the SRE Policy Action Research commissioned by Stoke-on-Trent LEA, Keele University.

David, M., Edwards, R. and Alldred, P. (2001) 'Children and school-based research: "informed consent" or "educated consent"', *British Educational Research Journal*, *27*, *3*: 347–365.

Davies, B. (1994) *Poststructuralist Theory and Classroom Practice*, Geelong: Deakin University Press.

Davies, B. and Harré, R. (1990) 'Positioning: the discursive production of selves', *Journal of the Theory of Social Behaviour*, *20*, *1*: 433.

Demie, F., Taplin, A. and Butler, R. (2003) 'Stages of English acquisition and attainment of bilingual pupils: implications for pupil achievement in schools', *Race Equality Teaching*, *21*, *2*: 42–48.

Demos, J. (1983) 'The changing faces of fatherhood: a new exploration in family history', pp. 158–181 in F. Kessel and A. Siegel (eds) *The Child and Other Cultural Inventions*, New York: Praeger.

Department for Education and Skills (DfES) (2003) *Every Child Matters: A Consultation Document*, London: The Stationery Office.

Department of Health (DoH) (2004) *National Service Framework for Children, Young People and Maternity Services*, London: The Stationery Office.

Dingwall, R. (1989) 'Labelling children as abused or neglected', pp. 158–164 in W. Stainton Rogers, D. Hevey, J. Roche and E. Ash (eds) *Child Abuse and Neglect: Facing the Challenge*, London: Batsford.

Dingwall, R. and Eekelaar, J. (1986) 'Judgements of Solomon: developmental psychology and family law', in M. Richards and P. Light (eds) *Children of Social Worlds*, Oxford: Polity.

Dingwall, R., Eekelaar, J.M. and Murray, T. (1984) 'Childhood as a social problem: a survey of the history of legal regulation', *Journal of Law and Society*, *11*, *2*: 207–232.

Dinnerstein, D. (1978) *The Rocking of the Cradle and the Ruling of the World*, London: Souvenir Press.

DiPietro, J., Larron, S. and Porges, S. (1987) 'Behavioral and heart rate pattern differences between breast-fed and bottle-fed neonates', *Developmental Psychology*, *23*, *4*: 467–474.

Dodge, K. (2006) 'Translational science in action: hostile attributional style and the development of aggressive behavior problems', *Development and Psychopathology*, *18*: 791–818.

Doi, T. (1973) *The Anatomy of Dependence* (trans. J. Bester), Tokyo: Kodansha International.

—— (1986) *The Anatomy of Self: The Individual Versus Society* (trans. J.A. Harbison), Tokyo: Kodansha International.

Dolev, R. and Zeedyk, M.S. (2006) 'How to be a good parent in bad times: constructing parenting advice about terrorism', *Child Care, Health and Development*, *32*, 4: 467–476.

Donaldson, M. (1978) *Children's Minds*, London: Fontana.

Dornbush, S. and Strober, M. (eds) (1988) *Feminism, Children and the New Families*, New York: Guilford Press.

Drennan, G., Levett, A. and Swartz, L. (1991) 'Hidden dimensions of power and resistance in the translation process: a South African study', *Culture, Medicine and Psychiatry*, *15*: 361–381.

Dubas, J. and Gerris, J. (2002) 'Longitudinal changes in the time parents spend in activities with their adolescent children as a function of child age, pubertal status, and gender', *Journal of Family Psychology*, *16*: 415–427.

Duffield, M. (2001) *Global Governance and the New Wars: The Merging of Development and Security*, London: Zed Books.

Dunn, J. and Kendrick, C. (1982) *Siblings: Love, Envy and Understanding*, London: Grant McIntyre.

Dunn, J., Brown, J., Slomkowski, E., Tesla, C. and Youngblade, L. (1991) 'Young children's understanding of other people's feelings and beliefs: individual differences and their antecedents', *Child Development*, *62*: 13526.

Durham, M. (1991) *Sex and Politics: The Family and Morality in the Thatcher Years*, London: Macmillan.

Durkin, K. (1987) 'Minds and language: social cognition, social interaction and the acquisition of language', *Mind and Language*, *2*: 1050.

Dutton Conn, J. (1995) 'Autonomy and connection: gendered thinking in a statutory agency dealing with child sexual abuse', pp. 100–119 in C. Burck and B. Speed (eds) *Gender, Power and Relationships*, London and New York: Routledge.

Dworetzky, J. (1990) *Introduction to Child Development*, St Paul, MN: West.

Dworetzky, J. and Davis, N. (1989) *Human Development: A Lifespan Approach*, St Paul, MN: West.

Edhborg, M., Matthiesen, A.-S., Lundh, W. and Widstrom, A.-M. (2005) 'Some early indications for depressive symptoms and bonding two months postpartum – a study of new mothers and fathers', *Archives of Women's Mental Health*, *8*, 4: 221–231.

Edwards, C.P. (1981) 'The comparative study of the development of moral judgement and reasoning', in R.H. Munroe, R.L. Munroe and B.B. Whiting (eds) *Handbook of Cross Cultural Human Development*, New York: Garland.

Edwards, D. and Mercer, N. (1987) *Common Knowledge: The Development of Understanding in the Classroom*, London: Sage.

Egerton, J. (1991) 'The family way: Labour's policy on the family', *Trouble and Strife*, *20*: 3–7.

Elam, D. (1994) *Feminism and Deconstruction: ms. en abyme*, London and New York: Routledge.

Elgin, S. (1985) *Native Tongue*, London: Women's Press.

Elias, N. (2000) *The Civilising Process*, Oxford: Oxford University Press.

Elson, D. (1992) 'The differentiation of children's labour in the capitalist labour market', *Development and Change*, *13*, 4: 479–497.

Engestrom, Y., Miettinen, R. and Punamaki, R. (eds) (1999) *Perspectives on Activity Theory*, Cambridge: Cambridge University Press.

Ennew, J. and Milne, B. (1989) *The Next Generation: Lives of Third World Children*, London: Zed Books.

Epstein, D. (ed.) (1998) *Failing Boys? Issues in Gender and Achievement*, Buckingham: Open University Press.

Equal Opportunities Commission (1991) *Some Facts about Women 1991*, Manchester: EOC.

Ervin Tripp, S., O'Connor, M. and Rosenberg, J. (1984) 'Language and power in the family', in C. Kramerae, M. Schultz and W. O'Barr (eds) *Language and Power*, Beverly Hills, CA: Sage.

Fairclough, N. (2003) *Analyzing Discourse – Textual Analysis for Social Research*, London: Routledge.

Fanon, F. (1952) *Black Skins, White Masks*, London: Pluto Press.

Fantz, R. (1961) 'The origin of form perception', *Scientific American*, *204*: 66–72.

Farrar, M. (1990) 'Discourse and the acquisition of grammatical morphemes', *Journal of Child Language*, *17*: 607–624.

Featherstone, B. (1997) ' "I wouldn't do your job!": women, social work and child abuse', pp. 176–192 in W. Hollway and B. Featherstone (eds) *Mothering and Ambivalence*, London: Routledge.

—— (2006) 'Why gender matters in child welfare and protection', *Critical Social Policy*, *26*, 2: 294–314.

Feldman, R. (2003) 'Paternal socio-psychological factors and infant attachment: the mediating role of synchrony in father–infant interactions', *Infant Behavior and Development*, *25*: 221–236.

Fendler, F. (2001) 'Educating flexible souls: the construction of subjectivity through developmentality and interaction', pp. 119–142 in K. Hultqvist and G. Dahlberg (eds) *Governing the Child in the New Millenium*, New York and London: RoutledgeFalmer.

Fenton, B. (2006) 'Junk culture "is poisoning our children"', *Daily Telegraph*, 12 September.

Ferguson, C. (1977) 'Baby talk as a simplified register', in C. Snow and C. Ferguson (eds) *Talking to Children*, Cambridge: Cambridge University Press.

Finch, J. (1989) *Family Obligations and Social Change*, Cambridge: Polity.

Finch, J. and Groves, D. (1983) *A Labour of Love*, London: Routledge & Kegan Paul.

Fineman, M. (1989) 'The politics of custody and gender: child advocacy and the transformation of custody decision making in the USA', in C. Smart and S. Sevenhuijsen (eds) *Child Custody and the Politics of Gender*, London: Routledge.

Flavell, J. (1963) *The Developmental Psychology of Jean Piaget*, New York: Van Nostrand.

Fletcher, H. (1982) 'A social worker's view', in *No Accountability, No Redress: The Powers of Social Workers and the Rights of Parents*, London: One Parent Families.

Fogel, A. (1991) *Infancy: Infant, Family and Society*, St Paul, MN: West.

Fonagy, P. (2001) *Attachment and Psychoanalysis*, New York: The Other Press.

—— (2003a) 'The interpersonal interpretive mechanism', pp. 107–128 in V. Green (ed.) *Emotional Development in Psychoanalysis, Attachment Theory and Neuroscience: Creating Connections*, London: Brunner-Routledge.

—— (2003b) 'Attachment to ideas: the status of attachment theory in psychoanalytic thought', unpublished paper to Centre for the Advancement of Psychoanalytic Studies, 14 November.

Fonagy, P. and Target, M. (2004) 'What can developmental psychopathology tell psychoanalysts about the mind?', pp. 307–342 in A. Casement (ed.) *Who Owns Psychoanalysis?*, London: Karnac.

Fonagy, P., Steele, H. and Steele, M. (1991) 'Maternal representations of attachment during pregnancy predict the organisation of infant–mother attachment at one year of age', *Child Development*, *62*: 891–905.

Fonagy, P., Gergely, G., Jurist, E. and Target, M. (2004) *Affect Regulation, Mentalization and the Development of the Self*, London: Karnac.

Ford, J. (1982) *Special Education and Social Control: Invisible Disasters*, London: Routledge & Kegan Paul.

Foucault, M. (1972) *The Archaeology of Knowledge*, London: Tavistock.

Franklin, B. (2002a) 'Children's rights and media wrongs: changing representations of children and the developing rights agenda', pp. 15–42 in B. Franklin (ed.) *The New Handbook of Children's Rights*, Oxford: Routledge.

—— (2002b) 'Children's rights: an introduction', pp. 1–12 in B. Franklin (ed.) *The New Handbook of Children's Rights*, Oxford: Routledge.

Franklin, J. (2000) 'What's wrong with New Labour politics', *Feminist Review*, *66*: 138–142.

Franklin, S. (1997) *Embodied Progress: A Cultural Account of Assisted Conception*, London and New York: Routledge.

Freeman, M. (1989) 'Principles and processes of the law in child protection', in W. Stainton Rogers, D. Hevey, J. Roche and E. Ash (eds) *Child Abuse and Neglect: Facing the Challenge*, London: Batsford.

—— (2000) 'The future of children's rights', *Children and Society*, *14*: 277–293.

—— (2002) 'Children's rights ten years after ratification', pp. 97–118 in B. Franklin (ed.) *The New Handbook of Children's Rights*, Oxford: Routledge.

French, E.P. and MacLure, M. (eds) (1981) *Adult–Child Conversation*, London: Croom Helm.

Freud, S. (1922/1981) 'Beyond the pleasure principle', in *On Metapsychology*, Penguin Freud Library, Vol. 11, Harmondsworth: Penguin.

Frosh, S. (1997) *For and Against Psychoanalysis*, London and New York: Routledge.

Frosh, S., Phoenix, A. and Pattman, R. (2002) *Young Masculinities*, London: Palgrave.

Fuchs, E. (1973) 'How teachers learn to help children fail', in N. Keddie (ed.) *Tinker, Tailor . . . the Myth of Cultural Deprivation*, Harmondsworth: Penguin.

Furedi, F. (2004) *Therapy Culture*, London and New York: Routledge.

Gammon, P. (2003) 'Using bilingual strategies to raise achievement: the experience of a Birmingham primary school', *Race Equality Teaching*, *21*, 3: 18–20.

Gamsa, A. (1987) 'A note on the modification of the Parental Bonding Instrument', *British Journal of Medical Psychology*, *69*: 291–294.

Gardner, H. (1982) *Developmental Psychology*, Boston, MA: Little, Brown.

Garland, C. and White, S. (1980) *Children and Day Nurseries*, London: Grant McIntyre.

Gesell, A. (1950) *The First Five Years of Life: A Guide to the Study of the Pre-school Child*, London: Methuen.

Gibson, E. and Walk, R.D. (1973) 'The "visual cliff"', in T. Greenough (ed.) *The Nature and Nurture of Behavior: Developmental Psychobiology*, San Francisco: Freeman.

Gillen, J. (2000) 'Listening to young children talking on the telephone: a reassessment of Vygotsky's notion of egocentric speech', *Contemporary Issues in Early Childhood*, *1*, *2*: 171–184.

Gilligan, C. (1982) *In a Different Voice: Psychological Theory and Women's Development*, Cambridge, MA: Harvard University Press.

Ginsberg, H. and Opper, S. (1979) *Piaget's Theory of Intellectual Development*, Englewood Cliffs, NJ: Prentice-Hall.

Gittins, D. (1985) *The Family in Question*, London: Macmillan.

Gjerde, P. (2001) 'Attachment, culture and *amae*', *American Psychologist*, *56*: 826–827.

—— (2004) 'Culture, power and experience: towards a person-centred cultural psychology', *Human Development*, *47*: 138–157.

Glauser, B. (1990) 'Street children: deconstructing a construct', pp. 138–156 in A. James and A. Prout (eds) *Constructing and Reconstructing Childhood*, London: Falmer Press.

Goldberg, S. (2000) *Attachment and Development*, London: Arnold.

Goldstein, H. (1987) 'Gender bias and test norms in educational selection', pp. 122–126 in M. Arnot and G. Weiner (eds) *Gender and the Politics of Schooling*, Basingstoke: Hutchinson.

Goleman, D. (1996) *Emotional Intelligence: Why It Can Matter more than IQ*, London: Bloomsbury.

Golombok, S. (2000) *Parenting: What Really Counts?*, London: Routledge.

Goodnow, J. and Collins, W. (1990) *Development According to Parents: The Nature, Sources and Consequences of Parents' Ideas*, Hove: LEA.

Gopnik, A. and Choi, S. (1990) 'Do linguistic differences lead to cognitive differences? A cross-linguistic study of semantic and cognitive development', *First Language*, *10*: 199–215.

Gordo Lopez, A. and Burman E. (2004) 'Emotional capital and information technologies in the changing rhetorics around children and childhoods', *New Directions in Child Development*, *105*: 63–80.

Gould, S. (1984) *The Mismeasure of Man*, Harmondsworth: Penguin.

Gravelle, M. (2003) 'Weighing the turkey does not make it fat: a reappraisal of assessment of bilingual learners', *Race Equality Teaching*, *21*, *2*: 37–41.

Graycar, R. (1989) 'Equal rights versus fathers' rights: the child custody debate in Australia', in C. Smart and S. Sevenhuijsen (eds) *Child Custody and the Politics of Gender*, London: Routledge.

Green, V. (ed.) (2003) *Emotional Development in Psychoanalysis, Attachment Theory and Neuroscience: Creating Connections*, London: Brunner-Routledge.

Greene, S. (2003) *The Psychological Development of Girls and Women: Rethinking Change in Time*, London and New York: Routledge.

Greenough, T. (ed.) (1973) *The Nature and Nurture of Behavior: Developmental Psychology*, San Francisco: Freeman.

Griffifth Fontaine, R., Salzer Burks, V. and Dodge, K. (2002) 'Response decision processes and externalizing behavior and problems in adolescents', *Development and Psychopathology*, *18*: 107–122.

Grosjean, F. (1989) 'Neurolinguists beware! The bilingual is not two monolinguals in one person', *Brain and Language*, *36*: 3–15.

—— (1998) 'Studying bilinguals: methodological and conceptual issues', *Bilingualism: Language and Cognition*, *1*, 2: 131–149.

Gruber, H. and Vonèche, J. (1977) *The Essential Piaget: An Interpretive Reference and Guide*, London: Routledge & Kegan Paul.

Grutier, U. (1987) 'German psychology during the Nazi period', in M. Ash and W. Woodwood (eds) *Psychology in Twentieth Century Thought and Society*, Cambridge, MA: Cambridge University Press.

Guishard-Pine, J. (2006) 'Men in black families: the impact of fathering on children's development', *Race Equality Teaching*, *24*, 2: 45–49.

Haaken, J. (1998) *Pillar of Salt: Gender, Memory and the Perils of Looking Back*, London: Free Association Books.

Haavind, H. and Magnusson, E. (2005a) 'The Nordic countries – welfare paradises for women and children?', *Feminism & Psychology*, *15*, 2: 237–247.

—— (2005b) 'Feminism, psychology and identity transformations in Nordic countries', *Feminism & Psychology*, *15*, 2: 227–236.

Hakuta, K. (1986) *Mirror of Language: The Debate on Bilingualism*, New York: Basic Books.

Hall, D.M.B., Hill, P. and Elliman D. (1990) *Handbook of Child Surveillance*, Oxford: Radcliffe Medical.

Halliday, M.A.K. (1973) 'Foreword', in B. Bernstein (ed.) *Class, Codes and Control*, Vol. 2, London: Routledge & Kegan Paul.

—— (1975) *Learning How to Mean: Explorations in the Development of Language*, London: Arnold.

Hallpike, C. (1979) *The Foundations of Primitive Thought*, Cambridge: Cambridge University Press.

Handelman, D. (1989) 'Bureaucracy and the maltreatment of the child: interpretive and structural issues', in N. Scheper-Hughes (ed.) *Child Survival and Neglect: Anthropological Perspectives on the Treatment and Maltreatment of Children*, Dordrecht: Reidel.

Haraway, D. (1989) 'Metaphors into hardware: Harry Harlow and the technology of love', in D. Haraway (ed.) *Primate Visions: Gender, Race and Nature in the World of Modern Science*, London: Verso.

Hardyment, C. (1983) *Dream Babies*, Oxford: Oxford University Press.

Harlow, H. (1959) 'Love in infant monkeys', reprinted in T. Greenough (ed.) (1973) *The Nature and Nurture of Behavior: Developmental Psychobiology*, San Francisco: Freeman.

Harlow, H., Harlow, M. and Suomi, S. (1971) 'From thought to therapy: lessons from a primate laboratory', *American Scientist*, *659*: 538–549.

Harré, R. (1983) *Personal Being: A Theory for Individual Psychology*, Oxford: Blackwell.

—— (1986) 'Steps towards social construction', in M. Richards and P. Light (eds) *Children of Social Worlds*, Oxford: Polity.

Harris, A. (1987) 'The rationalisation of infancy', in J. Broughton (ed.) *Critical Theories of Psychological Development*, New York: Plenum Press.

Hawkins, A. and Dollahite, D. (eds) (1997) *Generative Fathering: Beyond Deficit Perspectives*, Thousand Oaks: Sage.

Haworth, D. (2000) *Discourse*, Maidenhead: Open University Press.

Hearnshaw, L.S. (1980) *Cyril Burt, Psychologist*, London: Hodder & Stoughton.

Hendrick, H. (1990) 'Constructions and reconstructions of British childhood: an interpretive survey, 1800 to the present', pp. 35–59 in A. James and A. Prout (eds) *Constructing and Reconstructing Childhood: Contemporary Issues in the Sociological Study of Childhood*, Basingstoke: Falmer Press.

—— (2003) *Child Welfare: Historical Dimensions, Contemporary Debate*, University of Bristol: The Policy Press.

—— (ed.) (2005) *Child Welfare and Social Policy*, Bristol: The Policy Press.

Hennessy, E., Martin, S., Moss, P. and Melhuish, E. (1992) *Children and Day Care: Lessons from Research*, London: Paul Chapman.

Henriques, J., Hollway, W., Urwin, C., Venn, C. and Walkerdine, V. (1984; 1998) *Changing the Subject: Psychology, Social Regulation and Subjectivity*, London: Methuen.

Henwood, K. and Proctor, J. (2003) 'The "good father": reading men's accounts of paternal involvement during the transition to first-time fatherhood', *British Journal of Social Psychology*, *42*: 337–355.

Hepper, P. (2005) 'Unravelling our beginnings', *The Psychologist*, *18*, *8*: 474–477.

Hétu, S. (2004) *The Song of the Child*, Norfolk and Montreal: Ur Publications.

Hill Collins, P. (1990) *Black Feminist Thought*, New York and London: Routledge.

Hinde, R. (1983) 'Ethology and child development', in M.M. Haith and J.J. Campos (eds) *Infancy and Developmental Psychobiology*, New York: Wiley.

Hobson, B. (ed.) (2002) *Making Men into Fathers: Men, Masculinities and the Social Politics of Fatherhood*, Cambridge: Cambridge University Press.

Hochschild, A.R. (1983) *The Managed Heart*, Berkeley, CA: University of California Press.

—— (2000) 'Global care chains and emotional surplus value', pp. 130–146 in W. Hutton and A. Giddens (eds) *On the Edge: Living with Global Capitalism*, London: Jonathan Cape.

—— (2003) 'Let them eat war', *European Journal of Psychotherapy, Counselling and Health*, *6*, *3*: 175–186.

Hoff-Ginsberg, E. (1991) 'Mother–child conversation in different social classes and communicative settings', *Child Development*, *63*: 782–796.

Hogan, J. and Sussman, B. (2001). 'Cross cultural psychology in historical perspective', pp. 15–28 in L. Adler and U. Gielen (eds) *Cross-cultural Topics in Psychology*, Westport, CT and London: Praeger.

Hogen, R. (1975) 'Moral development and the structure of personality', in D. DePalma and J. Foley (eds) *Moral Development: Current Theory and Research*, New York: Lawrence Erlbaum Associates, Inc.

Holtrust, N., Sevenhuijsen, S. and Verbraken, A. (1989) 'Rights for fathers and the state: recent developments in custody politics in the Netherlands', in C. Smart and S. Sevenhuijsen (eds) *Child Custody and the Politics of Gender*, London: Routledge.

Holzman, L. (2006) 'Activating postmodernism', *Theory and Psychology*, *16*, *1*: 109–123.

—— (ed.) (1999) *Performing Psychology: A Postmodern Culture of the Mind*, New York and London: Routledge.

Homel, P., Palij, M. and Aaronson, D. (1987) 'Introduction', in P. Homel, M. Palij and D. Aaronson (eds) *Childhood Bilingualism: Aspects of Linguistic, Cognitive, and Social Development*, New York: Lawrence Erlbaum Associates, Inc.

Hook, D., Kiguwe, P., Mkhize, N. and Collins, A. (eds) (2004) *Critical Psychology*, Cape Town: UCT Press.

Horna, J. and Lupri, E. (1987) 'Fathers' participation in work, family life and leisure: a Canadian experience', pp. 54–73 in C. Lewis and M. O'Brien (eds) *Reassessing Fatherhood: New Observations on Fatherhood and the Modern Family*, London: Sage.

Hoyles, M. (1989) *The Politics of Childhood*, London: Journeyman.

Hrdy, S. (2003) 'The optimal number of fathers: evolution, demography and history in the shaping of female mate preferences', in D. LeCroy and P. Moller (eds) *Evolutionary Perspectives on Human Reproductive Behavior*, New York: Kluwer.

Hultqvist, K. and Dahlberg, G. (eds) (2001) *Governing the Child in the New Millennium*, New York and London: RoutledgeFalmer.

Hunt, F. (ed.) (1985) *Lessons for Life*, Oxford: Blackwell.

Hunt, J.M. and Uzgiris, L.C. (1964) 'Cathexis from recognitive familiarity: an exploratory study', paper presented at the Convention of the American Psychological Association, Los Angeles, California, September.

Hutchings, J. and Lane, E. (2006) 'Reaching those who need it most', *The Psychologist*, *19*, 8: 480–483.

Hymes, J. (1955) *A Child Development Point of View*, Englewood Cliffs, NJ: Prentice Hall.

Ingleby, D. (1985) 'Professionals as socializers: the "psy complex"', *Research in Law, Deviance and Social Control*, 7: 79–109.

Issa, T. (2005) 'Supplementary schools: language? Whose language?', *Race Equality Teaching*, *24*, 1: 37–42.

James, A. and Prout, A. (1990) 'Re-presenting childhood: time and transition in the study of childhood', pp. 216–238 in A. James and A. Prout (eds) *Constructing and Reconstructing Childhood: Contemporary Issues in the Sociological Study of Childhood*, London: Falmer Press.

James, A., Jenks, C. and Prout, A. (1998) *Theorizing Childhood*, Oxford: Polity Press.

Jaworksi, A. and Coupland, N. (eds) (1999) *The Discourse Reader*, London and New York: Routledge.

Jenks, C. (1996) *Childhood*, London: Routledge.

—— (ed.) (2005) *Childhood*, 2nd edn, London: Routledge.

Jenson, J. and Saint-Martin, D. (2002) 'Building blocks for a new welfare architecture: is LEGO TM the model for an active society?', paper prepared from the delivery at the 2002 Annual Meeting of the American Political Science Association, Boston, 20 August–1 September.

Jones, A. (1998) *The Child Welfare Implications of UK Immigration and Asylum Policy*, Manchester: MMU.

Jones, D. (1987) 'The choice to breast feed or bottle feed and influences upon that choice: a survey of 1525 mothers', *Child Care, Health and Development*, *13*, 1: 75–85.

Jones, K. (1989) *Right Turn: The Conservative Revolution in Education*, London: Radius.

Joravsky, D. (1987) 'L.S. Vgotskii: muffled deity of Soviet psychology', pp. 189–213 in M. Ash and M. Woodward (eds) *Psychology in Twentieth Century Thought and Society*, Cambridge: Cambridge University Press.

Joseph, G., Reddy, V. and Searle-Chatterjee, M. (1990) 'Eurocentrism in the social sciences', *Race & Class*, *31*, *4*: 1–26.

Kagan, J. (1984) *The Nature of the Child*, New York: Basic Books.

Kaplan, P. (1991) A *Child's Odyssey: Child and Adolescent Development*, St Paul, MN: West.

Karmiloff Smith, A. (1979) *A Functional Approach to Child Language: A Study of Determiners and Reference*, Cambridge: Cambridge University Press.

Karpf, A. (2006) 'Generation stressed', *Guardian*, 13 September: 12–13.

Kaye, K. (1982) *The Mental and Social Life of Babies: How Parents Make Persons*, London: Methuen.

Keller, H. (2003) 'Socialization for competence: cultural models of infancy', *Human Development*, *46*: 288–311.

Kepler, K. and Randall, J. (1981) 'Individualization: the subversive of elementary schooling', in H. Clarizio, R. Craig and W.A. Mehrens (eds) *Contemporary Issues in Educational Psychology*, Boston, MA: Allyn & Bacon.

Kershaw, A. (1991) 'How the new man became the new lad', *Independent on Sunday*, 14 April: 19.

Kessel, F. and Siegel, A. (eds) (1983) *The Child and Other Cultural Inventions*, New York: Praeger.

Kessen, W. (1979) 'The American child and other cultural inventions', *American Psychologist*, *34*, *10*: 815–820.

—— (1993) 'Avoiding the emptiness: the full child', *Theory and Psychology*, *3*, *4*: 415–427.

Kitzinger, C. (ed.) (1994) 'Should psychologists study sex differences?', *Feminism and Psychology*, *4*, *4*: 501–538.

Kitzinger, J. (1990) 'Who are you, kidding? Children, power and the struggle against sexual abuse', pp. 157–183 in A. James and A. Prout (eds) *Constructing and Reconstructing Childhood: Contemporary Issues in the Sociological Study of Childhood*, Basingstoke: Falmer Press.

Kjorholt, A.T. (2005) 'The competent child and the "right to be oneself": reflections on children as fellow citizens in an early childhood centre', pp. 151–175 in A. Clark, A. Kjorhold and P. Moss (eds) *Beyond Listening: Children's Perspectives on Early Children's Services*, Bristol: The Policy Press.

Klaus, M. and Kennell, J. (1976) *Maternal–Infant Bonding*, New York: Wiley.

Kleeberg-Niepage, A. (2005) 'Is there a childhood for children who work? Child labour and the Western construction of childhood', paper presented at the International Society for Theoretical Psychology, University of the Western Cape, Cape Town.

Kofsky Scholnick, E. (2000) 'Engendering development: metaphors of change', pp. 11–28 in P. Miller and E. Kofsky Scholnick (eds) *Towards a Feminist Developmental Psychology*, New York and London: Routledge.

Kohlberg, L. (1969a) 'The child as moral philosopher', in J. Sants (ed.) *Developmental Psychology*, Harmondsworth: Penguin.

Kohlberg, L. (1969b) 'Stage and sequence: the cognitive developmental approach', in D.A. Goslin (ed.) *The Handbook of Socialization Theory and Research*, Chicago: Rand McNally.

—— (1976) 'Moral stages and moralisation', in T. Lickona (ed.) *Moral Development and Moral Behaviour: Theory, Research and Social Issues*, New York: Holt, Rinehart & Winston.

Kondo-Ikemura, K. (2001) 'Insufficient evidence', *American Psychologist*, 56: 825–826.

Konner, M. (1977) 'Infancy among the Kalahari desert San', in P.H. Leiderman, S.R. Tulkin and A. Rosenfeld (eds) *Culture and Infancy*, New York: Academic Press.

Kozulin, A. (1990) *Vygotsky's Psychology: A Biography of Ideas*, Hemel Hempstead: Harvester Wheatsheaf.

Kuhn, T. (1962) *The Structure of Scientific Revolutions*, Chicago: University of Chicago Press.

Kurtz, S. (1992) *All the Mothers are One: Hindu India and the Cultural Reshaping of Psychoanalysis*, New York: Academic Press.

Lafargue, P. (1883) *The Right to be Lazy*, http://www.marxists.org/archive/lafargue/1883/lazy/index.htm (accessed 6 August 2006).

Lamb, M. (ed.) (1982) *Non-traditional Families: Parenting and Child Development*, Hillsdale, NJ: Lawrence Erlbaum Associates, Inc.

—— (1988) 'Social and emotional development in infancy', in M.H. Bornstein and M.E. Lamb (eds) *Social, Emotional and Personality Development*, Hillsdale, NJ: Lawrence Erlbaum Associates, Inc.

—— (1997) 'Fathers and child development: an introductory overview' pp. 1–19 in M. Lamb (ed.) *The Role of the Father in Child Development*, 3rd edn, Chichester: Wiley.

Lansford, J., Criss, M., Pettit, G. Dodge, K. and Bates, J. (2003) 'Friendship quality, peer group affiliation and peer antisocial behavior as moderators of the link between negative parenting and adolescent externalizing behavior', *Journal of Research on Adolescence*, 13, 2: 161–184.

Lavalette, M. (2000) 'Child employment in a capitalist labour market', pp. 214–230 in B. Schlemmer (ed.) *The Exploited Child*, London: Zed Books.

Lave, J. and Wenger, E. (1991) *Situated Learning: Legitimate Peripheral Participation*, Cambridge: Cambridge University Press.

Lawrence, D.H. (1973) 'Education and sex in man, woman and child', in J. Williams and R. Williams (eds) *Lawrence on Education*, Harmondsworth: Penguin.

Leiser, D. and Gilliéron, C. (1990) *Cognitive Science and Genetic Epistemology: A Case Study of Understanding*, New York: Plenum Press.

Leudar, I., Costall, A. and Francis, D. (2004) 'Theory of mind: a critical assessment', *Theory and Psychology*, 14, 5: 571–578.

Levett, A. (2003) 'Problems of cultural imperialism in the study of child sexual abuse', pp. 52–76 in P. Reavey and S. Warner (eds) *New Feminist Stories of Child Sexual Abuse*, London: Routledge.

Levine, C., Kohlberg, L. and Hewer, A. (1985) 'The current formulation of Kohlberg's theory and a response to critics', *Human Development*, 28: 94–100.

Lewis, C. (1982) 'The observation of father–infant relationships: an "attachment" to outmoded concepts', pp. 153–170 in L. McKee and M. O'Brien (eds) *The Father Figure*, London: Tavistock.

Lewis, C. and Lamb, M. (2003) 'Fathers' influences on children's development: the evidence from two parent families', *European Journal of Psychology of Education*, 18: 211–228.

Lewis, S. and Cooper, C. (1991) *Dual Earner Couples*, London: Unwin Hyman.

Licht, B. and Dweck, C. (1987) 'Sex differences in achievement orientations', pp. 95–107 in M. Arnot and G. Weiner (eds) *Gender and the Politics of Schooling*, London: Hutchinson.

Lichtman, R. (1987) 'The illusion of maturation in an age of decline', in J. Broughton (ed.) *Critical Theories of Psychological Development*, New York: Plenum Press.

Lieven, E. (1981) 'If it's natural we can't change it', in Cambridge Women's Studies Group (eds) *Women In Society*, London: Virago.

—— (1982) 'Context, process and progress in young children's speech', pp. 7–26 in M. Beveridge (ed.) *Children Thinking through Language*, London: Arnold.

—— (1994) 'Crosslinguistic and crosscultural aspects of language addressed to children', pp. 56–72 in C. Gallaway and B. Richards (eds) *Input and Interaction in Language Acquisition*, Cambridge: Cambridge University Press.

Lieven, E. and Pine, J. (1990) 'Review of E. Bates, I. Bretherton and L. Snyder, *From First Words to Grammar: Individual Differences and Dissociable Mechanisms, C.U.P.*, 1988', *Journal of Child Language*, 17: 495–501.

Light, P. (1979) *The Development of Social Sensitivity*, London: Cambridge University Press.

Linebaugh, P. (2003) *The London Hanged*, London: Verso.

Lister, R. (2005) 'Investing in the citizen workers of the future', pp. 449–462 in H. Hendrick (ed.) *Child Welfare and Social Policy*, Bristol: The Policy Press.

—— (2006) 'Children (but not women) first: New Labour, child welfare and gender', *Critical Social Policy*, 26, 2: 315–335.

Lloyd, N., O'Brien, M. and Lewis, C. (2003) *Fathers in Sure Start Local Programmes*, Nottingham: DfES Publications.

Lock, A. (ed.) (1978) *Action, Gesture and Symbol*, London: Academic Press.

Lok, M. and McMahon, C. (2006) 'Mothers' thoughts about their children: links between mind-mindedness and emotional availability', *British Journal of Developmental Psychology*, 24: 477–488.

Lourenco, O. and Machado, A. (1996) 'In defense of Piaget's theory: a reply to ten common criticisms', *Developmental Review*, 103, 1: 141–164.

Lowe, N. (1982) 'The legal status of fathers: past and present', pp. 26–42 in L. McKee and M. O'Brien (eds) *The Father Figure*, London: Tavistock.

Lowenfeld, M. (1935) *Play in Childhood*, London: Gollancz.

Lubeck, S. (1986) *Sandbox Society: Early Education in Black and White America – A Comparative Ethnography*, Lewes: Falmer Press.

Lucey, H. (2001) 'Social class, gender and schooling', pp. 177–188 in B. Francis and C. Skelton (eds) *Investigating Gender: Contemporary Perspectives in Education*, Maidenhead: Open University Press.

Lumnis, T. (1982) 'The historical dimension of fatherhood', pp. 43–56 in L. McKee and M. O'Brien (eds) *The Father Figure*, London: Tavistock.

Luscombe, R. (2006) 'Game over for toy guns in heart of the old west', *Guardian*, 14 August: 13.

Lutrell, W. (2003) *Pregnant Bodies, Fertile Minds: Gender, Race and the Schooling of Pregnant Teens*, New York: Routledge.

Lyon, C. (1989) 'The redefinition of parental rights – recent English developments relating to joint custodianship and adoption in England', *Journal of Social Welfare*, 3: 1387.

Mac an Ghaill, M. (1994) *The Making of Men: Masculinities, Sexualities and Schooling*, Buckingham: Open University Press.

McCabe, A. (1987) 'Failure in class inclusion reasoning in a university sample', *Journal of Psychology*, *121*, *4*: 351–358.

McClintock, A. (1995) *Imperial Leather: Race, Gender and Sexuality in the Colonial Contest*, New York and London: Routledge.

Macdonald, C. (2006) 'The properties of mediated action in three different literacy contexts in South Africa', *Theory and Psychology*, *16*, *1*: 51–80.

McDonald, L. and Pien, D. (1982) 'Mothers' conversational behaviour as a function of interactional intent', *Journal of Child Language*, *8*: 337–358.

McGuire, J. (1991) 'Sons and daughters', pp. 143–161 in A. Phoenix, A. Woollett and E. Lloyd (eds) *Motherhood: Meanings, Practices and Ideologies*, London: Sage.

McKee, L. (1982) 'Fathers' participation in infant care: a critique', pp. 120–138 in L. McKee and M. O'Brien (eds) *The Father Figure*, London: Tavistock.

McKee, L. and O'Brien, M. (1982) 'The father figure: some current orientations and historical perspectives', pp. 1–25 in L. McKee and M. O'Brien (eds) *The Father Figure*, London: Tavistock.

McLaughlin, B. (1984) *Second Language Acquisition in Childhood*, Vol. 1, Hillsdale, NJ: Lawrence Erlbaum Associates, Inc.

McLaughlin, K. (2006) 'The subject of social work: "diminished subjectivity" in contemporary theory and practice', unpublished PhD, Manchester Metropolitan University.

MacLure, M. (2003) *Discourse in Educational and Social Research*, Maidenhead: Open University Press.

MacNaughton, G. (2005) *Doing Foucault in Early Childhood Studies: Applying Poststructural Ideas*, Abingdon and New York: Routledge.

McNally, D.W. (1974) *Piaget, Education and Teaching*, Sydney: New Educational Press.

McShane, J. (1980) *Learning to Talk*, Cambridge: Cambridge University Press.

Marks, D. (1993a) 'Case conference analysis and action research', pp. 135–154 in E. Burman and I. Parker (eds) *Discourse Analytic Research*, London and New York: Routledge (download from www.discourseunit.com).

—— (1993b) 'Discourse analysis and education case conferences', unpublished PhD thesis, MMU Library.

—— (1996) 'Constructing a narrative: moral discourse and young people's experience of exclusion', pp. 114–130 in E. Burman, G. Aitken, P. Alldred, R. Allwood, T. Billington, A. Gordo-Lopez, C. Heenan, D. Marks and S. Warner (eds) *Psychology, Discourse Practice: From Regulation to Resistance*, London: Taylor & Francis.

Marks, D., Burman, E., Burman, L. and Parker, I. (1995) 'Collaborative Research into Education Case Conferences', *Educational Psychology in Practice*, *11*, *1*: 41–49.

Marks, M. (2001) Y*oung Warriors. Youth Politics, Identity and Violence in South Africa*, Johannesburg: Witwatersrand University Press.

Marshall, H. (1991) 'The social construction of motherhood: an analysis of childcare and parenting manuals', pp. 66–85 in A. Phoenix, A. Woollett and E. Lloyd (eds) *Motherhood: Meanings, Practices and Ideologies*, London: Sage.

Marshall, H. and Woollett, A. (2000) 'Fit to reproduce? The regulatory role of pregnancy texts', *Feminism & Psychology, 10, 3*: 351–366.

Martin, G. (1998) *The Effects of the UK's Reservation of Asylum and Immigration to the UN Convention on the Rights of the Child*, London: Committee for UNICEF.

Matthews, G., Zeidner, M. and Roberts, R. (2002) *Emotional Intelligence: Science and Myth*, Cambridge, MA and London: MIT Press.

Mearns, A.G. (1961) *The Whole Child*, London: National Children's Home.

Mehmet, O. (1995) *Westernizing the Third World: The Eurocentricity of Economic Development Theories*, London and New York: Routledge.

Meins, E. (1999) 'Sensitivity, security and internal working models: bridging the transmission gap', *Attachment and Human Development, 1*: 325–342.

Meins, E., Fernyhough, C., Fradley, E. and Tuckey, M. (2001) 'Rethinking maternal sensitivity: mothers' comments on infants; mental processes predict security of attachment at 12 months', *Journal of Child Psychology and Psychiatry, 42, 5*: 637–648.

Meins, E., Fernyhough, C., Johnson, F. and Lidstone, J. (2006) 'Mind-mindedness in children: individual differences in internal-state talk in middle childhood', *British Journal of Developmental Psychology, 24*: 181–196.

Meltzoff, A. (1981) 'Imitation, intermodal co-ordination and representation in early infancy', in G. Butterworth (ed.) *Infancy and Epistemology*, Brighton: Harvester.

Merchant, C. (1980) *The Death of Nature: Women, Ecology and the Scientific Revolution*, New York: Harper & Row.

Meyer, P. (1983) *The Child and the State: The Intervention of the State in the Family*, Cambridge: Cambridge University Press.

Middleton, D. and Edwards, D. (eds) (1990) *Collective Remembering*, London: Sage.

Middleton, N. and O'Keefe, P, (1998) *Disaster and Development. The Politics of Humanitarian Aid*, London: Pluto Press.

Miller, P. and Kofsky Scholnick, E. (2000a) 'Introduction: beyond gender as a variable', pp. 3–10 in P. Miller. and E. Kofsky Scholnick (eds) *Toward a Feminist Developmental Psychology*, New York and London: Routledge.

—— (eds) (2000b) *Toward a Feminist Developmental Psychology*, New York and London: Routledge.

Miller, S.A. (1976) 'Non-verbal assessment in Piagetian concepts', *Psychological Bulletin, 83*: 405–430.

Mitlenburg, R. and Singer, E. (2000) 'A concept becomes a passion: moral commitments and the affective development of the survivors of child abuse', *Theory and Psychology, 10, 1*: 503–526.

Mitter, S. (1988) *Common Fate, Common Bond*, London: Pluto Press.

Mizen, P., Bolton, A. and Pole, C. (1999) 'School age workers: the paid employment of children in Britain', *Work, Employment and Society, 13, 3*: 423–438.

Moll, L. (ed.) (1990) *Vygotsky and Education: Instructional Implications and Applications of Sociohistorical Psychology*, Cambridge: Cambridge University Press.

Moore, S. (1988) 'Getting a bit of the other: the pimps of postmodernism', in R. Chapman and J. Rutherford (eds) *Male Order: Unwrapping Masculinity*, London: Lawrence & Wishart.

Morgan, G. (1996) 'Learning to be a man: dilemmas and contradictions of masculine experience', in C. Luke (ed.) *Feminisms and Pedagogies of Everyday Life*, New York: SUNY.

Morice, A. (2000) 'Paternal domination: the typical relationship conditioning the exploitation of children', pp. 195–213 in B. Schlemmer (ed.) *The Exploited Child*, London: Zed Books.

Morokvasic, M. (2004) '"Settled in mobility": engendering post-wall migration in Europe', *Feminist Review*, *77*: 7–25.

Morris, L. (1987) 'The no-longer working class', *New Society*, 3 April: 16–18.

Morris, T. (1992) *The Despairing Developer: Diary of an Aid Worker in the Middle East*, London: IB Taurus.

Morss, J. (1990) *The Biologising of Childhood*, Hillsdale, NJ: Lawrence Erlbaum Associates, Inc.

—— (1996) *Growing Critical: Alternatives to Developmental Psychology*, London: Routledge.

Moss, P. (1990) 'Work, family and the care of children: issues of equality and responsibility', *Children and Society*, *4*, *2*: 1456.

Moss, P. and Petrie, P. (2002) *From Children's Services to Children's Spaces*, London: RoutledgeFalmer.

Moss, P., Dillon, J. and Statham, J. (2000) 'The "child in need" and "the rich child": discourses, constructions and practice', *Critical Social Policy*, *20*, *2*: 233–254.

Mullender, A. (2004) *Tackling Domestic Violence: Providing Support for Children who have Witnessed Violence*, Home Office Development and Practice Report no. 33, London: Home Office.

Munn, P. (1991) 'Mothering more than one child', pp. 162–177 in A. Phoenix, A. Woollett and E. Lloyd (eds) *Motherhood: Meanings, Practices and Ideologies*, London: Sage.

Munro, E. (2004) 'State regulation of parenting', *The Political Quarterly*, *75*, *2*: 180–188.

Murchison, C. (1933) 'Preface', in C. Murchison (ed.) *A Handbook of Child Psychology*, Worcester, MA: Clark University Press.

Myers, R. (1992) *The Twelve Who Survive: Strengthening Programmes of Early Childhood Development in the Third World*, London: Routledge/UNESCO.

Neff, K. (2003) 'Understanding how universal goals of independence and inter-dependence are manifested within particular cultural contexts', *Human Development*, *43*: 312–318.

Nelson, K. (1973) 'Structure and strategy in learning to talk', *Monographs of the Society for Research in Child Development*, *38*, *1–2*.

Nelson, K., Henseler, S. and Plesa, D. (2000) 'Entering a community of minds: theory of mind from a feminist standpoint', pp. 61–84 in P. Miller and E. Kofsky Scholnick (eds) *Towards a Feminist Developmental Psychology*, New York and London: Routledge.

New, C. and David, M. (1985) *For the Children's Sake: Making Childcare more than Women's Business*, Harmondsworth: Penguin.

Newman, D., Griffin, P. and Cole, M. (1989) *The Construction Zone: Working for Cognitive Change in School*, Cambridge: Cambridge University Press.

Newman, F. and Holzman, L. (1993) *Lev Vygotsky: Revolutionary Scientist*, London and New York: Routledge.

Newnes, C. and Radcliffe, N. (eds) (2005) *Making and Breaking Children's Lives*, Ross-on-Wye: PCCS Books.

Newport, E., Gleituran, H. and Gleituran, L. (1977) 'Mother I'd rather do it myself:

some effects and non-effects of maternal speech style', in C. Snow and C. Ferguson (eds) *Talking to Children*, Cambridge: Cambridge University Press.

Newson, J. and Newson, E. (1968) *Four Years Old in an Urban Community*, Harmondsworth: Penguin.

—— (1974) 'Cultural aspects of childrearing in the English-speaking world', pp. 53–82 in M. Richards (ed.) *The Integration of the Child into a Social World*, Cambridge: Cambridge University Press.

Newson, J. and Shotter, J. (1974) 'How babies communicate', *New Society*, 29: 345–357.

Niestroj, B. (1994) 'Women as mothers and the making of the European mind: a contribution to the history of developmental psychology and primary socialization', *Journal for the Theory of Social Behaviour*, 24, 2: 281–301.

Nieuwenhuys, O. (2000) 'The household economy and the commercial exploitation of children's work', pp. 278–290 in B. Schlemmer (ed.) *The Exploited Child*, London: Zed Books.

Nightingale, D. and Crombie, J. (eds) (1999) *Social Constructionist Psychology*, Buckingham: Open University Press.

Ninio, A. and Bruner, J. (1978) 'The achievement and antecedents of labelling', *Journal of Child Language*, S: 1–15.

Nobes, G., Martin, A. and Panagiotaki, G. (2005) 'The developmental of scientific knowledge of the earth', *British Journal of Developmental Psychology*, 23, 1: 47–64.

Oakley, A. (1980) *From Here to Maternity*, Harmondsworth: Penguin.

O'Brien, M. and Alldred, P. (1991) 'Children's representations of family life', paper presented to British Psychological Society Developmental Section Conference, September.

O'Brien, M. and L. Mckee (1983) 'Interviewing men: "taking gender seriously"', in E. Garmanikow, D. Morgan, J. Purvis and D. Taylorson (eds) *The Public and the Private*, London: Heinemann.

Ochs, E. (1979) 'Transcription as theory', in E. Ochs and B. Schieffelin (eds) *Developmental Pragmatics*, New York: Academic Press.

—— (1983) 'Cultural dimensions of language acquisition', in E. Ochs and B. Schieffelin (eds) *Acquiring Conversational Competence*, London: Routledge & Kegan Paul.

—— (1986) 'Introduction', in B. Schieffelin and E. Ochs (eds) *Language Socialisation across Cultures*, Cambridge: Cambridge University Press.

O'Hagan, S. (1991) 'Is the new lad a fitting model for the nineties?', *Arena, spring/summer*: 22–23.

O'Hara, M. (1991) 'The rights and wrongs of children', *Trouble and Strife, 20*: 28–33.

Olsen, R. (2000) 'Families under the microscope: parallels between the young carers debate of the 1990s and the transformation of childhood in the late nineteenth century', *Children and Society, 14*: 384–394.

Olsson, M. (1991) 'Producing the truth about people: science and the cult of the individual in educational psychology', pp. 188–209 in J. Morss and T. Linzey (eds) *Growing Up: The Politics of Human Learning*, Auckland: Longman.

O'Neil, T. (2004) 'Weaving wages, indebtedness, and remittances in the Nepalese carpet industry', *Human Organisation, 63, 2*: 211–220.

Onishi, M. and Gjerde, P. (2002) 'Attachment strategies in Japanese urban middle-class couples: a cultural theme analysis of asymmetry in marital relationships', *Personal Relationships*, *9*: 435–455.

Oppenheim, D. (2006) 'Child, parent, and parent–child emotion narratives: implications for developmental psychopathology', *Development and Psychopathology*, *18*: 771–790.

Orbach, S. (2001) *Towards Emotional Literacy*, London: Virago.

Orbach, S. and Eichenbaum, L. (1982) *Understanding Women*, Harmondsworth: Penguin.

Palmary, I. (2006) '(M)Othering women: unpacking refugee women's trauma and trauma service delivery', *International Journal of Critical Psychology*, *17*: 119–139.

Panagiotaki, G., Nobes, G. and Banerjee, R. (2006) 'Children's representations of the earth: a methodological comparison', *British Journal of Developmental Psychology*, *24*, *2*: 353–372.

Papert, S. (1980) *Mindstorms: Children, Computers and Powerful Ideas*, Brighton: Harvester.

Park, A. (2006) 'Children as risk or children at risk? International law, child soldiers and citizenship: the case of Sierra Leone', in S. Bittle and A. Doyle (eds) *Paradoxes of Risk: Inclusions and Exclusions*, Halifax: Fernwood.

Parke, R.D. (1984) *Fathering*, London: Fontana.

Parke, R. and Buriel, R. (1998) 'Socialization in the family: ethnic and ecological perspectives', pp. 463–552 in W. Damon and N. Eisenberg (eds) *Social, Emotional and Personality Development, Vol. 3: Handbook of Child Psychology*, New York: Wiley.

Parke, R.D., MacDonald, K.B., Burks, V.M., Bhavnagri, N., Barth, J.M. and Beitel, A. (1989) 'Family and peer systems: in search of the linkages', in K. Krepner and R.M. Lerner (eds) *Family Systems and Lifespan Development*, Hillsdale, NJ: Lawrence Erlbaum Associates, Inc.

Parker, G., Topling, H. and Brown, L. (1979) 'A parental bonding instrument', *British Journal of Medical Psychology*, *52*: 1–10.

Parker, I. (1989) *The Crisis in Social Psychology and How to End It*, London: Routledge.

—— (1992a) *Discourse Dynamics*, London and New York: Routledge (full text available on www.discourseunit.com).

—— (1992b) 'Wild men', paper presented at Psychoanalysis and the Public Sphere, 6th Annual Conference, University of East London, October.

—— (1997) *Psychoanalytic Culture*, London and Thousand Oaks: Sage.

—— (ed.) (1998) *Social Constructionism, Discourse and Realism*, London and Thousand Oaks: Sage.

—— (ed.) (1999) *Deconstructing Psychotherapy*, London and Thousand Oaks: Sage.

—— (2002) *Critical Discursive Psychology*, London: Palgrave.

—— (2004) 'Psychoanalysis and critical psychology', in N. Mkhize, P. Kiguwe and A. Collins (eds) *Critical Psychology*, Cape Town: UCT Press.

—— (2007) *Revolution in Psychology: Alienation to Emancipation*, London: Pluto Press.

Parker, I. and the Bolton Discourse Network (1999) *Critical Textwork: An Introduction to Varieties of Discourse and Analysis*, Buckingham: Open University Press.

Parker, I. and Shotter, J. (eds) (1990) *Deconstructing Social Psychology*, London: Routledge.

Parker, I., Georgaca, E., Harper, D., McLaughlin, T. and Stowell-Smith, M. (1995) *Deconstructing Psychopathology*, London and Thousand Oaks: Sage.

Parker, R. (1997) 'The production and purposes of maternal ambivalence', pp. 17–37 in W. Hollway and B. Featherstone (eds) *Mothering and Ambivalence*, London: Routledge.

Parsons, B. (1983) *The Expectant Father: A Practical Guide to Pregnancy and Childbirth for the Anxious Man*, Sunbury: Quartermaine House.

Parton, N. (1991) *Governing the Family: Child Care, Child Protection and the State*, London: Macmillan.

—— (2005) 'Risk, advanced liberalism and child welfare', pp. 127–142 in H. Hendrick (ed.) *Child Welfare and Social Policy*, Bristol: The Policy Press.

Pavlenko, A. (2005) *Emotions and Multilingualism*, New York: Cambridge University Press.

Pedersen, F.A., Cairn, R. and Zaslow, M. (1982) 'Variation in infant experience associated with alternative family roles', in L. Laosa and L. Segal (eds) *The Family as a Learning Environment*, New York: Plenum Press.

Penn, H. (2005) *Unequal Childhoods: Children's Lives in Poor Countries*, London: RoutledgeFalmer.

Phoenix, A. (1987) 'Theories of gender and black families', pp. 50–61 in G. Weiner and M. Arnot (eds) *Gender Under Scrutiny*, London: Hutchinson.

—— (1991) *Young Mothers?*, Oxford: Polity.

Phoenix, A. and Woollett, A. (1991) 'Motherhood: social construction, politics and psychology', pp. 13–27 in A. Phoenix, A. Woollett and E. Lloyd (eds) *Motherhood: Meanings, Practices and Ideologies*, London: Sage.

Phoenix, A., Woollett, A. and Lloyd, E. (eds) (1991) *Motherhood: Meanings, Practices and Ideologies*, London: Sage.

Piaget, J. (1918a) 'Biology and war', reprinted in H. Gruber and J. Vonèche (eds) (1977) *The Essential Piaget*, London: Routledge & Kegan Paul.

—— (1918b) 'Recherche', reprinted in H. Gruber and J. Vonèche (eds) (1977) *The Essential Piaget*, London: Routledge & Kegan Paul.

—— (1919) 'La psychanalyse dans ses rapports avec la psychologie de l'enfant', *Bulletin Mensuel de la Société Alfred Binet*, 18–34, 41–58.

—— (1926) *The Language and Thought of the Child*, London: Routledge & Kegan Paul.

—— (1929) *The Child's Conception of the World*, London: Routledge & Kegan Paul.

—— (1932) *The Moral Judgement of the Child*, London: Routledge & Kegan Paul.

—— (1933) 'Social evolution and the new education', *Education Tomorrow*, *4*: 3–25.

—— (1950) *Etudes Sociologiques*, partial unpublished translation by Carol Sherrard.

—— (1953) *The Origins of Intelligence in the Child*, London: Routledge & Kegan Paul.

—— (1957) 'The child and modern physics', *Scientific American*, *197*: 46–51.

Pine, J. (1992a) 'Maternal style at the early one-word stage: re-evaluating the stereotype of the directive mother', *First Language*, *12*: 169–186.

—— (1992b) 'The functional basis of referentiality: evidence from children's spontaneous speech', *First Language*, *12*: 39–55.

—— (1994) 'The language of primary caretakers', pp. 15–37 in C. Gallaway and B.

Richards (eds) *Input and Interaction in Language Acquisition*, Cambridge: Cambridge University Press.

Pine, J. and Lieven, E. (1990) 'Referential style at thirteen months: why age-defined cross-sectional measures are inappropriate for the study of strategy differences in early language development', *Journal of Child Language, 17*: 625–631.

Pinker, S. (1997) *How the Mind Works*, New York: Norton.

Pintner, R. (1933) 'The feebleminded child', in C. Murchison (ed.) *A Handbook of Child Psychology*, Worcester, MA: Clark University Press.

Platt, L. (2005) 'Fair but unequal? Children, ethnicity and the welfare state', pp. 355–366 in H. Hendrick (ed.) *Child Welfare and Social Policy*, Bristol: The Policy Press.

Plowden Report (1967) *Children in their Primary Schools: A Report of the Central Advisory Council for Education*, London: HMSO.

Pludderman, P. (1999) 'Multilingualism and education in South Africa: one year on', *International Journal of Educational Research, 31*: 327–340.

Pollack, L. (1983) *Forgotten Children*, Cambridge: Cambridge University Press.

Popkewitz, K. and Bloch, M. (2001) 'Administering freedom: a history of the present – rescuing the parent to rescue the child for society', pp. 85–118 in K. Hultqvist and G. Dahlberg (eds) *Governing the Child in the New Millenium*, New York and London: RoutledgeFalmer.

Potter, J. and Wetherell, M. (1987) *Discourse and Social Psychology*, London: Sage.

Powell, C. (2003) 'Lessons to be learnt from the Victoria Climbié inquiry', *British Journal of Nursing, 12, 3*: 137.

Prior, V. and Glaser, D. (2006) *Understanding Attachment and Attachment Disorders: Theory, Evidence and Practice*, London: Jessica Kingsley Publishers.

Pupavac, V. (1998) Children's rights and the infantilisation of citizenship', *Human Rights Law Review, March*: 3–8.

—— (2002a) 'The international children's rights regime', pp. 57–75 in D. Chandler (ed.) *Re-thinking Human Rights: Critical Approaches to International Politics*, London: Palgrave.

—— (2002b) 'Pathologizing populations and colonizing minds: International psychosocial programs in Kosovo', *Alternatives, 27*: 489–511.

—— (2004) 'Psychosocial interventions and the demoralization of humanitarianism', *Journal of Biosociological Science, 36*: 491–504.

—— (2005). The demoralised subject of global civil society, pp. 52–68 in G. Baker and D. Chandler (eds) *Global Civil Society: Contested Futures*, London: Routledge.

Qvortup, J. (2000) 'Does children's school work have a value? Colonisation of children through their school work', pp. 3–11 in Vol. 2 *Papers for International Conference on Rethinking Childhood: Working Children's Challenge to the Social Sciences*, Paris.

Radford, L., Sayer, S. and Amica, R. (1999) *Unreasonable Fears? Child Contact in the Context of Domestic Violence*, Bristol: WAFE.

Rahnema, M. with Bawtree, V. (eds) (1997) *The Post-Development Reader*, London: Zed Books.

Ramachandran, V. and Oberman, L. (2006) 'Broken mirrors: a theory of autism', *Scientific American, November*: 63–69.

Ramirez, A. (1992) 'Honduras: the traffic in children', *Central America Report, 55*: 5.

Read, J. (2005) 'The bio-bio-bio model of madness', *The Psychologist, 18, 19*: 596–597.

Reavey, P. and Warner, S. (eds) (2003) *New Feminist Stories of Child Sexual Abuse*, London: Sage.

Reddy, V. (2007) *Feeling Other Minds: How Babies Understand People*, Cambridge, MA: Harvard University Press.

Reddy, V. and Morris, P. (2004) 'Participants don't need theories: knowing minds in engagement', *Theory and Psychology, 14, 4*: 647–685.

Reeves, M. and Hammond, J. (eds) (1988) *Looking Beyond the Frame: Racism, Representation and Resistance*, Oxford: Third World First.

Renvoize, J. (1985) *Going Solo: Single Mothers by Choice*, London: Routledge & Kegan Paul.

Reyolds, T. (2005) *Caribbean Mothers: Identity and Experience in the UK*, London: Tufnell Press.

Ribbens, J. (1989) 'Interviewing – an "unnatural situation"?', *Women's Studies International Forum, 12, 6*: 579–592.

Rich, A. (1983) 'Compulsory heterosexuality and lesbian existence', in A. Snitow, C. Stansell and S. Thompson (eds) *Desire: The Politics of Sexuality*, London: Virago.

Richards, G. (1997) *'Race, Racism and Psychology: Towards a Reflexive History'*, London and New York: Routledge.

Richards, M.P.M. (1974) 'First steps in becoming social', pp. 83–98 in M.P.M. Richards (ed.) *The Integration of the Child into a Social World*, Cambridge: Cambridge University Press.

—— (1981) 'The myth of bonding', unpublished paper.

—— (1982) 'How should we approach the study of fathers?', pp. 57–71 in L. McKee and M. O'Brien (eds) *The Father Figure*, London: Tavistock.

Riegel, K. (ed.) (1975) *Structure and Transformation*, New York: Wiley.

—— (1976) 'The dialectics of human development', *American Psychologist*, 698–700.

—— (1977) 'A dialectical model of time and change', in B.S. Gorman and A.E. Weissmann (eds) *The Personal Experience of Time*, New York: Plenum Press.

—— (1979) *Foundations of Dialectical Psychology*, New York: Academic Press.

Riley, D. (1983) *War in the Nursery: Theories of Child and Mother*, London: Virago.

—— (1987) '"The serious burdens of love?" Some questions on childcare, feminism and socialism', pp. 176–198 in A. Phillips (ed.) *Feminism and Equality*, Oxford: Blackwell.

Rizzolatti, G., Fogassi, L. and Gallese, V. (2006) 'Mirrors in the mind', *Scientific American, November*: 54–61.

Robb, M. (2004) 'Exploring fatherhood: masculinity and intersubjectivity in the research process', *Journal of Social Work Practice, 18, 3*: 395–406.

Roberts, C., Green, R., Williams, K. and Goodman, M. (1987) 'Boyhood gender identity development: a statistical contrast of two family groups', *Developmental Psychology, 23, 4*: 544–557.

Robertson, J. (1958) *Young Children in Hospital*, London: Tavistock.

Roche, J. (1989) 'Children's rights and the welfare of the child', pp. 135–142 in W. Stainton Rogers, D. Hevey, J. Roche and E. Ash (eds) *Child Abuse and Neglect: Facing the Challenge*, London: Batsford.

Rodriguez Mora, I. (2003) 'Psychosocial interventions in emergences: theoretical models and their ethical and political implications in the Venezuelan context', unpublished PhD thesis, University of Cambridge.

Rogoff, B. (1990) *Apprenticeship in Thinking: Cognitive Development in Social Context*, New York: Cambridge University Press.

—— (2003) *The Cultural Organization of Development*, Cambridge, MA: Cambridge University Press.

Rorty, R. (1980) *Philosophy and the Mirror of Nature*, Oxford: Blackwell.

Rose, N. (1985) *The Psychological Complex: Psychology, Politics and Society in England 1869–1939*, London: Routledge & Kegan Paul.

—— (1990) *Governing the Soul: The Shaping of the Private Self*, London: Routledge.

Rose, S., Lewontin, R. and Kamin, L. (1984) *Not In Our Genes*, Harmondsworth: Penguin.

Rothbaum, F., Weisz, J., Pott, M., Miyake, K. and Morelli, G. (2000) 'Attachment and culture: security in the United States and Japan', *American Psychologist*, *55*: 1093–1104.

—— (2001) 'Deeper into attachment and culture', *American Psychologist*, *56*: 827–828.

Rotman, B. (1978) *Jean Piaget: Biologist of the Real*, New York: Academic Press.

Rowe, D. (2005) 'ADHD: adults fear of frightened children', *International Journal of Critical Psychology, Counselling and Psychotherapy*, *5*, *1*: 10–13.

Russell, G. (1983) *The Changing Role of Fathers?*, St Lucia: University of Queensland Press.

—— (1987) 'Problems in role-reversed families', pp. 161–182 in C. Lewis and M. O'Brien (eds) *Reassessing Fatherhood: New Observations on Fatherhood and the Modern Family*, London: Sage.

Russell, J. (1982) 'Propositional attitudes', pp. 75–98 in M. Beveridge (ed.) *Children Thinking through Language*, London: Edward Arnold.

Rustin, M. (2004) 'Learning from the Victoria Climbié inquiry', *Journal of Social Work Practice*, *18*, *1*: 9–18.

Rutkowska, J. (1993) *The Computational Infant*, Hemel Hempstead: Harvester.

Rutter, M. (1982) *Maternal Deprivation Reassessed*, Harmondsworth: Penguin.

—— (2002) 'Nature, nurture and development: from evangelism through science toward policy and practice', *Child Development*, *73*, *3*: 1–22.

Rutter, M., Maughan, B., Mortimore, P. and Ouston, J. (1979) *Fifteen Thousand Hours: Secondary Schools and their Effects on Children*, London: Open Books.

Rycroft, C. (1974) *A Critical Dictionary of Psychoanalysis*, Harmondsworth: Penguin.

Sachs, W. (ed.) (1992) *The Development Dictionary: A Guide to Knowledge as Power*, London: Zed Books.

Sacks, H. (1972) 'On the analyzability of stories by children', in J.J. Gumperz and D. Hymes (eds) *Directions in Sociolinguistics: The Ethnography of Communication*, New York: Holt, Rinehart & Winston.

Said, E. (1979) *Orientalism*, Harmondsworth: Penguin.

Salzberger-Wittenberg, I., Henry, G. and Osborne, E. (1983) *The Emotional Experience of Learning and Teaching*, London: Routledge & Kegan Paul.

Sampson, E. (1989) 'The deconstruction of self', in J. Shotter and K. Gergen (eds) *Texts of Identity*, London: Sage.

Sanders, M. and Morawska, A. (2006) 'Towards a public health approach to parenting', *The Psychologist*, *19*, *8*: 476–479.

Sandkvist, K. (1987) 'Swedish family policy and the attempt to change paternal roles', pp. 144–160 in C. Lewis and M. O'Brien (eds) *Reassessing Fatherhood: New Observations on Fatherhood and the Modern Family*, London: Sage.

Sandler, L.W., Strchler, G., Bums, P. and Julia, H. (1970) 'Early mother–infant interaction and 24 hour patterns of activity and sleep', *Journal of American Academic Child Psychiatry, 9*: 103–123.

Santiago-Delefosse, M. and Oderic Delefosse, J.-M. (2002) 'Spielrein, Piaget and Vygotsky: three positions on child thought and language', *Theory and Psychology, 12, 6*: 723–747.

Santrock, J.W. (1989) *Life-span Development*, Dubuque, IA: Wm. C. Brown.

Savva, H. (1990) 'The rights of bilingual children', in R. Carter (ed.) *Knowledge about Language and the Curriculum*, London: Hodder & Stoughton.

Sbert, J.M. (1992) 'Progress', in W. Sachs (ed.) *The Development Dictionary: A Guide to Knowledge as Power*, London: Zed Books.

Scaife, M. and Bruner, J. (1975) 'The capacity for joint visual attention in the infant', *Nature, 253, 5489*: 265–266.

Schaffer, H.R.H. (1971) *The Growth of Sociability*, Harmondsworth: Penguin.

—— (1977) *Mothering*, London: Fontana.

Schaffer, H.R.H. and Emerson, P.E. (1964) 'The development of social attachments in infancy', *Monograph of the Society for Research in Child Development, 29, 3*.

Schepeler, E. (1993) 'Jean Piaget's experiences on the couch: some clues to a mystery', *International Journal of Psycho-Analysis, 74*: 255–273.

Scheper-Hughes, N. (1989a) 'The cultural politics of child survival', in N. Scheper-Hughes (ed.) *Child Survival: Anthropological Perspectives on the Treatment and Maltreatment of Children*, Dordrecht: Reidel.

—— (1989b) 'Culture, scarcity and maternal thinking: motherlove and child death in Northeast Brazil', in N. Scheper-Hughes (ed.) *Child Survival: Anthropological Perspectives on the Treatment and Maltreatment of Children*, Dordrecht: Reidel.

—— (ed.) (1989c) *Child Survival: Anthropological Perspectives on the Treatment and Maltreatment of Children*, Dordrecht: Reidel.

Schieffelin, B. (1979) 'Getting it together: an ethnographic approach to the study of the development of communicative competence', in E. Ochs and B. Schieffelin (eds) *Developmental Pragmatics*, New York: Academic Press.

—— (1983) 'Talking like birds: sound play in a cultural perspective', in E. Ochs and B. Schieffelin, *Acquiring Conversational Competence*, London: Routledge & Kegan Paul.

—— (1990) *The Give and Take of Everyday Life: Language Socialisation of Kaluli Children*, Cambridge: Cambridge University Press.

Schieffelin, B. and Ochs, E. (eds) (1986) *Language Socialisation across Cultures*, Cambridge: Cambridge University Press.

Schwermer, B. (ed.) (2000) *The Exploited Child*, London: Zed Books.

Scott, S. (2006) 'Improving children's lives, preventing criminality: where next?', *The Psychologist, 19, 8*: 484–487.

Scourfield, J. (2006) 'The challenge of engaging fathers in the child protection process', *Critical Social Policy, 26, 2*: 440–449.

Scourfield, J. and Drakeford, M. (2002) 'New Labour and "the problem of men"', *Critical Social Policy, 22, 4*: 619–641.

Searle, J. (1972) 'What is a speech act?', in P. Giglio (ed.) *Language and Social Context*, Harmondsworth: Penguin.

Segal, L. (1990) *Slow Change: Changing Masculinities and Changing Men*, London: Virago.

Seifert, K.L. and Hoffnung, R.J. (1987) *Child and Adolescent Development*, Boston, MA: Houghton Mifflin.

Sewell, T. (1997) *Black Masculinity and Schooling: How Black Boys Survive Modern Schooling*, Stoke-on-Trent: Trentham Books.

Shapiro, J. (1987) *A Child, Your Choice*, London: Pandora.

Sharp, P. (2001) *Nurturing Emotional Literacy: A Practical Guide for Teachers, Parents and those in the Caring Professions*, London: David Fulton Publishers.

Sharp, R. and Green, A. (1975) *Education and Social Control*, London: Routledge & Kegan Paul.

Shatz, M. (1982) 'On the mechanisms of language development: can features of the communicative environment account for development?', in E. Wanner and L. Gleitman (eds) *Language Acquisition: The State of the Art*, Cambridge: Cambridge University Press.

Shefer, T., Boonzaier, F. and Kiguwe, P. (eds) (2006) *The Gender of Psychology*, Cape Town: UCT Press.

Shinn, M. (1978) 'Father absence and children's cognitive development', *Psychological Bulletin*, *85*, *3*: 286–224.

Shiva, V. (1997) 'Western science and its destruction of local knowledge', pp. 161–167 in M. Rahnema with V. Bawtree (eds) *The Post-Development Reader*, London: Zed Books.

Shonkoff, J. and Phillips, D. (eds) (2000) *From Neurons to Neighborhoods: The Science of Early Childhood Development*, Washington, DC: National Academy Press.

Shotter, J. (1973) 'Acquired powers: the transformation of natural into personal powers', *Journal for the Theory of Social Behaviour*, *3*: 141–156.

Siegel, L. (1978) 'The relationship of language and thought in the preoperational child: a reconsideration of non-verbal alternatives to Piagetian tasks', in L. Siegel and C. Brainerd (eds) *Alternatives to Piaget*, New York: Academic Press.

Siegler, R., Deloache, J. and Eisenberg, N. (2006) *How Children Develop*, New York: Worth.

Silverman, D., Baker, C. and Keogh, J. (1998) 'The case of the silent child: advice-giving and advice reception in parent–child interviews', pp. 220–240 in I. Hutchby and J. Moran-Ellis (eds) *Children and Social Competence: Arenas of Action*, London: Falmer Press.

Silverstein, M. (1991) 'A funny thing happened on the way to the form: a functionalist critique of functionalist developmentalism', *First Language*, *11*: 143–179.

Simpson, E. (1974) 'Moral development research: a case of scientific cultural bias', *Human Development*, *17*: 81–106.

Singer, E. (1992) *Child-care and the Psychology of Development*, London: Routledge.

—— (1993) 'Shared care for children', *Theory and Psychology*, *3*, *4*: 429–449.

—— (2005) 'The liberation of the child: a recurrent theme in the history of education in western societies', *Early Child Development and Care*, *165*, *6*: 611–620.

Singer, E. and Doorenebal, J. (2006) 'Learning morality in peer conflict: a study of schoolchildren's narratives about being betrayed by a friend', *Childhood*, *13*, *2*: 225–245.

Sinha, C. (1989) *Language and Representation: A Socio-naturalistic Approach to Human Development*, Brighton: Harvester.

Skeggs, B. and Wood, H. (2004) 'Notes on ethical scenarios of self on British reality TV', *Feminist Media Studies*, 4, 1: 201–208.

Skutnabb Kangas, T. (1981) *Bilingualism or Not: The Education of Minorities*, Clevedon: Multilingual Matters.

—— (1988) 'Multilingualism and the education of minority children', in T. Skutnabb Kangas and J. Cummins (eds) *Minority Education: From Shame to Struggle*, Clevedon: Multilingual Matters.

Skutnabb Kangas, T. and Cummins, J. (eds) (1988) *Minority Education: From Shame to Struggle*, Clevedon: Multilingual Matters.

Slaughter-Defoe, D., Akua Adda, W. and Bell, C. (2002) 'Toward the future schooling of girls: global status, issues and prospects', *Human Development*, 45: 34–53.

Slosberg Andersen, E. (1990) *Speaking with Style: The Sociolinguistic Skills of Children*, London: Routledge.

Smart, C. (1989) 'Power and the politics of child custody', in C. Smart and S. Sevenhuijsen (eds) *Child Custody and the Politics of Gender*, London: Routledge.

—— (2004) 'Equal shares: rights for fathers or recognition for children?', *Critical Social Policy*, 24, 4: 484–503.

Smith, D. and Tomlinson, S. (1989) *The School Effect: A Study of Multiracial Comprehensives*, London: Policy Studies Institute.

Smith, L. (ed.) (1965/1995) *Jean Piaget: Sociological Studies*, London; Routledge.

Snarey, J.R. (1985) 'Cross cultural universality of social-moral development: a critical review of Kohlbergian research', *Psychological Bulletin*, 97: 202–32.

Snow, C. (1972) 'Mothers' speech to children learning language', *Child Development*, 43: 549–565.

—— (1977) 'Mothers' speech research: from input to interaction', in C. Snow and C. Ferguson (eds) *Talking to Children*, Cambridge: Cambridge University Press.

Snow, C. and Ferguson, C. (eds) (1977) *Talking to Children*, Cambridge: Cambridge University Press.

Solberg, A. (1990) 'Negotiating childhood: changing constructions of age for Norwegian children', pp. 118–137 in A. James and A. Prout (eds) *Constructing and Reconstructing Childhood: Contemporary Issues in the Sociological Study of Childhood*, Basingstoke: Falmer Press.

Song, M.J., Smetana, J.G. and Kim, S.Y. (1987) 'Korean children's conceptions of moral and conventional transgressions', *Developmental Psychology*, 23, 4: 577–582.

Sorce, J.F., Emde, R.N., Campos, J. and Klinnert, M. (1985) 'Maternal emotional signalling: its effect on the visual cliff behaviour of one year olds', *Developmental Psychology*, 21, 1: 195–200.

Speekmann Klass, C. (1985) *The Autonomous Child: Daycare and the Transmission of Values*, Lewes: Falmer Press.

Spelman, E. (1990) *Inessential Woman: Problems of Exclusion in Feminist Thought*, London: The Women's Press.

Spivak, G.C. (1990) 'Practical politics at the open end', in S. Harasym (ed.) *The Postcolonial Critic: Interviews, Strategies, Dialogues*, London: Routledge.

—— (1993) 'Can the subaltern speak?', pp. 66–111 in P. Williams and L. Chrisman (eds) *Colonial Discourse and Postcolonial Theory: A Reader*, New York: Harvester Wheatsheaf.

Squire, C. (ed.) (2000) *Culture and Psychology*, London: Routledge.

Sroufe, L.A. and Waters, E. (1976) 'The ontogenesis of smiling and laughter: a perspective on the organisation of development in infancy', *Psychological Review*, *83*: 173–189.

Stainton Rogers, R. and Stainton Rogers, W. (1992) *Stories of Childhood: Shifting Agendas of Child Concern*, Hemel Hempstead: Harvester Wheatsheaf.

Stallibrass, A. (1974) *The Self-respecting Child: A Study of Children's Play and Development*, London: Thames & Hudson.

Stanway, P. and Stanway, A. (1983) *Breast is Best: A Commonsense Approach to Breastfeeding*, London: Pan.

Steedman, C. (1983) *The Tidy House: Little Girls' Writing*, London: Virago.

—— (1985) '"Listen how the caged bird sings": Amarjit's song', pp. 137–163 in C. Steedman, C. Urwin and V. Walkerdine (eds) *Language, Gender and Childhood*, London: Routlege & Kegan Paul.

—— (1995) *Strange Dislocations: Childhood and the Idea of Human Interiority 1780–1930*, London: Routledge.

Stein, N., Trabasso, T. and Garfin, D. (1979) 'Comprehending and remembering moral dilemmas', in S. Goldman (ed.) *Understanding Discourse: Interactions between Knowledge and Process*, symposium presented to American Psychological Association, September.

Stern, D. (1977) *The First Relationship*, Fontana: London.

—— (1985) *The Interpersonal World of the Infant: A View from Psychoanalysis and Developmental Psychology*, New York: Basic Books.

Stern, D., Sander, L., Nahum, J., Harrison, A., Lyons-Ruth, K., Morgan, A., Bruschweiler-Stern, N. and Tronick, E. (1998) 'Non-interpretive mechanisms in psychoanalytic therapy: the "something more" than interpretation', *Internal Journal of Psycho-Analysis*, *79*: 903–921.

Stetsenko, A. and Arievitch, I. (2004) 'Vygotskian collaborative project of social transformation: history, politics and practice in knowledge construction', *International Journal of Critical Psychology*, *12*: 58–80.

Stigler, J., Shweder, R. and Herdt, G. (eds) (1990) *Cultural Psychology: Essays on Comparative Human Development*, Cambridge: Cambridge University Press.

Stolorow, R., Atwood, G. and Brandschaft, B. (1994) *The Intersubjective Perspective*, New York: Jason Aronson.

Stone, L., Smith, H.T. and Murphy, L.B. (eds) (1973) *The Competent Infant: Research and Commentary*, New York: Basic Books.

Strang, R. (1959) *An Introduction to Child Study*, New York: Macmillan.

Strauble, I. (2005) 'Entangled in the eurocentric order of knowledge: why psychology is difficult to decolonise', paper presented at the International Society for Theoretical Psychology, University of the Western Cape, Cape Town.

Stronach, I. Frankham, J. and Stark, S. (2007) 'Sex, science and educational research: the unholy trinity', *Journal of Educational Policy*, *22*, 2: 215–235.

Sugarman, L. (1990) *Life Span Development: Concepts, Theories and Interventions*, London and New York: Routledge.

Sullivan, E. (1977) 'A study of Kohlberg's structural theory of moral development: a critique of liberal social science ideology', *Human Development*, *20*: 352–375.

Summerfield, D. (2001) 'The invention of post-traumatic stress disorder and the social usefulness of a psychiatric category', *British Medical Journal, 322*: 1105–1107.

Suomi, S. (1991) 'Up-tight and laid-back monkeys: individual differences in the response to social challenges', pp. 27–56 in S. Brauth, W. Hall and R. Dooling (eds) *Plasticity of Development*, Cambridge, MA: MIT Press.

—— (2000) 'A biobehavioral perspective on developmental psychopathology: excessive aggression and serotoenergic dysfunction in monkeys', pp. 237–256 in A. Sameroff, M. Lewis and S. Miller (eds) *Handbook of Developmental Psychopathology*, New York: Plenum Press.

Sutton, C., Utting, D. and Farrington, D. (2006) 'Nipping criminality in the bud', *The Psychologist, 19, 8*: 470–475.

Sutton-Smith, B. (1997) *The Ambiguity of Play*, London: Harvard.

Sutton Smith, B. and Kelly Byrne, D. (1984) 'The idealisation of play', pp. 305–322 in P. Smith (ed.) *Play in Animals and Humans*, Oxford: Blackwell.

Svejda, M.J., Campos, J.J. and Emde, R.R. (1980) 'Mother–infant bonding: a failure to generalise', *Child Development, 51*: 415–432.

Sylvester Bradley, B. (1983) 'The neglect of hatefulness in psychological studies of early infancy', unpublished manuscript.

—— (1985) 'Failure to distinguish between people and things in early infancy', *British Journal of Developmental Psychology, 3*: 281-292.

Takahashi, K. (1990) 'Are the key assumptions of the strange situation procedure universal? A view from Japanese research', *Human Development, 33*: 23–30.

Tasker, F. (2004) 'Lesbian parenting: experiencing pride and prejudice', *Psychology of Women Section Review, 6, 1*: 22–28.

Tasker, F. and Golombok, S. (1997) *Growing Up in a Lesbian Family: Effects on Child Development*, New York: Guilford Press.

Taylor, K. (1995) 'Keeping mum: the paradoxes of gendered power relations in interviewing', pp. 106–124 in E. Burman, P. Alldred, C. Bewley, B. Goldberg, C. Heenan, D. Marks, J. Marshall, K. Taylor, R. Ullah, and S. Warner (eds) *Challenging Women: Psychology's Exclusions, Feminist Possibilities*, Buckingham: Open University Press.

The Victoria Climbié Inquiry: Report of an Inquiry by Lord Laming (2003) Cmd 5730, London: The Stationery Office (www.victoria-climbie-inquiry.org.uk).

Theakston, A., Lieven, E., Pine, J. and Rowland, C. (2001) 'The role of performance limitations in the acquisition of verb-argument structure: an alternative account', *Journal of Child Language, 28*: 127–152.

—— (2004) 'Semantic generality, input frequency and the acquisition of syntax', *Journal of Child Language, 31*: 61–99.

Thom, D. (1992) 'Wishes, anxieties, play and gestures: child guidance in inter-war England', in R. Cooter (ed.) *In the Name of the Child: Health and Welfare 1880–1940*, London: Routledge.

Thorne, B. (1987) 'Revisioning women and social change: where are the children?', *Gender and Society, 1, 1*: 85–109.

Timimi, S. (2002) *Pathological Child Psychiatry and the Medicalisation of Childhood*, Hove and New York: Brunner-Routledge.

—— (2005) *Naughty Boys: Antisocial Behaviour, ADHD and the Role of Culture*, London: Palgrave.

Tittnich, E., Bloom, L., Schomberg, R. and Szekeres, S. (eds) (1990) *Facilitating*

Children's Language: Handbook for Child-related Professionals, New York: Haworth Press.

Tizard, B. (1991) 'Employed mothers and the care of young mothers', pp. 178–194 in A. Phoenix, A. Woollett and E. Lloyd (eds) *Motherhood: Meanings, Practices and Ideologies*, London: Sage.

Tizard, B. and Hughes, M. (1984) *Young Children Learning: Talking and Thinking at Home and School*, London: Fontana.

Torres, P. (1992) 'Els països Catalans, des del sud', *Demà, Periodic per la Revolta, 10*: 10–11.

Tosi, A. (1988) 'The jewel in the crown of the modern prince: the new approach to bilingualism in multicultural education in England', in T. Skutnabb Kangas and J. Cummins (eds) *Minority Education: From Shame to Struggle*, Clevedon: Multilingual Matters.

Trevarthen, C. (1977), 'Descriptive analyses of infant communicative behaviour', in H. Schaffer (ed.) *Studies in Mother–Infant Interaction*, London: Academic Press.

Tsou, J. (2006) 'Genetic epistemology and Piaget's philosophy of science: Piaget vs. Kuhn on scientific progress', *Theory and Psychology, 16*, 2: 203–224.

Turiel, E. *(1983) The Development of Social Knowledge: Morality and Convention*, Cambridge: Cambridge University Press.

UNICEF (2007) *Child Poverty in Perspective: An Overview of Child Well-Being in Rich Countries*, Florence: UNICEF Innocenti Research Centre.

Urwin, C. (1982) 'On the contribution of non-visual communication systems and language to knowing oneself, pp. 99–128 in M. Beveridge (ed.) *Children Thinking through Language*, London: Edward Arnold.

—— (1984) 'Power relations and the emergence of language', pp. 264–322 in J. Henriques, W. Hollway, C. Venn, C. Urwin and V. Walkerdine (eds) *Changing the Subject*, London: Methuen.

—— (1985a) 'Constructing motherhood: the persuasion of normal development', pp. 164–203 in C. Steedman, C. Urwin and V. Walkerdine (eds) *Language, Gender and Childhood*, London: Routledge & Kegan Paul.

—— (1985b) 'Review of *War in the Nursery* (D. Riley, Virago, 1983)', *Feminist Review, 19*: 95–100.

—— (1986) 'Developmental psychology and psychoanalysis: splitting the difference', in M. Richards and P. Light (eds) *Children of Social Worlds*, Oxford: Polity/Blackwell.

Urwin, C. and Sharland, E. (1992) 'From bodies to minds in childcare literature: advice to parents in inter-war Britain', in R. Cooter (ed.) *In the Name of the Child: Health and Welfare 1880–1940*, London: Routledge.

Valentine, C. (1956) *The Normal Child and some of his Abnormalities*, Harmondsworth: Penguin.

Valsiner, J. (1988) *Developmental Psychology in the Soviet Union*, Brighton: Harvester.

Van der Eyken, W. (ed.) (1973) *Education, the Child and Society*, Harmondsworth: Penguin.

Van Every, J. (1992) 'Who is "the family"? The assumptions of British social policy', *Critical Social Policy, 33*: 62–75.

van IJzenhoorn, M. and Sagi, A. (2001) 'Cultural blindness or selective inattention?', *American Psychologist, 56*: 824–825.

Vandenberg, B. (1993) 'Developmental psychology, God and the good', *Theory and Psychology*, *3*, *2*: 191–205.

Vedeler, D. (1991) 'Infant intentionality as object directedness: an alternative to representationalism', *Journal for the Theory of Social Behaviour*, *31*: 431–448.

Venn, C. (2000) *Occidentalism*, London: Sage.

Venn, C. and Walkerdine, V. (1978) 'The acquisition and production of knowledge: Piaget's theory reconsidered', *Ideology and Consciousness*, *3*: 67–94.

Venuti, L. (ed.) (2000) *The Translation Studies Reader*, London and New York: Routledge.

Vianna, E. and Stetsenko, A. (2006) 'Embracing history through transforming it: contrasting Piagetian versus Vygotskyan (activity) theories of learning and development to expand constructivism within a dialectical view of history', *Theory and Psychology*, *16*, *1*: 81–108.

Vidal, F. (1987) 'Jean Piaget and the liberal protestant tradition', in M. Ash and M. Woodward (eds) *Psychology in Twentieth Century Thought and Society*, Cambridge: Cambridge University Press.

Vukelich, C. and Kumar, D.S. (1985) 'Mature and teenage mothers' infant growth expectation and use of child development sources', *Family Relations: Journal of Applied Family and Child Studies*, *34*: 189–196.

Vygotsky, L.S. (1962) *Language and Thought*, Cambridge, MA: MIT Press.

—— (1978a) *Mind in Society: The Development of Higher Psychological Processes*, Cambridge, MA: Harvard University Press.

—— (1978b) 'Problems of method', pp. 58–78 in L.S. Vygotsky (ed.) *Mind in Society: The Development of Higher Psychological Processes*, Cambridge, MA: Harvard University Press.

Wachs, T.D. and Gruen, G.E. (1982) *Early Experience and Human Development*, New York: Plenum Press.

Waites, M. (2005) *The Age of Consent: Young People, Sexuality and Citizenship*, London: Palgrave.

Walker, L.J. (1989) 'A longitudinal study of moral reasoning', *Child Development*, *60*: 157–166.

Walkerdine, V. (1981) 'Sex, power and pedagogy', *Screen Education*, *38*: 14–21.

—— (1984; 1998) 'Developmental psychology and the child-centred pedagogy', pp. 153–202 in J. Henriques, W. Hollway, C. Urwin, C. Venn and V. Walkerdine (eds) *Changing the Subject: Psychology, Social Regulation and Subjectivity*, London: Methuen.

—— (1988) *The Mastery of Reason: Cognitive Development and the Production of Rationality*, London: Routledge.

—— (1990) *Schoolgirl Fictions*, London: Verso.

Walkerdine, V. and Lucey, H. (1989) *Democracy in the Kitchen: Regulating Mothers and Socialising Daughters*, London: Virago.

Walkerdine, V. and the Girls and Mathematics Unit (1990) *Counting Girls Out*, London: Virago.

Wallace, T. and March, C. (1991) *Changing Perceptions: Writings on Gender and Development*, Oxford: Oxfam.

Ware, V. (1992) *Beyond the Pale: White Women, Racism and History*, London: Verso.

Warner, S. (2000) *Understanding Child Sexual Abuse: Making the Tactics Visible*, Gloucester: Handsell Press.

Watson, J. (1973) 'Smiling, cooing and "the game"', *Merrill Palmer Quarterly*, *18*: 323–339.

Watt, D. (2002) 'Black motherhood in the diaspora: survival, power and identity amongst Jamaican women in Manchester', unpublished doctoral dissertation, Manchester Metropolitan University.

Wedge, P. and Prosser, H. (1973) *Born to Fail?*, London: Arrow Books.

Wells, G. and Robinson, W.P. (1982) 'The role of adult speech in language development', in C. Fraser and K. Scherer (eds) *The Social Psychology of Language*, Cambridge: Cambridge University press.

Wenger, E. (1998) *Communities of Practice. Learning, Meaning and Identity.* Cambridge: Cambridge University Press.

Wertsch, J. (1991) *Voices of the Mind: A Sociocultural Approach to Mediated Action*, Hemel Hempstead: Harvester.

—— (1998) *Mind as Action*, New York: Oxford University Press.

Wexler, P. (1983) *Critical Social Psychology*, London: Routledge & Kegan Paul.

Wheelock, J. (1990) *Husbands at Home: The Domestic Economy in a Post-industrial Society*, London: Routledge.

Wheldall, K. and Poborca, B. (1980) 'Conservation without conversation? An alternative non-verbal paradigm for conservation of liquid quantity', *British Journal of Psychology*, *71*: 117–134.

White, D. and Woollett, A. (1992) *Families: A Context for Development*, Basingstoke: Falmer Press.

Whiten, A. and Milner, P. (1986) 'The educational experiences of Nigerian infants', in H.V. Curran (ed.) *Nigerian Children: Developmental Perspectives*, London: Routledge & Kegan Paul.

Whitfield, R. (1980) *Education for Family Life: Some New Policies for Child Care*, London: Hodder & Stoughton.

Wilkinson, S. and Kitzinger, C. (eds) (1996) *Representing the Other*, London: Sage.

Willig, C. (ed.) (1999) *Applied Discourse Analysis: Social and Psychological Interventions*, Buckingham: Open University Press.

Winnicott, D.W. (1958) 'Hate in the counter-transference', in D.W. Winnicott (ed.) *Collected Papers: Through Pediatrics to Psychoanalysis*, London: Tavistock.

Wolman, B. (ed.) (1982) *Handbook of Developmental Psychology*, Englewood Cliffs, NJ: Prentice-Hall.

Wolfe, R. (1981) 'Maladjustment in the context of local authority decision making', in L. Barton and S. Tomlinson (eds) *Special Education: Policy, Practice and Social Issues*, London: Harper & Row.

Wolff, P.H. (1969) 'The natural history of crying and other vocalisations', in B. Foss (ed.) *Determinants of Infant Behaviour*, Vol. 4, London: Methuen.

Woodhead, M. (1988) 'When psychology informs public policy: the case of early childhood intervention', *American Psychologist*, *43*, 6: 443–454.

—— (1990) 'Psychology and the cultural construction of children's needs', pp. 60–77 in A. James and A. Prout (eds) *Constructing and Reconstructing Childhood: Contemporary Issues in the Sociological Study of Childhood*, Basingstoke: Falmer Press.

—— (1999) 'Reconstructing developmental psychology – some first steps', *Children and Society*, *13*: 3–19.

Woodhead, M., Faulkner, D. and Littleton, K. (eds) (1999) *Making Sense of Social Development*, London and New York: Routledge.

Woods, J.R. (2004) 'A study of children's meaning-making at a multicultural London primary school', unpublished PhD in psychology, Department of Human Sciences, Brunel University.

Wooffitt, R. (2005) *Conversation Analysis and Discourse Analysis: A Comparative and Critical Introduction*, London: Sage.

Woollett, A. (1986) 'The influence of older siblings on the language environment of young children', *British Journal of Developmental Psychology*, 4: 2355.

Yarrow, L.J., Rubenstein, J.L. and Pedersen, F.A. (1975) *Infant and Environment: Early Emotional and Motivational Development*, Washington, DC: Hemisphere/ Wiley.

Yeates, N. (2004) 'A dialogue with "global care chain" analysis: nurse migration in the Irish context', *Feminist Review*, 77: 79–95.

Yuval-Davis, N. (1997) *Gender and Nation*, London: Sage.

Yuval-Davis, N. and Anthias, F. (eds) (1989) *Woman–Nation–State*, London: Macmillan.

Zavos, A. (2005) '(Im)possible translations: challenging therapeutic authority through textual practices', *Group Analysis*, 38, 1: 115–127.

Zeedyk, M.S. (1996) 'Developmental accounts of intentionality: toward integration', *Developmental Review*, 16: 416–461.

Zelizer, V.A. (1985) *Pricing the Priceless Child: The Changing Social Value of Children*, New York: Basic Books.

Author index

Subject index

354   *Subject index*